EV4.00

W9-AVH-164

AN ASTROLOGICAL INDEX
TO THE WORLD'S
FAMOUS PEOPLE

AN ASTROLOGICAL INDEX
TO THE WORLD'S
FAMOUS PEOPLE

by Michael Cooper and Andrew Weaver

Doubleday & Company, Inc.
Garden City, New York
1975

Library of Congress Cataloging in Publication Data

Cooper, Michael, 1943–
    An astrological index to the world's famous people.

    1. Horoscopes. 2. Biography—Miscellanea.
I. Weaver, Andrew, 1946–   joint author. II. Title.
BF1728.A2C66   133.5′48
ISBN 0-385-00507-5
Library of Congress Catalog Card Number 74-3545

Copyright © 1975 by Michael Cooper and Andrew Weaver
All Rights Reserved
Printed in the United States of America
First Edition

CONTENTS

INTRODUCTION

Current popular interest in astrology has created a need for a simple reference giving names of famous people and their birthdays, which would satisfy the prevalent curiosity to know people's sun signs. Since the birthday is the only information necessary to determine a person's sun sign, it is possible to compile for this purpose a more comprehensive list than has been attempted in any biographical reference source; this is what we have done, including famous and notorious figures from the past as well as living persons.

The number of historical personages has necessarily been limited by the fact that their birthdays in many cases are not recorded; nineteenth-century dates, except for some individuals of obscure origins, are usually available, and many from the eighteenth and seventeenth centuries, but earlier than that they become increasingly scarce, until the European Middle Ages, when only birth dates of rulers were normally recorded. For the ancient Romans a few dates are known, thanks to the Romans' reliable calendar and clerical efficiency, and also to the Roman vogue for astrology, which prompted registration of some birth times for horoscopic purposes. Of the Greeks, we have three names with dates—Alexander, which is probably accurate, and Socrates and Euripides, which are doubtful. Outside of Europe and America, precise dates are entirely unobtainable until the present century, and thus, regrettably, we have no names from Asian or African history, and none of famous primitives such as American Indian leaders.

The older dates have had to be adjusted to conform to our modern Gregorian calendar, which was adopted in the sixteenth century in Europe, and in the eighteenth century in Great Britain. A birth date according to the old Julian calendar does not represent astrologically the same position of the sun as the same date on the Gregorian calendar; for example, in the middle of May, 1700, in England, the sun was in Gemini, but in the middle of May nowadays the sun is in Taurus. Therefore, in order that all dates indicate the sun's position consistently and as accurately as possible, we have altered the dates reckoned in the old style.

Contemporary birth dates have presented other difficulties. Many are not published in existing references such as Who's Who, Celebrity Register and Current Biography, and must be hunted elsewhere; this is the case, for instance, with rock musicians and many television personalities and sports stars. Another problem has been that of occasional discrepancies between dates given in various sources; confronted with such a situation, we have used the date most frequently given.

The names have been arranged in two lists, one of them an alphabetical index for reference to any particular person, and the other a calendar, so that it is possible to look up any date (one's own birthday, for example) to find out what celebrities were born on that day. Some names that are known mainly in special fields appear in the index for completeness' sake, but not in the day-by-day list.

In connection with the day-by-day section the question of cusps arises. A cusp is that point in time-space where a zodiacal sign begins; the sun is on the cusp of Aries, which is to say that it enters Aries, at the moment of the vernal equinox, of Libra at the autumnal equinox, and of Cancer and Capricorn at the summer and winter solstices, respectively, with the cusps of the signs in between calculated accordingly. However, these annual events in the earth-sun relationship do not occur at exactly the same time each calendar year, and not even always on the same date, so that for general purposes two days of each month must be considered "cuspal"; this means that on those days, in any year, the sun is at, or near, the point of entering a new sign. An individual born at such a time presumably shows characteristics of one sign merging into those of the next; in these instances we have indicated both signs.

The sun's position is the single most important factor of a birthchart, and with only this information certain general conclusions about a person's character may be drawn, but that is only the beginning; the next consideration is the moon's position, which will considerably modify the working out of tendencies indicated by the sun. The sun represents the central unifying principle of an individual's personality, while the moon shows how this inner will may be instrumented in daily life; depending on the strength of their respective positions in a chart, the characteristics of the moon sign may be more apparent in a person than those of the sun sign. Therefore, for the sake of greater completeness we have appended a rough table to be used for looking up the moon's position in the zodiac for any birth date from 1890 to 1950, in hopes that this will add to the book's usefulness.

New York, 1975   Michael Cooper
                                                    Andrew Weaver

AN ASTROLOGICAL INDEX
TO THE WORLD'S
FAMOUS PEOPLE

ALPHABETICAL INDEX

AARON, HANK (baseball player) 2 / 5 / 1934 AQUARIUS
ABBADO, CLAUDIO (conductor) 6 / 26 / 1933 CANCER
ABBOTT, BUD (comedian) 10 / 2 / 1898 LIBRA
ABBOTT, GEORGE (playwright and producer) 6 / 25 / 1887 CANCER
ABERNATHY, RALPH DAVID (civil rights leader) 3 / 11 / 1926 PISCES
ABOLAFIA, LOUIS (politician) 2 / 23 / 1943 PISCES
ABPLANALP, ROBERT (financier) 4 / 4 / 1922 ARIES
ABRAMOVITZ, MAX (architect) 5 / 23 / 1908 GEMINI
ABZUG, BELLA (politician) 7 / 24 / 1920 LEO
ACCARDO, TONY "BIG TUNA" (mobster) 4 / 28 / 1906 TAURUS
ACE, GOODMAN (radio personality) 1 / 15 / 1899 CAPRICORN
ACHESON, DEAN (government official) 4 / 11 / 1893 ARIES
ADAM, ADOLPHE (composer) 7 / 24 / 1803 LEO
ADAMS, ABIGAIL (first lady) 11 / 21 / 1744 SCORPIO
ADAMS, EDIE (singer) 4 / 16 / 1931 ARIES
ADAMS, EVANGELINE (astrologer) 2 / 8 / 1868 AQUARIUS
ADAMS, HENRY (writer) 2 / 16 / 1838 AQUARIUS
ADAMS, JOHN (politician) 10 / 30 / 1735 SCORPIO
ADAMS, JOHN QUINCY (politician) 7 / 11 / 1767 CANCER
ADAMS, JULIE (actress) 10 / 17 / 1928 LIBRA
ADAMS, SAMUEL (patriot) 10 / 8 / 1722 LIBRA
ADAMS, SHERMAN (government official) 1 / 8 / 1899 CAPRICORN
ADAMSON, JOY (wildlife conservationist) 1 / 20 / 1910
    CAPRICORN/AQUARIUS
ADDAMS, CHARLES (cartoonist) 1 / 7 / 1912 CAPRICORN
ADDAMS, JANE (social worker) 9 / 6 / 1860 VIRGO
ADDERLEY, CANNONBALL (jazz musician) 9 / 15 / 1928 VIRGO
ADDISON, JOSEPH (writer) 5 / 11 / 1672 TAURUS
ADENAUER, KONRAD (German politician) 1 / 5 / 1876 CAPRICORN

ADLER, ALFRED (psychologist) 2 / 7 / 1870 AQUARIUS
ADLER, MORTIMER (educator) 12 / 28 / 1902 CAPRICORN
ADLER, POLLY (procuress) 4 / 16 / 1900 ARIES
ADLER, RICHARD (composer and producer) 8 / 3 / 1921 LEO
AGA KHAN IV (Muslim leader) 12 / 13 / 1937 SAGITTARIUS
AGAR, JOHN (actor) 1 / 31 / 1921 AQUARIUS
AGEE, JAMES (writer) 11 / 27 / 1909 SAGITTARIUS
AGNEW, SPIRO (politician) 11 / 9 / 1918 SCORPIO
AHERNE, BRIAN (actor) 5 / 2 / 1902 TAURUS
AIKEN, CONRAD (poet) 8 / 5 / 1889 LEO
AILEY, ALVIN (choreographer) 1 / 5 / 1931 CAPRICORN
AIMEE, ANOUK (actress) 4 / 27 / 1932 TAURUS
AKIHITO (crown prince of Japan) 12 / 23 / 1933 CAPRICORN
ALBANESE, LICIA (soprano) 7 / 22 / 1913 CANCER
ALBEE, EDWARD (playwright) 3 / 12 / 1928 PISCES
ALBENIZ, ISAAC (composer) 5 / 29 / 1860 GEMINI
ALBERGHETTI, ANNA MARIA (actress) 5 / 15 / 1936 TAURUS
ALBERS, JOSEF (painter) 3 / 19 / 1888 PISCES
ALBERT, PRINCE (royal consort) 8 / 26 / 1819 VIRGO
ALBERT, CARL (politician) 5 / 10 / 1908 TAURUS
ALBERT, EDDIE (actor) 4 / 22 / 1908 TAURUS
ALBERT, EDWARD (actor) 2 / 20 / 1951 PISCES
ALBRIGHT, LOLA (actress) 7 / 20 / 1925 CANCER
ALCINDOR, LEW (basketball player) 4 / 16 / 1947 ARIES
ALCOTT, AMOS BRONSON (transcendentalist) 11 / 29 / 1799
    SAGITTARIUS
ALCOTT, LOUISA MAY (novelist) 11 / 29 / 1832 SAGITTARIUS
ALDA, ALAN (actor) 1 / 28 / 1936 AQUARIUS
ALDA, FRANCES (soprano) 5 / 31 / 1883 GEMINI
ALDRICH, TOMMY (rock musician) 8 / 15 / 1950 LEO
ALDRIN, EDWIN "BUZZ" (astronaut) 1 / 20 / 1930
    CAPRICORN/AQUARIUS
ALEICHEM, SHOLOM (writer) 2 / 18 / 1859 AQUARIUS/PISCES
ALEXANDER THE GREAT (conqueror) 7 / 16 / 356 B.C. CANCER
ALEXANDER, GROVER CLEVELAND (baseball player) 2 / 26 / 1887
    PISCES
ALEXANDER, JANE (actress) 10 / 28 / 1939 SCORPIO
ALEXANDRA OF RUSSIA, EMPRESS 6 / 6 / 1872 GEMINI
ALEXEI, PATRIARCH OF RUSSIA (Russian Orthodox leader)
    10 / 27 / 1877 SCORPIO

ALEXIS OF RUSSIA, CZAREVITCH 8 / 12 / 1904 LEO
ALGER, HORATIO (novelist) 1 / 13 / 1834 CAPRICORN
ALGREN, NELSON (writer) 3 / 28 / 1909 ARIES
ALI, MUHAMMAD (boxer) 1 / 17 / 1942 CAPRICORN
ALIOTO, JOSEPH (politician) 2 / 12 / 1916 AQUARIUS
ALLEN, DICK (baseball player) 3 / 8 / 1942 PISCES
ALLEN, ETHAN (patriot) 1 / 21 / 1738 CAPRICORN/AQUARIUS
ALLEN, FRED (comedian) 5 / 31 / 1894 GEMINI
ALLEN, GRACIE (comedienne) 7 / 26 / 1905 LEO
ALLEN, MEL (sportscaster) 2 / 14 / 1913 AQUARIUS
ALLEN, STEVE (TV personality) 12 / 26 / 1921 CAPRICORN
ALLEN, WOODY (comedian) 12 / 1 / 1935 SAGITTARIUS
ALLENDE, SALVADOR (Chilean politician) 7 / 26 / 1908 LEO
ALLEYN, EDWARD (actor) 9 / 11 / 1566 VIRGO
ALLILUYEVA, SVETLANA (dictator's daughter) 2 / 28 / 1926 PISCES
ALLMAN, DUANE (rock musician) 11 / 20 / 1946 SCORPIO
ALLMAN, GREG (rock musician) 12 / 8 / ? SAGITTARIUS
ALLYSON, JUNE (actress) 10 / 7 / 1923 LIBRA
ALONSO, ALICIA (ballet dancer) 12 / 21 / 1921
    SAGITTARIUS/CAPRICORN
ALPERT, HERB (bandleader) 3 / 31 / 1935 ARIES
ALPERT, RICHARD (drug experimenter) 4 / 6 / 1931 ARIES
ALSOP, JOSEPH (newsman) 10 / 11 / 1910 LIBRA
ALSOP, STEWART (newsman) 5 / 17 / 1914 TAURUS
ALSTON, SMOKEY (baseball manager) 12 / 1 / 1911 SAGITTARIUS
ALTMAN, ROBERT (film director) 2 / 20 / 1925 PISCES
ALVA, LUIGI (tenor) 4 / 10 / 1927 ARIES
ALVAREZ, LUIS (physicist) 6 / 13 / 1906 GEMINI
ALY KHAN, PRINCE (playboy) 6 / 13 / 1911 GEMINI
AMARA, LUCINE (soprano) 3 / 1 / 1925 PISCES
AMATO, PASQUALE (baritone) 3 / 21 / 1878 PISCES/ARIES
AMECHE, DON (actor) 5 / 31 / 1908 GEMINI
AMIES, HARDY (fashion designer) 7 / 17 / 1909 CANCER
AMIS, KINGSLEY (writer) 4 / 16 / 1922 ARIES
AMORY, CLEVELAND (TV critic) 9 / 2 / 1917 VIRGO
AMRAM, DAVID (composer) 11 / 17 / 1930 SCORPIO
AMUNDSEN, ROALD (explorer) 7 / 16 / 1872 CANCER
ANASTASIA OF RUSSIA, GRAND DUCHESS 6 / 18 / 1901 GEMINI
ANDA, GEZA (pianist) 11 / 19 / 1921 SCORPIO
ANDERSEN, HANS CHRISTIAN (writer) 4 / 2 / 1805 ARIES

ANDERSON, EDDIE (comedian) 9 / 18 / 1905 VIRGO
ANDERSON, JACK (columnist) 10 / 19 / 1922 LIBRA
ANDERSON, JUDITH (actress) 2 / 10 / 1898 AQUARIUS
ANDERSON, LEROY (composer) 6 / 29 / 1908 CANCER
ANDERSON, LYNN (singer) 10 / 26 / 1945 SCORPIO
ANDERSON, MARIAN (contralto) 2 / 27 / 1902 PISCES
ANDERSON, MAXWELL (playwright) 12 / 15 / 1888 SAGITTARIUS
ANDERSON, ROBERT (playwright) 4 / 28 / 1917 TAURUS
ANDERSON, SHERWOOD (novelist) 9 / 13 / 1876 VIRGO
ANDERSSON, BIBI (actress) 11 / 11 / 1935 SCORPIO
ANDERSSON, HARRIET (actress) 1 / 14 / 1932 CAPRICORN
ANDRESS, URSULA (actress) 3 / 19 / 1936 PISCES
ANDRETTI, MARIO (auto racer) 2 / 28 / 1940 PISCES
ANDREWS, DANA (actor) 1 / 1 / 1909 CAPRICORN
ANDREWS, HARRY (actor) 11 / 10 / 1911 SCORPIO
ANDREWS, JULIE (actress) 10 / 1 / 1935 LIBRA
ANDREWS, LAVERNE (singer) 7 / 6 / 1915 CANCER
ANDREWS, MAXENE (singer) 1 / 3 / 1918 CAPRICORN
ANDREWS, PATTY (singer) 2 / 16 / 1920 AQUARIUS
ANGELI, PIER (actress) 6 / 19 / 1932 GEMINI
ANGELOU, MAYA (writer) 4 / 4 / 1929 ARIES
ANIEVAS, AGUSTIN (pianist) 11 / 6 / 1934 SCORPIO
ANKA, PAUL (singer) 7 / 30 / 1941 LEO
ANN-MARGRET (actress) 4 / 28 / 1941 TAURUS
ANNE OF ENGLAND, PRINCESS 8 / 15 / 1950 LEO
ANNE OF ENGLAND, QUEEN 2 / 16 / 1665 AQUARIUS
ANOUILH, JEAN (playwright) 6 / 23 / 1910 CANCER
ANSELMI, GIUSEPPE (tenor) 11 / 12 / 1876 SCORPIO
ANSERMET, ERNEST (conductor) 11 / 11 / 1883 SCORPIO
ANSON, CAP (baseball player) 4 / 17 / 1851 ARIES
ANTHONY OF PADUA, ST. (monk) 8 / 22 / 1195 LEO
ANTHONY, LITTLE (singer) 1 / 8 / 1940 CAPRICORN
ANTHONY, RAY (bandleader) 1 / 22 / 1922 AQUARIUS
ANTHONY, SUSAN B. (feminist) 2 / 15 / 1820 AQUARIUS
ANTOINE (hairdresser) 12 / 24 / 1884 CAPRICORN
ANTONIONI, MICHELANGELO (film maker) 9 / 29 / 1912 LIBRA
APOLLINAIRE, GUILLAUME (writer) 8 / 26 / 1880 VIRGO
APPLESEED, JOHNNY (pioneer) 9 / 26 / 1775 LIBRA
ARAGON, LOUIS (writer) 10 / 3 / 1897 LIBRA
ARBUCKLE, FATTY (actor) 3 / 24 / 1887 ARIES

ARCARO, EDDIE (jockey) 2 / 19 / 1916 AQUARIUS/PISCES
ARCHIPENKO, ALEXANDER (sculptor) 5 / 30 / 1887 GEMINI
ARDEN, EVE (actress) 4 / 30 / 1912 TAURUS
ARDREY, ROBERT (anthropologist) 10 / 16 / 1908 LIBRA
ARENDT, HANNAH (writer) 10 / 14 / 1906 LIBRA
ARIAS NAVARRO, CARLOS (Spanish politician) 12 / 11 / 1908
    SAGITTARIUS
ARIOSTO, LODOVICO (poet) 9 / 17 / 1474 VIRGO
ARKIN, ALAN (actor) 3 / 26 / 1934 ARIES
ARLEN, HAROLD (composer) 2 / 15 / 1905 AQUARIUS
ARLETTY (actress) 5 / 15 / 1898 TAURUS
ARMITAGE, KENNETH (sculptor) 7 / 18 / 1916 CANCER
ARMSTRONG, LOUIS (jazz musician) 7 / 4 / 1900 CANCER
ARMSTRONG, NEIL (astronaut) 8 / 5 / 1930 LEO
ARMSTRONG-JONES, ANTONY (photographer) 3 / 7 / 1930 PISCES
ARNAZ, DESI (actor) 3 / 2 / 1917 PISCES
ARNAZ, DESI, JR. (actor) 1 / 19 / 1953 CAPRICORN
ARNESS, JAMES (actor) 5 / 26 / 1923 GEMINI
ARNOLD, BENEDICT (traitor) 1 / 25 / 1741 AQUARIUS
ARNOLD, EDDY (country singer) 5 / 15 / 1918 TAURUS
ARNOLD, MATTHEW (writer) 12 / 24 / 1822 CAPRICORN
ARP, JEAN (artist) 9 / 16 / 1887 VIRGO
ARPINO, GERALD (choreographer) 1 / 14 / 1928 CAPRICORN
ARQUETTE, CLIFF (actor) 12 / 28 / 1905 CAPRICORN
ARRABAL, FERNANDO (playwright) 8 / 11 / 1932 LEO
ARRAU, CLAUDIO (pianist) 2 / 6 / 1903 AQUARIUS
ARROYO, MARTINA (soprano) 2 / 6 / 1939 AQUARIUS
ARTHUR, BEATRICE (actress) 5 / 13 / 1926 TAURUS
ARTHUR, CHESTER ALAN (politician) 10 / 5 / 1829 LIBRA
ARTHUR, JEAN (actress) 10 / 17 / 1908 LIBRA
ASHCROFT, PEGGY (actress) 12 / 22 / 1907 SAGITTARIUS/CAPRICORN
ASHE, ARTHUR (tennis player) 7 / 10 / 1943 CANCER
ASHKENAZY, VLADIMIR (pianist) 7 / 6 / 1937 CANCER
ASHLEY, ELIZABETH (actress) 8 / 30 / 1941 VIRGO
ASHTON, FREDERICK (choreographer) 9 / 17 / 1906 VIRGO
ASIMOV, ISAAC (writer) 1 / 2 / 1920 CAPRICORN
ASKEW, REUBIN (politician) 9 / 11 / 1928 VIRGO
ASTAIRE, FRED (dancer) 5 / 10 / 1899 TAURUS
ASTOR, JOHN JACOB (fur merchant) 7 / 17 / 1763 CANCER
ASTOR, MARY (actress) 5 / 3 / 1906 TAURUS

ASTOR, LADY NANCY (politician) 5 / 19 / 1879 TAURUS
ATKINS, CHET (guitarist) 6 / 20 / 1924 GEMINI
ATKINS, EILEEN (actress) 6 / 16 / 1934 GEMINI
ATKINS, ROBERT C. (physician and author) 10 / 17 / 1930 LIBRA
ATKINSON, BROOKS (drama critic) 11 / 28 / 1894 SAGITTARIUS
ATLAS, CHARLES (bodybuilder) 10 / 30 / 1893 SCORPIO
ATTENBOROUGH, RICHARD (actor) 8 / 29 / 1923 VIRGO
AUBER, DANIEL (composer) 1 / 29 / 1782 AQUARIUS
AUBREY, JAMES, JR. (film executive) 12 / 14 / 1918 SAGITTARIUS
AUDEN, W. H. (poet) 2 / 21 / 1907 PISCES
AUDUBON, JOHN JAMES (naturalist) 4 / 26 / 1785 TAURUS
AUERBACH, ARNOLD (basketball executive) 9 / 20 / 1917 VIRGO
AUGUSTINE, ST. (theologian) 11 / 14 / A.D. 354 SCORPIO
AUGUSTUS CAESAR OF ROME, EMPEROR 9 / 19 / 63 B.C. VIRGO
AUROBINDO, SRI (mystic) 8 / 15 / 1872 LEO
AUSTEN, JANE (novelist) 12 / 16 / 1775 SAGITTARIUS
AUTRY, GENE (actor) 9 / 29 / 1907 LIBRA
AVALON, FRANKIE (singer) 9 / 8 / 1940 VIRGO
AVEDON, RICHARD (photographer) 5 / 13 / 1923 TAURUS
AVERY, MILTON (painter) 3 / 7 / 1893 PISCES
AYRES, LEW (actor) 12 / 28 / 1908 CAPRICORN
AZNAVOUR, CHARLES (singer) 5 / 22 / 1924 GEMINI

BACALL, LAUREN (actress) 9 / 16 / 1924 VIRGO
BACH, CARL PHILIPP EMANUEL (composer) 3 / 8 / 1714 PISCES
BACH, JOHANN CHRISTIAN (composer) 9 / 5 / 1735 VIRGO
BACH, JOHANN SEBASTIAN (composer) 3 / 31 / 1685 ARIES
BACH, RICHARD (writer and aviator) 6 / 23 / 1936 CANCER
BACHARACH, BURT (composer) 5 / 12 / 1929 TAURUS
BACHAUER, GINA (pianist) 5 / 21 / 1913 TAURUS/GEMINI
BACKHAUS, WILHELM (pianist) 3 / 26 / 1884 ARIES
BACKUS, JIM (actor) 2 / 25 / 1913 PISCES
BACON, FRANCIS (philosopher) 2 / 2 / 1561 AQUARIUS
BACQUIER, GABRIEL (baritone) 5 / 17 / 1924 TAURUS
BADDELEY, HERMIONE (actress) 11 / 13 / 1908 SCORPIO
BADEN-POWELL, ROBERT (Boy Scouts founder) 2 / 22 / 1857 PISCES
BADURA-SKODA, PAUL (pianist) 10 / 6 / 1927 LIBRA
BAEZ, JOAN (singer) 1 / 9 / 1941 CAPRICORN
BAILEY, ALICE (theosophist) 6 / 16 / 1880 GEMINI

BAILEY, F. LEE (lawyer) 6 / 10 / 1933 GEMINI
BAILEY, PEARL (singer) 3 / 29 / 1918 ARIES
BAIRD, BILL (puppeteer) 8 / 15 / 1904 LEO
BAIRD, CORA (puppeteer) 1 / 26 / 1912 AQUARIUS
BAKER, CARROLL (actress) 5 / 28 / 1931 GEMINI
BAKER, DIANE (actress) 2 / 25 / 1940 PISCES
BAKER, GINGER (rock musician) 8 / 18 / 1939 LEO
BAKER, HOWARD (politician) 11 / 15 / 1925 SCORPIO
BAKER, JANET (mezzo-soprano) 8 / 21 / 1933 LEO
BAKER, JOSEPHINE (dancer) 6 / 3 / 1906 GEMINI
BAKER, LAVERN (singer) 11 / 11 / 1929 SCORPIO
BAKER, RUSSELL (journalist) 8 / 14 / 1925 LEO
BAKUNIN, MICHAEL (Russian revolutionary) 5 / 30 / 1814 GEMINI
BALANCHINE, GEORGE (choreographer) 1 / 9 / 1904 CAPRICORN
BALDWIN, FAITH (novelist) 10 / 1 / 1893 LIBRA
BALDWIN, JAMES (writer) 8 / 2 / 1924 LEO
BALIN, INA (actress) 11 / 12 / 1937 SCORPIO
BALIN, MARTY (singer) 1 / 30 / 1943 AQUARIUS
BALL, LUCILLE (comedienne) 8 / 6 / 1911 LEO
BALLARD, KAYE (comedienne) 11 / 20 / 1926 SCORPIO
BALSAM, MARTIN (actor) 11 / 4 / 1919 SCORPIO
BALZAC, HONORE DE (novelist) 5 / 20 / 1799 TAURUS
BAMPTON, ROSE (soprano) 11 / 28 / 1909 SAGITTARIUS
BANCROFT, ANNE (actress) 9 / 17 / 1931 VIRGO
BANDARANAIKE, SIRIMAVO (Ceylonese politician) 4 / 17 / 1916 ARIES
BANKHEAD, TALLULAH (actress) 1 / 31 / 1902 AQUARIUS
BANKS, ERNIE (baseball player) 1 / 31 / 1931 AQUARIUS
BANNISTER, ROGER (runner) 3 / 23 / 1929 ARIES
BARBER, JERRY (golfer) 4 / 25 / 1916 TAURUS
BARBER, RED (sportscaster) 2 / 17 / 1908 AQUARIUS
BARBER, SAMUEL (composer) 3 / 9 / 1910 PISCES
BARBIERI, FEDORA (mezzo-soprano) 6 / 4 / 1919 GEMINI
BARBIROLLI, JOHN (conductor) 12 / 2 / 1899 SAGITTARIUS
BARDOT, BRIGITTE (actress) 9 / 28 / 1934 LIBRA
BARENBOIM, DANIEL (conductor) 11 / 15 / 1942 SCORPIO
BARKER, LEX (actor) 5 / 8 / 1919 TAURUS
BARNARD, CHRISTIAAN (surgeon) 11 / 8 / 1922 SCORPIO
BARNES, CLIVE (critic) 5 / 13 / 1927 TAURUS
BARNES, DJUNA (writer) 6 / 12 / 1892 GEMINI
BARNUM, P. T. (showman) 7 / 5 / 1810 CANCER

BARRAULT, JEAN-LOUIS (actor) 9 / 8 / 1910 VIRGO
BARRETT, RONA (columnist) 10 / 8 / 1936 LIBRA
BARRIE, BARBARA (actress) 5 / 23 / 1931 GEMINI
BARRIE, JAMES (writer) 5 / 9 / 1860 TAURUS
BARRIE, WENDY (actress) 4 / 18 / 1913 ARIES
BARRIENTOS, MARIA (soprano) 3 / 10 / 1883 PISCES
BARROW, CLYDE (outlaw) 3 / 24 / 1909 ARIES
BARRY, GENE (actor) 6 / 14 / 1922 GEMINI
BARRY, JACK (TV personality) 3 / 20 / 1918 PISCES/ARIES
BARRY, RICK (basketball player) 3 / 28 / 1944 ARIES
BARRYMORE, ETHEL (actress) 8 / 15 / 1879 LEO
BARRYMORE, JOHN (actor) 2 / 15 / 1882 AQUARIUS
BARRYMORE, LIONEL (actor) 4 / 28 / 1878 TAURUS
BART, LIONEL (composer) 8 / 1 / 1930 LEO
BARTH, JOHN (novelist) 5 / 27 / 1930 GEMINI
BARTH, KARL (theologian) 10 / 5 / 1886 LIBRA
BARTHOLOMEW, FREDDIE (child actor) 3 / 28 / 1924 ARIES
BARTOK, BELA (composer) 3 / 25 / 1881 ARIES
BARTON, CLARA (nurse) 12 / 25 / 1821 CAPRICORN
BARUCH, BERNARD (financier) 8 / 19 / 1870 LEO
BARYSHNIKOV, MIKHAIL (ballet dancer) 1 / 27 / 1948 AQUARIUS
BARZINI, LUIGI (writer) 12 / 21 / 1908 SAGITTARIUS/CAPRICORN
BARZUN, JACQUES (writer) 11 / 30 / 1907 SAGITTARIUS
BASEHART, RICHARD (actor) 8 / 31 / 1914 VIRGO
BASIE, COUNT (jazz musician) 8 / 21 / 1906 LEO
BASSEY, SHIRLEY (singer) 1 / 8 / 1937 CAPRICORN
BASTIANINI, ETTORE (baritone) 9 / 24 / 1922 VIRGO/LIBRA
BATES, ALAN (actor) 2 / 17 / 1934 AQUARIUS
BATHGATE, ANDY (hockey player) 8 / 28 / 1932 VIRGO
BATISTA, FULGENCIO (dictator) 1 / 16 / 1901 CAPRICORN
BATTISTINI, MATTIA (baritone) 2 / 27 / 1857 PISCES
BAUDELAIRE, CHARLES (poet) 4 / 9 / 1821 ARIES
BAUER, HANK (baseball manager) 7 / 31 / 1922 LEO
BAUM, KURT (tenor) 3 / 15 / 1908 PISCES
BAUM, L. FRANK (writer) 5 / 15 / 1856 TAURUS
BAXLEY, BARBARA (actress) 1 / 1 / 1927 CAPRICORN
BAXTER, ANNE (actress) 5 / 7 / 1923 TAURUS
BEAME, ABRAHAM (politician) 3 / 20 / 1906 PISCES
BEAN, ORSON (actor) 7 / 22 / 1928 CANCER
BEARD, FRANK (golfer) 5 / 1 / 1939 TAURUS

BEARD, JAMES (gourmet) 5 / 5 / 1903 TAURUS
BEARDEN, ROMARE (artist) 9 / 2 / 1914 VIRGO
BEARDSLEY, AUBREY (artist) 8 / 24 / 1872 VIRGO
BEATON, CECIL (stage designer) 1 / 14 / 1904 CAPRICORN
BEATTY, JIM (runner) 10 / 28 / 1934 SCORPIO
BEATTY, WARREN (actor) 3 / 30 / 1937 ARIES
BEAUMARCHAIS, PIERRE AUGUSTIN (playwright) 1 / 24 / 1732
    AQUARIUS
BEAUVOIR, SIMONE DE (writer) 1 / 9 / 1908 CAPRICORN
BEBAN, GARY (football player) 8 / 5 / 1946 LEO
BECHI, GINO (baritone) 10 / 16 / 1913 LIBRA
BECK, JEFF (rock musician) 6 / 24 / ? CANCER
BECK, JULIAN (actor) 5 / 31 / 1925 GEMINI
BECKET, THOMAS (clergyman) 1 / 4 / 1119 CAPRICORN
BECKETT, SAMUEL (writer) 4 / 13 / 1906 ARIES
BEDFORD, BRIAN (actor) 2 / 16 / 1935 AQUARIUS
BEECHAM, THOMAS (conductor) 4 / 29 / 1879 TAURUS
BEECHER, HENRY WARD (preacher) 6 / 24 / 1813 CANCER
BEERBOHM, MAX (writer) 8 / 24 / 1872 VIRGO
BEETHOVEN, LUDWIG VAN (composer) 12 / 16 / 1770 SAGITTARIUS
BEGLEY, ED (actor) 3 / 25 / 1901 ARIES
BEHAN, BRENDAN (writer) 2 / 9 / 1923 AQUARIUS
BEJART, MAURICE (choreographer) 1 / 1 / 1927 CAPRICORN
BELAFONTE, HARRY (singer) 3 / 1 / 1927 PISCES
BEL GEDDES, BARBARA (actress) 10 / 31 / 1922 SCORPIO
BEL GEDDES, NORMAN (producer and stage designer) 4 / 27 / 1893
    TAURUS
BELL, ALEXANDER GRAHAM (inventor) 3 / 3 / 1847 PISCES
BELL, BERT (football commissioner) 2 / 25 / 1894 PISCES
BELLAMY, RALPH (actor) 6 / 17 / 1904 GEMINI
BELLI, MELVIN (lawyer) 7 / 29 / 1907 LEO
BELLINI, VINCENZO (composer) 11 / 3 / 1801 SCORPIO
BELLOW, SAUL (novelist) 6 / 10 / 1915 GEMINI
BELLUSCHI, PIETRO (architect) 8 / 18 / 1899 LEO
BELMONDO, JEAN-PAUL (actor) 4 / 9 / 1933 ARIES
BELMONT, MRS. AUGUST (philanthropist) 12 / 13 / 1879
    SAGITTARIUS
BEMELMANS, LUDWIG (writer) 4 / 27 / 1898 TAURUS
BENCH, JOHNNY (baseball player) 12 / 7 / 1947 SAGITTARIUS
BENDIX, WILLIAM (actor) 1 / 14 / 1906 CAPRICORN

BENEDICT, RUTH (anthropologist) 6 / 5 / 1887 GEMINI
BENET, STEPHEN VINCENT (writer) 7 / 22 / 1898 CANCER
BEN-GURION, DAVID (Israeli statesman) 10 / 16 / 1886 LIBRA
BENJAMIN, RICHARD (actor) 5 / 22 / 1938 GEMINI
BENNETT, ARNOLD (novelist) 5 / 27 / 1867 GEMINI
BENNETT, CONSTANCE (actress) 10 / 22 / 1905 LIBRA
BENNETT, JOAN (actress) 2 / 27 / 1910 PISCES
BENNETT, RICHARD RODNEY (composer) 3 / 29 / 1936 ARIES
BENNETT, ROBERT RUSSELL (composer) 6 / 15 / 1894 GEMINI
BENNETT, TONY (singer) 8 / 3 / 1926 LEO
BENNY, JACK (comedian) 2 / 14 / 1894 AQUARIUS
BENTHAM, JEREMY (philosopher) 2 / 15 / 1748 AQUARIUS
BENTON, THOMAS HART (painter) 3 / 14 / 1782 PISCES
BEN-VENISTE, RICHARD (lawyer) 1 / 3 / 1943 CAPRICORN
BERDYAEV, NICHOLAS (philosopher) 3 / 6 / 1874 PISCES
BERENSON, BERNARD (art critic) 6 / 26 / 1865 CANCER
BERG, ALBAN (composer) 2 / 9 / 1885 AQUARIUS
BERG, GERTRUDE (actress) 10 / 3 / 1899 LIBRA
BERG, PATTY (golfer) 2 / 13 / 1918 AQUARIUS
BERGANZA, TERESA (mezzo-soprano) 3 / 16 / 1935 PISCES
BERGEN, EDGAR (ventriloquist) 2 / 16 / 1903 AQUARIUS
BERGEN, POLLY (actress) 7 / 14 / 1930 CANCER
BERGER, ERNA (soprano) 10 / 19 / 1900 LIBRA
BERGERAC, CYRANO DE (soldier and writer) 3 / 6 / 1620 PISCES
BERGHOF, HERBERT (acting teacher) 9 / 13 / 1909 VIRGO
BERGMAN, INGMAR (film maker) 7 / 14 / 1918 CANCER
BERGMAN, INGRID (actress) 8 / 29 / 1916 VIRGO
BERGONZI, CARLO (tenor) 7 / 13 / 1924 CANCER
BERIOSOVA, SVETLANA (ballet dancer) 9 / 24 / 1932 VIRGO/LIBRA
BERKELEY, BUSBY (film director) 11 / 29 / 1895 SAGITTARIUS
BERLE, MILTON (comedian) 7 / 12 / 1908 CANCER
BERLIN, IRVING (composer) 5 / 11 / 1888 TAURUS
BERLIN, JEANNIE (actress) 11 / 1 / 1949 SCORPIO
BERLIOZ, HECTOR (composer) 12 / 11 / 1803 SAGITTARIUS
BERLITZ, CHARLES (educator) 11 / 23 / 1914 SCORPIO/SAGITTARIUS
BERMAN, EUGENE (artist) 11 / 4 / 1899 SCORPIO
BERMAN, SHELLEY (comedian) 2 / 3 / 1924 AQUARIUS
BERNADETTE OF LOURDES, ST. (nun) 1 / 7 / 1844 CAPRICORN
BERNANOS, GEORGES (writer) 2 / 20 / 1888 PISCES
BERNHARDT, SARAH (actress) 10 / 23 / 1844 LIBRA

BERNINI, GIOVANNI (artist) 12 / 7 / 1598 SAGITTARIUS
BERNSTEIN, CARL (reporter) 2 / 14 / 1944 AQUARIUS
BERNSTEIN, ELMER (composer) 4 / 4 / 1922 ARIES
BERNSTEIN, LEONARD (conductor) 8 / 25 / 1918 VIRGO
BERRA, YOGI (baseball player) 5 / 12 / 1925 TAURUS
BERRIGAN, DANIEL (clergyman) 5 / 9 / 1921 TAURUS
BERRIGAN, PHILIP (clergyman) 10 / 5 / 1923 LIBRA
BERRY, CHUCK (singer) 10 / 18 / 1926 LIBRA
BERRY, WALTER (baritone) 4 / 8 / 1929 ARIES
BERTOLUCCI, BERNARDO (film maker) 3 / 16 / 1940 PISCES
BESANT, ANNIE (theosophist) 10 / 1 / 1847 LIBRA
BEST, EDNA (actress) 3 / 3 / 1900 PISCES
BETANCOURT, ROMULO (Venezuelan politician) 2 / 22 / 1908 PISCES
BETTELHEIM, BRUNO (sociologist) 8 / 25 / 1903 VIRGO
BETTI, UGO (writer) 2 / 4 / 1892 AQUARIUS
BETTS, RICHARD (rock musician) 12 / 12 / ? SAGITTARIUS
BEYMER, RICHARD (actor) 2 / 21 / 1939 PISCES
BIDAULT, GEORGES (French politician) 10 / 5 / 1899 LIBRA
BIERCE, AMBROSE (writer) 6 / 24 / 1842 CANCER
BIERSTADT, ALBERT (painter) 1 / 7 / 1830 CAPRICORN
BIGGS, E. POWER (organist) 3 / 29 / 1906 ARIES
BIKEL, THEODORE (folk singer) 5 / 2 / 1924 TAURUS
BILLY THE KID (outlaw) 11 / 23 / 1859 SAGITTARIUS
BING, RUDOLF (operatic impresario) 1 / 9 / 1902 CAPRICORN
BIRDFEATHER, BARBARA (astrologer) 9 / 24 / 1940 LIBRA
BIRREN, FABER (color theorist) 9 / 21 / 1900 VIRGO
BISHOP, JOEY (TV personality) 2 / 3 / 1918 AQUARIUS
BISMARCK, OTTO VON (German statesman) 4 / 1 / 1815 ARIES
BISSET, JACQUELINE (actress) 9 / 13 / 1944 VIRGO
BIZET, GEORGES (composer) 10 / 25 / 1838 SCORPIO
BJOERLING, JUSSI (tenor) 2 / 5 / 1911 AQUARIUS
BJOERNSTRAND, GUNNAR (actor) 11 / 13 / 1909 SCORPIO
BLACK, CILLA (singer) 5 / 27 / 1943 GEMINI
BLACK, HUGO (jurist) 2 / 27 / 1886 PISCES
BLACK, KAREN (actress) 7 / 1 / 1942 CANCER
BLACK, SHIRLEY TEMPLE (actress and politician) 4 / 23 / 1928
    TAURUS
BLACKMER, SIDNEY (actor) 7 / 13 / 1898 CANCER
BLACKMUN, HARRY (jurist) 11 / 12 / 1908 SCORPIO
BLADD, STEVEN JO (rock musician) 6 / 13 / 1942 GEMINI

BLAINE, VIVIAN (actress) 11 / 21 / 1924 SCORPIO
BLAIR, DAVID (ballet dancer) 7 / 27 / 1932 LEO
BLAIR, FRANK (newscaster) 5 / 30 / 1915 GEMINI
BLAIR, JANET (actress) 4 / 22 / 1921 TAURUS
BLAIR, LINDA (actress) 1 / 22 / 1959 AQUARIUS
BLAKE, AMANDA (actress) 2 / 20 / 1931 PISCES
BLAKE, EUBIE (songwriter) 2 / 7 / 1873 AQUARIUS
BLAKE, WILLIAM (poet and artist) 11 / 28 / 1757 SAGITTARIUS
BLANDA, GEORGE (football player) 9 / 17 / 1927 VIRGO
BLANKSHINE, ROBERT (ballet dancer) 12 / 22 / 1948
    SAGITTARIUS/CAPRICORN
BLASS, BILL (fashion designer) 6 / 22 / 1922 GEMINI/CANCER
BLATTY, WILLIAM PETER (novelist) 1 / 7 / 1928 CAPRICORN
BLAVATSKY, MME. HELENA (theosophist) 8 / 12 / 1831 LEO
BLIGH, WILLIAM (British naval officer) 9 / 9 / 1754 VIRGO
BLISS, ARTHUR (composer) 8 / 2 / 1891 LEO
BLOCH, ERNEST (composer) 7 / 24 / 1880 LEO
BLONDELL, JOAN (actress) 8 / 30 / 1909 VIRGO
BLOOM, CLAIRE (actress) 2 / 15 / 1931 AQUARIUS
BLOOMER, AMELIA (feminist) 5 / 27 / 1818 GEMINI
BLOOMFIELD, MIKE (blues musician) 7 / 28 / 1943 LEO
BLOOMINGDALE, AL (merchant) 4 / 15 / 1916 ARIES
BLUE, VIDA (baseball player) 7 / 28 / 1949 LEO
BLYDEN, LARRY (actor) 6 / 23 / 1925 CANCER
BLYTH, ANNE (actress) 8 / 16 / 1928 LEO
BOCCHERINI, LUIGI (composer) 2 / 19 / 1743 AQUARIUS/PISCES
BOCK, JERRY (composer) 11 / 23 / 1928 SCORPIO/SAGITTARIUS
BOEHM, KARL (conductor) 8 / 28 / 1894 VIRGO
BOELL, HEINRICH (writer) 12 / 21 / 1917 SAGITTARIUS/CAPRICORN
BOGAN, LOUISE (sculptress) 8 / 11 / 1897 LEO
BOGARDE, DIRK (actor) 3 / 28 / 1921 ARIES
BOGARDUS, JAMES (architect) 3 / 14 / 1800 PISCES
BOGART, HUMPHREY (actor) 12 / 25 / 1899 CAPRICORN
BOGDANOVITCH, PETER (film director) 7 / 30 / 1939 LEO
BOHR, NIELS (physicist) 10 / 7 / 1885 LIBRA
BOITO, ARRIGO (composer and poet) 2 / 24 / 1842 PISCES
BOLAN, MARC (singer) 9 / 30 / 1947 LIBRA
BOLGER, RAY (actor) 1 / 10 / 1904 CAPRICORN
BOLIVAR, SIMON (liberator) 7 / 24 / 1783 LEO
BOLT, ROBERT (playwright) 8 / 15 / 1924 LEO

BONCI, ALESSANDRO (tenor) 2 / 10 / 1870 AQUARIUS
BOND, CARRIE JACOBS (composer) 8 / 11 / 1862 LEO
BOND, JULIAN (politician) 1 / 14 / 1940 CAPRICORN
BOND, RUDY (actor) 10 / 1 / 1915 LIBRA
BOND, WARD (actor) 4 / 9 / 1905 ARIES
BONINSEGNA, CELESTINA (soprano) 2 / 26 / 1877 PISCES
BONNARD, PIERRE (painter) 10 / 3 / 1867 LIBRA
BONO, CHASTITY (entertainers' daughter) 3 / 4 / 1969 PISCES
BONO, SONNY (entertainer) 2 / 16 / 1935 AQUARIUS
BONYNGE, RICHARD (conductor) 9 / 29 / 1930 LIBRA
BOONE, DANIEL (frontiersman) 11 / 2 / 1734 SCORPIO
BOONE, PAT (singer) 6 / 1 / 1934 GEMINI
BOONE, RICHARD (actor) 6 / 18 / 1917 GEMINI
BOOTH, EDWIN (actor) 11 / 13 / 1833 SCORPIO
BOOTH, JOHN WILKES (assassin) 5 / 10 / 1838 TAURUS
BOOTH, SHIRLEY (actress) 8 / 30 / 1907 VIRGO
BORGE, VICTOR (entertainer) 1 / 3 / 1909 CAPRICORN
BORGES, JORGE LUIS (writer) 8 / 24 / 1899 VIRGO
BORGIA, CESARE (Italian politician) 10 / 4 / 1478 LIBRA
BORGIOLI, DINO (tenor) 2 / 15 / 1891 AQUARIUS
BORGNINE, ERNEST (actor) 1 / 24 / 1917 AQUARIUS
BORI, LUCREZIA (soprano) 12 / 24 / 1888 CAPRICORN
BORKH, INGE (soprano) 5 / 26 / 1917 GEMINI
BORMAN, FRANK (astronaut) 3 / 14 / 1928 PISCES
BORN, MAX (physicist) 12 / 11 / 1882 SAGITTARIUS
BORODIN, ALEXANDER (composer) 11 / 12 / 1834 SCORPIO
BOROS, JULIUS (golfer) 3 / 3 / 1920 PISCES
BORTOLUZZI, PAOLO (ballet dancer) 5 / 17 / 1938 TAURUS
BOSLEY, TOM (actor) 10 / 1 / 1927 LIBRA
BOSWELL, JAMES (writer) 11 / 9 / 1740 SCORPIO
BOUCHER, FRANÇOIS (painter) 9 / 29 / 1703 LIBRA
BOUDREAU, LOU (baseball player) 7 / 17 / 1917 CANCER
BOULANGER, NADIA (music teacher) 9 / 16 / 1887 VIRGO
BOULEZ, PIERRE (conductor) 3 / 26 / 1925 ARIES
BOULT, ADRIAN (conductor) 4 / 8 / 1889 ARIES
BOUTON, JIM (baseball player) 3 / 8 / 1939 PISCES
BOVASSO, JULIE (playwright and director) 8 / 1 / 1930 LEO
BOW, CLARA (actress) 7 / 29 / 1905 LEO
BOWDLER, THOMAS (editor) 7 / 11 / 1754 CANCER
BOWEN, ELIZABETH (novelist) 6 / 7 / 1899 GEMINI

BOWIE, DAVID (singer) 1 / 8 / 1948 CAPRICORN
BOWLES, CHESTER (politician) 4 / 5 / 1901 ARIES
BOYD, MALCOLM (clergyman) 6 / 8 / 1923 GEMINI
BOYD, STEPHEN (actor) 7 / 4 / 1928 CANCER
BOYD, WILLIAM (actor) 6 / 5 / 1898 GEMINI
BOYER, CHARLES (actor) 8 / 28 / 1899 VIRGO
BOYER, KEN (baseball player) 5 / 20 / 1931 TAURUS
BOYINGTON, PAPPY (flying ace) 12 / 4 / 1906 SAGITTARIUS
BOYLE, ROBERT (scientist) 2 / 4 / 1627 AQUARIUS
BOYLE, W. A. "TONY" (labor leader) 12 / 1 / 1904 SAGITTARIUS
BRACKEN, EDDIE (actor) 2 / 7 / 1920 AQUARIUS
BRADBURY, RAY (writer) 8 / 22 / 1920 LEO
BRADLEY, BILL (basketball player) 7 / 28 / 1943 LEO
BRADLEY, OMAR (army officer) 2 / 12 / 1893 AQUARIUS
BRADLEY, THOMAS (politician) 12 / 29 / 1917 CAPRICORN
BRADY, DIAMOND JIM (financier) 8 / 12 / 1856 LEO
BRADY, SCOTT (actor) 9 / 13 / 1924 VIRGO
BRAHE, TYCHO (astronomer) 12 / 23 / 1546 CAPRICORN
BRAHMS, JOHANNES (composer) 5 / 7 / 1833 TAURUS
BRAILLE, LOUIS (teacher of the blind) 1 / 4 / 1806 CAPRICORN
BRAILOWSKY, ALEXANDER (pianist) 2 / 16 / 1896 AQUARIUS
BRAMLETT, BONNIE (singer) 11 / 19 / ? SCORPIO
BRAMLETT, DELANEY (singer) 7 / 1 / ? CANCER
BRANCUSI, CONSTANTIN (sculptor) 2 / 21 / 1876 PISCES
BRANDO, MARLON (actor) 4 / 3 / 1924 ARIES
BRANDT, WILLY (German politician) 12 / 18 / 1913 SAGITTARIUS
BRAQUE, GEORGES (painter) 5 / 13 / 1882 TAURUS
BRAUN, EVA (dictator's mistress) 2 / 6 / 1912 AQUARIUS
BRAZZI, ROSSANO (actor) 9 / 18 / 1916 VIRGO
BREAM, JULIAN (guitarist) 7 / 15 / 1933 CANCER
BRECHT, BERTOLT (playwright) 2 / 10 / 1898 AQUARIUS
BREEDLOVE, CRAIG (auto racer) 3 / 23 / 1938 ARIES
BREL, JACQUES (composer) 4 / 8 / 1929 ARIES
BRENNAN, WALTER (actor) 6 / 25 / 1894 CANCER
BRENNAN, WILLIAM (jurist) 4 / 25 / 1906 TAURUS
BRENT, GEORGE (actor) 3 / 15 / 1904 PISCES
BRESLIN, JIMMY (journalist) 10 / 17 / 1930 LIBRA
BRESSON, ROBERT (film director) 9 / 25 / 1907 LIBRA
BRETON, ANDRE (writer) 2 / 19 / 1896 AQUARIUS/PISCES
BREUER, MARCEL (architect) 5 / 22 / 1902 TAURUS/GEMINI

BREWER, TERESA (singer) 5 / 7 / 1931 TAURUS
BREZHNEV, LEONID (Soviet politician) 12 / 19 / 1906 SAGITTARIUS
BRICE, FANNY (comedienne) 10 / 29 / 1891 SCORPIO
BRIDGES, BEAU (actor) 12 / 9 / 1941 SAGITTARIUS
BRIDGES, HARRY (labor leader) 7 / 28 / 1901 LEO
BRIDGES, LLOYD (actor) 1 / 15 / 1913 CAPRICORN
BRINKLEY, DAVID (newsman) 7 / 10 / 1920 CANCER
BRITT, MAY (actress) 3 / 22 / 1936 ARIES
BRITTEN, BENJAMIN (composer) 11 / 22 / 1913 SAGITTARIUS
BRONSON, CHARLES (actor) 11 / 3 / 1922 SCORPIO
BRONTE, ANNE (novelist) 1 / 17 / 1820 CAPRICORN
BRONTE, CHARLOTTE (novelist) 4 / 21 / 1816 TAURUS
BRONTE, EMILY (novelist) 7 / 30 / 1818 LEO
BRONZINO (painter) 11 / 27 / 1503 SAGITTARIUS
BROOK, PETER (director) 3 / 21 / 1925 PISCES/ARIES
BROOKS, DONALD (fashion and costume designer) 1 / 10 / 1928
    CAPRICORN
BROOKS, LOUISE (actress) 11 / 14 / 1906 SCORPIO
BROOKS, VAN WYCK (writer) 2 / 16 / 1886 AQUARIUS
BROPHY, BRIGID (writer) 6 / 12 / 1929 GEMINI
BROTHERS, JOYCE (TV personality) 10 / 20 / 1928 LIBRA
BROWN, EDMOND, JR. (politician) 4 / 7 / 1938 ARIES
BROWN, EDMUND "PAT" (politician) 4 / 21 / 1905 TAURUS
BROWN, H. RAP (black militant) 10 / 4 / 1943 LIBRA
BROWN, HELEN GURLEY (writer) 2 / 18 / 1922 AQUARIUS
BROWN, JAMES (actor) 3 / 22 / 1920 ARIES
BROWN, JIM (football player) 2 / 17 / 1936 AQUARIUS
BROWN, JOE E. (comedian) 7 / 28 / 1892 LEO
BROWN, JOHN (abolitionist) 5 / 9 / 1800 TAURUS
BROWN, LARRY (football player) 9 / 19 / 1947 VIRGO
BROWN, NORMAN O. (writer) 10 / 25 / 1913 SCORPIO
BROWN, PAMELA (actress) 7 / 8 / 1917 CANCER
BROWN, TALLY (singer) 8 / 1 / 1934 LEO
BROWNE, CORAL (actress) 7 / 23 / 1913 CANCER/LEO
BROWNE, JACKSON (singer) 10 / 9 / 1948 LIBRA
BROWNING, ELIZABETH BARRETT (poet) 3 / 6 / 1806 PISCES
BROWNING, JOHN (pianist) 5 / 23 / 1933 GEMINI
BROWNING, ROBERT (poet) 5 / 7 / 1812 TAURUS
BROWNLEE, JOHN (baritone) 1 / 7 / 1900 CAPRICORN
BRUBECK, DAVE (jazz musician) 12 / 6 / 1920 SAGITTARIUS

BURNS, GEORGE (comedian) 1 / 20 / 1896 AQUARIUS
BURNS, JOHN A. (politician) 3 / 30 / 1909 ARIES
BURNS, ROBERT (poet) 1 / 25 / 1759 AQUARIUS
BURPEE, DAVID (horticulturist) 4 / 5 / 1893 ARIES
BURR, AARON (politician) 2 / 6 / 1756 AQUARIUS
BURR, RAYMOND (actor) 5 / 21 / 1917 GEMINI
BURROUGHS, EDGAR RICE (novelist) 9 / 1 / 1875 VIRGO
BURROUGHS, WILLIAM (writer) 2 / 5 / 1914 AQUARIUS
BURROWS, ABE (producer) 12 / 18 / 1910 SAGITTARIUS
BURTON, RICHARD (actor) 11 / 10 / 1925 SCORPIO
BURTON, RICHARD (explorer) 3 / 19 / 1821 PISCES
BUSCH, FRITZ (conductor) 3 / 13 / 1890 PISCES
BUSH, GEORGE (government official) 6 / 12 / 1924 GEMINI
BUSHMAN, FRANCIS X. (actor) 1 / 10 / 1883 CAPRICORN
BUSONI, FERRUCCIO (composer) 4 / 1 / 1866 ARIES
BUTLER, JOHN (choreographer) 9 / 29 / 1920 LIBRA
BUTLER, MICHAEL (producer) 11 / 26 / 1926 SAGITTARIUS
BUTLER, SAMUEL (novelist) 12 / 4 / 1835 SAGITTARIUS
BUTTONS, RED (actor) 2 / 5 / 1919 AQUARIUS
BUTZ, EARL (government official) 7 / 3 / 1909 CANCER
BUZHARDT, J. FRED (lawyer) 2 / 21 / 1924 PISCES
BUZZI, RUTH (comedienne) 7 / 24 / 1936 LEO
BYINGTON, SPRING (actress) 10 / 17 / 1893 LIBRA
BYRD, CHARLIE (guitarist) 9 / 16 / 1925 VIRGO
BYRD, RICHARD E. (explorer) 10 / 25 / 1888 SCORPIO
BYRNE, BRENDAN (politician) 4 / 1 / 1924 ARIES
BYRON, LORD (poet) 1 / 22 / 1788 AQUARIUS

CAAN, JAMES (actor) 3 / 26 / 1939 ARIES
CABALLE, MONTSERRAT (soprano) 4 / 12 / 1933 ARIES
CABRINI, MOTHER (nun) 7 / 15 / 1850 CANCER
CACOYANNIS, MICHAEL (director) 6 / 11 / 1922 GEMINI
CADMUS, PAUL (painter) 12 / 17 / 1904 SAGITTARIUS
CAEN, HERB (columnist) 4 / 3 / 1916 ARIES
CAESAR, JULIUS, EMPEROR 7 / 8 / 102 B.C. CANCER
CAESAR, SID (comedian) 9 / 8 / 1922 VIRGO
CAGE, JOHN (composer) 9 / 5 / 1912 VIRGO
CAGNEY, JAMES (actor) 7 / 17 / 1904 CANCER
CAGNEY, JEANNE (actress) 3 / 25 / 1919 ARIES

CAHILL, WILLIAM (politician) 6 / 25 / 1912 CANCER
CAHN, SAMMY (songwriter) 6 / 18 / 1913 GEMINI
CAINE, MICHAEL (actor) 3 / 14 / 1933 PISCES
CALDER, ALEXANDER (sculptor) 7 / 22 / 1898 CANCER
CALDERON DE LA BARCA, PEDRO (playwright) 1 / 17 / 1600
    CAPRICORN
CALDERONE, MARY (sex educator) 7 / 1 / 1904 CANCER
CALDWELL, ERSKINE (novelist) 12 / 17 / 1903 SAGITTARIUS
CALDWELL, TAYLOR (novelist) 9 / 7 / 1900 VIRGO
CALDWELL, ZOE (actress) 9 / 14 / 1933 VIRGO
CALHOUN, JOHN C. (politician) 3 / 18 / 1782 PISCES
CALHOUN, RORY (actor) 8 / 8 / 1922 LEO
CALIGULA OF ROME, EMPEROR 8 / 30 / A.D. 12 VIRGO
CALLAS, MARIA (soprano) 12 / 3 / 1923 SAGITTARIUS
CALLEY, WILLIAM L., JR. (army officer) 6 / 8 / 1943 GEMINI
CALLOWAY, CAB (singer) 12 / 24 / 1907 CAPRICORN
CALVE, EMMA (soprano) 8 / 15 / 1858 LEO
CALVET, CORINNE (actress) 4 / 30 / 1925 TAURUS
CALVIN, JOHN (theologian) 7 / 21 / 1509 CANCER
CAMBRIDGE, GODFREY (comedian) 2 / 26 / 1933 PISCES
CAMERON, ROD (actor) 12 / 7 / 1912 SAGITTARIUS
CAMPANELLA, ROY (baseball player) 11 / 19 / 1921 SCORPIO
CAMPBELL, GLEN (singer) 4 / 22 / 1938 TAURUS
CAMPBELL, JOSEPH (writer) 3 / 26 / 1904 ARIES
CAMPBELL, MRS. PATRICK (actress) 2 / 9 / 1865 AQUARIUS
CAMUS, ALBERT (writer) 11 / 7 / 1913 SCORPIO
CANADAY, JOHN (art critic) 2 / 1 / 1907 AQUARIUS
CANALETTO (painter) 10 / 18 / 1697 LIBRA
CANBY, VINCENT (film critic) 7 / 27 / 1924 LEO
CANIFF, MILTON (cartoonist) 2 / 28 / 1907 PISCES
CANNON, DYAN (actress) 1 / 4 / 1929 CAPRICORN
CANOVA, ANTONIO (sculptor) 11 / 1 / 1757 SCORPIO
CANOVA, JUDY (comedienne) 11 / 20 / 1916 SCORPIO
CANTINFLAS (comedian) 8 / 12 / 1911 LEO
CANTOR, EDDIE (comedian) 1 / 31 / 1892 AQUARIUS
CANTRELL, LANA (singer) 8 / 7 / 1944 LEO
CAPOBIANCO, TITO (director) 8 / 28 / 1931 VIRGO
CAPONE, AL (mobster) 1 / 17 / 1899 CAPRICORN
CAPOTE, TRUMAN (writer) 9 / 30 / 1924 LIBRA
CAPP, AL (cartoonist) 9 / 28 / 1909 LIBRA

CAPRA, FRANK (film maker) 5 / 18 / 1897 TAURUS
CAPUCINE (actress) 1 / 6 / 1933 CAPRICORN
CARAVAGGIO, MICHELANGELO (painter) 10 / 8 / 1573 LIBRA
CARDIN, PIERRE (fashion designer) 7 / 7 / 1922 CANCER
CARDINALE, CLAUDIA (actress) 4 / 15 / 1938 ARIES
CAREY, HUGH (politician) 4 / 11 / 1919 ARIES
CAREY, MACDONALD (actor) 3 / 15 / 1913 PISCES
CARL XVI GUSTAVUS OF SWEDEN, KING 4 / 30 / 1946 TAURUS
CARLIN, GEORGE (comedian) 5 / 12 / 1937 TAURUS
CARLISLE, KITTY (actress) 9 / 3 / 1914 VIRGO
CARLOTA OF MEXICO, EMPRESS 6 / 7 / 1840 GEMINI
CARLTON, STEVE (baseball player) 12 / 22 / 1944
    SAGITTARIUS/CAPRICORN
CARLYLE, THOMAS (writer) 12 / 4 / 1795 SAGITTARIUS
CARMICHAEL, HOAGY (composer) 11 / 22 / 1899 SAGITTARIUS
CARMICHAEL, STOKELY (black militant) 6 / 29 / 1941 CANCER
CARMINES, AL (clergyman and composer) 7 / 25 / 1936 LEO
CARNE, MARCEL (film maker) 8 / 18 / 1906 LEO
CARNEGIE, ANDREW (tycoon) 11 / 25 / 1835 SAGITTARIUS
CARNEGIE, DALE (writer) 11 / 24 / 1888 SAGITTARIUS
CARNEY, ART (actor) 11 / 4 / 1918 SCORPIO
CARON, LESLIE (actress) 7 / 1 / 1931 CANCER
CARPENTER, SCOTT (astronaut) 5 / 1 / 1925 TAURUS
CARRADINE, DAVID (actor) 12 / 8 / 1940 SAGITTARIUS
CARRADINE, JOHN (actor) 2 / 5 / 1906 AQUARIUS
CARRADINE, KEITH (actor) 8 / 8 / 1949 LEO
CARRERO BLANCO, LUIS (Spanish politician) 3 / 4 / 1903 PISCES
CARROLL, DIAHANN (singer) 7 / 17 / 1935 CANCER
CARROLL, LEWIS (writer) 1 / 27 / 1832 AQUARIUS
CARROLL, MADELEINE (actress) 2 / 26 / 1909 PISCES
CARROLL, PAT (actress) 5 / 5 / 1927 TAURUS
CARSON, JACK (actor) 10 / 27 / 1910 SCORPIO
CARSON, JOHNNY (TV personality) 10 / 23 / 1925 SCORPIO
CARSON, KIT (frontiersman) 12 / 24 / 1809 CAPRICORN
CARSON, RACHEL (naturalist) 5 / 27 / 1907 GEMINI
CARTER THE GREAT (magician) 6 / 14 / 1874 GEMINI
CARTER, C. E. O. (astrologer) 1 / 31 / 1887 AQUARIUS
CARTER, DON (bowler) 7 / 29 / 1926 LEO
CARTER, ELLIOTT (composer) 12 / 11 / 1908 SAGITTARIUS
CARTIER-BRESSON, HENRI (photographer) 8 / 22 / 1908 LEO

CERF, BENNETT (publisher) 5 / 25 / 1898 GEMINI
CERNAN, EUGENE (astronaut) 3 / 14 / 1934 PISCES
CERVANTES, MIGUEL DE (writer) 10 / 17 / 1547 LIBRA
CEZANNE, PAUL (painter) 1 / 19 / 1839 CAPRICORN
CHABRIER, EMMANUEL (composer) 1 / 18 / 1841 CAPRICORN
CHABROL, CLAUDE (film maker) 6 / 24 / 1930 CANCER
CHADWICK, FLORENCE (swimmer) 11 / 9 / 1918 SCORPIO
CHAGALL, MARC (painter) 7 / 7 / 1887 CANCER
CHAKIRIS, GEORGE (actor) 9 / 16 / 1933 VIRGO
CHALIAPIN, FEODOR (basso) 2 / 13 / 1873 AQUARIUS
CHAMBERLAIN, RICHARD (actor) 3 / 31 / 1935 ARIES
CHAMBERLAIN, WILT (basketball player) 8 / 21 / 1936 LEO
CHAMPION, GOWER (choreographer) 6 / 22 / 1921 CANCER
CHAMPION, MARGE (dancer) 9 / 2 / 1923 VIRGO
CHANCE, DEAN (baseball player) 6 / 1 / 1941 GEMINI
CHANCELLOR, JOHN (TV personality) 7 / 14 / 1927 CANCER
CHANDLER, JEFF (actor) 12 / 15 / 1918 SAGITTARIUS
CHANDLER, RAYMOND (writer) 7 / 23 / 1888 LEO
CHANEL, COCO (fashion designer) 8 / 19 / 1883 LEO
CHANEY, LON (actor) 4 / 1 / 1883 ARIES
CHANEY, LON, JR. (actor) 2 / 10 / 1915 AQUARIUS
CHANNING, CAROL (actress) 1 / 30 / 1921 AQUARIUS
CHAPIN, HARRY (singer) 12 / 7 / 1942 SAGITTARIUS
CHAPIN, SCHUYLER G. (operatic impresario) 2 / 13 / 1923 AQUARIUS
CHAPLIN, CHARLIE (comedian) 4 / 16 / 1889 ARIES
CHAPLIN, GERALDINE (actress) 7 / 31 / 1944 LEO
CHAPLIN, SYDNEY (actor) 3 / 31 / 1926 ARIES
CHARDIN, JEAN BAPTISTE (painter) 11 / 2 / 1699 SCORPIO
CHARISSE, CYD (actress) 3 / 8 / 1923 PISCES
CHARLEMAGNE, EMPEROR 4 / 6 / 742 ARIES
CHARLES OF ENGLAND, PRINCE 11 / 14 / 1948 SCORPIO
CHARLES I OF ENGLAND, KING 11 / 30 / 1600 SAGITTARIUS
CHARLES II OF ENGLAND, KING 6 / 10 / 1630 GEMINI
CHARLES V, EMPEROR 3 / 6 / 1500 PISCES
CHARLES, EZZARD (boxer) 7 / 7 / 1921 CANCER
CHARLES, RAY (singer) 9 / 23 / 1932 LIBRA
CHARPENTIER, GUSTAVE (composer) 6 / 25 / 1860 CANCER
CHARUBEL (seer) 11 / 9 / 1826 SCORPIO
CHASE, ILKA (actress) 4 / 8 / 1905 ARIES
CHATEAUBRIAND, FRANÇOIS RENE (writer) 9 / 4 / 1768 VIRGO

CHAVEZ, CARLOS (composer) 6 / 13 / 1899 GEMINI
CHAVEZ, CESAR (labor reformer) 3 / 31 / 1927 ARIES
CHAYEFSKY, PADDY (playwright) 1 / 29 / 1923 AQUARIUS
CHECKER, CHUBBY (singer) 10 / 3 / 1941 LIBRA
CHEECH (comedian) 7 / 13 / 1946 CANCER
CHEEVER, JOHN (novelist) 5 / 27 / 1912 GEMINI
CHEKHOV, ANTON (writer) 1 / 17 / 1860 CAPRICORN
CHENIER, ANDRE (poet) 10 / 30 / 1762 SCORPIO
CHER (entertainer) 5 / 20 / 1946 TAURUS
CHERUBINI, LUIGI (composer) 9 / 14 / 1760 VIRGO
CHESTERFIELD, LORD (writer) 10 / 2 / 1694 LIBRA
CHEVALIER, MAURICE (actor) 9 / 12 / 1888 VIRGO
CHIANG KAI-SHEK (army officer) 10 / 31 / 1886 SCORPIO
CHIANG KAI-SHEK, MME. (sociologist) 6 / 4 / 1899 GEMINI
CHILD, JULIA (cook) 8 / 15 / 1912 LEO
CHIRICO, GIORGIO DE (painter) 7 / 10 / 1888 CANCER
CHISHOLM, SHIRLEY (politician) 11 / 30 / 1924 SAGITTARIUS
CHOISNARD, PAUL (astrologer) 2 / 13 / 1867 AQUARIUS
CHOMSKY, NOAM (writer) 12 / 7 / 1928 SAGITTARIUS
CHONG (comedian) 5 / 24 / 1939 GEMINI
CHOPIN, FREDERIC (composer) 2 / 22 / 1810 PISCES
CHRISTIAN, LINDA (actress) 11 / 13 / 1923 SCORPIO
CHRISTIE, AGATHA (writer) 9 / 15 / 1890 VIRGO
CHRISTIE, JULIE (actress) 4 / 14 / 1941 ARIES
CHRISTOFF, BORIS (basso) 5 / 18 / 1919 TAURUS
CHRISTOPHER, JORDAN (actor) 10 / 23 / 1940 LIBRA/SCORPIO
CHURCH, FRANK (politician) 7 / 25 / 1924 LEO
CHURCH, FREDERICK EDWIN (painter) 5 / 4 / 1826 TAURUS
CHURCHILL, SARAH (actress) 10 / 7 / 1914 LIBRA
CHURCHILL, WINSTON (British statesman) 11 / 30 / 1874
    SAGITTARIUS
CIARDI, JOHN (poet) 6 / 24 / 1916 CANCER
CICERO, MARCUS TULLIUS (Roman statesman) 1 / 1 / 106 B.C.
    CAPRICORN
CILEA, FRANCESCO (composer) 7 / 29 / 1866 LEO
CILENTO, DIANE (actress) 10 / 5 / 1933 LIBRA
CIMAROSA, DOMENICO (composer) 12 / 17 / 1749 SAGITTARIUS
CLAIBORNE, CRAIG (gourmet) 9 / 4 / 1920 VIRGO
CLAIR, RENE (film maker) 11 / 11 / 1898 SCORPIO
CLAIRE, INA (actress) 10 / 15 / 1895 LIBRA

CLANCY, PAUL G. (astrologer) 6 / 29 / 1897 CANCER
CLAPTON, ERIC (rock musician) 3 / 30 / 1945 ARIES
CLARK, DANE (actor) 2 / 18 / 1915 AQUARIUS/PISCES
CLARK, DICK (TV personality) 11 / 30 / 1929 SAGITTARIUS
CLARK, GEORGE ROGERS (soldier) 11 / 19 / 1752 SCORPIO
CLARK, JIM (auto racer) 3 / 4 / 1936 PISCES
CLARK, KATHY LENNON (singer) 8 / 2 / 1943 LEO
CLARK, KENNETH (art historian) 7 / 13 / 1903 CANCER
CLARK, MAE (actress) 8 / 16 / 1910 LEO
CLARK, MARK (army officer) 5 / 1 / 1896 TAURUS
CLARK, PETULA (singer) 11 / 15 / 1932 SCORPIO
CLARK, RAMSEY (politician) 12 / 18 / 1927 SAGITTARIUS
CLARK, WILLIAM (explorer) 8 / 1 / 1770 LEO
CLARKE, ARTHUR C. (writer) 12 / 16 / 1917 SAGITTARIUS
CLARKE, RON (runner) 2 / 21 / 1937 PISCES
CLARKE, SHIRLEY (film maker) 10 / 2 / 1927 LIBRA
CLAUDIUS I OF ROME, EMPEROR 7 / 30 / 10 B.C. LEO
CLAY, HENRY (statesman) 4 / 12 / 1777 ARIES
CLAY, LUCIUS D. (army officer) 4 / 23 / 1897 TAURUS
CLEAVER, ELDRIDGE (writer) 8 / 31 /1935 VIRGO
CLEMENCEAU, GEORGES (French statesman) 9 / 28 / 1841 LIBRA
CLEMENT, RENE (film maker) 3 / 18 / 1913 PISCES
CLEMENTE, ROBERTO (baseball player) 8 / 18 / 1934 LEO
CLEMENTI, MUZIO (composer) 1 / 23 / 1752 AQUARIUS
CLEVA, FAUSTO (conductor) 5 / 17 / 1902 TAURUS
CLEVELAND, GROVER (politician) 3 / 18 / 1837 PISCES
CLIBURN, VAN (pianist) 7 / 12 / 1934 CANCER
CLIFFORD, CLARK (government official) 12 / 25 / 1906 CAPRICORN
CLIFT, MONTGOMERY (actor) 10 / 17 / 1920 LIBRA
CLINE, PATSY (country singer) 9 / 8 / 1932 VIRGO
CLOONEY, ROSEMARY (singer) 5 / 23 / 1928 GEMINI
CLOUZOT, HENRI-GEORGES (film director) 11 / 20 / 1907 SCORPIO
CLURMAN, HAROLD (drama critic) 9 / 18 / 1901 VIRGO
CLUYTENS, ANDRE (conductor) 3 / 26 / 1905 ARIES
COBB, JERRIE (pilot) 3 / 5 / 1931 PISCES
COBB, LEE J. (actor) 12 / 9/ 1911 SAGITTARIUS
COBB, TY (baseball player) 12 / 18 / 1886 SAGITTARIUS
COBURN, CHARLES (actor) 6 / 19 / 1877 GEMINI
COBURN, JAMES (actor) 8 / 31 / 1928 VIRGO
COCA, IMOGENE (comedienne) 11 / 18 / 1908 SCORPIO

COCHRAN, EDDIE (singer) 10 / 3 / 1938 LIBRA
COCHRAN, STEVE (actor) 5 / 25 / 1917 GEMINI
COCKER, JOE (singer) 5 / 20 / 1944 TAURUS
COCO, JAMES (actor) 3 / 21 / 1929 PISCES/ARIES
COCTEAU, JEAN (writer) 7 / 5 / 1891 CANCER
CODY, BUFFALO BILL (showman) 2 / 26 / 1846 PISCES
COHAN, GEORGE M. (producer) 7 / 4 / 1878 CANCER
COHEN, ALEXANDER H. (producer) 7 / 24 / 1920 LEO
COHEN, LEONARD (poet) 9 / 21 / 1934 VIRGO
COHN, ROY (lawyer) 2 / 20 / 1927 PISCES
COLBERT, CLAUDETTE (actress) 9 / 13 / 1905 VIRGO
COLBY, WILLIAM E. (government official) 1 / 4 / 1920 CAPRICORN
COLE, NAT KING (singer) 3 / 17 / 1919 PISCES
COLEMAN, ORNETTE (jazz musician) 3 / 19 / 1930 PISCES
COLERIDGE, SAMUEL TAYLOR (poet) 10 / 21 / 1772 LIBRA
COLETTE (writer) 1 / 28 / 1873 AQUARIUS
COLLIER, CONSTANCE (actress) 1 / 22 / 1880 AQUARIUS
COLLIER, MARIE (soprano) 4 / 16 / 1927 ARIES
COLLINS, DOROTHY (singer) 11 / 18 / 1926 SCORPIO
COLLINS, JOAN (actress) 5 / 23 / 1933 GEMINI
COLLINS, JUDY (singer) 5 / 1 / 1939 TAURUS
COLLINS, MICHAEL (astronaut) 10 / 31 / 1930 SCORPIO
COLMAN, RONALD (actor) 2 / 9 / 1891 AQUARIUS
COLSON, CHARLES W. (government official) 10 / 16 / 1931 LIBRA
COLT, SAMUEL (inventor) 7 / 19 / 1814 CANCER
COLUMBUS, CHRISTOPHER (explorer) 10 / 30 / 1451 SCORPIO
COMDEN, BETTY (lyricist) 5 / 3 / 1915 TAURUS
COMER, ANJANETTE (actress) 8 / 7 / 1942 LEO
COMFORT, ALEX (physician and author) 2 / 10 / 1920 AQUARIUS
COMMAGER, HENRY STEELE (historian) 10 / 25 / 1902 SCORPIO
COMO, PERRY (singer) 5 / 18 / 1913 TAURUS
CONDON, EDDIE (jazz musician) 11 / 16 / 1905 SCORPIO
CONERLY, CHARLES (football player) 9 / 19 / 1922 VIRGO
CONGDON, WILLIAM (painter) 4 / 15 / 1912 ARIES
CONIGLIARO, TONY (baseball player) 1 / 7 / 1945 CAPRICORN
CONNALLY, JOHN (politician) 2 / 27 / 1917 PISCES
CONNELLY, MARC (writer) 12 / 13 / 1890 SAGITTARIUS
CONNERY, SEAN (actor) 8 / 25 / 1930 VIRGO
CONNIFF, RAY (bandleader) 11 / 6 / 1916 SCORPIO
CONNORS, CHUCK (actor) 4 / 10 / 1921 ARIES

CONNORS, JIMMY (tennis player) 9 / 2 / 1952 VIRGO
CONRAD, CHARLES, JR. (astronaut) 6 / 2 / 1930 GEMINI
CONRAD, JOSEPH (writer) 12 / 3 / 1857 SAGITTARIUS
CONSTABLE, JOHN (painter) 6 / 11 / 1776 GEMINI
CONSTANTINE II OF GREECE, KING 6 / 2 / 1940 GEMINI
CONTE, RICHARD (actor) 3 / 24 / 1914 ARIES
CONVY, BERT (actor) 7 / 23 / 1935 CANCER/LEO
COOGAN, JACKIE (actor) 10 / 26 / 1914 SCORPIO
COOK, BARBARA (singer) 10 / 25 / 1927 SCORPIO
COOK, DONALD (actor) 9 / 26 / 1901 LIBRA
COOK, CAPTAIN JAMES (explorer) 11 / 7 / 1728 SCORPIO
COOKE, ALISTAIR (journalist) 11 / 20 / 1908 SCORPIO
COOLIDGE, CALVIN (politician) 7 / 4 / 1872 CANCER
COOPER, ALICE (rock musician) 2 / 4 / 1948 AQUARIUS
COOPER, GARY (actor) 5 / 7 / 1901 TAURUS
COOPER, GLADYS (actress) 12 / 18 / 1888 SAGITTARIUS
COOPER, GORDON (astronaut) 3 / 6 / 1927 PISCES
COOPER, JACKIE (actor) 9 / 15 / 1922 VIRGO
COOPER, JAMES FENIMORE (novelist) 9 / 15 / 1789 VIRGO
COOPER, MICHAEL (author) 3 / 21 / 1943 ARIES
COOPER, PETER (inventor) 2 / 12 / 1791 AQUARIUS
COPERNICUS, NICOLAUS (astronomer) 3 / 1 / 1473 PISCES
COPLAND, AARON (composer) 11 / 14 / 1900 SCORPIO
COPLEY, JOHN SINGLETON (painter) 7 / 14 / 1738 CANCER
COPPOLA, FRANCIS FORD (film director) 4 / 7 / 1939 ARIES
CORBETT, GENTLEMAN JIM (boxer) 9 / 1 / 1866 VIRGO
CORDAY, CHARLOTTE (assassin) 7 / 27 / 1768 LEO
CORELLI, ARCANGELO (composer) 2 / 17 / 1653 AQUARIUS
CORELLI, FRANCO (tenor) 4 / 8 / 1923 ARIES
CORENA, FERNANDO (basso) 12 / 22 / 1923 SAGITTARIUS/CAPRICORN
COREY, WENDELL (actor) 3 / 20 / 1914 PISCES/ARIES
CORMAN, ROGER (film director) 4 / 5 / 1926 ARIES
CORNEILLE, PIERRE (playwright) 6 / 6 / 1606 GEMINI
CORNELL, KATHARINE (actress) 2 / 16 / 1898 AQUARIUS
CORNWALLIS, CHARLES (army officer) 1 / 10 / 1739 CAPRICORN
COROT, JEAN BAPTISTE (painter) 7 / 28 / 1796 LEO
CORSARO, FRANK (director) 12 / 22 / 1924 SAGITTARIUS/CAPRICORN
CORTOT, ALFRED (pianist) 9 / 26 / 1877 LIBRA
COSBY, BILL (comedian) 7 / 12 / 1937 CANCER
COSELL, HOWARD (sportscaster) 3 / 25 / 1920 ARIES

COSSOTTO, FIORENZA (mezzo-soprano) 4 / 22 / 1936 TAURUS
COSTAIN, THOMAS B. (writer) 5 / 8 / 1885 TAURUS
COSTELLO, FRANK (mobster) 1 / 26 / 1893 AQUARIUS
COSTELLO, LOU (comedian) 3 / 6 / 1908 PISCES
COTTEN, JOSEPH (actor) 5 / 15 / 1905 TAURUS
COUPERIN, FRANÇOIS (composer) 11 / 10 / 1668 SCORPIO
COURBET, GUSTAVE (painter) 6 / 10 / 1819 GEMINI
COURREGES, ANDRE (fashion designer) 3 / 9 / 1923 PISCES
COURT, MARGARET (tennis player) 7 / 16 / 1942 CANCER
COURTENAY, TOM (actor) 2 / 25 / 1937 PISCES
COURTNEIDGE, CICELY (actress) 4 / 1 / 1893 ARIES
COUSINS, NORMAN (publisher) 6 / 24 / 1915 CANCER
COUSTEAU, JACQUES-YVES (oceanographer) 6 / 11 / 1910 GEMINI
COUSY, BOB (basketball player) 8 / 9 / 1928 LEO
COWARD, NOEL (playwright) 12 / 16 / 1899 SAGITTARIUS
COWELL, HENRY (composer) 3 / 11 / 1897 PISCES
COWPER, WILLIAM (poet) 12 / 7 / 1731 SAGITTARIUS
COX, ARCHIBALD (lawyer) 5 / 17 / 1912 TAURUS
COX, EDWARD F. (politician's son-in-law) 10 / 2 / 1946 LIBRA
COX, HARVEY (clergyman) 5 / 19 / 1929 TAURUS
COX, TRICIA NIXON (politician's daughter) 2 / 21 / 1946 PISCES
COX, WALLY (actor) 12 / 6 / 1924 SAGITTARIUS
COZZENS, JAMES GOULD (novelist) 8 / 19 / 1903 LEO
CRABBE, BUSTER (actor) 2 / 7 / 1908 AQUARIUS
CRAIG, GORDON (producer and stage designer) 1 / 16 / 1872
    CAPRICORN
CRAIN, JEANNE (actress) 5 / 25 / 1925 GEMINI
CRANACH, LUCAS (painter) 10 / 4 / 1472 LIBRA
CRANE, HART (poet) 7 / 21 / 1899 CANCER
CRANE, STEPHEN (writer) 11 / 1 / 1871 SCORPIO
CRANMER, THOMAS (clergyman) 7 / 11 / 1489 CANCER
CRANSTON, ALAN (politician) 6 / 19 / 1914 GEMINI
CRAWFORD, BRODERICK (actor) 12 / 9 / 1911 SAGITTARIUS
CRAWFORD, CHERYL (producer and director) 9 / 24 / 1902
    VIRGO/LIBRA
CRAWFORD, JOAN (actress) 3 / 23 / 1908 ARIES
CRESPIN, REGINE (soprano) 3 / 23 / 1927 ARIES
CRICHTON, MICHAEL (novelist) 10 / 23 / 1942 LIBRA/SCORPIO
CRIST, JUDITH (film critic) 5 / 22 / 1922 GEMINI

CROCE, BENEDETTO (philosopher) 2 / 25 / 1866 PISCES
CROCE, JIM (singer) 1 / 10 / 1943 CAPRICORN
CROCKETT, DAVY (frontiersman) 8 / 17 / 1786 LEO
CROMWELL, OLIVER (Puritan statesman) 5 / 5 / 1599 TAURUS
CRONIN, JOE (sports executive) 10 / 12 / 1906 LIBRA
CRONKITE, WALTER (newsman) 11 / 4 / 1916 SCORPIO
CRONYN, HUME (actor) 7 / 18 / 1911 CANCER
CROOKS, RICHARD (tenor) 6 / 26 / 1900 CANCER
CROSBY, BING (singer) 5 / 2 / 1904 TAURUS
CROSBY, DAVID (rock musician) 8 / 14 / 1941 LEO
CROSBY, GARY (singer) 6 / 27 / 1933 CANCER
CROSBY, JOHN (TV critic) 5 / 18 / 1912 TAURUS
CROSETTI, FRANK (baseball coach) 10 / 4 / 1910 LIBRA
CROSS, MILTON (radio commentator) 4 / 16 / 1897 ARIES
CROUSE, RUSSEL (playwright) 2 / 20 / 1893 PISCES
CROWLEY, ALEISTER (occultist) 10 / 12 / 1875 LIBRA
CROWLEY, MART (playwright) 8 / 21 / 1936 LEO
CROWTHER, BOSLEY (film critic) 7 / 13 / 1905 CANCER
CRUIKSHANK, GEORGE (illustrator) 9 / 27 / 1792 LIBRA
CRUMB, R. (cartoonist) 8 / 30 / 1943 VIRGO
CUENOD, HUGUES (tenor) 6 / 26 / 1902 CANCER
CUGAT, XAVIER (bandleader) 1 / 1 / 1900 CAPRICORN
CUKOR, GEORGE (film director) 7 / 7 / 1899 CANCER
CULLEN, BILL (TV personality) 2 / 18 / 1920 AQUARIUS
CULP, ROBERT (actor) 8 / 16 / 1930 LEO
CUMMINGS, CONSTANCE (actress) 5 / 15 / 1910 TAURUS
CUMMINGS, E. E. (poet) 10 / 14 / 1894 LIBRA
CUMMINGS, ROBERT (actor) 6 / 9 / 1910 GEMINI
CUNNINGHAM, BILLY (basketball player) 6 / 13 / 1943 GEMINI
CUNNINGHAM, MERCE (choreographer) 4 / 16 / 1919 ARIES
CURIE, MARIE (physicist) 11 / 7 / 1867 SCORPIO
CURIE, PIERRE (physicist) 5 / 15 / 1859 TAURUS
CURTIN, PHYLLIS (soprano) 12 / 3 / 1922 SAGITTARIUS
CURTIS, JACKIE (actress) 2 / 8 / 1948 AQUARIUS
CURTIS, TONY (actor) 6 / 3 / 1925 GEMINI
CURZON, CLIFFORD (pianist) 5 / 18 / 1907 TAURUS
CUSAK, CYRIL (actor) 11 / 26 / 1910 SAGITTARIUS
CUSHING, PETER (actor) 5 / 26 / 1913 GEMINI
CUSHING, RICHARD (clergyman) 8 / 24 / 1895 VIRGO

CUSTER, GEORGE (army officer) 12 / 5 / 1839 SAGITTARIUS
CZERNY, KARL (pianist) 2 / 20 / 1791 PISCES
CZIFFRA, GYORGY (pianist) 11 / 5 / 1921 SCORPIO

DACOSTA, MORTON (producer) 3 / 7 / 1918 PISCES
DA COSTA GOMES, FRANCISCO (Portuguese politician) 6 / 30 / 1914
    CANCER
DAGUERRE, LOUIS (inventor) 11 / 18 / 1789 SCORPIO
DAHL, ARLENE (actress) 8 / 11 / 1927 LEO
DAHL, ROALD (writer) 9 / 13 / 1916 VIRGO
DAILEY, DAN (actor) 12 / 14 / 1917 SAGITTARIUS
DAILEY, IRENE (actress) 9 / 12 / 1920 VIRGO
DALAI LAMA XIV (Buddhist leader) 6 / 6 / 1935 GEMINI
DALEY, RICHARD (politician) 5 / 15 / 1902 TAURUS
DALI, SALVADOR (painter) 5 / 11 / 1904 TAURUS
DALIS, IRENE (mezzo-soprano) 10 / 8 / 1929 LIBRA
DALLAPICCOLA, LUIGI (composer) 2 / 3 / 1904 AQUARIUS
DALLESANDRO, JOE (actor) 12 / 31 / 1948 CAPRICORN
DAL MONTE, TOTI (soprano) 6 / 27 / 1893 CANCER
DALRYMPLE, JEAN (producer and director) 9 / 2 / 1910 VIRGO
DALY, JOHN (TV personality) 2 / 20 / 1914 PISCES
DALTREY, ROGER (rock musician) 3 / 1 / 1945 PISCES
D'AMBOISE, JACQUES (ballet dancer) 7 / 28 / 1934 LEO
DAMONE, VIC (singer) 6 / 12 / 1928 GEMINI
DANA, RICHARD HENRY (writer) 8 / 1 / 1815 LEO
DANCER, STANLEY (harness racing driver) 7 / 25 / 1927 LEO
DANIEL, CLIFTON (newsman) 9 / 19 / 1912 VIRGO
DANILOVA, ALEXANDRA (ballet dancer) 11 / 20 / 1904 SCORPIO
D'ANNUNZIO, GABRIELE (poet) 3 / 12 / 1863 PISCES
DANTE ALIGHIERI (poet) 5 / 22 / 1265 GEMINI
DANTON, GEORGES JACQUES (revolutionary leader) 10 / 28 / 1759
    SCORPIO
DA PONTE, LORENZO (poet and librettist) 3 / 10 / 1749 PISCES
DARBY, KIM (actress) 7 / 8 / 1948 CANCER
DARIN, BOBBY (singer) 5 / 14 / 1936 TAURUS
DARNELL, LINDA (actress) 10 / 16 / 1923 LIBRA
DARRIEUX, DANIELLE (actress) 5 / 1 / 1917 TAURUS
DARROW, CLARENCE (lawyer) 4 / 18 / 1857 ARIES
DARWIN, CHARLES (naturalist) 2 / 12 / 1809 AQUARIUS

DASH, SARAH (singer) 8 / 18 / 1948 LEO
DA SILVA, HOWARD (actor) 5 / 4 / 1909 TAURUS
DASSIN, JULES (film director) 12 / 12 / 1911 SAGITTARIUS
DAUDET, ALPHONSE (poet) 5 / 13 / 1840 TAURUS
DAUGHERTY, PAT "DIRTY" (rock musician) 11 / 11 / 1947 SCORPIO
DAUMIER, HONORE (painter) 2 / 20 / 1808 PISCES
DAVENPORT, MARCIA (writer) 6 / 9 / 1903 GEMINI
DAVID, JACQUES LOUIS (painter) 8 / 30 / 1748 VIRGO
DAVIES, MARION (actress) 1 / 3 / 1900 CAPRICORN
DAVIS, ADELLE (nutritionist) 2 / 25 / 1904 PISCES
DAVIS, ANGELA (black militant) 1 / 26 / 1944 AQUARIUS
DAVIS, BETTE (actress) 4 / 5 / 1908 ARIES
DAVIS, COLIN (conductor) 9 / 25 / 1927 LIBRA
DAVIS, IVAN (pianist) 2 / 4 / 1932 AQUARIUS
DAVIS, JEFF (hobo king) 8 / 22 / 1883 LEO
DAVIS, JEFFERSON (Confederate politician) 6 / 3 / 1808 GEMINI
DAVIS, JOAN (comedienne) 6 / 29 / 1907 CANCER
DAVIS, MILES (jazz musician) 5 / 25 / 1926 GEMINI
DAVIS, OSSIE (actor) 2 / 18 / 1917 AQUARIUS/PISCES
DAVIS, SAMMY, JR. (singer) 12 / 8 / 1925 SAGITTARIUS
DAVIS, SKEETER (country singer) 12 / 30 / 1931 CAPRICORN
DAVIS, STUART (painter) 12 / 7 / 1894 SAGITTARIUS
DAY, DENNIS (singer) 5 / 21 / 1917 TAURUS/GEMINI
DAY, DORIS (actress) 4 / 3 / 1924 ARIES
DAY, LARAINE (actress) 10 / 13 / 1920 LIBRA
DAYAN, MOSHE (Israeli army officer) 5 / 20 / 1915 TAURUS
DEAN, DIZZY (sportscaster) 1 / 16 / 1911 CAPRICORN
DEAN, JAMES (actor) 2 / 8 / 1931 AQUARIUS
DEAN, JIMMY (country singer) 8 / 10 / 1928 LEO
DEAN, JOHN W., III (government official) 10 / 14 / 1938 LIBRA
DEANE, MARTHA (radio personality) 11 / 21 / 1902 SCORPIO
DEBAKEY, MICHAEL (surgeon) 9 / 7 / 1908 VIRGO
DEBS, EUGENE (labor leader) 11 / 5 / 1855 SCORPIO
DEBUSSCHERE, DAVE (basketball player) 10 / 16 / 1940 LIBRA
DEBUSSY, CLAUDE (composer) 8 / 22 / 1862 LEO
DE CARLO, YVONNE (actress) 9 / 1 / 1922 VIRGO
DEE, JOEY (actor) 6 / 11 / 1940 GEMINI
DEE, RUBY (actress) 10 / 27 / 1924 SCORPIO
DEE, SANDRA (actress) 4 / 23 / 1942 TAURUS
DEERE, JOHN (inventor) 2 / 7 / 1804 AQUARIUS

DEGAS, HILAIRE (painter) 7 / 19 / 1834 CANCER
DE GAULLE, CHARLES (French statesman) 11 / 22 / 1890 SCORPIO
DEHAVEN, GLORIA (actress) 7 / 23 / 1925 CANCER/LEO
DEHAVILLAND, OLIVIA (actress) 7 / 1 / 1916 CANCER
DE KOONING, WILLEM (painter) 4 / 24 / 1904 TAURUS
DE KRUIF, PAUL (writer) 3 / 2 / 1890 PISCES
DELACROIX, FERDINAND (painter) 4 / 26 / 1799 TAURUS
DE LA MARE, WALTER (poet) 4 / 25 / 1873 TAURUS
DE LA RENTA, OSCAR (fashion designer) 7 / 22 / 1932 CANCER/LEO
DELAROCHE, PAUL (painter) 6 / 17 / 1797 GEMINI
DE LAURENTIIS, DINO (film producer) 8 / 8 / 1919 LEO
DE LAVALLADE, CARMEN (dancer) 3 / 6 / 1931 PISCES
DELIBES, LEO (composer) 2 / 21 / 1836 PISCES
DELIUS, FREDERICK (composer) 1 / 29 / 1862 AQUARIUS
DELLA CASA, LISA (soprano) 2 / 2 / 1921 AQUARIUS
DELLER, ALFRED (countertenor) 5 / 31 / 1912 GEMINI
DELLO JOIO, NORMAN (composer) 1 / 24 / 1913 AQUARIUS
DEL MONACO, MARIO (tenor) 7 / 27 / 1915 LEO
DELON, ALAIN (actor) 11 / 8 / 1935 SCORPIO
DE LOS ANGELES, VICTORIA (soprano) 11 / 1 / 1923 SCORPIO
DEL RIO, DOLORES (actress) 8 / 3 / 1905 LEO
DE LUCA, GIUSEPPE (baritone) 12 / 25 / 1876 CAPRICORN
DE LUCIA, FERNANDO (tenor) 10 / 11 / 1860 LIBRA
DEMILLE, CECIL B. (film producer) 8 / 12 / 1881 LEO
DEMPSEY, JACK (boxer) 6 / 24 / 1895 CANCER
DENEUVE, CATHERINE (actress) 10 / 22 / 1943 LIBRA
DE NIRO, ROBERT (actor) 8 / 17 / 1943 LEO
DENNIS, PATRICK (novelist) 5 / 18 / 1921 TAURUS
DENNIS, SANDY (actress) 4 / 27 / 1937 TAURUS
DENNY, MARTIN (composer) 4 / 10 / 1915 ARIES
DENT, EDWARD (musicologist) 7 / 18 / 1876 CANCER
DENVER, JOHN (singer) 12 / 31 / 1943 CAPRICORN
DE QUINCEY, THOMAS (writer) 8 / 15 / 1785 LEO
DEREK, JOHN (actor) 8 / 12 / 1926 LEO
DE RESZKE, EDOUARD (basso) 12 / 23 / 1855 CAPRICORN
DE RESZKE, JEAN (tenor) 1 / 14 / 1850 CAPRICORN
DERMOTA, ANTON (tenor) 6 / 4 / 1910 GEMINI
DERNESCH, HELGA (soprano) 3 / 2 / 1940 PISCES
DE SABATA, VICTOR (conductor) 4 / 10 / 1892 ARIES
DESCARTES, RENE (philosopher) 3 / 31 / 1596 ARIES

DE SICA, VITTORIO (film director) 7 / 7 / 1901 CANCER

DESTINN, EMMY (soprano) 2 / 26 / 1878 PISCES

DEUTEKOM, CRISTINA (soprano) 8 / 28 / 1934 VIRGO

DE VALOIS, NINETTE (choreographer) 6 / 6 / 1898 GEMINI

DEVEREUX, ROBERT (courtier) 11 / 29 / 1566 SAGITTARIUS

DEVINE, ANDY (actor) 10 / 7 / 1905 LIBRA

DEVLIN, BERNADETTE (Irish politician) 4 / 23 / 1947 TAURUS

DE VRIES, PETER (writer) 2 / 27 / 1910 PISCES

DEWEY, JOHN (philosopher) 10 / 20 / 1859 LIBRA

DEWEY, THOMAS E. (politician) 3 / 24 / 1902 ARIES

DEWHURST, COLLEEN (actress) 6 / 3 / 1926 GEMINI

DE WILDE, BRANDON (actor) 4 / 9 / 1942 ARIES

DIAGHILEV, SERGEI (impresario) 3 / 19 / 1872 PISCES

DIANE DE POITIERS (king's mistress) 9 / 13 / 1499 VIRGO

DIAMOND, LEGS (mobster) 7 / 10 / 1897 CANCER

DIAMOND, NEIL (singer) 1 / 24 / 1941 AQUARIUS

DIBELIUS, OTTO (Lutheran leader) 5 / 15 / 1880 TAURUS

DICKENS, CHARLES (novelist) 2 / 7 / 1812 AQUARIUS

DICKEY, JAMES (poet) 2 / 2 / 1923 AQUARIUS

DICKINSON, ANGIE (actress) 9 / 30 / 1931 LIBRA

DICKINSON, EMILY (poet) 12 / 10 / 1830 SAGITTARIUS

DIDDLEY, BO (rock musician) 12 / 30 / 1928 CAPRICORN

DIDEROT, DENIS (philosopher) 10 / 5 / 1713 LIBRA

DIEBENKORN, RICHARD (artist) 4 / 22 / 1922 TAURUS

DIEFENBAKER, JOHN (Canadian politician) 9 / 18 / 1895 VIRGO

DIENER, JOAN (actress) 2 / 24 / 1934 PISCES

DIESEL, RUDOLF (engineer) 3 / 18 / 1858 PISCES

DIETRICH, MARLENE (actress) 12 / 27 / 1904 CAPRICORN

DILLER, PHYLLIS (comedienne) 7 / 17 / 1917 CANCER

DILLINGER, JOHN (outlaw) 6 / 22 / 1903 GEMINI

DILLMAN, BRADFORD (actor) 4 / 14 / 1930 ARIES

DILLON, MELINDA (actress) 10 / 13 / 1939 LIBRA

DIMAGGIO, JOE (baseball player) 11 / 25 / 1914 SAGITTARIUS

DIMUCCI, DION (singer) 7 / 18 / 1939 CANCER

DINE, JIM (painter) 6 / 16 / 1935 GEMINI

DINESEN, ISAK (writer) 10 / 17 / 1885 LIBRA

DIONNE, YVONNE (quintuplet) 5 / 28 / 1934 GEMINI

DIOR, CHRISTIAN (fashion designer) 1 / 21 / 1905 CAPRICORN/
    AQUARIUS

DIRKSEN, EVERETT (politician) 1 / 4 / 1896 CAPICORN

DISNEY, WALT (film producer) 12 / 5 / 1901 SAGITTARIUS
DISRAELI, BENJAMIN (British statesman) 12 / 21 / 1804
    SAGITTARIUS
DI STEFANO, GIUSEPPE (tenor) 7 / 24 / 1921 LEO
DITTERSDORF, KARL DITTERS VON (composer) 11 / 2 / 1739 SCORPIO
DIX, DOROTHEA (prison reformer) 4 / 4 / 1802 ARIES
DIXON, JEANE (psychic) 11 / ? / 1918 SCORPIO
DMITRI, IVAN (artist) 2 / 3 / 1900 AQUARIUS
DOBBS, MATTIWILDA (soprano) 7 / 11 / 1925 CANCER
DODD, THOMAS C. (politician) 5 / 15 / 1907 TAURUS
DOHNANYI, ERNST VON (composer) 7 / 27 / 1877 LEO
DOHRN, BERNARDINE (revolutionary) 1 / 12 / 1942 CAPRICORN
DOLIN, ANTON (ballet dancer) 7 / 27 / 1904 LEO
DOMINGO, PLACIDO (tenor) 1 / 21 / 1941 CAPRICORN/AQUARIUS
DOMINGUEZ, ORALIA (mezzo-soprano) 6 / 24 / 1928 CANCER
DOMINGUIN, LUIS MIGUEL (bullfighter) 12 / 9 / 1926 SAGITTARIUS
DOMINO, FATS (singer) 2 / 26 / 1928 PISCES
DONAHUE, TROY (actor) 1 / 27 / 1937 AQUARIUS
DONAT, ROBERT (actor) 3 / 18 / 1905 PISCES
DONEN, STANLEY (film director) 4 / 13 / 1924 ARIES
DONIZETTI, GAETANO (composer) 11 / 29 / 1797 SAGITTARIUS
DONLEVY, BRIAN (actor) 2 / 9 / 1903 AQUARIUS
DONN, JORGE (ballet dancer) 2 / 28 / 1947 PISCES
DONOVAN (singer) 2 / 10 / 1946 AQUARIUS
DOOLEY, THOMAS (physician) 1 / 17 / 1927 CAPRICORN
DORATI, ANTAL (conductor) 4 / 9 / 1906 ARIES
DORE, GUSTAVE (artist) 1 / 6 / 1832 CAPRICORN
DORS, DIANA (actress) 10 / 23 / 1931 LIBRA/SCORPIO
DORSEY, TOMMY (bandleader) 11 / 10 / 1905 SCORPIO
DOS PASSOS, JOHN (novelist) 1 / 14 / 1896 CAPRICORN
DOSTOYEVSKY, FEODOR (novelist) 11 / 11 / 1821 SCORPIO
DOUBLEDAY, FRANK NELSON (publisher) 1 / 8 / 1862 CAPRICORN
DOUBLEDAY, NELSON (publisher) 7 / 20 / 1933 CANCER
DOUGLAS, KIRK (actor) 12 / 9 / 1916 SAGITTARIUS
DOUGLAS, MELVYN (actor) 4 / 5 / 1901 ARIES
DOUGLAS, MIKE (TV personality) 8 / 11 / 1925 LEO
DOUGLAS, PAUL (actor) 11 / 4 / 1907 SCORPIO
DOUGLAS, STEPHEN A. (politician) 4 / 23 / 1813 TAURUS
DOUGLAS, WILLIAM O. (jurist) 10 / 16 / 1898 LIBRA
DOVE, ARTHUR (artist) 8 / 2 / 1880 LEO

DOVZHENKO, ALEXANDER (film maker) 9 / 11 / 1894 VIRGO
DOWELL, ANTHONY (ballet dancer) 2 / 16 / 1943 AQUARIUS
DOWNES, OLIN (music critic) 1 / 27 / 1886 AQUARIUS
DOWNEY, MORTON (singer) 11 / 14 / 1902 SCORPIO
DOWNS, HUGH (TV personality) 2 / 14 / 1921 AQUARIUS
DOYLE, ARTHUR CONAN (writer) 5 / 22 / 1859 GEMINI
DOYLE, DESMOND (ballet dancer) 6 / 16 / 1932 GEMINI
DRAKE, ALFRED (actor) 10 / 7 / 1914 LIBRA
DRAPER, PAUL (dancer) 10 / 25 / 1909 SCORPIO
DRAPER, RUTH (monologuist) 12 / 2 / 1884 SAGITTARIUS
DREIFUS, CLAUDIA (feminist) 11 / 24 / 1944 SAGITTARIUS
DREISER, THEODORE (novelist) 8 / 27 / 1871 LEO
DRESSEN, CHUCK (baseball manager) 9 / 20 / 1898 VIRGO
DRESSLER, MARIE (actress) 11 / 9 / 1871 SCORPIO
DREYER, CARL (film maker) 2 / 3 / 1889 AQUARIUS
DREYFUS, ALFRED (French army officer) 10 / 9 / 1859 LIBRA
DRISCOLL, BOBBY (actor) 3 / 3 / 1937 PISCES
DRISCOLL, PADDY (football coach) 1 / 11 / 1896 CAPRICORN
DRU, JOANNE (actress) 1 / 31 / 1923 AQUARIUS
DRURY, ALLEN (novelist) 9 / 2 / 1918 VIRGO
DRYDEN, JOHN (writer) 8 / 19 / 1631 LEO
DRYDEN, SPENCER (rock musician) 4 / 4 / ? ARIES
DRYSDALE, DON (baseball player) 7 / 23 / 1936 LEO
DU BARRY, MME. (courtesan) 8 / 19 / 1746 LEO
DUBCEK, ALEXANDER (Czech politician) 11 / 27 / 1921 SAGITTARIUS
DUBUFFET, JEAN (painter) 7 / 31 / 1901 LEO
DUCHAMP, MARCEL (artist) 7 / 28 / 1887 LEO
DUCHIN, EDDY (pianist) 4 / 1 / 1909 ARIES
DUCHIN, PETER (bandleader) 7 / 28 / 1937 LEO
DUERER, ALBRECHT (artist) 5 / 30 / 1471 GEMINI
DUERRENMATT, FRIEDRICH (writer) 1 / 5 / 1921 CAPRICORN
DUFF, HOWARD (actor) 11 / 24 / 1917 SAGITTARIUS
DUFY, RAOUL (painter) 6 / 3 / 1877 GEMINI
DUKAS, PAUL (composer) 10 / 1 / 1865 LIBRA
DUKE, DORIS (heiress) 11 / 22 /1912 SCORPIO/SAGITTARIUS
DUKE, PATTY (actress) 12 / 14 / 1946 SAGITTARIUS
DULLEA, KEIR (actor) 5 / 30 / 1936 GEMINI
DULLES, JOHN FOSTER (government official) 2 / 25 / 1888 PISCES
DUMAS, ALEXANDRE (*fils*) (writer) 7 / 27 / 1824 LEO
DUMAS, ALEXANDRE (*père*) (writer) 7 / 24 / 1802 LEO

DU MAURIER, DAPHNE (writer) 5 / 13 / 1907 TAURUS
DUNAWAY, FAYE (actress) 1 / 14 / 1941 CAPRICORN
DUNCAN, ISADORA (dancer) 5 / 27 / 1878 GEMINI
DUNCAN, TODD (actor) 2 / 12 / 1903 AQUARIUS
DUNHAM, KATHERINE (choreographer) 6 / 22 / 1910 GEMINI/CANCER
DUNN, MICHAEL (actor) 10 / 20 / 1934 LIBRA
DUNN, MIGNON (mezzo-soprano) 6 / 17 / 1931 GEMINI
DUNNE, IRENE (actress) 12 / 20 / 1904 SAGITTARIUS
DUNNINGER (magician) 4 / 28 / 1896 TAURUS
DUNNOCK, MILDRED (actress) 1 / 25 / 1906 AQUARIUS
DUPARC, HENRI (composer) 1 / 21 / 1858 CAPRICORN/AQUARIUS
DU PRE, JACQUELINE (cellist) 1 / 26 / 1945 AQUARIUS
DUPRE, MARCEL (organist) 5 / 3 / 1886 TAURUS
DUPREZ, GILBERT (tenor) 12 / 6 / 1806 SAGITTARIUS
DURANT, WILL (writer) 11 / 5 / 1885 SCORPIO
DURANTE, JIMMY (comedian) 2 / 10 / 1893 AQUARIUS
DURAS, MARGUERITE (writer) 4 / 4 / 1914 ARIES
DURBIN, DEANNA (actress) 12 / 4 / 1922 SAGITTARIUS
DUROCHER, LEO (baseball manager) 7 / 27 / 1906 LEO
DURRELL, LAWRENCE (writer) 2 / 27 / 1912 PISCES
DURUFLE, MAURICE (composer) 1 / 11 / 1902 CAPRICORN
DURYEA, DAN (actor) 1 / 23 / 1907 AQUARIUS
DUSE, ELEANORA (actress) 10 / 3 / 1859 LIBRA
DUVALIER, JEAN-CLAUDE (dictator) 7 / 3 / 1951 CANCER
DUVALIER, FRANÇOIS (dictator) 4 / 14 / 1907 ARIES
DVORAK, ANTONIN (composer) 9 / 8 / 1841 VIRGO
DYER-BENNET, RICHARD (folk singer) 10 / 6 / 1913 LIBRA
DYLAN, BOB (singer) 5 / 24 / 1941 GEMINI

EAGELS, JEANNE (actress) 6 / 26 / 1890 CANCER
EAGLETON, THOMAS (politician) 9 / 4 / 1929 VIRGO
EAKINS, THOMAS (painter) 8 / 25 / 1844 VIRGO
EAMES, EMMA (soprano) 8 / 13 / 1865 LEO
EARHART, AMELIA (aviatrix) 7 / 24 / 1898 LEO
EARP, WYATT (lawman) 3 / 19 / 1848 PISCES
EASTLAND, JAMES (politician) 11 / 28 / 1904 SAGITTARIUS
EASTMAN, GEORGE (inventor and industrialist) 7 / 12 / 1854 CANCER
EASTWOOD, CLINT (actor) 5 / 31 / 1931 GEMINI
EBERHART, RICHARD (poet) 4 / 5 / 1904 ARIES

ECKART, JEAN (stage designer) 8 / 18 / 1921 LEO
ECKSTINE, BILLY (singer) 7 / 8 / 1914 CANCER
EDDY, MARY BAKER (Christian Scientist) 7 / 16 / 1821 CANCER
EDDY, NELSON (actor) 6 / 29 / 1901 CANCER
EDEN, ANTHONY (British politician) 6 / 12 / 1897 GEMINI
EDGE, GRAEME (rock musician) 3 / 30 / ? ARIES
EDISON, THOMAS ALVA (inventor) 2 / 11 / 1847 AQUARIUS
EDWARD I OF ENGLAND, KING 6 / 24 / 1239 CANCER
EDWARD II OF ENGLAND, KING 5 / 3 / 1284 TAURUS
EDWARD VII OF ENGLAND, KING 11 / 9 / 1841 SCORPIO
EDWARDS, DOUGLAS (newscaster) 7 / 14 / 1917 CANCER
EDWARDS, JONATHAN (clergyman) 10 / 16 / 1703 LIBRA
EDWARDS, RALPH (TV personality) 6 / 13 / 1913 GEMINI
EDWARDS, VINCE (actor) 7 / 7 / 1928 CANCER
EGAN, RICHARD (actor) 7 / 29 / 1923 LEO
EGGAR, SAMANTHA (actress) 3 / 5 / 1939 PISCES
EHRENBURG, ILYA (writer) 1 / 27 / 1891 AQUARIUS
EHRLICH, PAUL (environmentalist) 5 / 29 / 1932 GEMINI
EHRLICHMAN, JOHN D. (government official) 3 / 20 / 1925 PISCES
EICHENDORFF, JOSEPH VON (poet) 3 / 10 / 1788 PISCES
EICHMANN, ADOLF (Nazi official) 3 / 19 / 1906 PISCES
EIFFEL, ALEXANDRE GUSTAVE (engineer) 12 / 15 / 1882
    SAGITTARIUS
EIGSTI, KARL (stage designer) 9 / 19 / 1938 VIRGO
EINSTEIN, ALBERT (physicist) 3 / 14 / 1879 PISCES
EINSTEIN, ALFRED (musicologist) 12 / 30 / 1880 CAPRICORN
EISELEY, LOREN (anthropologist) 9 / 3 / 1907 VIRGO
EISENHOWER, DAVID (politician's grandson) 3 / 31 / 1948 ARIES
EISENHOWER, DWIGHT DAVID (politician) 10 / 14 / 1890 LIBRA
EISENHOWER, JULIE NIXON (politician's daughter) 7 / 5 / 1948
    CANCER
EISENHOWER, MAMIE (first lady) 11 / 14 / 1896 SCORPIO
EISENHOWER, MILTON (government official) 9 / 15 / 1899 VIRGO
EISENSTEIN, SERGEI (film maker) 1 / 23 / 1898 AQUARIUS
EKBERG, ANITA (actress) 9 / 29 / 1931 LIBRA
ELAINE (proprietress) 2 / 10 / 1939 AQUARIUS
EL CORDOBES (bullfighter) 5 / 4 / 1936 TAURUS
ELDRIDGE, FLORENCE (actress) 9 / 5 / 1901 VIRGO
ELGAR, EDWARD (composer) 6 / 2 / 1857 GEMINI
ELIAS, ROSALIND (mezzo-soprano) 3 / 13 / 1931 PISCES

ELIOT, GEORGE (novelist) 11 / 22 / 1819 SCORPIO
ELIOT, T. S. (poet) 9 / 26 / 1888 LIBRA
ELIZABETH I OF ENGLAND, QUEEN 9 / 17 / 1533 VIRGO
ELIZABETH II OF ENGLAND, QUEEN 4 / 21 / 1926 TAURUS
ELIZABETH OF VALOIS, QUEEN 4 / 23 / 1545 TAURUS
ELLINGTON, DUKE (jazz musician) 4 / 29 / 1899 TAURUS
ELLIOT, CASS (singer) 2 / 19 / 1941 AQUARIUS/PISCES
ELLIOTT, BOB (comedian) 3 / 26 / 1923 ARIES
ELLIS, ALBERT (sexologist) 9 / 27 / 1913 LIBRA
ELLIS, HAVELOCK (psychologist) 2 / 2 / 1859 AQUARIUS
ELLISON, RALPH (writer) 3 / 1 / 1914 PISCES
ELLSBERG, DANIEL (economist) 4 / 7 / 1931 ARIES
ELMAN, MISCHA (violinist) 1 / 21 / 1891 CAPRICORN/AQUARIUS
ELY, RON (actor) 6 / 21 / 1938 GEMINI/CANCER
EMERSON, FAYE (actress) 7 / 8 / 1917 CANCER
EMERSON, KEITH (rock musician) 11 / 2 / 1944 SCORPIO
EMERSON, RALPH WALDO (writer) 5 / 25 / 1803 GEMINI
EMERSON, ROY (tennis player) 11 / 3 / 1936 SCORPIO
ENESCO, GEORGES (composer) 8 / 19 / 1881 LEO
ENGELS, FRIEDRICH (socialist) 9 / 28 / 1820 LIBRA
ENSOR, JAMES (painter) 4 / 13 / 1860 ARIES
ENTERS, ANGNA (artist) 4 / 28 / 1907 TAURUS
ENTREMONT, PHILIPPE (pianist) 6 / 6 / 1934 GEMINI
ENTWISTLE, JOHN (rock musician) 10 / 9 / 1944 LIBRA
EPSTEIN, BRIAN (rock musicians' agent) 9 / 19 / 1934 VIRGO
ERASMUS, DESIDERIUS (humanist) 11 / 6 / 1467 SCORPIO
ERDMAN, JEAN (dancer) 2 / 20 / 1917 PISCES
ERHARD, LUDWIG (German politician) 2 / 4 / 1897 AQUARIUS
ERIKSON, ERIK H. (psychologist) 6 / 15 / 1902 GEMINI
ERNST, JIMMY (artist) 6 / 24 / 1920 CANCER
ERNST, MAX (painter) 4 / 2 / 1891 ARIES
ERVIN, SAM, JR. (politician) 9 / 27 / 1896 LIBRA
ESCHER, M. C. (graphic artist) 6 / 18 / 1898 GEMINI
ESPOSITO, JOSEPH "DIAMOND JOE" (mobster) 4 / 28 / 1872 TAURUS
ESPOSITO, PHIL (hockey player) 2 / 20 / 1942 PISCES
EURIPIDES (playwright) 9 / 23 / 480 B.C. VIRGO/LIBRA
EVANS, BERGEN (etymologist) 9 / 19 / 1904 VIRGO
EVANS, DALE (actress) 10 / 31 / 1912 SCORPIO
EVANS, EDITH (actress) 2 / 8 / 1888 AQUARIUS
EVANS, GERAINT (baritone) 2 / 16 / 1922 AQUARIUS

EVANS, MAURICE (actor) 6 / 3 / 1901 GEMINI
EVANS, ROWLAND, JR. (columnist) 4 / 28 / 1921 TAURUS
EVANS, WALKER (photographer) 11 / 3 / 1903 SCORPIO
EVELYN, JUDITH (actress) 3 / 13 / 1913 PISCES
EVERETT, CHAD (actor) 6 / 11 / 1936 GEMINI
EVERGOOD, PHILIP (painter) 10 / 26 / 1901 SCORPIO
EVERLY, DON (singer) 2 / 1 / 1937 AQUARIUS
EVERLY, PHIL (singer) 1 / 19 / 1939 CAPRICORN
EVERS, CHARLES (black leader) 9 / 11 / 1922 VIRGO
EVERS, MEDGAR W. (black leader) 7 / 2 / 1925 CANCER
EVERT, CHRIS (tennis player) 12 / 21 / 1954
    SAGITTARIUS/CAPRICORN
EWBANK, WEEB (football coach) 5 / 6 / 1907 TAURUS
EWELL, TOM (actor) 4 / 29 / 1909 TAURUS

FABIAN (singer) 2 / 6 / 1943 AQUARIUS
FABIAN, FRANÇOISE (actress) 5 / 10 / 1935 TAURUS
FABRAY, NANETTE (actress) 10 / 27 / 1922 SCORPIO
FADEYECHEV, NIKOLAI (ballet dancer) 1 / 27 / 1933 AQUARIUS
FADIMAN, CLIFTON (literary critic) 5 / 15 / 1904 TAURUS
FAHRENHEIT, GABRIEL (physicist) 5 / 14 / 1686 TAURUS
FAIRBANKS, DOUGLAS (actor) 5 / 23 / 1883 GEMINI
FAIRBANKS, DOUGLAS, JR. (actor) 12 / 9 / 1909 SAGITTARIUS
FAITH, PERCY (bandleader) 4 / 7 / 1908 ARIES
FALK, PETER (actor) 9 / 16 / 1927 VIRGO
FALLA, MANUEL DE (composer) 11 / 23 / 1876 SCORPIO/
    SAGITTARIUS
FARADAY, MICHAEL (physicist) 9 / 22 / 1791 VIRGO
FARINELLI (castrato) 1 / 24 / 1705 AQUARIUS
FARMER, JAMES (black leader) 1 / 12 / 1920 CAPRICORN
FAROUK OF EGYPT, KING 2 / 11 / 1920 AQUARIUS
FARR, FELICIA (actress) 10 / 4 / 1932 LIBRA
FARRAGUT, DAVID (naval officer) 7 / 5 / 1801 CANCER
FARRAR, GERALDINE (soprano) 2 / 28 / 1882 PISCES
FARRELL, EILEEN (soprano) 2 / 13 / 1920 AQUARIUS
FARRELL, JAMES T. (novelist) 2 / 27 / 1904 PISCES
FARRELL, SUZANNE (ballet dancer) 8 / 16 / 1945 LEO
FARROW, MIA (actress) 2 / 9 / 1945 AQUARIUS
FAST, HOWARD (novelist) 11 / 11 / 1914 SCORPIO

FAUBUS, ORVAL (politician) 1 / 7 / 1910 CAPRICORN
FAULKNER, BRIAN (Irish politician) 2 / 18 / 1921 AQUARIUS/PISCES
FAULKNER, WILLIAM (novelist) 9 / 25 / 1897 LIBRA
FAURE, GABRIEL (composer) 5 / 13 / 1845 TAURUS
FAY, FRANK (actor) 11 / 17 / 1897 SCORPIO
FAYE, ALICE (actress) 5 / 5 / 1915 TAURUS
FEIFFER, JULES (humorist) 1 / 26 / 1929 AQUARIUS
FEININGER, ANDREAS (photographer) 12 / 27 / 1906 CAPRICORN
FELICIANO, JOSE (singer) 9 / 10 / 1945 VIRGO
FELLER, BOB (baseball player) 11 / 3 / 1918 SCORPIO
FELLINI, FEDERICO (film maker) 1 / 20 / 1920 AQUARIUS
FENTON, BEATRICE (sculptress) 7 / 12 / 1887 CANCER
FERBER, EDNA (novelist) 8 / 15 / 1887 LEO
FERBER, HERBERT (sculptor) 4 / 30 / 1906 TAURUS
FERDINAND OF AUSTRIA, ARCHDUKE 12 / 18 / 1863 SAGITTARIUS
FERDINAND OF CASTILE, KING 3 / 20 / 1452 PISCES/ARIES
FERLINGHETTI, LAWRENCE (poet) 3 / 24 / 1919 ARIES
FERMI, ENRICO (physicist) 9 / 29 / 1901 LIBRA
FERNANDEL (comedian) 5 / 8 / 1903 TAURUS
FERNANDEZ, ROYES (ballet dancer) 6 / 15 / 1929 GEMINI
FERRARI, ENZO (automobile executive) 2 / 20 / 1898 PISCES
FERRER, JOSE (actor) 1 / 8 / 1912 CAPRICORN
FERRER, MEL (actor) 8 / 25 / 1917 VIRGO
FERRIER, KATHLEEN (contralto) 4 / 22 / 1912 TAURUS
FEYDEAU, GEORGES (playwright) 12 / 8 / 1862 SAGITTARIUS
FIEDLER, ARTHUR (conductor) 12 / 17 / 1894 SAGITTARIUS
FIELD, BETTY (actress) 2 / 8 / 1918 AQUARIUS
FIELD, EUGENE (poet) 9 / 2 / 1850 VIRGO
FIELD, MARSHALL (merchant) 8 / 18 / 1834 LEO
FIELD, SALLY (actress) 11 / 6 / 1946 SCORPIO
FIELDING, HENRY (novelist) 5 / 3 / 1707 TAURUS
FIELDS, DOROTHY (lyricist) 7 / 15 / 1905 CANCER
FIELDS, GRACIE (singer) 1 / 9 / 1898 CAPRICORN
FIELDS, W. C. (comedian) 1 / 29 / 1880 AQUARIUS
FILLMORE, MILLARD (politician) 1 / 7 / 1800 CAPRICORN
FILMUS, TULLY (painter) 8 / 29 / 1908 VIRGO
FINCH, PETER (actor) 9 / 28 / 1916 LIBRA
FINLEY, CHARLES O. (baseball manager) 2 / 22 / 1918 PISCES
FINNEY, ALBERT (actor) 5 / 9 / 1936 TAURUS
FIRESTONE, HARVEY S. (industrialist) 12 / 20 / 1868 SAGITTARIUS

FISCHER, BOBBY (chess player) 3 / 9 / 1943 PISCES
FISCHER, EDWIN (pianist) 10 / 6 / 1886 LIBRA
FISCHER-DIESKAU, DIETRICH (baritone) 5 / 28 / 1925 GEMINI
FISHER, EDDIE (singer) 8 / 10 / 1928 LEO
FITZGERALD, BARRY (actor) 3 / 10 / 1888 PISCES
FITZGERALD, ELLA (jazz singer) 4 / 25 / 1918 TAURUS
FITZGERALD, F. SCOTT (novelist) 9 / 24 / 1896 LIBRA
FITZGERALD, GERALDINE (actress) 11 / 24 / 1914 SAGITTARIUS
FITZGERALD, ZELDA (novelist) 7 / 24 / 1900 LEO
FLACK, ROBERTA (singer) 2 / 10 / 1940 AQUARIUS
FLAGSTAD, KIRSTEN (soprano) 7 / 12 / 1895 CANCER
FLAHERTY, ROBERT (film maker) 2 / 16 / 1884 AQUARIUS
FLANAGAN, FATHER (clergyman) 7 / 13 / 1886 CANCER
FLANDERS, MICHAEL (comedian) 3 / 1 / 1922 PISCES
FLATT, LESTER (country singer) 6 / 28 / 1914 CANCER
FLAUBERT, GUSTAVE (novelist) 12 / 12 / 1821 SAGITTARIUS
FLEISCHER, LEON (pianist) 7 / 23 / 1928 CANCER/LEO
FLEMING, IAN (novelist) 5 / 28 / 1908 GEMINI
FLEMING, PEGGY (skater) 7 / 27 / 1948 LEO
FLEMING, RHONDA (actress) 8 / 10 / 1923 LEO
FLEMING, VICTOR (film director) 2 / 23 / 1883 PISCES
FLETA, MIGUEL (tenor) 12 / 28 / 1893 CAPRICORN
FLINDT, FLEMMING (ballet dancer) 9 / 30 / 1936 LIBRA
FLOTOW, FRIEDRICH VON (composer) 4 / 26 / 1812 TAURUS
FLOYD, CARLISLE (composer) 6 / 11 / 1926 GEMINI
FLYNN, ERROL (actor) 6 / 20 / 1909 GEMINI
FOCH, NINA (actress) 4 / 20 / 1924 ARIES/TAURUS
FOGARTY, ANNE (fashion designer) 2 / 2 / 1919 AQUARIUS
FOKINE, MICHEL (choreographer) 4 / 26 / 1880 TAURUS
FOLEY, RED (country singer) 6 / 17 / 1910 GEMINI
FONDA, HENRY (actor) 5 / 16 / 1905 TAURUS
FONDA, JANE (actress) 12 / 21 / 1937 SAGITTARIUS/CAPRICORN
FONDA, PETER (actor) 2 / 23 / 1939 PISCES
FONTAINE, JOAN (actress) 10 / 22 / 1917 LIBRA
FONTANNE, LYNN (actress) 12 / 6 / 1887 SAGITTARIUS
FONTEYN, MARGOT (ballet dancer) 5 / 18 / 1919 TAURUS
FORD, BETTY (first lady) 4 / 8 / 1918 ARIES
FORD, EDSEL (automobile executive) 11 / 6 / 1893 SCORPIO
FORD, EILEEN (modeling agent) 3 / 25 / 1922 ARIES
FORD, FORD MADOX (writer) 12 / 17 / 1873 SAGITTARIUS

FORD, GERALD R. (politician) 7 / 14 / 1913 CANCER
FORD, GLENN (actor) 5 / 1 / 1916 TAURUS
FORD, HENRY (automobile manufacturer) 7 / 30 / 1863 LEO
FORD, HENRY, II (automobile executive) 9 / 4 / 1917 VIRGO
FORD, JOHN (film director) 2 / 1 / 1895 AQUARIUS
FORD, MARY (singer) 7 / 7 / 1924 CANCER
FORD, PAUL (actor) 11 / 2 / 1901 SCORPIO
FORD, SUSAN (politician's daughter) 7 / 6 / 1957 CANCER
FORD, TENNESSEE ERNIE (singer) 2 / 13 / 1919 AQUARIUS
FORD, WHITEY (baseball player) 10 / 21 / 1928 LIBRA
FOREMAN, GEORGE (boxer) 1 / 10 / 1949 CAPRICORN
FORMAN, MILOS (film maker) 2 / 18 / 1932 AQUARIUS
FORMAN, PERCY (lawyer) 6 / 21 / 1902 GEMINI/CANCER
FORRESTER, MAUREEN (contralto) 7 / 25 / 1930 LEO
FORSTER, E. M. (novelist) 1 / 1 / 1879 CAPRICORN
FORSYTHE, JOHN (actor) 1 / 29 / 1918 AQUARIUS
FORTAS, ABE (jurist) 6 / 19 / 1910 GEMINI
FOSDICK, HARRY EMERSON (preacher) 5 / 24 / 1878 GEMINI
FOSS, LUKAS (composer) 8 / 15 / 1922 LEO
FOSSE, BOB (director) 6 / 23 / 1927 CANCER
FOSTER, STEPHEN (composer) 7 / 4 / 1826 CANCER
FOUNTAIN, PETE (jazz musician) 7 / 3 / 1930 CANCER
FOURNIER, PIERRE (cellist) 6 / 24 / 1906 CANCER
FOWLES, JOHN (novelist) 3 / 31 / 1926 ARIES
FOX, NELLIE (baseball player) 12 / 25 / 1927 CAPRICORN
FOX, VIRGIL (organist) 5 / 3 / 1912 TAURUS
FOX, WILLIAM (film executive) 1 / 1 / 1879 CAPRICORN
FOXX, JIMMY (baseball player) 10 / 22 / 1907 LIBRA
FOYT, A. J. (auto racer) 1 / 16 / 1935 CAPRICORN
FRACCI, CARLA (ballet dancer) 8 / 20 / 1938 LEO
FRAGONARD, JEAN HONORE (painter) 4 / 5 / 1732 ARIES
FRANCE, ANATOLE (writer) 4 / 16 / 1844 ARIES
FRANCESCATTI, ZINO (violinist) 8 / 9 / 1905 LEO
FRANCIOSA, TONY (actor) 10 / 25 / 1928 SCORPIO
FRANCIS I OF FRANCE, KING 9 / 21 / 1494 VIRGO
FRANCIS, ANNE (actress) 9 / 16 / 1932 VIRGO
FRANCIS, ARLENE (TV personality) 10 / 20 / 1908 LIBRA
FRANCIS, CONNIE (singer) 12 / 12 / 1938 SAGITTARIUS
FRANCK, CESAR (composer) 12 / 10 / 1822 SAGITTARIUS
FRANCO, FRANCISCO (dictator) 12 / 4 / 1892 SAGITTARIUS

FRANJU, GEORGES (film maker) 4 / 12 / 1912 TAURUS
FRANKENHEIMER, JOHN (film director) 2 / 19 / 1930
AQUARIUS/PISCES
FRANKENTHALER, HELEN (painter) 12 / 12 / 1928 SAGITTARIUS
FRANKFURTER, FELIX (jurist) 11 / 15 / 1882 SCORPIO
FRANKLIN, ARETHA (singer) 3 / 25 / 1942 ARIES
FRANKLIN, BENJAMIN (statesman and inventor) 1 / 17 / 1706
CAPRICORN
FRANZ JOSEF OF AUSTRIA, EMPEROR 8 / 18 / 1830 LEO
FRANZBLAU, ROSE N. (advice columnist) 1 / 6 / 1904 CAPRICORN
FRANZEN, ULRICH (architect) 1 / 15 / 1921 CAPRICORN
FRASCONI, ANTONIO (artist) 4 / 28 / 1919 TAURUS
FRAZER, JAMES (anthropologist) 1 / 1 / 1854 CAPRICORN
FRAZIER, JOE (boxer) 1 / 17 / 1944 CAPRICORN
FRAZIER, WALT (basketball player) 3 / 29 / 1945 ARIES
FREDERICK THE GREAT OF PRUSSIA, KING 1 / 24 / 1712 AQUARIUS
FREDERIK IX OF DENMARK, KING 3 / 11 / 1899 PISCES
FREDERIKA OF GREECE, QUEEN 4 / 18 / 1917 ARIES
FREED, ALAN (disc jockey) 12 / 15 / 1921 SAGITTARIUS
FREEMAN, MONA (actress) 6 / 9 / 1926 GEMINI
FREMONT, JOHN CHARLES (explorer) 1 / 21 / 1813
CAPRICORN/AQUARIUS
FREMSTAD, OLIVE (soprano) 3 / 14 / 1871 PISCES
FRENI, MIRELLA (soprano) 2 / 27 / 1935 PISCES
FREUD, ANNA (psychologist) 12 / 3 / 1895 SAGITTARIUS
FREUD, SIGMUND (psychologist) 5 / 6 / 1856 TAURUS
FRICK, GOTTLOB (basso) 7 / 28 / 1906 LEO
FRICK, HENRY CLAY (industrialist) 12 / 19 / 1849 SAGITTARIUS
FRICSAY, FERENC (conductor) 8 / 9 / 1914 LEO
FRIEDAN, BETTY (feminist) 2 / 4 / 1921 AQUARIUS
FRIEDMAN, BRUCE JAY (writer) 4 / 26 / 1930 TAURUS
FRIENDLY, FRED W. (TV producer) 10 / 30 / 1915 SCORPIO
FRISCH, MAX (writer) 5 / 15 / 1911 TAURUS
FROMAN, JANE (singer) 11 / 10 / 1917 SCORPIO
FROMM, ERICH (psychologist) 3 / 23 / 1900 ARIES
FROST, DAVID (TV personality) 4 / 7 / 1939 ARIES
FROST, ROBERT (poet) 3 / 26 / 1875 ARIES
FRUEHBECK DE BURGOS, RAFAEL (conductor) 9 / 15 / 1933 VIRGO
FRY, CHRISTOPHER (playwright) 12 / 18 / 1907 SAGITTARIUS
FUCHS, JOSEPH (violinist) 4 / 26 / 1900 TAURUS

FUCHS, VIVIAN (geologist) 2 / 11 / 1908 AQUARIUS
FULBRIGHT, J. WILLIAM (politician) 4 / 9 / 1905 ARIES
FULLER, ALFRED (brush manufacturer) 1 / 13 / 1885 CAPRICORN
FULLER, BUCKMINSTER (engineer and writer) 7 / 12 / 1895 CANCER
FULTON, ROBERT (inventor) 11 / 14 / 1765 SCORPIO
FUNICELLO, ANNETTE (actress) 10 / 22 / 1942 LIBRA
FUNT, ALLEN (TV personality) 9 / 16 / 1914 VIRGO
FURNESS, BETTY (TV personality and consumer advocate)
    1 / 3 / 1916 CAPRICORN
FURTWAENGLER, WILHELM (conductor) 1 / 25 / 1886 AQUARIUS
FUSELI, JOHN HENRY (painter) 2 / 7 / 1741 AQUARIUS

GABEL, MARTIN (actor) 6 / 19 / 1912 GEMINI
GABIN, JEAN (actor) 5 / 17 / 1904 TAURUS
GABLE, CLARK (actor) 2 / 1 / 1901 AQUARIUS
GABO, NAUM (sculptor) 8 / 5 / 1890 LEO
GABOR, EVA (actress) 2 / 11 / 1926 AQUARIUS
GABOR, ZSA ZSA (actress) 2 / 6 / 1923 AQUARIUS
GADES, ANTONIO (dancer) 11 / 16 / 1936 SCORPIO
GADSKI, JOHANNA (soprano) 6 / 15 / 1871 GEMINI
GAGARIN, YURI (cosmonaut) 3 / 9 / 1934 PISCES
GAINSBOROUGH, THOMAS (painter) 5 / 25 / 1727 GEMINI
GALANOS, JAMES (fashion designer) 9 / 20 / 1924 VIRGO
GALBRAITH, JOHN KENNETH (economist) 10 / 15 / 1908 LIBRA
GALILEI, GALILEO (astronomer) 2 / 25 / 1564 PISCES
GALLAGHER, HELEN (actress) 7 / 19 / 1926 CANCER
GALLI-CURCI, AMELITA (soprano) 11 / 18 / 1889 SCORPIO
GALLUP, GEORGE (pollster) 11 / 18 / 1901 SCORPIO
GALSWORTHY, JOHN (novelist) 8 / 14 / 1867 LEO
GAM, RITA (actress) 4 / 2 / 1928 ARIES
GAMOW, GEORGE (physicist) 3 / 4 / 1904 PISCES
GANDHI, INDIRA (Indian politician) 11 / 19 / 1917 SCORPIO
GANDHI, MOHANDAS K. (Hindu leader) 10 / 2 / 1869 LIBRA
GARAGIOLA, JOE (TV personality) 2 / 12 / 1926 AQUARIUS
GARBO, GRETA (actress) 9 / 18 / 1905 VIRGO
GARCIA, JERRY (rock musician) 8 / 1 / 1941 LEO
GARCIA, MANUEL (singing teacher) 1 / 22 / 1775 AQUARIUS
GARCIA, MANUEL, II (singing teacher) 3 / 17 / 1805 PISCES
GARDEN, MARY (soprano) 2 / 20 / 1877 PISCES

GARDNER, AVA (actress) 12 / 24 / 1922 CAPRICORN
GARDNER, ERLE STANLEY (novelist) 7 / 17 / 1889 CANCER
GARFIELD, JAMES ABRAM (politician) 11 / 19 / 1831 SCORPIO
GARFIELD, JOHN (actor) 3 / 14 / 1913 PISCES
GARFUNKEL, ART (singer) 11 / 5 / 1941 SCORPIO
GARIBALDI, GIUSEPPE (Italian patriot) 7 / 4 / 1807 CANCER
GARLAND, JUDY (singer) 6 / 10 / 1922 GEMINI
GARNER, ERROLL (jazz musician) 6 / 15 / 1921 GEMINI
GARNER, JAMES (actor) 4 / 7 / 1928 ARIES
GARRICK, DAVID (actor) 3 / 2 / 1717 PISCES
GARRISON, JIM (public official) 11 / 20 / 1921 SCORPIO
GARRISON, WILLIAM LLOYD (abolitionist) 12 / 10 / 1805
     SAGITTARIUS
GARROWAY, DAVE (TV personality) 7 / 13 / 1913 CANCER
GARSON, GREER (actress) 9 / 29 / 1908 LIBRA
GARY, JOHN (singer) 11 / 29 / 1932 SAGITTARIUS
GASKELL, ELIZABETH (novelist) 9 / 29 / 1810 LIBRA
GASSMAN, VITTORIO (actor) 9 / 1 / 1922 VIRGO
GATCH, LEE (artist) 9 / 10 / 1902 VIRGO
GATTI-CASAZZA, GIULIO (operatic impresario) 2 / 3 / 1869 AQUARIUS
GAUDI, ANTONIO (architect) 6 / 25 / 1852 CANCER
GAUGUIN, PAUL (painter) 6 / 7 / 1848 GEMINI
GAVAZZENI, GIANANDREA (conductor) 7 / 25 / 1909 LEO
GAVIN, JOHN (actor) 4 / 8 / 1928 ARIES
GAY, JOHN (composer) 9 / 26 / 1685 LIBRA
GAYE, MARVIN (singer) 4 / 2 / 1939 ARIES
GAYNOR, JANET (actress) 10 / 6 / 1906 LIBRA
GAYNOR, MITZI (actress) 9 / 4 / 1931 VIRGO
GAZZARA, BEN (actor) 8 / 28 / 1930 VIRGO
GEDDA, NICOLAI (tenor) 7 / 11 / 1925 CANCER
GEER, WILL (actor) 3 / 9 / 1902 PISCES
GEHRIG, LOU (baseball player) 6 / 19 / 1903 GEMINI
GEIGER, HANS (physicist) 9 / 30 / 1882 LIBRA
GEILS, J. (rock musician) 2 / 20 / 1946 PISCES
GELBER, JACK (playwright) 4 / 12 / 1932 ARIES
GENCER, LEYLA (soprano) 10 / 10 / 1928 LIBRA
GENET, JEAN (writer) 12 / 19 / 1910 SAGITTARIUS
GENOVESE, VITO (mobster) 11 / 21 / 1897 SCORPIO
GENTELE, GOERAN (operatic impresario) 9 / 20 / 1917 VIRGO
GENTRY, BOBBIE (singer) 7 / 27 / 1944 LEO

GEORGE III OF ENGLAND, KING 6 / 15 / 1738 GEMINI
GEORGE V OF ENGLAND, KING 6 / 3 / 1865 GEMINI
GEORGE VI OF ENGLAND, KING 12 / 14 / 1895 SAGITTARIUS
GEORGE, LLEWELLYN (astrologer) 8 / 17 / 1876 LEO
GERICAULT, JEAN LOUIS (painter) 9 / 26 / 1791 LIBRA
GERNREICH, RUDI (fashion designer) 8 / 8 / 1922 LEO
GERSHWIN, GEORGE (composer) 9 / 26 / 1898 LIBRA
GERSHWIN, IRA (lyricist) 12 / 6 / 1896 SAGITTARIUS
GESELL, GERHARD A. (jurist) 6 / 16 / 1910 GEMINI
GETTY, J. PAUL (tycoon) 12 / 15 / 1892 SAGITTARIUS
GETZ, STAN (jazz musician) 2 / 2 / 1927 AQUARIUS
GHIAUROV, NICOLAI (basso) 9 / 13 / 1929 VIRGO
GHISLANZONI, ANTONIO (librettist) 11 / 25 / 1824 SAGITTARIUS
GIACOMETTI, ALBERTO (sculptor) 10 / 10 / 1901 LIBRA
GIACOMIN, EDWARD (hockey player) 6 / 6 / 1939 GEMINI
GIANNINI, DUSOLINA (soprano) 12 / 19 / 1902 SAGITTARIUS
GIBB, BARRY (singer) 9 / 1 / 1947 VIRGO
GIBB, MARY-MARGARET (Siamese twins) 5 / 20 / 1912 TAURUS
GIBB, MAURICE (rock musician) 12 / 22 / 1949
    SAGITTARIUS/CAPRICORN
GIBB, ROBIN (rock musician) 12 / 22 / 1949
    SAGITTARIUS/CAPRICORN
GIBBON, EDWARD (historian) 4 / 27 / 1737 TAURUS
GIBRAN, KAHLIL (poet) 1 / 6 / 1883 CAPRICORN
GIBSON, ALTHEA (tennis player) 8 / 25 / 1927 VIRGO
GIBSON, BOB (singer) 11 / 16 / 1931 SCORPIO
GIBSON, JOSHUA (baseball player) 12 / 21 / 1911
    SAGITTARIUS/CAPRICORN
GIBSON, ROBERT (baseball player) 11 / 9 / 1935 SCORPIO
GIDE, ANDRE (writer) 11 / 22 / 1869 SAGITTARIUS
GIELGUD, JOHN (actor) 4 / 14 / 1904 ARIES
GIESEKING, WALTER (pianist) 11 / 5 / 1895 SCORPIO
GIFFORD, FRANK (sportscaster) 8 / 16 / 1930 LEO
GIGLI, BENIAMINO (tenor) 3 / 20 / 1890 PISCES/ARIES
GILBERT, ROD (hockey player) 7 / 1 / 1941 CANCER
GILBERT, WILLIAM (librettist) 11 / 18 / 1836 SCORPIO
GILELS, EMIL (pianist) 10 / 19 / 1916 LIBRA
GILFORD, JACK (actor) 7 / 25 / 1913 LEO
GILLESPIE, DIZZY (jazz musician) 10 / 21 / 1917 LIBRA
GILMORE, DAVID (rock musician) 3 / 6 / ? PISCES

GILROY, FRANK D. (playwright) 10 / 13 / 1925 LIBRA
GIMBEL, BERNARD F. (merchant) 4 / 10 / 1885 ARIES
GINASTERA, ALBERTO (composer) 4 / 11 / 1916 ARIES
GINGOLD, HERMIONE (actress) 12 / 9 / 1897 SAGITTARIUS
GINSBERG, ALLEN (poet) 6 / 3 / 1926 GEMINI
GIORDANO, UMBERTO (composer) 8 / 27 / 1867 VIRGO
GIRAUDOUX, JEAN (playwright) 10 / 29 / 1882 SCORPIO
GIRODIAS, MAURICE (publisher) 4 / 12 / 1919 ARIES
GISCARD D'ESTAING, VALERY (French politician) 2 / 2 / 1926
     AQUARIUS
GISH, DOROTHY (actress) 3 / 11 / 1898 PISCES
GISH, LILLIAN (actress) 10 / 14 / 1896 LIBRA
GIULINI, CARLO MARIA (conductor) 5 / 9 / 1914 TAURUS
GIVENCHY, HUBERT DE (fashion designer) 2 / 21 / 1927 PISCES
GLADSTONE, WILLIAM (British statesman) 12 / 29 / 1809 CAPRICORN
GLAZUNOV, ALEXANDER (composer) 8 / 10 / 1865 LEO
GLEASON, JACKIE (comedian) 2 / 26 / 1916 PISCES
GLENN, JOHN (astronaut) 7 / 18 / 1921 CANCER
GLIERE, REINHOLD (composer) 12 / 30 / 1874 CAPRICORN
GLINKA, MIKHAIL (composer) 6 / 2 / 1804 GEMINI
GLITTER, GARY (singer) 5 / 8 / 1944 TAURUS
GLOSSOP, PETER (baritone) 7 / 6 / 1928 CANCER
GLUCK, ALMA (soprano) 5 / 11 / 1866 TAURUS
GLUCK, CHRISTOPH WILLIBALD VON (composer) 7 / 2 / 1714 CANCER
GOBBI, TITO (baritone) 10 / 24 / 1915 LIBRA/SCORPIO
GOBEL, GEORGE (comedian) 5 / 20 / 1920 TAURUS
GODARD, JEAN-LUC (film maker) 12 / 3 / 1930 SAGITTARIUS
GODDARD, PAULETTE (actress) 6 / 3 / 1911 GEMINI
GODFREY, ARTHUR (radio and TV personality) 8 / 31 / 1903 VIRGO
GOEBBELS, PAUL JOSEPH (Nazi official) 10 / 29 / 1897 SCORPIO
GOERING, HERMANN WILHELM (Nazi official) 1 / 12 / 1893
     CAPRICORN
GOETHALS, GEORGE WASHINGTON (engineer) 6 / 29 / 1858 CANCER
GOETHE, JOHANN WOLFGANG VON (poet) 8 / 28 / 1749 VIRGO
GOGOL, NIKOLAI (writer) 3 / 31 / 1809 ARIES
GOLD, HERBERT (writer) 3 / 9 / 1924 PISCES
GOLDBERG, ARTHUR (jurist) 8 / 8 / 1908 LEO
GOLDEN, HARRY (writer) 5 / 6 / 1902 TAURUS
GOLDING, WILLIAM (novelist) 9 / 19 / 1911 VIRGO
GOLDMARK, KARL (composer) 5 / 18 / 1830 TAURUS

GOLDONI, CARLO (playwright) 2 / 25 / 1707 PISCES
GOLDOVSKY, BORIS (impresario) 6 / 7 / 1908 GEMINI
GOLDSBORO, BOBBY (singer) 1 / 11 / 1941 CAPRICORN
GOLDSMITH, OLIVER (writer) 11 / 21 / 1728 SCORPIO
GOLDSTEIN, AL (publisher) 1 / 10 / 1936 CAPRICORN
GOLDWATER, BARRY (politician) 1 / 1 / 1909 CAPRICORN
GOLDWYN, SAMUEL (film executive) 8 / 27 / 1882 VIRGO
GOLTZ, CHRISTEL (soprano) 7 / 8 / 1912 CANCER
GOMPERS, SAMUEL (labor leader) 1 / 27 / 1850 AQUARIUS
GONCHAROV, IVAN (novelist) 6 / 18 / 1812 GEMINI
GONZALES, PANCHO (tennis player) 5 / 9 / 1928 TAURUS
GOODELL, CHARLES ELLSWORTH (politician) 3 / 16 / 1926 PISCES
GOODING, CYNTHIA (folk singer) 8 / 12 / 1924 LEO
GOODMAN, BENNY (clarinetist) 5 / 30 / 1909 GEMINI
GOODMAN, LINDA (astrologer) ? ARIES
GOODMAN, PAUL (writer) 9 / 9 / 1911 VIRGO
GOODYEAR, CHARLES (inventor) 12 / 29 / 1800 CAPRICORN
GOOLAGONG, EVONNE (tennis player) 7 / 31 / 1951 LEO
GORDON, RUTH (actress) 10 / 30 / 1896 SCORPIO
GORE, ALBERT (politician) 12 / 26 / 1907 CAPRICORN
GORE, LESLEY (singer) 5 / 2 / 1946 TAURUS
GOREN, CHARLES (bridge player) 3 / 4 / 1901 PISCES
GORGAS, WILLIAM CRAWFORD (epidemiologist) 10 / 3 / 1854 LIBRA
GORKI, MAXIM (writer) 3 / 28 / 1868 ARIES
GORMAN, CLIFF (actor) 10 / 13 / 1936 LIBRA
GORME, EYDIE (singer) 8 / 16 / 1932 LEO
GORR, RITA (mezzo-soprano) 2 / 18 / 1926 AQUARIUS/PISCES
GORTNER, MARJOE (evangelist) 1 / 14 / 1944 CAPRICORN
GOTTSCHALK, LOUIS (composer) 5 / 18 / 1829 TAURUS
GOULD, CHESTER (cartoonist) 11 / 20 / 1900 SCORPIO
GOULD, ELLIOTT (actor) 8 / 29 / 1938 VIRGO
GOULD, GLENN (pianist) 9 / 25 / 1932 LIBRA
GOULD, JAY (financier) 5 / 27 / 1836 GEMINI
GOULD, MORTON (composer) 12 / 10 / 1913 SAGITTARIUS
GOULDING, RAY (comedian) 3 / 20 / 1922 PISCES/ARIES
GOULET, ROBERT (singer) 11 / 26 / 1933 SAGITTARIUS
GOUNOD, CHARLES (composer) 6 / 17 / 1818 GEMINI
GOYA, FRANCISCO DE (painter) 3 / 30 / 1746 ARIES
GRABLE, BETTY (actress) 12 / 18 / 1916 SAGITTARIUS
GRAEBNER, CLARK (tennis player) 11 / 4 / 1943 SCORPIO

GRAF, HERBERT (director) 4 / 10 / 1903 ARIES
GRAFFMAN, GARY (pianist) 10 / 14 / 1928 LIBRA
GRAHAM, BILL (rock impresario) 1 / 8 / 1931 CAPRICORN
GRAHAM, BILLY (evangelist) 11 / 7 / 1918 SCORPIO
GRAHAM, KATHARINE (publisher) 6 / 16 / 1917 GEMINI
GRAHAM, MARTHA (dancer and choreographer) 5 / 11 / 1894
    TAURUS
GRAHAM, VIRGINIA (TV personality) 7 / 4 / 1913 CANCER
GRAHAME, GLORIA (actress) 11 / 28 / 1925 SAGITTARIUS
GRAHAME, KENNETH (writer) 3 / 8 / 1859 PISCES
GRAINGER, PERCY (composer) 7 / 8 / 1882 CANCER
GRANADOS, ENRIQUE (composer) 7 / 27 / 1867 LEO
GRANGE, RED (football player) 6 / 13 / 1903 GEMINI
GRANGER, FARLEY (actor) 7 / 1 / 1925 CANCER
GRANGER, STEWART (actor) 5 / 6 / 1913 TAURUS
GRANT, CARY (actor) 1 / 18 / 1904 CAPRICORN
GRANT, LEE (actress) 10 / 31 / 1927 SCORPIO
GRANT, ULYSSES S. (politician) 4 / 27 / 1822 TAURUS
GRANT, W. T. (merchant) 6 / 27 / 1876 CANCER
GRASS, GUENTER (novelist) 10 / 16 / 1927 LIBRA
GRASSO, ELLA (politician) 5 / 10 / 1919 TAURUS
GRAUER, BEN (newscaster) 6 / 2 / 1908 GEMINI
GRAVEL, MIKE (politician) 5 / 13 / 1930 TAURUS
GRAVES, PETER (actor) 3 / 18 / 1926 PISCES
GRAVES, ROBERT (writer) 7 / 26 / 1895 LEO
GRAY, DOLORES (actress) 6 / 7 / 1924 GEMINI
GRAY, L. PATRICK, III (government official) 7 / 18 / 1916 CANCER
GRAY, THOMAS (poet) 1 / 6 / 1717 CAPRICORN
GRAYSON, KATHRYN (actress) 2 / 9 / 1923 AQUARIUS
GRECO, JOSE (dancer) 12 / 23 / 1918 CAPRICORN
GREELEY, HORACE (journalist) 2 / 3 / 1811 AQUARIUS
GREEN, ADOLPH (lyricist) 12 / 2 / 1915 SAGITTARIUS
GREEN, HETTY (financier) 11 / 21 / 1835 SCORPIO
GREENBERG, HANK (baseball player) 1 / 1 / 1911 CAPRICORN
GREENE, GRAHAM (novelist) 10 / 2 / 1904 LIBRA
GREENE, LORNE (actor) 2 / 12 / 1915 AQUARIUS
GREENE, NANCY (skier) 5 / 11 / 1943 TAURUS
GREENE, RICHARD (actor) 8 / 25 / 1918 VIRGO
GREENWOOD, JOAN (actress) 3 / 4 / 1921 PISCES
GREER, GERMAINE (feminist) 1 / 29 / 1939 AQUARIUS

GREER, MICHAEL (actor) 4 / 20 / 1943 ARIES/TAURUS
GREGORY, CYNTHIA (ballet dancer) 7 / 8 / 1945 CANCER
GREGORY, DICK (comedian) 10 / 12 / 1932 LIBRA
GREGORY, LADY (playwright) 3 / 15 / 1852 PISCES
GRENFELL, JOYCE (actress) 2 / 10 / 1910 AQUARIUS
GREUZE, JEAN (painter) 8 / 21 / 1875 LEO
GREY, JOEL (actor) 4 / 11 / 1932 ARIES
GREY, ZANE (novelist) 1 / 31 / 1875 AQUARIUS
GRIEG, EDVARD (composer) 6 / 15 / 1843 GEMINI
GRIFFIES, ETHEL (actress) 4 / 26 / 1878 TAURUS
GRIFFIN, MERV (TV personality) 7 / 6 / 1925 CANCER
GRIFFITH, ANDY (actor) 6 / 1 / 1926 GEMINI
GRIFFITH, D. W. (film maker) 1 / 22 / 1875 AQUARIUS
GRIFFITH, HUGH (actor) 5 / 30 / 1912 GEMINI
GRIGOROVICH, YURI (choreographer) 1 / 1 / 1927 CAPRICORN
GRILLPARZER, FRANZ (poet) 1 / 15 / 1791 CAPRICORN
GRIMES, TAMMY (actress) 1 / 30 / 1936 AQUARIUS
GRIMM, JAKOB (folklorist) 1 / 4 / 1785 CAPRICORN
GRIMM, WILHELM (folklorist) 2 / 24 / 1786 PISCES
GRISI, GIUDITTA (mezzo-soprano) 7 / 28 / 1805 LEO
GRISI, GIULIA (soprano) 7 / 28 / 1811 LEO
GRISSOM, VIRGIL (astronaut) 4 / 3 / 1926 ARIES
GRIZZARD, GEORGE (actor) 4 / 1 / 1928 ARIES
GROAT, DICK (baseball player) 11 / 4 / 1930 SCORPIO
GROFE, FERDE (composer) 3 / 27 / 1892 ARIES
GROMYKO, ANDREI (Soviet official) 7 / 6 / 1909 CANCER
GROPIUS, WALTER (architect) 5 / 18 / 1883 TAURUS
GROSS, CHAIM (artist) 3 / 17 / 1904 PISCES
GROTOWSKI, JERZY (director) 8 / 11 / 1933 LEO
GROVE, ROBERT "LEFTY" (baseball player) 3 / 6 / 1900 PISCES
GRUEMMER, ELISABETH (soprano) 3 / 31 / 1911 ARIES
GUARDI, FRANCESCO (painter) 10 / 5 / 1712 LIBRA
GUARDINO, HARRY (actor) 12 / 23 / 1925 CAPRICORN
GUARNERI, GIUSEPPE ANTONIO (violin maker) 10 / 16 / 1687 LIBRA
GUCCI, ALDO (shoe merchant) 5 / 26 / 1909 GEMINI
GUEDEN, HILDE (soprano) 9 / 15 / 1923 VIRGO
GUEST, EDGAR A. (poet) 8 / 20 / 1881 LEO
GUEVARA, CHE (revolutionary leader) 6 / 14 / 1928 GEMINI
GUGGENHEIM, PEGGY (art collector) 8 / 26 / 1898 VIRGO
GUI, VITTORIO (conductor) 9 / 14 / 1885 VIRGO

GUINNESS, ALEC (actor) 4 / 2 / 1914 ARIES
GUITRY, SACHA (actor and playwright) 2 / 21 / 1885 PISCES
GUNN, MOSES (actor) 10 / 2 / 1929 LIBRA
GUNTHER, JOHN (writer) 8 / 30 / 1901 VIRGO
GURDJIEFF, G. I. (philosopher) 1 / 13 / 1877 CAPRICORN
GURNEY, EDWARD (politician) 1 / 12 / 1914 CAPRICORN
GUSTAVUS III OF SWEDEN, KING 1 / 24 / 1746 AQUARIUS
GUSTAVUS VI OF SWEDEN, KING 11 / 11 / 1882 SCORPIO
GUSTAVUS ADOLPHUS OF SWEDEN, KING 12 / 9 / 1594 SAGITTARIUS
GUSTON, PHILIP (painter) 6 / 27 / 1913 CANCER
GUTHRIE, ARLO (singer) 7 / 10 / 1947 CANCER
GUTHRIE, TYRONE (director) 7 / 2 / 1900 CANCER
GUTHRIE, WOODY (folk singer) 7 / 14 / 1912 CANCER
GUY, BUDDY (blues musician) 7 / 30 / 1936 LEO
GWENN, EDMUND (actor) 9 / 26 / 1875 LIBRA
GWYN, NELL (courtesan) 2 / 12 / 1560 AQUARIUS

HACKETT, BUDDY (comedian) 8 / 31 / 1924 VIRGO
HACKMAN, GENE (actor) 1 / 30 / 1931 AQUARIUS
HADAS, MOSES (classicist) 6 / 25 / 1900 CANCER
HADRIAN OF ROME, EMPEROR 1 / 22 / A.D. 76 AQUARIUS
HAGEN, UTA (actress) 6 / 12 / 1919 GEMINI
HAGEN, WALTER (golfer) 12 / 21 / 1892 SAGITTARIUS/CAPRICORN
HAGGARD, HENRY RIDER (writer) 6 / 22 / 1856 GEMINI/CANCER
HAGGARD, MERLE (country singer) 4 / 5 / 1937 ARIES
HAHN, OTTO (physicist) 3 / 8 / 1879 PISCES
HAHN, REYNALDO (composer) 8 / 9 / 1875 LEO
HAIG, ALEXANDER (government official) 12 / 2 / 1924 SAGITTARIUS
HAILE SELASSIE OF ETHIOPIA, EMPEROR 7 / 23 / 1891 LEO
HAILEY, ARTHUR (novelist) 4 / 5 / 1920 ARIES
HALDEMAN, H. R. (government official) 10 / 27 / 1926 SCORPIO
HALE, BARBARA (actress) 4 / 18 / 1922 ARIES
HALE, NATHAN (patriot) 6 / 6 / 1755 GEMINI
HALEVY, FROMENTAL (composer) 5 / 27 / 1799 GEMINI
HALL, MANLY PALMER (occultist) 3 / 18 / 1901 PISCES
HALL, PETER (director) 11 / 22 / 1930 SAGITTARIUS
HALLEY, EDMUND (astronomer) 11 / 18 / 1656 SCORPIO
HALSMAN, PHILIPPE (photographer) 5 / 2 / 1906 TAURUS
HAMILL, PETE (columnist) 6 / 24 / 1935 CANCER

HAMILTON, DUKE OF (British air force officer) 2 / 3 / 1903
    AQUARIUS

HAMILTON, ALEXANDER (statesman) 1 / 11 / 1757 CAPRICORN

HAMILTON, CHICO (guitarist) 9 / 21 / 1921 VIRGO

HAMILTON, EDITH (classicist) 8 / 12 / 1867 LEO

HAMILTON, LADY EMMA (naval officer's mistress) 4 / 26 / 1763
    TAURUS

HAMILTON, GEORGE (actor) 8 / 12 / 1939 LEO

HAMILTON, MARGARET (actress) 12 / 9 / 1902 SAGITTARIUS

HAMMARSKJOELD, DAG (UN official) 7 / 29 / 1905 LEO

HAMMERSTEIN, OSCAR (impresario) 5 / 8 / 1846 TAURUS

HAMMERSTEIN, OSCAR, II (lyricist) 7 / 12 / 1895 CANCER

HAMMETT, DASHIELL (writer) 5 / 27 / 1894 GEMINI

HAMPSHIRE, SUSAN (actress) 5 / 12 / 1941 TAURUS

HAMPTON, LIONEL (xylophonist) 4 / 20 / 1914 ARIES/TAURUS

HANCOCK, JOHN (patriot) 1 / 23 / 1737 AQUARIUS

HAND, LEARNED (jurist) 1 / 27 / 1872 AQUARIUS

HANDEL, GEORGE FREDERICK (composer) 2 / 23 / 1685 PISCES

HANDY, W. C. (composer) 11 / 16 / 1873 SCORPIO

HANEY, FRED (baseball player) 4 / 25 / 1898 TAURUS

HANSBERRY, LORRAINE (playwright) 5 / 19 / 1930 TAURUS

HANSEN, FRED (athlete) 12 / 29 / 1940 CAPRICORN

HANSON, HARRY (actor) 3 / 3 / 1895 PISCES

HANSON, HOWARD (composer) 10 / 28 / 1896 SCORPIO

HARBACH, OTTO (lyricist) 8 / 16 / 1873 LEO

HARD, DARLENE (tennis player) 1 / 6 / 1936 CAPRICORN

HARDIN, JOHN WESLEY (outlaw) 5 / 26 / 1853 GEMINI

HARDING, ANN (actress) 8 / 7 / 1902 LEO

HARDING, WARREN G. (politician) 11 / 2 / 1865 SCORPIO

HARDWICKE, CEDRIC (actor) 2 / 19 / 1893 AQUARIUS/PISCES

HARDY, OLIVER (comedian) 1 / 18 / 1892 CAPRICORN

HARDY, THOMAS (novelist) 6 / 2 / 1840 GEMINI

HARGIS, BILLY JAMES (evangelist) 8 / 3 / 1925 LEO

HARKNESS, REBEKAH (composer and patron of dance) 4 / 17 / 1915
    ARIES

HARLOW, JEAN (actress) 3 / 3 / 1911 PISCES

HARNICK, SHELDON (lyricist) 4 / 30 / 1924 TAURUS

HARPER, VALERIE (actress) 8 / 22 / 1940 LEO

HARRELSON, KEN (baseball player) 9 / 4 / 1941 VIRGO

HARRIMAN, AVERELL (government official) 11 / 15 / 1891 SCORPIO

HARRINGTON, MICHAEL (socialist) 2 / 24 / 1928 PISCES
HARRIS, BUCKY (baseball manager) 11 / 8 / 1896 SCORPIO
HARRIS, JOEL CHANDLER (writer) 12 / 9 / 1848 SAGITTARIUS
HARRIS, JULIE (actress) 12 / 2 / 1925 SAGITTARIUS
HARRIS, LOUIS (pollster) 1 / 6 / 1921 CAPRICORN
HARRIS, PHIL (actor) 6 / 24 / 1906 CANCER
HARRIS, RICHARD (actor) 10 / 1 / 1930 LIBRA
HARRIS, ROSEMARY (actress) 9 / 19 / 1930 VIRGO
HARRIS, ROY (composer) 2 / 12 / 1898 AQUARIUS
HARRISON, BENJAMIN (politician) 8 / 20 / 1833 LEO
HARRISON, GEORGE (rock musician) 2 / 25 / 1943 PISCES
HARRISON, JAY (music critic) 1 / 25 / 1927 AQUARIUS
HARRISON, NOEL (actor) 1 / 29 / 1936 AQUARIUS
HARRISON, REX (actor) 3 / 5 / 1908 PISCES
HARRISON, WALLACE K. (architect) 10 / 28 / 1895 SCORPIO
HARRISON, WILLIAM HENRY (politician) 2 / 9 / 1773 AQUARIUS
HART, LORENZ (lyricist) 5 / 2 / 1895 TAURUS
HART, MOSS (playwright) 10 / 24 / 1904 SCORPIO
HART, WILLIAM S. (actor) 12 / 6 / 1872 SAGITTARIUS
HARTACK, WILLIE (jockey) 12 / 9 / 1932 SAGITTARIUS
HARTE, BRET (writer) 8 / 25 / 1839 VIRGO
HARTFORD, HUNTINGTON (art patron) 4 / 18 / 1911 ARIES
HARTIGAN, GRACE (artist) 3 / 28 / 1922 ARIES
HARTMAN, ELIZABETH (actress) 12 / 23 / 1941 SAGITTARIUS/
    CAPRICORN
HARTZ, JIM (TV personality) 2 / 3 / 1940 AQUARIUS
HARVEY, LAURENCE (actor) 10 / 1 / 1928 LIBRA
HARVEY, PETER (stage designer) 1 / 2 / 1933 CAPRICORN
HARVEY, WILLIAM (physician) 4 / 11 / 1578 ARIES
HASKIL, CLARA (pianist) 1 / 7 / 1895 CAPRICORN
HATFIELD, MARK (politician) 7 / 12 / 1922 CANCER
HAUK, MINNIE (soprano) 11 / 14 / 1852 SCORPIO
HAUPTMANN, GERHART (playwright) 11 / 15 / 1862 SCORPIO
HAVEL, VACLAV (playwright) 10 / 5 / 1936 LIBRA
HAVENS, RICHIE (rock musician) 1 / 21 / 1941 CAPRICORN/
    AQUARIUS
HAVOC, JUNE (actress) 11 / 8 / 1916 SCORPIO
HAWKINS, JACK (actor) 9 / 14 / 1910 VIRGO
HAWKS, HOWARD (film director) 5 / 30 / 1896 GEMINI
HAWN, GOLDIE (actress) 11 / 21 / 1945 SCORPIO

HAWTHORNE, NATHANIEL (writer) 7 / 4 / 1804 CANCER
HAYAKAWA, S. I. (philologist) 7 / 18 / 1906 CANCER
HAYAKAWA, SESSUE (actor) 6 / 10 / 1890 GEMINI
HAYDEN, GAIL (actress) 12 / 26 / 1944 CAPRICORN
HAYDEN, MELISSA (ballet dancer) 4 / 25 / 1928 TAURUS
HAYDEN, STERLING (actor) 3 / 26 / 1916 ARIES
HAYDN, FRANZ JOSEF (composer) 3 / 31 / 1732 ARIES
HAYES, BOB (football player) 12 / 20 / 1942 SAGITTARIUS
HAYES, DAVID (sculptor) 3 / 15 / 1931 PISCES
HAYES, GABBY (actor) 5 / 7 / 1885 TAURUS
HAYES, HELEN (actress) 10 / 10 / 1900 LIBRA
HAYES, ISAAC (composer) 8 / 20 / 1942 LEO
HAYES, PETER LIND (TV personality) 6 / 25 / 1915 CANCER
HAYES, RUTHERFORD B. (politician) 10 / 4 / 1822 LIBRA
HAYWARD, JUSTIN (rock musician) 10 / 14 / 1946 LIBRA
HAYWARD, LELAND (producer) 9 / 13 / 1902 VIRGO
HAYWARD, SUSAN (actress) 6 / 30 / 1919 CANCER
HAYWORTH, RITA (actress) 10 / 17 / 1918 LIBRA
HAZLITT, WILLIAM (writer) 4 / 10 / 1778 ARIES
HEAD, EDITH (costume designer) 10 / 28 / 1907 SCORPIO
HEALY, MARY (TV personality) 4 / 14 / 1918 ARIES
HEARST, PATRICIA "TANIA" (outlaw) 2 / 20 / 1954 PISCES
HEARST, RANDOLPH (publisher) 12 / 2 / 1915 SAGITTARIUS
HEARST, WILLIAM RANDOLPH (publisher) 4 / 29 / 1863 TAURUS
HEARST, WILLIAM RANDOLPH, JR. (publisher) 1 / 27 / 1908
     AQUARIUS
HEATH, EDWARD (British politician) 7 / 9 / 1916 CANCER
HECHT, BEN (writer) 2 / 28 / 1894 PISCES
HECKART, EILEEN (actress) 3 / 29 / 1919 ARIES
HEDISON, DAVID (actor) 5 / 20 / 1929 TAURUS
HEFLIN, VAN (actor) 12 / 13 / 1910 SAGITTARIUS
HEFNER, HUGH (publisher) 4 / 9 / 1926 ARIES
HEGEL, GEORG WILHELM FRIEDRICH (philosopher) 8 / 27 / 1770
     VIRGO
HEIDEGGER, MARTIN (philosopher) 9 / 26 / 1889 LIBRA
HEIFETZ, JASCHA (violinist) 2 / 2 / 1901 AQUARIUS
HEINDEL, MAX (occultist) 7 / 23 / 1865 LEO
HEINE, HEINRICH (poet) 12 / 13 / 1797 SAGITTARIUS
HEINLEIN, ROBERT A. (writer) 7 / 7 / 1907 CANCER
HEISS, CAROL E. (skater) 1 / 20 / 1940 CAPRICORN/AQUARIUS

HELD, ANNA (actress) 3 / 18 / 1873 PISCES
HELLER, JOSEPH (novelist) 5 / 1 / 1923 TAURUS
HELLMAN, LILLIAN (writer) 6 / 20 / 1905 GEMINI
HELMHOLTZ, HERMANN LUDWIG VON (physicist) 8 / 31 / 1821 VIRGO
HELMS, RICHARD (government official) 3 / 30 / 1913 ARIES
HELPMANN, ROBERT (ballet dancer) 4 / 9 / 1909 ARIES
HEMINGWAY, ERNEST (writer) 7 / 21 / 1899 CANCER
HEMINGWAY, MARY (writer's wife) 4 / 5 / 1908 ARIES
HEMMINGS, DAVID (actor) 11 / 21 / 1941 SCORPIO
HEMPEL, FRIEDA (soprano) 6 / 26 / 1885 CANCER
HENDERSON, FLORENCE (actress) 2 / 14 / 1934 AQUARIUS
HENDERSON, JIMMY (rock musician) 5 / 20 / 1954 TAURUS
HENDERSON, RAY (composer) 12 / 1 / 1896 SAGITTARIUS
HENDERSON, ROY (baritone) 7 / 4 / 1899 CANCER
HENDERSON, SKITCH (bandleader) 1 / 27 / 1918 AQUARIUS
HENDRIX, JIMI (rock musician) 11 / 27 / 1942 SAGITTARIUS
HENDRYX, NONA (singer) 10 / 9 / 1947 LIBRA
HENIE, SONJA (skater) 4 / 8 / 1912 ARIES
HENREID, PAUL (actor) 1 / 10 / 1908 CAPRICORN
HENRI DE NAVARRE, KING 12 / 23 / 1533 CAPRICORN
HENRY THE NAVIGATOR, PRINCE 3 / 12 / 1394 PISCES
HENRY II OF ENGLAND, KING 3 / 19 / 1133 PISCES
HENRY IV OF ENGLAND, KING 3 / 19 / 1367 PISCES
HENRY V OF ENGLAND, KING 8 / 17 / 1387 LEO
HENRY VIII OF ENGLAND, KING 7 / 7 / 1491 CANCER
HENRY, O. (writer) 9 / 11 / 1862 VIRGO
HENRY, PATRICK (patriot) 6 / 9 / 1735 GEMINI
HENZE, HANS WERNER (composer) 7 / 1 / 1926 CANCER
HEPBURN, AUDREY (actress) 5 / 4 / 1929 TAURUS
HEPBURN, KATHARINE (actress) 11 / 8 / 1909 SCORPIO
HERBER, ARNIE (football player) 4 / 2 / 1910 ARIES
HERBERT, GEORGE (poet) 4 / 13 / 1593 ARIES
HERBERT, VICTOR (composer) 2 / 1 / 1859 AQUARIUS
HERBLOCK (cartoonist) 10 / 13 / 1909 LIBRA
HERLIE, EILEEN (actress) 3 / 8 / 1920 PISCES
HERLIHY, JAMES LEO (novelist) 2 / 27 / 1927 PISCES
HERMAN, JERRY (composer) 7 / 10 / 1933 CANCER
HERMAN, WOODY (bandleader) 5 / 16 / 1913 TAURUS
HERRMANN, BERNARD (composer) 6 / 29 / 1911 CANCER
HERSCHEL, WILLIAM (astronomer) 11 / 15 / 1738 SCORPIO

HERSEY, JOHN (writer) 6 / 17 / 1914 GEMINI
HERSHEY, LEWIS (government official) 9 / 12 / 1893 VIRGO
HERTER, CHRISTIAN (government official) 3 / 28 / 1895 ARIES
HERZOG, MAURICE (mountain climber) 1 / 15 / 1919 CAPRICORN
HESS, MYRA (pianist) 2 / 25 / 1890 PISCES
HESS, RUDOLF (Nazi official) 4 / 26 / 1894 TAURUS
HESSE, HERMANN (novelist) 7 / 2 / 1877 CANCER
HESTON, CHARLTON (actor) 10 / 4 / 1924 LIBRA
HEYERDAHL, THOR (ethnologist) 10 / 6 / 1914 LIBRA
HEYWOOD, ANNE (actress) 12 / 11 / 1933 SAGITTARIUS
HICKEL, WALTER (government official) 8 / 18 / 1919 LEO
HICKMAN, DARRYL (actor) 7 / 28 / 1933 LEO
HICKMAN, DWAYNE (actor) 5 / 18 / 1934 TAURUS
HICKOK, WILD BILL (frontiersman) 5 / 27 / 1837 GEMINI
HICKS, GRANVILLE (writer) 9 / 9 / 1901 VIRGO
HILDEGARDE (singer) 2 / 1 / 1906 AQUARIUS
HILL, GRAHAM (auto racer) 2 / 15 / 1929 AQUARIUS
HILL, STEVEN (actor) 2 / 24 / 1922 PISCES
HILLARY, EDMUND (explorer) 7 / 20 / 1919 CANCER
HILLER, WENDY (actress) 8 / 15 / 1912 LEO
HILTON, CONRAD (hotel executive) 12 / 25 / 1887 CAPRICORN
HIMMLER, HEINRICH (Nazi official) 10 / 7 / 1900 LIBRA
HINDEMITH, PAUL (composer) 11 / 16 / 1895 SCORPIO
HINDENBURG, PAUL VON (German statesman) 10 / 2 / 1847 LIBRA
HINES, DUNCAN (merchant) 3 / 26 / 1880 ARIES
HINES, EARL (jazz musician) 12 / 28 / 1903 CAPRICORN
HINES, JEROME (basso) 11 / 8 / 1921 SCORPIO
HINGLE, PAT (actor) 7 / 19 / 1924 CANCER
HINKSON, MARY (dancer) 3 / 16 / 1930 PISCES
HIROHITO OF JAPAN, EMPEROR 4 / 29 / 1901 TAURUS
HIRSCHFELD, AL (caricaturist) 6 / 21 / 1903 CANCER
HIRT, AL (jazz musician) 11 / 7 / 1922 SCORPIO
HISS, ALGER (public official) 11 / 11 / 1904 SCORPIO
HITCHCOCK, ALFRED (film director) 8 / 13 / 1899 LEO
HITLER, ADOLF (dictator) 4 / 20 / 1889 TAURUS
HOBBES, THOMAS (philosopher) 4 / 15 / 1588 ARIES
HOBBY, OVETA CULP (publisher and government official)
    1 / 19 / 1905 CAPRICORN
HOCHHUTH, ROLF (playwright) 4 / 1 / 1931 ARIES
HO CHI MINH (Vietnamese politician) 5 / 19 / 1890 TAURUS

HOCKNEY, DAVID (artist) 7 / 9 / 1937 CANCER
HODGES, GIL (baseball player) 4 / 4 / 1924 ARIES
HOELDERLIN, JOHANN C. F. (poet) 3 / 20 / 1770 PISCES/ARIES
HOFFA, JIMMY (labor leader) 2 / 14 / 1913 AQUARIUS
HOFFER, ERIC (writer) 7 / 25 / 1902 LEO
HOFFMAN, ABBIE (revolutionary) 11 / 30 / 1936 SAGITTARIUS
HOFFMAN, DUSTIN (actor) 8 / 8 / 1937 LEO
HOFFMAN, JULIUS (jurist) 7 / 7 / 1895 CANCER
HOFFMAN, MALVINA (sculptress) 6 / 15 / 1887 GEMINI
HOFFMANN, E. T. A. (writer) 1 / 24 / 1776 AQUARIUS
HOFFMANN, HANS (painter) 3 / 21 / 1880 PISCES/ARIES
HOFHEINZ, ROY (entrepreneur) 4 / 10 / 1912 ARIES
HOFMANN, JOSEF (pianist) 1 / 20 / 1876 CAPRICORN/AQUARIUS
HOFMANNSTHAL, HUGO VON (poet) 2 / 1 / 1874 AQUARIUS
HOGAN, BEN (golfer) 8 / 13 / 1912 LEO
HOGAN, FRANK (public official) 1 / 17 / 1902 CAPRICORN
HOGARTH, WILLIAM (painter) 11 / 20 / 1697 SCORPIO
HOLBROOK, HAL (actor) 2 / 17 / 1925 AQUARIUS
HOLDEN, WILLIAM (actor) 4 / 17 / 1918 ARIES
HOLIDAY, BILLIE (jazz singer) 4 / 7 / 1915 ARIES
HOLLANDER, XAVIERA (procuress) 6 / 15 / 1943 GEMINI
HOLLIDAY, JUDY (actress) 6 / 21 / 1922 GEMINI/CANCER
HOLLOWAY, STANLEY (actor) 10 / 1 / 1890 LIBRA
HOLLY, BUDDY (singer) 9 / 7 / 1936 VIRGO
HOLM, CELESTE (actress) 4 / 29 / 1919 TAURUS
HOLMES, OLIVER WENDELL (poet) 8 / 29 / 1809 VIRGO
HOLMES, OLIVER WENDELL (jurist) 3 / 8 / 1841 PISCES
HOLST, GUSTAV (composer) 9 / 21 / 1874 VIRGO
HOMER (country singer) 7 / 27 / 1920 LEO
HOMER, LOUISE (contralto) 4 / 28 / 1871 TAURUS
HOMER, WINSLOW (painter) 2 / 24 / 1836 PISCES
HOMOLKA, OSCAR (actor) 8 / 12 / 1898 LEO
HONEGGER, ARTHUR (composer) 3 / 10 / 1892 PISCES
HOOK, SIDNEY (writer) 12 / 20 / 1902 SAGITTARIUS
HOOKER, JOHN LEE (blues musician) 8 / 22 / 1917 LEO
HOOKS, ROBERT (actor) 4 / 18 / 1937 ARIES
HOOVER, HERBERT (politician) 8 / 10 / 1874 LEO
HOOVER, J. EDGAR (government official) 1 / 1 / 1895 CAPRICORN
HOPE, BOB (comedian) 5 / 29 / 1904 GEMINI
HOPKINS, GERARD MANLEY (poet) 6 / 11 / 1844 GEMINI

HOPKINS, LIGHTNIN (blues singer) 3 / 15 / 1912 PISCES
HOPKINS, MIRIAM (actress) 10 / 18 / 1902 LIBRA
HOPPER, DENNIS (actor) 5 / 17 / 1936 TAURUS
HOPPER, EDWARD (painter) 7 / 22 / 1882 CANCER/LEO
HOPPER, HEDDA (columnist) 6 / 2 / 1890 GEMINI
HORACE (poet) 12 / 6 / 65 B.C. SAGITTARIUS
HORNE, LENA (singer) 6 / 30 / 1917 CANCER
HORNE, MARILYN (mezzo-soprano) 1 / 16 / 1934 CAPRICORN
HORNSBY, ROGERS (baseball manager) 4 / 27 / 1896 TAURUS
HORNUNG, PAUL (football player) 12 / 23 / 1935 CAPRICORN
HOROWITZ, VLADIMIR (pianist) 10 / 1 / 1904 LIBRA
HORTON, EDWARD EVERETT (actor) 3 / 18 / 1887 PISCES
HORTON, JOHNNY (actor) 4 / 3 / 1929 ARIES
HORTON, ROBERT (actor) 7 / 29 / 1924 LEO
HOTTER, HANS (baritone) 1 / 19 / 1909 CAPRICORN
HOUDINI, HARRY (magician) 4 / 6 / 1874 ARIES
HOUGHTON, KATHARINE (actress) 3 / 10 / 1945 PISCES
HOUK, RALPH (baseball manager) 8 / 9 / 1919 LEO
HOUSMAN, A. E. (poet) 5 / 26 / 1859 GEMINI
HOUSTON, CISCO (folk singer) 8 / 18 / 1918 LEO
HOUSTON, SAM (soldier and politician) 3 / 2 / 1793 PISCES
HOVHANESS, ALAN (composer) 3 / 8 / 1911 PISCES
HOVING, THOMAS P. F. (art museum manager) 1 / 15 / 1931
    CAPRICORN
HOWARD, ELSTON (baseball player) 2 / 23 / 1930 PISCES
HOWARD, FRANK (baseball player) 8 / 8 / 1936 LEO
HOWARD, LESLIE (actor) 4 / 3 / 1893 ARIES
HOWARD, TREVOR (actor) 9 / 29 / 1916 LIBRA
HOWE, ELIAS (inventor) 7 / 9 / 1819 CANCER
HOWE, GORDIE (hockey player) 3 / 31 / 1928 ARIES
HOWE, IRVING (writer) 6 / 11 / 1920 GEMINI
HOWE, JULIA WARD (writer) 5 / 27 / 1819 GEMINI
HOWELLS, WILLIAM DEAN (writer) 3 / 1 / 1837 PISCES
HOWES, SALLY ANN (actress) 7 / 20 / 1930 CANCER
HUBBARD, L. RON (Scientologist) 3 / 13 / 1911 PISCES
HUDSON, ROCK (actor) 11 / 17 / 1925 SCORPIO
HUDSON, WILLIAM HENRY (writer) 8 / 4 / 1841 LEO
HUGHES, HOWARD (tycoon) 12 / 24 / 1905 CAPRICORN
HUGHES, LANGSTON (writer) 2 / 1 / 1902 AQUARIUS
HUGO, VICTOR (writer) 2 / 26 / 1802 PISCES

HULL, BOBBY (hockey player) 1 / 3 / 1939 CAPRICORN
HULL, JOSEPHINE (actress) 1 / 3 / 1886 CAPRICORN
HUME, DAVID (philosopher) 5 / 7 / 1711 TAURUS
HUMPERDINCK, ENGELBERT (composer) 9 / 1 / 1854 VIRGO
HUMPERDINCK, ENGELBERT (singer) 5 / 3 / 1937 TAURUS
HUMPHREY, HUBERT (politician) 5 / 27 / 1911 GEMINI
HUNT, E. HOWARD (intelligence agent) 10 / 9 / 1918 LIBRA
HUNT, H. L. (tycoon) 2 / 17 / 1889 AQUARIUS
HUNT, MARSHA (actress) 10 / 17 / 1917 LIBRA
HUNT, MARTITA (actress) 1 / 30 / 1900 AQUARIUS
HUNTER, IAN (actor) 6 / 13 / 1900 GEMINI
HUNTER, JEFFREY (actor) 11 / 25 / 1927 SAGITTARIUS
HUNTER, JIM "CATFISH" (baseball player) 4 / 8 / 1946 ARIES
HUNTER, KIM (actress) 11 / 12 / 1922 SCORPIO
HUNTER, ROSS (producer) 5 / 6 / 1924 TAURUS
HUNTER, TAB (actor) 7 / 11 / 1931 CANCER
HUNTINGTON, ANNA HYATT (sculptress) 3 / 10 / 1876 PISCES
HUNTLEY, CHET (newsman) 12 / 10 / 1911 SAGITTARIUS
HUROK, SOL (impresario) 4 / 9 / 1888 ARIES
HURST, FANNY (novelist) 10 / 18 / 1889 LIBRA
HURT, MISSISSIPPI JOHN (folk singer) 3 / 8 / 1892 PISCES
HUSSEIN OF JORDAN, KING 11 / 14 / 1935 SCORPIO
HUSSEY, RUTH (actress) 10 / 30 / 1917 SCORPIO
HUSTON, JOHN (film director) 8 / 5 / 1906 LEO
HUSTON, WALTER (actor) 4 / 6 / 1884 ARIES
HUTTON, BARBARA (heiress) 11 / 14 / 1912 SCORPIO
HUTTON, BETTY (actress) 2 / 26 / 1921 PISCES
HUTTON, LAUREN (model and actress) 11 / 17 / 1943 SCORPIO
HUXLEY, ALDOUS (writer) 7 / 26 / 1894 LEO
HUXLEY, JULIAN (biologist) 6 / 22 / 1887 CANCER
HUXLEY, THOMAS (biologist) 5 / 4 / 1825 TAURUS
HUYSMANS, JORIS KARL (writer) 2 / 5 / 1848 AQUARIUS
HYDE-WHITE, WILFRID (actor) 5 / 12 / 1903 TAURUS
HYER, MARTHA (actress) 8 / 10 / 1934 LEO

IAN, JANIS (singer) 4 / 7 / 1951 ARIES
IBERT, JACQUES (composer) 8 / 15 / 1890 LEO
IBSEN, HENRIK (playwright) 3 / 20 / 1828 ARIES
IGLESIAS, ROBERTO (dancer) 10 / 27 / 1927 SCORPIO

ILLICA, LUIGI (librettist) 5 / 9 / 1857 TAURUS
INDIANA, ROBERT (painter) 9 / 13 / 1928 VIRGO
INDY, VINCENT D' (composer) 3 / 27 / 1851 ARIES
INGE, WILLIAM (playwright) 5 / 3 / 1913 TAURUS
INGRES, JEAN AUGUSTE (painter) 8 / 29 / 1780 VIRGO
INNESS, GEORGE (painter) 5 / 1 / 1825 TAURUS
INNIS, ROY (black leader) 6 / 6 / 1934 GEMINI
INOUYE, DANIEL (politician) 9 / 7 / 1924 VIRGO
IONESCO, EUGENE (playwright) 11 / 13 / 1912 SCORPIO
IRELAND, JOHN (actor) 1 / 30 / 1914 AQUARIUS
IRVING, CLIFFORD (writer) 11 / 5 / 1930 SCORPIO
IRVING, HENRY (actor) 2 / 6 / 1838 AQUARIUS
IRVING, WASHINGTON (writer) 4 / 3 / 1783 ARIES
ISABELLA OF CASTILE, QUEEN 5 / 1 / 1451 TAURUS
ISHERWOOD, CHRISTOPHER (writer) 8 / 26 / 1904 VIRGO
ISTOMIN, EUGENE (pianist) 11 / 26 / 1925 SAGITTARIUS
ITURBI, JOSE (pianist) 11 / 28 / 1895 SAGITTARIUS
IVAN THE TERRIBLE OF RUSSIA, CZAR 9 / 4 / 1530 VIRGO
IVES, BURL (folk singer and actor) 6 / 14 / 1909 GEMINI
IVES, CHARLES (composer) 10 / 20 / 1874 LIBRA

JACKSON, ANDREW (politician) 3 / 15 / 1767 PISCES
JACKSON, ANNE (actress) 9 / 3 / 1926 VIRGO
JACKSON, GLENDA (actress) 5 / 9 / 1936 TAURUS
JACKSON, HENRY (politician) 5 / 31 / 1912 GEMINI
JACKSON, MAHALIA (gospel singer) 10 / 26 / 1911 SCORPIO
JACKSON, REGGIE (baseball player) 5 / 18 / 1946 TAURUS
JACKSON, SHIRLEY (writer) 12 / 14 / 1919 SAGITTARIUS
JACKSON, STONEWALL (army officer) 1 / 21 / 1824 AQUARIUS
JACOBI, LOU (actor) 12 / 28 / 1913 CAPRICORN
JAFFE, SAM (actor) 3 / 8 / 1897 PISCES
JAGGER, CHRIS (singer) 12 / 19 / 1947 SAGITTARIUS
JAGGER, DEAN (actor) 11 / 7 / 1903 SCORPIO
JAGGER, MICK (singer) 7 / 26 / 1943 LEO
JAMAL, AHMAD (jazz musician) 7 / 2 / 1930 CANCER
JAMES I OF ENGLAND, KING 6 / 29 / 1566 CANCER
JAMES II OF ENGLAND, KING 10 / 26 / 1633 SCORPIO
JAMES, HARRY (trumpeter) 3 / 15 / 1916 PISCES
JAMES, HENRY (novelist) 4 / 15 / 1843 ARIES

JAMES, JESSE (outlaw) 9 / 5 / 1847 VIRGO
JAMES, JONI (singer) 9 / 22 / 1930 VIRGO
JAMES, WILLIAM (philosopher) 1 / 11 / 1842 CAPRICORN
JAMISON, JUDITH (dancer) 5 / 10 / 1944 TAURUS
JANACEK, LEOS (composer) 7 / 3 / 1854 CANCER
JANIS, BYRON (pianist) 3 / 24 / 1928 ARIES
JANNINGS, EMIL (actor) 7 / 23 / 1886 CANCER/LEO
JANOWITZ, GUNDULA (soprano) 8 / 2 / 1937 LEO
JANSSEN, DAVID (actor) 3 / 27 / 1930 ARIES
JARMAN, CLAUDE, JR. (actor) 9 / 27 / 1934 LIBRA
JAROFF, SERGE (choral conductor) 3 / 20 / 1896 PISCES/ARIES
JAVITS, JACOB (politician) 5 / 18 / 1904 TAURUS
JAWORSKI, LEON (lawyer) 9 / 19 / 1905 VIRGO
JAY, JOHN (jurist) 12 / 23 / 1745 CAPRICORN
JAZY, MICHEL (runner) 6 / 13 / 1936 GEMINI
JEAN, GLORIA (actress) 4 / 14 / 1928 ARIES
JEANS, ISABEL (actress) 9 / 16 / 1891 VIRGO
JEANS, URSULA (actress) 5 / 5 / 1906 TAURUS
JEFFERS, ROBINSON (poet) 1 / 10 / 1887 CAPRICORN
JEFFERSON, THOMAS (politician) 4 / 13 / 1743 ARIES
JEFFREYS, ANNE (singer) 1 / 26 / 1923 AQUARIUS
JENNER, EDWARD (physician) 5 / 28 / 1749 GEMINI
JENS, SALOME (actress) 5 / 8 / 1935 TAURUS
JENSEN, JACKIE (baseball player) 3 / 9 / 1927 PISCES
JERITZA, MARIA (soprano) 10 / 6 / 1887 LIBRA
JESSEL, GEORGE (actor) 4 / 3 / 1898 ARIES
JETHRO (country singer) 3 / 10 / 1920 PISCES
JEWETT, SARAH ORNE (writer) 9 / 3 / 1849 VIRGO
JOAN OF ARC, ST. (soldier) 1 / 15 / 1412 CAPRICORN
JOCHUM, EUGEN (conductor) 11 / 1 / 1902 SCORPIO
JOFFREY, ROBERT (choreographer) 12 / 24 / 1930 CAPRICORN
JOHANSSON, INGEMAR (boxer) 9 / 22 / 1932 VIRGO
JOHN OF CAPISTRANO, ST. (preacher) 7 / 2 / 1386 CANCER
JOHN OF ENGLAND, KING 12 / 31 / 1167 CAPRICORN
JOHN OF THE CROSS, ST. (mystic) 7 / 4 / 1542 CANCER
JOHN XXIII, POPE 11 / 27 / 1881 SAGITTARIUS
JOHN, ELTON (singer) 3 / 25 / 1947 ARIES
JOHNS, GLYNIS (actress) 10 / 5 / 1923 LIBRA
JOHNS, JASPER (artist) 5 / 15 / 1930 TAURUS
JOHNSON, ANDREW (politician) 12 / 29 / 1808 CAPRICORN

JOHNSON, CELIA (actress) 12 / 18 / 1908 SAGITTARIUS
JOHNSON, EDWARD (operatic impresario) 8 / 22 / 1881 LEO
JOHNSON, J. J. (rock musician) 7 / 8 / ? CANCER
JOHNSON, JACK (boxer) 3 / 31 / 1878 ARIES
JOHNSON, LADY BIRD (first lady) 12 / 22 / 1912 SAGITTARIUS/
    CAPRICORN
JOHNSON, LYNDON BAINES (politician) 8 / 27 / 1908 VIRGO
JOHNSON, PHILIP (architect) 7 / 8 / 1906 CANCER
JOHNSON, OSA (explorer) 3 / 14 / 1894 PISCES
JOHNSON, RAFER (athlete) 8 / 18 / 1935 LEO
JOHNSON, SAMUEL (writer) 9 / 18 / 1709 VIRGO
JOHNSON, VAN (actor) 8 / 20 / 1916 LEO
JOHNSON, VIRGINIA E. (sexologist) 2 / 11 / 1925 AQUARIUS
JOHNSON, WALTER P. (baseball player) 11 / 6 / 1887 SCORPIO
JOLSON, AL (singer) 5 / 26 / 1886 GEMINI
JONES, BARRY (actor) 3 / 6 / 1893 PISCES
JONES, BRIAN (rock musician) 2 / 28 / 1942 PISCES
JONES, CANDY (cosmetologist) 12 / 31 / 1925 CAPRICORN
JONES, CAROLYN (actress) 4 / 28 / 1933 TAURUS
JONES, CASEY (railroadsman) 3 / 14 / 1864 PISCES
JONES, CHRISTOPHER (actor) 8 / 18 / 1941 LEO
JONES, DEAN (actor) 1 / 25 / 1936 AQUARIUS
JONES, GWYNETH (soprano) 11 / 7 / 1936 SCORPIO
JONES, INIGO (architect and stage designer) 7 / 25 / 1573 LEO
JONES, JACK (singer) 1 / 14 / 1938 CAPRICORN
JONES, JAMES (novelist) 11 / 6 / 1921 SCORPIO
JONES, JAMES EARL (actor) 1 / 17 / 1931 CAPRICORN
JONES, JENNIFER (actress) 3 / 2 / 1919 PISCES
JONES, JOHN PAUL (naval officer) 7 / 17 / 1747 CANCER
JONES, LEROI (writer) 10 / 7 / 1934 LIBRA
JONES, MARC EDMUND (astrologer) 10 / 1 /1888 LIBRA
JONES, QUINCY (jazz musician) 3 / 14 / 1933 PISCES
JONES, SHIRLEY (actress) 3 / 31 / 1934 ARIES
JONES, SPIKE (comedian) 12 / 14 / 1911 SAGITTARIUS
JONES, TOM (singer) 6 / 7 / 1940 GEMINI
JONG, ERICA (novelist) 3 / 26 / 1942 ARIES
JONSON, BEN (playwright) 6 / 21 / 1572 GEMINI/CANCER
JOPLIN, JANIS (singer) 1 / 19 / 1943 CAPRICORN
JOPLIN, SCOTT (composer) 11 / 24 / 1868 SAGITTARIUS
JORDA, ENRIQUE (composer) 3 / 24 / 1911 ARIES

JORDAN, BARBARA (politician) 2 / 21 / 1936 PISCES
JORGENSEN, CHRISTINE (transsexual) 5 / 30 / 1926 GEMINI
JORY, VICTOR (actor) 11 / 23 / 1902 SCORPIO/SAGITTARIUS
JOSEPHINE OF FRANCE, EMPRESS 6 / 23 / 1763 CANCER
JOURDAN, LOUIS (actor) 6 / 18 / 1921 GEMINI
JOURNET, MARCEL (basso) 7 / 25 / 1867 LEO
JOUVET, LOUIS (actor) 12 / 24 / 1887 CAPRICORN
JOYCE, JAMES (writer) 2 / 2 / 1882 AQUARIUS
JUAREZ, BENITO (Mexican politician) 3 / 21 / 1806 PISCES/ARIES
JUDD, WINNIE RUTH (murderess) 1 / 30 / 1905 AQUARIUS
JULIA, RAUL (actor) 3 / 9 / 1940 PISCES
JULIANA OF THE NETHERLANDS, QUEEN 4 / 30 / 1909 TAURUS
JUNG, CARL (psychologist) 7 / 26 / 1875 LEO
JURINAC, SENA (soprano) 10 / 24 / 1921 LIBRA/SCORPIO
JUSTINIAN OF ROME, EMPEROR 5 / 12 / A.D. 483 TAURUS
JUSTMAN, SETH (rock musician) 1 / 27 / 1951 AQUARIUS

KABALEVSKY, DMITRI (composer) 12 / 30 / 1904 CAPRICORN
KAEL, PAULINE (film critic) 6 / 19 / 1919 GEMINI
KAFKA, FRANZ (writer) 7 / 3 / 1883 CANCER
KAHN, ALBERT (architect) 3 / 21 / 1869 PISCES/ARIES
KAHN, ELY (architect) 6 / 1 / 1884 GEMINI
KAHN, GUS (composer) 11 / 6 / 1886 SCORPIO
KAHN, LOUIS I. (architect) 2 / 20 / 1901 PISCES
KAHN, MADELINE (actress) 9 / 29 / 1942 LIBRA
KAISER, HENRY J. (industrialist) 5 / 9 / 1882 TAURUS
KALINE, AL (baseball player) 12 / 19 / 1934 SAGITTARIUS
KALMBACH, HERBERT (lawyer) 10 / 19 / 1921 LIBRA
KAMINSKA, IDA (actress) 11 / 4 / 1899 SCORPIO
KANDINSKY, WASSILY (painter) 12 / 5 / 1866 SAGITTARIUS
KANGAROO, CAPTAIN (TV personality) 6 / 27 / 1927 CANCER
KANIN, GARSON (director) 11 / 24 / 1912 SAGITTARIUS
KANT, IMMANUEL (philosopher) 4 / 22 / 1724 TAURUS
KANTNER, PAUL (rock musician) 3 / 17 / 1942 PISCES
KARINSKA (costume designer) 10 / 3 / 1886 LIBRA
KARLOFF, BORIS (actor) 11 / 23 / 1887 SAGITTARIUS
KASZNAR, KURT (actor) 8 / 12 / 1913 LEO
KATZIR, EPHRAIM (Israeli politician) 5 / 16 / 1916 TAURUS
KAUFMAN, GEORGE S. (playwright) 11 / 16 / 1889 SCORPIO

KAUFMANN, CHRISTINE (actress) 1 / 11 / 1945 CAPRICORN
KAUKONEN, JORMA (rock musician) 12 / 23 / 1940 CAPRICORN
KAY, JOHN (rock musician) 4 / 12 / 1944 ARIES
KAYE, DANNY (comedian) 1 / 18 / 1913 CAPRICORN
KAYE, SAMMY (orchestra leader) 3 / 13 / 1913 PISCES
KAZAN, ELIA (director) 9 / 7 / 1909 VIRGO
KAZAN, LAINIE (singer) 5 / 16 / 1940 TAURUS
KAZANTZAKIS, NIKOS (writer) 12 / 2 / 1885 SAGITTARIUS
KEACH, STACY (actor) 6 / 2 / 1941 GEMINI
KEAN, EDMUND (actor) 3 / 17 / 1787 PISCES
KEAR, DENNIS (actor) 4 / 8 / 1944 ARIES
KEATING, KENNETH (politician) 5 / 18 / 1900 TAURUS
KEATON, BUSTER (comedian) 10 / 4 / 1895 LIBRA
KEATS, JOHN (poet) 10 / 29 / 1795 SCORPIO
KEEL, HOWARD (actor) 4 / 13 / 1917 ARIES
KEELER, RUBY (dancer) 8 / 25 / 1909 VIRGO
KEELER, WEE WILLIE (baseball player) 3 / 3 / 1872 PISCES
KEITH, BRIAN (actor) 11 / 14 / 1921 SCORPIO
KELLER, HELEN (lecturer) 6 / 27 / 1880 CANCER
KELLERMAN, SALLY (actress) 6 / 2 / 1938 GEMINI
KELLEY, CLARENCE MARION (government official) 11 / 24 / 1911
    SAGITTARIUS
KELLY, ELLSWORTH (painter) 5 / 31 / 1923 GEMINI
KELLY, EMMETT (clown) 12 / 9 / 1898 SAGITTARIUS
KELLY, GENE (dancer) 8 / 23 / 1912 VIRGO
KELLY, GRACE (actress) 11 / 12 / 1929 SCORPIO
KELLY, NANCY (actress) 3 / 25 / 1921 ARIES
KELLY, PATSY (actress) 1 / 12 / 1910 CAPRICORN
KELLY, WALT (cartoonist) 8 / 25 / 1913 VIRGO
KELVIN, BARON (physicist) 6 / 26 / 1824 CANCER
KEMBLE, CHARLES (actor) 11 / 25 / 1775 SAGITTARIUS
KEMBLE, JOHN PHILIP (actor) 2 / 1 / 1757 AQUARIUS
KEMPE, RUDOLF (conductor) 6 / 14 / 1910 GEMINI
KEMPFF, WILHELM (pianist) 11 / 25 / 1895 SAGITTARIUS
KENNEDY, ARTHUR (actor) 2 / 17 / 1914 AQUARIUS
KENNEDY, CAROLINE (politician's daughter) 11 / 27 / 1957
    SAGITTARIUS
KENNEDY, EDWARD (politician) 2 / 22 / 1932 PISCES
KENNEDY, ETHEL (politician's widow) 4 / 11 / 1928 ARIES

KENNEDY, FLORYNCE (feminist) 2 / 11 / 1916 AQUARIUS
KENNEDY, GEORGE (actor) 2 / 18 / 1925 AQUARIUS/PISCES
KENNEDY, JOAN (politician's wife) 9 / 5 / 1936 VIRGO
KENNEDY, JOHN F. (politician) 5 / 29 / 1917 GEMINI
KENNEDY, JOHN, JR. (politician's son) 11 / 25 / 1960 SAGITTARIUS
KENNEDY, JOSEPH (financier) 9 / 6 / 1888 VIRGO
KENNEDY, ROBERT (politician) 11 / 20 / 1925 SCORPIO
KENNEDY, ROSE (politicians' mother) 7 / 22 / 1890 CANCER
KENNETH (hairdresser) 4 / 19 / 1927 ARIES
KENT, ALLEGRA (ballet dancer) 8 / 11 / 1938 LEO
KENT, CORITA (artist) 11 / 20 / 1918 SCORPIO
KENT, ROCKWELL (painter) 6 / 21 / 1882 CANCER
KENTON, STAN (jazz musician) 2 / 19 / 1912 AQUARIUS/PISCES
KEPLER, JOHANN (astronomer) 1 / 6 / 1572 CAPRICORN
KERENSKY, ALEXANDER (revolutionary leader) 4 / 22 / 1881 TAURUS
KERN, JEROME (composer) 1 / 27 / 1885 AQUARIUS
KEROUAC, JACK (novelist) 3 / 12 / 1922 PISCES
KERR, CLARK (university official) 5 / 17 / 1911 TAURUS
KERR, DEBORAH (actress) 9 / 30 / 1921 LIBRA
KERR, JEAN (writer) 7 / 10 / 1923 CANCER
KERR, JOHN (actor) 11 / 15 / 1931 SCORPIO
KERR, WALTER (drama critic) 7 / 8 / 1913 CANCER
KERT, LARRY (actor) 12 / 5 / 1934 SAGITTARIUS
KERTESZ, ISTVAN (conductor) 8 / 28 / 1929 VIRGO
KESEY, KEN (novelist) 9 / 11 / 1935 VIRGO
KETCHAM, HANK (cartoonist) 3 / 14 / 1920 PISCES
KEY, FRANCIS SCOTT (lawyer) 8 / 1 / 1779 LEO
KEYES, FRANCES PARKINSON (writer) 7 / 21 / 1885 CANCER
KEYNES, JOHN MAYNARD (economist) 6 / 5 / 1883 GEMINI
KHACHATURIAN, ARAM (composer) 6 / 6 / 1903 GEMINI
KHRUSHCHEV, NIKITA (Soviet politician) 4 / 17 / 1894 ARIES
KIERKEGAARD, SOREN (philosopher) 5 / 5 / 1813 TAURUS
KILEY, RICHARD (actor) 3 / 31 / 1922 ARIES
KILGALLEN, DOROTHY (journalist) 7 / 3 / 1913 CANCER
KILLEBREW, HARMON (baseball player) 6 / 29 / 1936 CANCER
KILLY, JEAN-CLAUDE (skier) 8 / 30 / 1943 VIRGO
KILMER, JOYCE (poet) 12 / 6 / 1886 SAGITTARIUS
KING, ALAN (comedian) 12 / 26 / 1927 CAPRICORN
KING, ALBERT (blues musician) 4 / 25 / 1925 TAURUS

KING, B. B. (blues musician) 9 / 16 / 1925 VIRGO
KING, BILLIE JEAN (tennis player) 11 / 22 / 1943
    SCORPIO/SAGITTARIUS
KING, CAROLE (singer) 2 / 9 / 1941 AQUARIUS
KING, CORETTA SCOTT (civil rights leader) 4 / 27 / 1927 TAURUS
KING, JAMES (tenor) 5 / 22 / 1925 TAURUS/GEMINI
KING, MARTIN LUTHER, JR. (civil rights leader) 1 / 15 / 1929
    CAPRICORN
KINKAID, ARON (actor) 6 / 15 / 1943 GEMINI
KINSEY, ALFRED (sexologist) 6 / 23 / 1894 CANCER
KIPLING, RUDYARD (writer) 12 / 30 / 1865 CAPRICORN
KIPLINGER, W. M. (writer) 1 / 8 / 1891 CAPRICORN
KIPNIS, ALEXANDER (basso) 2 / 1 / 1891 AQUARIUS
KIRK, GRAYSON (university official) 10 / 12 / 1903 LIBRA
KIRKLAND, SALLY (actress) 10 / 31 / 1944 SCORPIO
KIRKPATRICK, RALPH (harpsichordist) 6 / 10 / 1911 GEMINI
KIRSTEN, DOROTHY (soprano) 7 / 6 / 1917 CANCER
KISSINGER, HENRY (government official) 5 / 27 / 1923 GEMINI
KITT, EARTHA (singer) 1 / 26 / 1928 AQUARIUS
KLEE, PAUL (painter) 12 / 18 / 1879 SAGITTARIUS
KLEIBER, CARLOS (conductor) 7 / 3 / 1930 CANCER
KLEIBER, ERICH (conductor) 8 / 5 / 1890 LEO
KLEIN, DANIEL (rock musician) 5 / 23 / 1946 GEMINI
KLEINDIENST, RICHARD (government official) 8 / 5 / 1923 LEO
KLEIST, HEINRICH VON (playwright) 10 / 18 / 1777 LIBRA
KLEMPERER, OTTO (conductor) 5 / 14 / 1885 TAURUS
KLOPSTOCK, FRIEDRICH GOTTLIEB (poet) 7 / 2 / 1724 CANCER
KNAPPERTSBUSCH, HANS (conductor) 3 / 12 / 1888 PISCES
KNIEVEL, EVEL (daredevil) 10 / 17 / 1938 LIBRA
KNIGHT, SHIRLEY (actress) 7 / 5 / 1937 CANCER
KNIGHT, STANLEY "GOOBER GRIN" (rock musician) 2 / 12 / 1949
    AQUARIUS
KNOPF, ALFRED A. (publisher) 9 / 12 / 1892 VIRGO
KOCH, JOHN (artist) 8 / 18 / 1909 LEO
KOCH, ROBERT (bacteriologist) 12 / 11 / 1843 SAGITTARIUS
KODALY, ZOLTAN (composer) 12 / 16 / 1882 SAGITTARIUS
KOESTLER, ARTHUR (novelist) 9 / 5 / 1905 VIRGO
KOETH, ERIKA (soprano) 9 / 15 / 1927 VIRGO
KOHNER, SUSAN (actress) 11 / 11 / 1936 SCORPIO
KOKOSCHKA, OSKAR (painter) 10 / 1 / 1886 LIBRA

KOLODIN, IRVING (music critic) 2 / 22 / 1908 PISCES
KONDRASHIN, KIRIL (conductor) 2 / 21 / 1914 PISCES
KONSTANTY, JIM (baseball player) 3 / 2 / 1917 PISCES
KOOPER, AL (singer) 2 / 5 / 1944 AQUARIUS
KOPECHNE, MARY JO (secretary) 7 / 26 / 1940 LEO
KOPIT, ARTHUR (playwright) 5 / 10 / 1937 TAURUS
KORBUT, OLGA (gymnast) 5 / 16 / 1955 TAURUS
KORFF, BARUCH M. (rabbi) 7 / 4 / 1914 CANCER
KOSCIUSKO, TADEUSZ (Polish patriot) 2 / 12 / 1746 AQUARIUS
KOSTELANETZ, ANDRE (conductor) 12 / 22 / 1901
    SAGITTARIUS/CAPRICORN
KOSYGIN, ALEXEI (Soviet politician) 2 / 20 / 1904 PISCES
KOTT, JAN (literary critic) 10 / 27 / 1914 SCORPIO
KOUFAX, SANDY (baseball player) 12 / 30 / 1935 CAPRICORN
KOUSSEVITSKY, SERGE (conductor) 7 / 26 / 1874 LEO
KOVACS, ERNIE (comedian) 1 / 23 / 1919 AQUARIUS
KOZOL, JONATHAN (writer) 9 / 5 / 1936 VIRGO
KRAMER, JACK (tennis player) 8 / 1 / 1921 LEO
KRAMER, STANLEY (film producer) 9 / 29 / 1913 LIBRA
KRAUS, LILI (pianist) 3 / 4 / 1908 PISCES
KRAUSS, CLEMENS (conductor) 3 / 31 / 1893 ARIES
KREISLER, FRITZ (violinist) 2 / 2 / 1875 AQUARIUS
KRESGE, S. S. (merchant) 7 / 31 / 1867 LEO
KRIPS, JOSEF (conductor) 4 / 8 / 1902 ARIES
KRISHNAMURTI, JIDDU (lecturer) 5 / 12 / 1895 TAURUS
KRISTOFFERSON, KRIS (singer) 6 / 22 / 1936 CANCER
KROGH, EGIL "BUD" (lawyer) 8 / 3 / 1939 LEO
KRUGER, HARDY (actor) 4 / 12 / 1928 ARIES
KRUPA, GENE (drummer) 1 / 15 / 1909 CAPRICORN
KRUPP, ALFRED (industrialist) 8 / 13 / 1907 LEO
KRUPP, GUSTAV (industrialist) 8 / 7 / 1870 LEO
KRUTCH, JOSEPH WOOD (writer) 11 / 25 / 1893 SAGITTARIUS
KUBELIK, RAFAEL (conductor) 6 / 29 / 1914 CANCER
KUBRICK, STANLEY (film maker) 7 / 26 / 1928 LEO
KUNSTLER, WILLIAM (lawyer) 7 / 7 / 1919 CANCER
KUROSAWA, AKIRA (film maker) 3 / 23 / 1910 ARIES
KURTZ, EFREM (conductor) 11 / 7 / 1900 SCORPIO
KURZ, SELMA (soprano) 11 / 15 / 1875 SCORPIO
KUTUZOV, MIKHAIL (Russian army officer) 9 / 16 / 1745 VIRGO
KWAN, NANCY (actress) 5 / 19 / 1939 TAURUS

KY, NGUYEN CAO (Vietnamese politician) 9 / 8 / 1930 VIRGO
KYO, MACHIKO (actress) 3 / 25 / 1924 ARIES
KYSER, KAY (bandleader) 6 / 18 / 1906 GEMINI

LABELLE, PATTI (singer) 5 / 24 / 1947 GEMINI
LABLACHE, LUIGI (basso) 12 / 6 / 1794 SAGITTARIUS
LACEY, CATHERINE (actress) 5 / 6 / 1904 TAURUS
LACLOS, CHODERLOS DE (writer) 10 / 19 / 1741 LIBRA
LADD, ALAN (actor) 9 / 3 / 1913 VIRGO
LA FARGE, OLIVER (writer) 12 / 19 / 1901 SAGITTARIUS
LAFAYETTE, MARQUIS DE (army officer) 9 / 6 / 1757 VIRGO
LA FAYETTE, MME. DE (novelist) 3 / 16 / 1634 PISCES
LA FONTAINE, JEAN DE (poet and fabulist) 7 / 8 / 1621 CANCER
LAGERLOEF, SELMA (writer) 11 / 20 / 1858 SCORPIO
LA GUARDIA, FIORELLO (politician) 12 / 11 / 1882 SAGITTARIUS
LAHR, BERT (comedian) 8 / 13 / 1895 LEO
LAINE, CLEO (singer) 10 / 28 / 1927 SCORPIO
LAINE, FRANKIE (singer) 3 / 30 / 1913 ARIES
LAING, CORKY (rock musican) 1 / 28 / 1948 AQUARIUS
LAING, R. D. (psychologist) 10 / 7 / 1927 LIBRA
LAIRD, MELVIN (government official) 9 / 1 / 1922 VIRGO
LAKE, GREG (rock musician) 10 / 10 / 1947 LIBRA
LAKE, VERONICA (actress) 11 / 14 / 1919 SCORPIO
LALANNE, JACK (physical culturist) 10 / 3 / 1914 LIBRA
LALO, EDOUARD (composer) 1 / 27 / 1823 AQUARIUS
LAMARR, HEDY (actress) 11 / 9 / 1913 SCORPIO
LAMARTINE, ALPHONSE DE (poet) 10 / 21 / 1790 LIBRA
LAMAS, FERNANDO (actor) 1 / 9 / 1920 CAPRICORN
LAMB, CHARLES (writer) 2 / 10 / 1775 AQUARIUS
LAMBRAKIS, CHRISTOS (journalist) 2 / 24 / 1934 PISCES
LAMOUR, DOROTHY (actress) 12 / 10 / 1914 SAGITTARIUS
LAMPERT, ZOHRA (actress) 5 / 13 / 1936 TAURUS
LAMPERTI, FRANCESCO (singing teacher) 3 / 11 / 1811 PISCES
LANCASTER, BURT (actor) 11 / 2 / 1913 SCORPIO
LANCHESTER, ELSA (actress) 10 / 28 / 1902 SCORPIO
LANDAU, MARTIN (actor) 12 / 17 / 1917 SAGITTARIUS
LANDER, TONI (ballet dancer) 6 / 19 / 1931 GEMINI
LANDERS, ANN (advice columnist) 7 / 4 / 1918 CANCER
LANDIS, JESSIE ROYCE (actress) 11 / 25 / 1904 SAGITTARIUS

LANDOWSKA, WANDA (harpsichordist) 7 / 5 / 1877 CANCER
LANDRY, TOM (baseball player) 9 / 11 / 1924 VIRGO
LANE, ABBIE (actress) 12 / 14 / 1935 SAGITTARIUS
LANE, BURTON (composer) 2 / 2 / 1912 AQUARIUS
LANE, KENNETH JAY (fashion designer) 4 / 22 / 1932 TAURUS
LANG, ANDREW (fairy tale collector) 3 / 31 / 1844 ARIES
LANG, FRITZ (film maker) 12 / 5 / 1890 SAGITTARIUS
LANG, PEARL (dancer) 5 / 29 / 1922 GEMINI
LANGDON, HARRY (actor) 6 / 15 / 1884 GEMINI
LANGE, HOPE (actress) 11 / 28 / 1933 SAGITTARIUS
LANGER, SUSANNE (philosopher) 12 / 20 / 1895 SAGITTARIUS
LANGTRY, LILLIE (actress) 10 / 13 / 1852 LIBRA
LANSBURY, ANGELA (actress) 10 / 16 / 1925 LIBRA
LANSKY, MEYER (mobster) 7 / 4 / 1902 CANCER
LANSON, SNOOKY (singer) 4 / 27 / 1914 TAURUS
LANTZ, WALTER (cartoonist) 4 / 27 / 1900 TAURUS
LANZA, MARIO (singer) 1 / 20 / 1921 CAPRICORN/AQUARIUS
LAPCHICK, JOSEPH (basketball coach) 4 / 12 / 1900 ARIES
LA PUMA, JOSEPHINE (operatic impresario) 5 / 18 / 1895 TAURUS
LARDNER, RING (writer) 3 / 6 / 1885 PISCES
LA ROCHEFOUCAULD, DUC DE (epigrammatist) 9 / 15 / 1613 VIRGO
LA ROSA, JULIUS (singer) 1 / 2 / 1930 CAPRICORN
LARROCHA, ALICIA DE (pianist) 5 / 23 / 1923 GEMINI
LA SALLE, ROBERT DE (explorer) 11 / 22 / 1643 SAGITTARIUS
LA TOUR, GEORGES DE (painter) 3 / 19 / 1593 PISCES
LA TOURNEAUX, ROBERT (actor) 8 / 10 / 1946 LEO
LAUD, WILLIAM (clergyman) 10 / 17 / 1573 LIBRA
LAUGHTON, CHARLES (actor) 7 / 1 / 1899 CANCER
LAUREL, STAN (comedian) 6 / 16 / 1895 GEMINI
LAURENTS, ARTHUR (playwright) 7 / 14 / 1920 CANCER
LAURI-VOLPI, GIACOMO (tenor) 12 / 11 / 1892 SAGITTARIUS
LAURIE, PIPER (actress) 1 / 22 / 1932 AQUARIUS
LAVIN, LINDA (actress) 10 / 15 / 1939 LIBRA
LAVOISIER, ANTOINE (chemist) 8 / 16 / 1743 LEO
LAW, JOHN PHILLIP (actor) 9 / 7 / 1937 VIRGO
LAW, VERNON (baseball player) 3 / 12 / 1930 PISCES
LAWFORD, PETER (actor) 9 / 7 / 1923 VIRGO
LAWRENCE, BARBARA (actress) 2 / 24 / 1930 PISCES
LAWRENCE, CAROL (actress) 9 / 5 / 1934 VIRGO
LAWRENCE, D. H. (writer) 9 / 11 / 1885 VIRGO

LAWRENCE, ERNEST (physicist) 8 / 8 / 1901 LEO
LAWRENCE, GERTRUDE (actress) 7 / 4 / 1901 CANCER
LAWRENCE, JACOB (painter) 9 / 7 / 1917 VIRGO
LAWRENCE, JEROME (playwright) 7 / 14 / 1915 CANCER
LAWRENCE, MARJORIE (soprano) 2 / 17 / 1909 AQUARIUS
LAWRENCE, STEVE (singer) 7 / 8 / 1935 CANCER
LAWRENCE, T. E. (adventurer) 8 / 15 / 1888 LEO
LAYTON, JOE (choreographer) 5 / 3 / 1931 TAURUS
LEACHMAN, CLORIS (actress) 4 / 30 / 1930 TAURUS
LEADBELLY (folk singer) 12 / 24 / 1922 CAPRICORN
LEAN, DAVID (film director) 3 / 25 / 1908 ARIES
LEAR, EDWARD (humorist) 5 / 12 / 1812 TAURUS
LEAR, EVELYN (soprano) 1 / 8 / 1929 CAPRICORN
LEARY, TIMOTHY (psychedelicist) 10 / 22 / 1920 LIBRA
LE CARRE, JOHN (novelist) 10 / 19 / 1931 LIBRA
LE CORBUSIER (architect) 10 / 6 / 1887 LIBRA
LECOUVREUR, ADRIENNE (actress) 4 / 5 / 1692 ARIES
LEE, BRENDA (singer) 12 / 11 / 1944 SAGITTARIUS
LEE, BRUCE (actor) 11 / 27 / 1940 SAGITTARIUS
LEE, CHRISTOPHER (actor) 5 / 27 / 1922 GEMINI
LEE, GYPSY ROSE (stripper) 1 / 9 / 1914 CAPRICORN
LEE, HARPER (novelist) 4 / 28 / 1926 TAURUS
LEE, PEGGY (singer) 5 / 26 / 1920 GEMINI
LEE, ROBERT E. (army officer) 1 / 19 / 1807 CAPRICORN
LEEK, SYBIL (occultist) 2 / 22 / 1922 PISCES
LEEUWENHOEK, ANTON VAN (microscopist) 10 / 24 / 1632 SCORPIO
LE GALLIENNE, EVA (actress) 1 / 11 / 1899 CAPRICORN
LEGER, FERNAND (artist) 2 / 4 / 1881 AQUARIUS
LEHAR, FRANZ (composer) 4 / 30 / 1870 TAURUS
LEHMANN, LILLI (soprano) 11 / 24 / 1848 SAGITTARIUS
LEHMANN, LOTTE (soprano) 2 / 27 / 1888 PISCES
LEIBMAN, RON (actor) 10 / 11 / 1937 LIBRA
LEIBNITZ, GOTTFRIED WILHELM VON (philosopher) 7 / 1 / 1646
    CANCER
LEIDER, FRIDA (soprano) 4 / 18 / 1888 ARIES
LEIGH, JANET (actress) 7 / 6 / 1927 CANCER
LEIGH, VIVIEN (actress) 11 / 5 / 1913 SCORPIO
LEIGHTON, MARGARET (actress) 2 / 26 / 1922 PISCES
LEINSDORF, ERICH (conductor) 2 / 4 / 1912 AQUARIUS
LEMAY, CURTIS (air force officer) 11 / 15 / 1906 SCORPIO

LEMMON, JACK (actor) 2 / 8 / 1925 AQUARIUS
LEMNITZ, TIANA (soprano) 10 / 26 / 1897 SCORPIO
LENIN, NIKOLAI (revolutionary leader) 4 / 22 / 1870 TAURUS
LENNON, JOHN (rock musician) 10 / 9 / 1940 LIBRA
LENYA, LOTTE (singer) 10 / 18 / 1900 LIBRA
LEO, ALAN (astrologer) 8 / 7 / 1860 LEO
LEONARD, BILL (newsman) 4 / 9 / 1916 ARIES
LEONARDO DA VINCI (artist and inventor) 4 / 24 / 1452 TAURUS
LEONCAVALLO, RUGGIERO (composer) 3 / 8 / 1858 PISCES
LEOPARDI, GIACOMO (poet) 6 / 29 / 1798 CANCER
LERNER, ALAN JAY (lyricist) 8 / 31 / 1918 VIRGO
LERNER, MAX (columnist) 12 / 20 / 1902 SAGITTARIUS
LE ROUX, MADELEINE (actress) 5 / 28 / 1946 GEMINI
LESLIE, BETHEL (actress) 8 / 3 / 1929 LEO
LESSEPS, FERDINAND DE (engineer) 11 / 19 / 1805 SCORPIO
LESSING, GOTTHOLD EPHRAIM (writer) 1 / 22 / 1729 AQUARIUS
LESTER, MARK (actor) 7 / 11 / 1958 CANCER
LESTER, RICHARD (film director) 1 / 19 / 1932 CAPRICORN
LEVANT, OSCAR (pianist) 12 / 27 / 1906 CAPRICORN
LEVENSON, SAM (TV personality) 12 / 28 / 1911 CAPRICORN
LEVI-STRAUSS, CLAUDE (anthropologist) 11 / 28 / 1908 SAGITTARIUS
LEVIN, IRA (novelist) 8 / 27 / 1929 VIRGO
LEVINE, JACK (painter) 1 / 3 / 1915 CAPRICORN
LEVINE, JAMES (conductor) 6 / 23 / 1943 CANCER
LEVY, MARVIN DAVID (composer) 8 / 2 / 1937 LEO
LEWI, GRANT (astrologer) 6 / 8 / 1902 GEMINI
LEWIS, HENRY (conductor) 10 / 16 / 1932 LIBRA
LEWIS, JERRY (comedian) 3 / 16 / 1926 PISCES
LEWIS, JERRY LEE (singer) 9 / 29 / 1935 LIBRA
LEWIS, JOHN (jazz musician) 5 / 3 / 1920 TAURUS
LEWIS, JOHN L. (labor leader) 2 / 12 / 1880 AQUARIUS
LEWIS, MERIWETHER (explorer) 8 / 18 / 1774 LEO
LEWIS, OSCAR (sociologist) 12 / 25 / 1914 CAPRICORN
LEWIS, SHARI (entertainer) 1 / 17 / 1934 CAPRICORN
LEWIS, SINCLAIR (writer) 2 / 7 / 1885 AQUARIUS
LHEVINNE, JOSEF (pianist) 12 / 3 / 1874 SAGITTARIUS
LHEVINNE, ROSINA (piano teacher) 3 / 29 / 1880 ARIES
LIBERACE (pianist) 5 / 16 / 1920 TAURUS
LICHTENSTEIN, ROY (painter) 10 / 27 / 1923 SCORPIO
LIDDY, G. GORDON (lawyer) 11 / 30 / 1930 SAGITTARIUS

LIEBERMANN, ROLF (impresario) 9 / 14 / 1910 VIRGO
LIGHTFOOT, GORDON (singer) 11 / 17 / 1938 SCORPIO
LILIUOKALANI OF HAWAII, QUEEN 9 / 2 / 1838 VIRGO
LILLIE, BEATRICE (comedienne) 5 / 29 / 1898 GEMINI
LILLY, DORIS (writer) 12 / 26 / 1926 CAPRICORN
LILLY, WILLIAM (astrologer) 5 / 11 / 1602 TAURUS
LIMON, JOSE (choreographer) 1 / 12 / 1908 CAPRICORN
LINCOLN, ABRAHAM (politician) 2 / 12 / 1809 AQUARIUS
LINCOLN, MARY TODD (first lady) 12 / 13 / 1818 SAGITTARIUS
LIND, JENNY (soprano) 10 / 6 / 1820 LIBRA
LINDBERGH, ANNE MORROW (writer) 6 / 22 / 1906 CANCER
LINDBERGH, CHARLES A. (aviator) 2 / 4 / 1902 AQUARIUS
LINDEN, HAL (actor) 3 / 20 / 1931 PISCES
LINDFORS, VIVECA (actress) 12 / 29 / 1920 CAPRICORN
LINDSAY, JOHN V. (politician) 11 / 24 / 1921 SAGITTARIUS
LINKLETTER, ART (TV personality) 7 / 17 / 1912 CANCER
LINNAEUS, CAROLUS (botanist) 5 / 13 / 1707 TAURUS
LIPATTI, DINU (pianist) 3 / 19 / 1917 PISCES
LIPCHITZ, JACQUES (sculptor) 8 / 22 / 1891 LEO
LIPPMANN, WALTER (journalist) 9 / 23 / 1889 LIBRA
LIPSCOMB, MANCE (blues musician) 4 / 9 / 1895 ARIES
LIPTON, SEYMOUR (sculptor) 11 / 6 / 1903 SCORPIO
LISTER, JOSEPH (surgeon) 4 / 5 / 1827 ARIES
LISTON, SONNY (boxer) 5 / 8 / 1932 TAURUS
LISZT, FRANZ (composer) 10 / 22 / 1811 LIBRA
LITTLE, CLEAVON (actor) 6 / 1 / 1939 GEMINI
LIVINGSTONE, DAVID (explorer) 3 / 19 / 1813 PISCES
LLOYD, HAROLD (actor) 4 / 20 / 1894 ARIES/TAURUS
LLOYD GEORGE, DAVID (British statesman) 1 / 17 / 1863 CAPRICORN
LOCKE, JOHN (philosopher) 9 / 8 / 1632 VIRGO
LOCKHART, GENE (actor) 7 / 18 / 1891 CANCER
LOCKHART, JUNE (actress) 6 / 25 / 1925 CANCER
LOCKWOOD, MARGARET (actress) 9 / 15 / 1916 VIRGO
LODEN, BARBARA (actress and director) 7 / 8 / 1937 CANCER
LODGE, HENRY CABOT, JR. (government official) 7 / 5 / 1902
    CANCER
LODGE, JOHN (rock musician) 7 / 20 / ? CANCER
LOEB, RICHARD (murderer) 6 / 11 / 1905 GEMINI
LOESSER, FRANK (composer) 6 / 29 / 1910 CANCER
LOEWE, FREDERICK (composer) 6 / 10 / 1904 GEMINI

LOGAN, JOSHUA (director) 10 / 5 / 1908 LIBRA
LOLLOBRIGIDA, GINA (actress) 7 / 4 / 1928 CANCER
LOMAX, ALAN (folk song collector) 1 / 15 / 1915 CAPRICORN
LOMBARD, CAROLE (actress) 10 / 6 / 1908 LIBRA
LOMBARDI, VINCE (football coach) 6 / 11 / 1913 GEMINI
LOMBARDO, GUY (bandleader) 6 / 19 / 1902 GEMINI
LONDON, GEORGE (basso) 5 / 30 / 1920 GEMINI
LONDON, JACK (writer) 1 / 12 / 1876 CAPRICORN
LONDON, JULIE (singer) 9 / 26 / 1926 LIBRA
LONG, EARL (politician) 8 / 26 / 1895 VIRGO
LONG, HUEY P. (politician) 8 / 30 / 1893 VIRGO
LONG, RICHARD (actor) 12 / 17 / 1927 SAGITTARIUS
LONGFELLOW, HENRY WADSWORTH (poet) 2 / 27 / 1807 PISCES
LONGWORTH, ALICE ROOSEVELT (politician's daughter) 2 / 12 / 1884
    AQUARIUS
LOOS, ANITA (writer) 4 / 26 / 1893 TAURUS
LOPEZ, AL (baseball manager) 8 / 20 / 1908 LEO
LOPEZ, TRINI (bandleader) 5 / 15 / 1937 TAURUS
LOPEZ, VINCENT (bandleader) 12 / 30 / 1895 CAPRICORN
LORCA, FEDERICO GARCIA (writer) 6 / 5 / 1899 GEMINI
LORD, JACK (actor) 12 / 30 / 1930 CAPRICORN
LOREN, SOPHIA (actress) 9 / 20 / 1934 VIRGO
LORENGAR, PILAR (soprano) 1 / 16 / 1933 CAPRICORN
LORRE, PETER (actor) 6 / 26 / 1904 CANCER
LOSEY, JOSEPH (film director) 1 / 14 / 1909 CAPRICORN
LOUIS XIII OF FRANCE, KING 9 / 27 / 1601 LIBRA
LOUIS XIV OF FRANCE, KING 9 / 5 / 1638 VIRGO
LOUIS XV OF FRANCE, KING 2 / 15 / 1710 AQUARIUS
LOUIS XVI OF FRANCE, KING 8 / 23 / 1754 VIRGO
LOUIS, JOE (boxer) 5 / 13 / 1914 TAURUS
LOUISE, ANITA (actress) 1 / 29 / 1915 AQUARIUS
LOUISE, TINA (actress) 2 / 11 / 1934 AQUARIUS
LOUYS, PIERRE (writer) 12 / 10 / 1870 SAGITTARIUS
LOVEJOY, FRANK (actor) 3 / 28 / 1914 ARIES
LOVELL, JAMES A., JR. (astronaut) 3 / 25 / 1928 ARIES
LOWELL, AMY (poet) 2 / 9 / 1874 AQUARIUS
LOWELL, JAMES RUSSELL (writer) 2 / 22 / 1819 PISCES
LOWELL, PERCIVAL (astronomer) 3 / 13 / 1855 PISCES
LOWELL, ROBERT (poet) 3 / 1 / 1917 PISCES
LOWRY, MALCOLM (writer) 7 / 28 / 1909 LEO

LOY, MYRNA (actress) 8 / 2 / 1905 LEO

LOYOLA, ST. IGNATIUS OF (Jesuit) 1 / 2 / 1492 CAPRICORN

LUBITSCH, ERNST (film director) 1 / 29 / 1892 AQUARIUS

LUBOFF, NORMAN (choral conductor) 5 / 14 / 1917 TAURUS

LUCAS, JERRY (basketball player) 3 / 30 / 1940 ARIES

LUCE, CLARE BOOTHE (playwright) 4 / 10 / 1903 ARIES

LUCE, HENRY (publisher) 4 / 3 / 1898 ARIES

LUCIANO, LUCKY (mobster) 11 / 11 / 1897 SCORPIO

LUDWIG I OF BAVARIA, KING 8 / 25 / 1786 VIRGO

LUDWIG II OF BAVARIA, KING 8 / 25 / 1845 VIRGO

LUDWIG, CHRISTA (mezzo-soprano) 3 / 16 / 1928 PISCES

LUGOSI, BELA (actor) 10 / 20 / 1882 LIBRA

LUKAS, PAUL (actor) 5 / 26 / 1895 GEMINI

LULLY, JEAN BAPTISTE (composer) 11 / 29 / 1633 SAGITTARIUS

LUMET, SIDNEY (film director) 6 / 25 / 1924 CANCER

LUMIERE, LOUIS JEAN (film maker) 10 / 5 / 1864 LIBRA

LUMUMBA, PATRICE (Congolese politician) 7 / 2 / 1925 CANCER

LUNDIGAN, WILLIAM (actor) 6 / 12 / 1914 GEMINI

LUNT, ALFRED (actor) 8 / 19 / 1893 LEO

LUPINO, IDA (actress and film director) 2 / 4 / 1918 AQUARIUS

LUTHER, MARTIN (religious reformer) 11 / 19 / 1483 SCORPIO

LYMPANY, MOURA (pianist) 8 / 18 / 1916 LEO

LYNCH, JACK (Irish politician) 8 / 15 / 1917 LEO

LYNDE, PAUL (actor) 6 / 13 / 1926 GEMINI

LYNLEY, CAROL (actress) 2 / 13 / 1943 AQUARIUS

LYNN, DIANA (actress) 10 / 7 / 1926 LIBRA

LYNN, LORETTA (singer) 4 / 14 / 1932 ARIES

LYON, SUE (actress) 7 / 10 / 1946 CANCER

LYONS, LEONARD (columnist) 9 / 10 / 1906 VIRGO

MAAZEL, LORIN (conductor) 3 / 6 / 1930 PISCES

MABLEY, MOMS (comedienne) 3 / 19 / 1894 PISCES

MACARTHUR, CHARLES (writer) 11 / 5 / 1895 SCORPIO

MACARTHUR, DOUGLAS (army officer) 1 / 26 / 1880 AQUARIUS

MACARTHUR, JAMES (actor) 12 / 8 / 1937 SAGITTARIUS

MACCOLL, EWAN (folk singer) 1 / 25 / 1915 AQUARIUS

MACDERMOT, GALT (composer) 12 / 19 / 1928 SAGITTARIUS

MACDONALD, DWIGHT (writer) 3 / 24 / 1906 ARIES

MACDONALD, JEANETTE (actress) 6 / 18 / 1907 GEMINI

MACDOWELL, EDWARD (composer) 12 / 18 / 1861 SAGITTARIUS
MACGOWRAN, JACK (actor) 10 / 13 / 1918 LIBRA
MACGRAW, ALI (actress) 4 / 1 / 1939 ARIES
MACHIAVELLI, NICCOLO (Italian statesman) 5 / 12 / 1469 TAURUS
MACINNES, HELEN (novelist) 10 / 7 / 1907 LIBRA
MACK, CONNIE (baseball manager) 12 / 22 / 1862 SAGITTARIUS/
    CAPRICORN
MACK, TED (TV personality) 2 / 12 / 1904 AQUARIUS
MACKENZIE, GISELE (singer) 1 / 10 / 1927 CAPRICORN
MACKERRAS, CHARLES (conductor) 11 / 17 / 1925 SCORPIO
MACLAINE, SHIRLEY (actress) 4 / 24 / 1934 TAURUS
MACLEARY, DONALD (ballet dancer) 8 / 22 / 1937 LEO
MACLEISH, ARCHIBALD (writer) 5 / 7 / 1892 TAURUS
MAC LIAMMOIR, MICHEAL (actor) 10 / 25 / 1899 SCORPIO
MACMILLAN, HAROLD (British politician) 2 / 10 / 1894 AQUARIUS
MACMURRAY, FRED (actor) 8 / 30 / 1908 VIRGO
MACNEIL, CORNELL (baritone) 9 / 24 / 1922 VIRGO/LIBRA
MACRAE, GORDON (singer) 3 / 12 / 1921 PISCES
MADDEN, DONALD (actor) 11 / 5 / 1933 SCORPIO
MADDOX, LESTER (politician) 9 / 30 / 1915 LIBRA
MADEIRA, JEAN (mezzo-soprano) 11 / 14 / 1924 SCORPIO
MADISON, DOLLEY (first lady) 5 / 20 / 1768 GEMINI
MADISON, GUY (actor) 1 / 19 / 1922 CAPRICORN
MADISON, JAMES (politician) 3 / 16 / 1751 PISCES
MAETERLINCK, MAURICE (playwright) 8 / 29 / 1862 VIRGO
MAGNANI, ANNA (actress) 3 / 7 / 1908 PISCES
MAGRITTE, RENE (painter) 11 / 21 / 1898 SCORPIO
MAGRUDER, JEB STUART (government official) 11 / 5 / 1935
    SCORPIO
MAHAN, LARRY (rodeo cowboy) 11 / 21 / 1943 SCORPIO
MAHARAJ JI (guru) 12 / 10 / 1957 SAGITTARIUS
MAHARIS, GEORGE (actor) 9 / 1 / 1933 VIRGO
MAHLER, GUSTAV (composer) 7 / 7 / 1860 CANCER
MAILER, NORMAN (writer) 1 / 31 / 1923 AQUARIUS
MAILLOL, ARISTIDE (sculptor) 12 / 25 / 1861 CAPRICORN
MAIMONIDES, MOSES (rabbi) 4 / 6 / 1135 ARIES
MAIN, MARJORIE (actress) 2 / 24 / 1890 PISCES
MAKARIOS III, ARCHBISHOP (Greek Orthodox prelate) 8 / 13 / 1913
    LEO
MAKAROVA, NATALIA (ballet dancer) 11 / 21 / 1940 SCORPIO

MAKEBA, MIRIAM (singer) 3 / 4 / 1932 PISCES
MALAMUD, BERNARD (novelist) 4 / 26 / 1914 TAURUS
MALCOLM X. (black leader) 5 / 19 / 1925 TAURUS
MALCUZYNSKI, WITOLD (pianist) 8 / 10 / 1914 LEO
MALDEN, KARL (actor) 3 / 22 / 1914 ARIES
MALIBRAN, MARIA (soprano) 3 / 24 / 1808 ARIES
MALINA, JUDITH (actress) 6 / 4 / 1926 GEMINI
MALINOWSKY, BRONISLAW (anthropologist) 4 / 7 / 1884 ARIES
MALLARME, STEPHANE (poet) 3 / 18 / 1842 PISCES
MALLE, LOUIS (film maker) 10 / 30 / 1932 SCORPIO
MALONE, DOROTHY (actress) 1 / 30 / 1925 AQUARIUS
MALRAUX, ANDRE (writer) 11 / 3 / 1901 SCORPIO
MANCHESTER, WILLIAM (writer) 4 / 1 / 1922 ARIES
MANCINI, HENRY (composer) 4 / 16 / 1924 ARIES
MANET, EDOUARD (painter) 1 / 23 / 1832 AQUARIUS
MANGANO, SILVANA (actress) 4 / 21 / 1930 TAURUS
MANGRUM, JIM "DANDY" (rock musician) 3 / 30 / 1948 ARIES
MANKIEWICZ, JOSEPH (film producer) 2 / 11 / 1909 AQUARIUS
MANN, DANIEL (film director) 8 / 8 / 1912 LEO
MANN, HERBIE (jazz musician) 4 / 16 / 1930 ARIES
MANN, HORACE (educational reformer) 5 / 4 / 1796 TAURUS
MANN, MANFRED (jazz musician) 10 / 21 / 1940 LIBRA
MANN, THEODORE (director) 5 / 13 / 1924 TAURUS
MANN, THOMAS (writer) 6 / 6 / 1875 GEMINI
MANNES, MARYA (writer) 11 / 14 / 1904 SCORPIO
MANSFIELD, KATHERINE (writer) 10 / 14 / 1888 LIBRA
MANSFIELD, JAYNE (actress) 4 / 19 / 1933 ARIES
MANSFIELD, MIKE (politician) 3 / 16 / 1903 PISCES
MANSON, CHARLES (criminal) 11 / 12 / 1934 SCORPIO
MANTLE, MICKEY (baseball player) 10 / 20 / 1931 LIBRA
MANTOVANI (orchestra leader) 11 / 15 / 1905 SCORPIO
MANZONI, ALESSANDRO (writer) 3 / 7 / 1785 PISCES
MAO TSE-TUNG (revolutionary leader) 12 / 26 / 1893 CAPRICORN
MARAIS, JEAN (actor) 12 / 11 / 1913 SAGITTARIUS
MARAIS, JOSEF (folk singer) 10 / 17 / 1905 LIBRA
MARAIS, MIRANDA (folk singer) 1 / 9 / 1912 CAPRICORN
MARANVILLE, RABBIT (baseball player) 11 / 11 / 1891 SCORPIO
MARAT, JEAN PAUL (revolutionary leader) 5 / 24 / 1744 GEMINI
MARAVICH, PETE (basketball player) 6 / 22 / 1948 GEMINI/CANCER
MARC, FRANZ (painter) 2 / 8 / 1880 AQUARIUS

MARCA-RELLI, CONRAD (artist) 6 / 5 / 1913 GEMINI
MARCEAU, MARCEL (mime) 3 / 22 / 1923 ARIES
MARCH, FREDRIC (actor) 8 / 31 / 1897 VIRGO
MARCH, HAL (quizmaster) 4 / 22 / 1920 TAURUS
MARCHAND, NANCY (actress) 6 / 19 / 1928 GEMINI
MARCHESI, MATHILDE (singing teacher) 3 / 24 / 1821 ARIES
MARCIANO, ROCKY (boxer) 9 / 1 / 1924 VIRGO
MARCONI, GUGLIELMO (inventor) 4 / 25 / 1874 TAURUS
MARCUS AURELIUS OF ROME, EMPEROR 4 / 26 / A.D. 121 TAURUS
MARCUS, STANLEY (merchant) 4 / 20 / 1905 ARIES/TAURUS
MARCUSE, HERBERT (philosopher) 7 / 19 / 1898 CANCER
MARGARET OF ENGLAND, PRINCESS 8 / 21 / 1930 LEO
MARGO (actress) 5 / 10 / 1920 TAURUS
MARGOLIN, JANET (actress) 7 / 25 / 1943 LEO
MARIA THERESA OF AUSTRIA, EMPRESS 5 / 13 / 1717 TAURUS
MARIE ANTOINETTE OF FRANCE, QUEEN 11 / 2 / 1755 SCORPIO
MARIE DE MEDECIS OF FRANCE, QUEEN 5 / 6 / 1573 TAURUS
MARIN, JOHN (painter) 12 / 23 / 1870 CAPRICORN
MARIS, ROGER (baseball player) 9 / 10 / 1934 VIRGO
MARISOL (artist) 5 / 22 / 1930 TAURUS/GEMINI
MARITAIN, JACQUES (philosopher) 11 / 18 / 1882 SCORPIO
MARKEVITCH, IGOR (conductor) 7 / 27 / 1912 LEO
MARKOVA, ALICIA (ballet dancer) 12 / 1 / 1910 SAGITTARIUS
MARLOWE, CHRISTOPHER (playwright) 2 / 16 / 1564 AQUARIUS
MARLOWE, HUGH (actor) 1 / 30 / 1911 AQUARIUS
MARQUAND, J. P. (novelist) 11 / 10 / 1893 SCORPIO
MARSHALL, CATHERINE (writer) 9 / 27 / 1914 LIBRA
MARSHALL, E. G. (actor) 6 / 18 / 1910 GEMINI
MARSHALL, GEORGE (army officer) 12 / 31 / 1880 CAPRICORN
MARSHALL, HERBERT (actor) 5 / 23 / 1890 GEMINI
MARSHALL, JOHN (jurist) 9 / 24 / 1755 VIRGO/LIBRA
MARSHALL, PETER (chaplain) 5 / 27 / 1902 GEMINI
MARSHALL, THURGOOD (jurist) 7 / 10 / 1908 CANCER
MARTIN, DEAN (singer) 6 / 17 / 1917 GEMINI
MARTIN, DICK (comedian) 1 / 30 / 1922 AQUARIUS
MARTIN, MARY (actress) 12 / 1 / 1913 SAGITTARIUS
MARTIN, MICHAEL "CAPTAIN LIGHTFOOT" (highwayman) 4 / 9 / 1775
    ARIES
MARTIN, PEPPER (baseball player) 2 / 29 / 1904 PISCES
MARTIN, TONY (singer) 12 / 25 / 1913 CAPRICORN

MARTINELLI, GIOVANNI (tenor) 10 / 22 / 1885 LIBRA
MARTINON, JEAN (conductor) 1 / 10 / 1910 CAPRICORN
MARVELL, ANDREW (poet) 4 / 10 / 1621 ARIES
MARVIN, LEE (actor) 2 / 19 / 1924 PISCES
MARX, CHICO (comedian) 3 / 22 / 1891 ARIES
MARX, GROUCHO (comedian) 10 / 2 / 1895 LIBRA
MARX, HARPO (comedian) 11 / 23 / 1893 SAGITTARIUS
MARX, KARL (philosopher) 5 / 5 / 1818 TAURUS
MARX, ZEPPO (comedian) 2 / 25 / 1901 PISCES
MARY STUART, QUEEN OF SCOTS 12 / 16 / 1542 SAGITTARIUS
MARY I OF ENGLAND, QUEEN 2 / 28 / 1516 PISCES
MASACCIO (painter) 12 / 30 / 1401 CAPRICORN
MASCAGNI, PIETRO (composer) 12 / 7 / 1863 SAGITTARIUS
MASEFIELD, JOHN (poet) 6 / 1 / 1878 GEMINI
MASIELLO, ALBERTA (vocal coach) 11 / 20 / 1915 SCORPIO
MASINA, GIULIETTA (actress) 2 / 22 / 1921 PISCES
MASON, JAMES (actor) 5 / 15 / 1909 TAURUS
MASON, NICK (rock musician) 1 / 27 / ? AQUARIUS
MASON, PAMELA (actress) 3 / 10 / 1918 PISCES
MASSENA, ANDRE (army officer) 5 / 6 / 1758 TAURUS
MASSENET, JULES (composer) 5 / 12 / 1842 TAURUS
MASSEY, DANIEL (actor) 10 / 10 / 1933 LIBRA
MASSEY, RAYMOND (actor) 8 / 30 / 1896 VIRGO
MASSINE, LEONIDE (choreographer) 8 / 9 / 1896 LEO
MASSON, ANDRE (artist) 1 / 4 / 1896 CAPRICORN
MASTERS, EDGAR LEE (poet) 8 / 23 / 1869 VIRGO
MASTERS, WILLIAM H. (sexologist) 12 / 27 / 1915 CAPRICORN
MASTROIANNI, MARCELLO (actor) 9 / 28 / 1924 LIBRA
MASTROIANNI, UMBERTO (sculptor) 9 / 21 / 1910 VIRGO
MATA HARI (spy) 8 / 7 / 1876 LEO
MATHER, COTTON (clergyman) 2 / 22 / 1663 PISCES
MATHER, INCREASE (clergyman) 7 / 1 / 1639 CANCER
MATHEWS, CARMEN (singer) 5 / 8 / 1918 TAURUS
MATHEWS, EDDIE (baseball player) 10 / 13 / 1931 LIBRA
MATHEWSON, CHRISTY (baseball player) 8 / 12 / 1880 LEO
MATHIS, JOHNNY (singer) 9 / 30 / 1935 LIBRA
MATISSE, HENRI (painter) 12 / 31 / 1869 CAPRICORN
MATSON, RANDY (athlete) 3 / 5 / 1945 PISCES
MATTHAU, WALTER (actor) 10 / 1 / 1920 LIBRA
MATURE, VICTOR (actor) 1 / 29 / 1916 AQUARIUS

MATZENAUER, MARGARETE (mezzo-soprano) 6 / 1 / 1881 GEMINI
MAUGHAM, W. SOMERSET (novelist) 1 / 25 / 1874 AQUARIUS
MAULDIN, BILL (cartoonist) 10 / 29 / 1921 SCORPIO
MAUPASSANT, GUY DE (writer) 8 / 5 / 1850 LEO
MAUREL, VICTOR (baritone) 6 / 17 / 1848 GEMINI
MAURIAC, FRANÇOIS (writer) 10 / 11 / 1885 LIBRA
MAUROIS, ANDRE (writer) 7 / 26 / 1885 LEO
MAX, PETER (artist) 10 / 19 / 1937 LIBRA
MAXIMILIAN OF MEXICO, EMPEROR 7 / 6 / 1832 CANCER
MAXIMOVA, EKATERINA (ballet dancer) 2 / 1 / 1939 AQUARIUS
MAX MUELLER, FRIEDRICH (Sanskrit scholar) 12 / 6 / 1823
     SAGITTARIUS
MAXWELL, ELSA (socialite) 5 / 24 / 1883 GEMINI
MAXWELL, MARILYN (actress) 8 / 3 / 1922 LEO
MAY, ELAINE (comedienne) 4 / 21 / 1932 TAURUS
MAY, LEE (baseball player) 3 / 23 / 1943 ARIES
MAYALL, JOHN (blues singer) 11 / 29 / 1933 SAGITTARIUS
MAYNOR, DOROTHY (soprano) 9 / 3 / 1910 VIRGO
MAYO, CHARLES (surgeon) 7 / 19 / 1865 CANCER
MAYO, WILLIAM (surgeon) 6 / 29 / 1861 CANCER
MAYR, JOHANN SIMON (composer) 6 / 14 / 1763 GEMINI
MAYS, WILLIE (baseball player) 5 / 6 / 1931 TAURUS
MAZZO, KAY (ballet dancer) 1 / 17 / 1947 CAPRICORN
MCBRIDE, MARY MARGARET (radio commentator) 11 / 16 / 1899
     SCORPIO
MCBRIDE, PATRICIA (ballet dancer) 8 / 23 / 1942 LEO/VIRGO
MCCALLUM, DAVID (actor) 9 / 19 / 1933 VIRGO
MCCAMBRIDGE, MERCEDES (actress) 3 / 17 / 1918 PISCES
MCCAREY, LEO (film director) 10 / 3 / 1898 LIBRA
MCCARTHY, EUGENE (politician) 3 / 29 / 1916 ARIES
MCCARTHY, JOE (baseball manager) 4 / 21 / 1887 TAURUS
MCCARTHY, JOSEPH (politician) 11 / 14 / 1909 SCORPIO
MCCARTHY, KEVIN (actor) 2 / 15 / 1914 AQUARIUS
MCCARTHY, MARY (writer) 6 / 21 / 1912 CANCER
MCCARTNEY, PAUL (rock musician) 6 / 18 / 1942 GEMINI
MCCLURE, DOUG (actor) 5 / 11 / 1938 TAURUS
MCCORMACK, JOHN (tenor) 6 / 14 / 1884 GEMINI
MCCORMACK, JOHN (politician) 12 / 21 / 1891 SAGITTARIUS
MCCORMACK, PATTY (actress) 8 / 21 / 1945 LEO
MCCORMICK, CYRUS (inventor) 2 / 15 / 1809 AQUARIUS

MCCOVEY, WILLIE (baseball player) 1 / 10 / 1938 CAPRICORN

MCCOWEN, ALEC (actor) 5 / 26 / 1925 GEMINI

MCCRACKEN, JAMES (tenor) 12 / 16 / 1926 SAGITTARIUS

MCCREA, JOEL (actor) 11 / 5 / 1905 SCORPIO

MCCULLERS, CARSON (novelist) 2 / 19 / 1917 AQUARIUS/PISCES

MCDANIEL, HATTIE (actress) 6 / 10 / 1895 GEMINI

MCDERMOTT, PATRICK (actor) 3 / 20 / 1908 PISCES/ARIES

MCDEVITT, RUTH (actress) 9 / 13 / 1895 VIRGO

MCDIVITT, JAMES (astronaut) 6 / 10 / 1929 GEMINI

MCDOWALL, RODDY (actor) 9 / 17 / 1928 VIRGO

MCDOWELL, MALCOLM (actor) 6 / 19 / 1943 GEMINI

MCEWAN, GERALDINE (actress) 5 / 9 / 1932 TAURUS

MCGAVIN, DARREN (actor) 5 / 7 / 1922 TAURUS

MCGEE, FRANK (newsman) 9 / 12 / 1921 VIRGO

MCGHEE, BROWNIE (blues musician) 11 / 30 / 1915 SAGITTARIUS

MCGINLEY, PHYLLIS (writer) 3 / 21 / 1905 PISCES/ARIES

MCGIVER, JOHN (actor) 11 / 5 / 1913 SCORPIO

MCGOVERN, GEORGE (politician) 7 / 19 / 1922 CANCER

MCGUFFEY, WILLIAM HOLMES (educator) 9 / 23 / 1800 VIRGO/LIBRA

MCGUIRE, DOROTHY (actress) 6 / 14 / 1918 GEMINI

MCHENRY, DON (actor) 2 / 25 / 1908 PISCES

MCINTIRE, CARL (evangelist) 5 / 17 / 1906 TAURUS

MCKAY, GARDNER (actor) 6 / 10 / 1932 GEMINI

MCKAY, JIM (sportscaster) 9 / 24 / 1921 LIBRA

MCKAYLE, DONALD (choreographer) 7 / 6 / 1930 CANCER

MCKENNA, SIOBHAN (actress) 5 / 24 / 1923 GEMINI

MCKENNA, VIRGINIA (actress) 6 / 7 / 1931 GEMINI

MCKERN, LEO (actor) 3 / 16 / 1920 PISCES

MCKINLEY, CHUCK (tennis player) 1 / 5 / 1941 CAPRICORN

MCKINLEY, WILLIAM (politician) 1 / 29 / 1843 AQUARIUS

MCKISSICK, FLOYD (civil rights leader) 3 / 9 / 1922 PISCES

MCKUEN, ROD (poet and singer) 4 / 29 / 1933 TAURUS

MCLAIN, DENNIS (baseball player) 3 / 29 / 1944 ARIES

MCLEAN, DON (singer) 10 / 2 / 1945 LIBRA

MCLUHAN, MARSHALL (writer) 7 / 21 / 1911 CANCER

MCMAHON, ED (TV personality) 3 / 6 / 1923 PISCES

MCNAIR, BARBARA (singer) 3 / 4 / 1939 PISCES

MCNALLY, TERRENCE (playwright) 11 / 3 / 1939 SCORPIO

MCNAMARA, ROBERT (government official) 6 / 9 / 1916 GEMINI

MCNEIL, CLAUDIA (actress) 8 / 13 / 1917 LEO

MCNEILL, DON (radio personality) 12 / 23 / 1907 CAPRICORN
MCPHERSON, AIMEE SEMPLE (evangelist) 10 / 9 / 1899 LIBRA
MCQUEEN, BUTTERFLY (actress) 1 / 8 / 1911 CAPRICORN
MCQUEEN, STEVE (actor) 3 / 24 / 1930 ARIES
MEACHAM, ANNE (actress) 7 / 21 / 1925 CANCER
MEAD, MARGARET (anthropologist) 12 / 16 / 1901 SAGITTARIUS
MEAD, TAYLOR (actor) 12 / 31 / 1924 CAPRICORN
MEADE, JULIA (actress) 12 / 17 / 1928 SAGITTARIUS
MEADOWS, JAYNE (actress) 9 / 27 / 1923 LIBRA
MEANY, GEORGE (labor leader) 8 / 16 / 1894 LEO
MEDFORD, KAY (actress) 9 / 14 / 1920 VIRGO
MEDICI, COSIMO DE (Italian statesman) 6 / 21 / 1519
    GEMINI/CANCER
MEDINA, PATRICIA (actress) 7 / 19 / 1923 CANCER
MEEKER, RALPH (actor) 11 / 21 / 1920 SCORPIO
MEHER BABA (mystic) 2 / 25 / 1894 PISCES
MEHTA, ZUBIN (conductor) 4 / 29 / 1936 TAURUS
MEIR, GOLDA (Israeli politician) 5 / 3 / 1898 TAURUS
MEKAS, JONAS (film critic) 12 / 24 / 1922 CAPRICORN
MELANIE (singer) 2 / 3 / 1947 AQUARIUS
MELBA, NELLIE (soprano) 5 / 19 / 1861 TAURUS
MELCHIOR, LAURITZ (tenor) 3 / 20 / 1890 PISCES/ARIES
MELIES, GEORGES (film maker) 12 / 8 / 1861 SAGITTARIUS
MELVILLE, HERMAN (novelist) 8 / 1 / 1819 LEO
MENCKEN, H. L. (writer) 9 / 12 / 1880 VIRGO
MENDEL, GREGOR JOHANN (biologist) 7 / 22 / 1822 CANCER/LEO
MENDELSSOHN, FELIX (composer) 2 / 3 / 1809 AQUARIUS
MENJOU, ADOLPHE (actor) 2 / 18 / 1890 PISCES
MENNINGER, KARL (psychiatrist) 7 / 22 / 1893 CANCER/LEO
MENOTTI, GIAN CARLO (composer) 7 / 7 / 1911 CANCER
MENUHIN, YEHUDI (violinist) 4 / 22 / 1916 TAURUS
MERCER, JOHNNY (singer) 11 / 18 / 1909 SCORPIO
MERCER, MABEL (singer) 2 / 3 / 1900 AQUARIUS
MERCER, MARIAN (singer) 11 / 26 / 1935 CAPRICORN
MERCHANT, VIVIEN (actress) 7 / 22 / 1929 CANCER/LEO
MERCOURI, MELINA (actress) 10 / 18 / 1925 LIBRA
MEREDITH, BURGESS (actor) 11 / 16 / 1908 SCORPIO
MEREDITH, GEORGE (writer) 2 / 12 / 1828 AQUARIUS
MEREDITH, JAMES (civil rights leader) 6 / 25 / 1933 CANCER
MERIDA, CARLOS (painter) 12 / 2 / 1891 SAGITTARIUS

MERIMEE, PROSPER (writer) 9 / 28 / 1803 LIBRA

MERIWETHER, DELANO (sprinter) 4 / 23 / 1943 TAURUS

MERKEL, UNA (actress) 12 / 10 / 1903 SAGITTARIUS

MERMAN, ETHEL (singer) 1 / 16 / 1908 CAPRICORN

MERRICK, DAVID (producer) 11 / 27 / 1912 SAGITTARIUS

MERRILL, BOB (songwriter) 5 / 17 / 1920 TAURUS

MERRILL, DINA (actress) 12 / 9 / 1925 SAGITTARIUS

MERRILL, GARY (actor) 8 / 2 / 1915 LEO

MERRILL, JOHN OGDEN (architect) 8 / 10 / 1896 LEO

MERRILL, ROBERT (baritone) 6 / 4 / 1919 GEMINI

MERRIMAN, NAN (mezzo-soprano) 4 / 28 / 1920 TAURUS

MERTON, THOMAS (writer) 1 / 31 / 1915 AQUARIUS

MESKILL, THOMAS J. (politician) 1 / 30 / 1928 AQUARIUS

MESMER, ANTON (hypnotist) 5 / 23 / 1733 GEMINI

MESSIAEN, OLIVIER (composer) 12 / 10 / 1908 SAGITTARIUS

MESTA, PERLE (hostess) 10 / 12 / 1891 LIBRA

METALIOUS, GRACE (novelist) 9 / 8 / 1924 VIRGO

METASTASIO, PIETRO (poet) 1 / 3 / 1698 CAPRICORN

METTERNICH, KLEMENS VON (Austrian statesman) 5 / 15 / 1773
    TAURUS

MEYER, DEBBIE (swimmer) 8 / 14 / 1952 LEO

MEYERBEER, GIACOMO (composer) 9 / 5 / 1791 VIRGO

MICHELANGELI, ARTURO BENEDETTI (pianist) 1 / 5 / 1920
    CAPRICORN

MICHELANGELO BUONARROTI (artist) 3 / 15 / 1475 PISCES

MICHELET, JULES (historian) 8 / 21 / 1798 LEO

MICHELL, KEITH (actor) 12 / 1 / 1928 SAGITTARIUS

MICHENER, JAMES (novelist) 2 / 3 / 1907 AQUARIUS

MIDDLETON, OLIVE TOWNEND (soprano) 6 / 20 / 1891 GEMINI

MIDDLETON, RAY (actor) 2 / 8 / 1907 AQUARIUS

MIDLER, BETTE (singer) 12 / 1 / 1944 SAGITTARIUS

MIELZINER, JO (stage designer) 3 / 19 / 1901 PISCES

MIES VAN DER ROHE, LUDWIG (architect) 3 / 27 / 1886 ARIES

MIFUNE, TOSHIRO (actor) 4 / 1 / 1920 ARIES

MIKITA, STAN (hockey player) 5 / 20 / 1940 TAURUS

MIKOYAN, ANASTAS (Soviet official) 11 / 25 / 1895 SAGITTARIUS

MILANOV, ZINKA (soprano) 5 / 17 / 1906 TAURUS

MILES, SARAH (actress) 12 / 31 / 1943 CAPRICORN

MILES, SYLVIA (actress) 9 / 9 / 1932 VIRGO

MILES, VERA (actress) 8 / 23 / 1930 LEO/VIRGO

MILHAUD, DARIUS (composer) 9 / 4 / 1892 VIRGO

MILL, JOHN STUART (philosopher) 5 / 20 / 1806 TAURUS

MILLAIS, J. E. (painter) 6 / 8 / 1829 GEMINI

MILLAND, RAY (actor) 1 / 3 / 1908 CAPRICORN

MILLAY, EDNA ST. VINCENT (poet) 2 / 22 / 1892 PISCES

MILLER, MRS. (TV personality) 5 / 26 / 1897 GEMINI

MILLER, ANN (dancer) 4 / 12 / 1919 ARIES

MILLER, ARNOLD (labor leader) 4 / 25 / 1923 TAURUS

MILLER, ARTHUR (playwright) 10 / 17 / 1915 LIBRA

MILLER, GLENN (bandleader) 3 / 1 / 1909 PISCES

MILLER, HENRY (novelist) 12 / 26 / 1891 CAPRICORN

MILLER, JASON (actor and playwright) 4 / 22 / 1939 TAURUS

MILLER, JOHNNY (golfer) 4 / 29 / 1947 TAURUS

MILLER, JONATHAN (comedian) 7 / 21 / 1934 CANCER

MILLER, MITCH (musician) 7 / 4 / 1911 CANCER

MILLER, ROGER (country singer) 1 / 2 / 1936 CAPRICORN

MILLER, STEVE (rock musician) 10 / 5 / 1943 LIBRA

MILLET, JEAN (painter) 10 / 4 / 1814 LIBRA

MILLETT, KATE (feminist) 9 / 14 / 1934 VIRGO

MILLS, HAYLEY (actress) 4 / 18 / 1946 ARIES

MILLS, JOHN (actor) 2 / 22 / 1908 PISCES

MILLS, JULIET (actress) 11 / 21 / 1941 SCORPIO

MILNE, A. A. (writer) 1 / 18 / 1882 CAPRICORN

MILNES, SHERRILL (baritone) 1 / 10 / 1935 CAPRICORN

MILSTEIN, NATHAN (violinist) 12 / 31 / 1904 CAPRICORN

MILTON, JOHN (poet) 12 / 20 / 1608 SAGITTARIUS

MIMIEUX, YVETTE (actress) 1 / 8 / 1941 CAPRICORN

MINEO, SAL (actor) 1 / 10 / 1939 CAPRICORN

MING CHO LEE (stage designer) 10 / 3 / 1930 LIBRA

MINGUS, CHARLIE (jazz musician) 4 / 22 / 1922 TAURUS

MINK, PATSY (politician) 12 / 6 / 1927 SAGITTARIUS

MINNELLI, LIZA (singer) 3 / 12 / 1946 PISCES

MINNELLI, VINCENTE (film director) 2 / 28 / 1913 PISCES

MINOSO, ORESTES (baseball player) 11 / 22 / 1922
    SCORPIO/SAGITTARIUS

MINOTIS, ALEXIS (actor and director) 8 / 21 / 1906 LEO

MIRANDA, CARMEN (singer) 2 / 9 / 1914 AQUARIUS

MIRO, JOAN (painter) 4 / 20 / 1893 ARIES/TAURUS

MISHIMA, YUKIO (writer) 1 / 14 / 1925 CAPRICORN

MITCHELL, ARTHUR (choreographer) 3 / 27 / 1934 ARIES

MITCHELL, CAMERON (actor) 11 / 4 / 1918 SCORPIO
MITCHELL, CHAD (singer) 12 / 5 / 1936 SAGITTARIUS
MITCHELL, GEORGE (actor) 2 / 21 / 1905 PISCES
MITCHELL, HOWARD (actor) 3 / 11 / 1911 PISCES
MITCHELL, JAMES (actor) 2 / 29 / 1920 PISCES
MITCHELL, JOHN (government official) 9 / 15 / 1913 VIRGO
MITCHELL, JONI (singer) 11 / 7 / 1943 SCORPIO
MITCHELL, MARGARET (novelist) 11 / 8 / 1900 SCORPIO
MITCHELL, MARTHA (public figure) 9 / 2 / 1918 VIRGO
MITCHELL, THOMAS (actor) 7 / 11 / 1892 CANCER
MITCHUM, ROBERT (actor) 8 / 6 / 1917 LEO
MITFORD, JESSICA (writer) 9 / 11 / 1917 VIRGO
MITFORD, NANCY (writer) 11 / 28 / 1904 SAGITTARIUS
MITROPOULOS, DMITRI (conductor) 3 / 1 / 1896 PISCES
MIX, TOM (actor) 1 / 6 / 1880 CAPRICORN
MIZOGUCHI, KENJI (film maker) 5 / 16 / 1898 TAURUS
MODIGLIANI, AMEDEO (painter) 7 / 12 / 1884 CANCER
MODJESKA, HELENA (actress) 10 / 12 / 1844 LIBRA
MOEDL, MARTHA (soprano) 3 / 22 / 1912 ARIES
MOFFAT, DONALD (actor) 12 / 26 / 1930 CAPRICORN
MOFFO, ANNA (soprano) 6 / 26 / 1935 CANCER
MOISEIWITSCH, TANYA (stage designer) 12 / 3 / 1914 SAGITTARIUS
MOLIERE (playwright) 1 / 15 / 1622 CAPRICORN
MOLINA, JOSE (choreographer) 11 / 19 / 1937 SCORPIO
MOLINARI-PRADELLI, FRANCESCO (conductor) 7 / 4 / 1911 CANCER
MOLOTOV, VYACHESLAV (Soviet official) 3 / 9 / 1890 PISCES
MONDRIAAN, PIET (painter) 3 / 7 / 1872 PISCES
MONET, CLAUDE (painter) 11 / 14 / 1840 SCORPIO
MONK, THELONIOUS (jazz musician) 10 / 10 / 1918 LIBRA
MONROE, JAMES (politician) 4 / 28 / 1758 TAURUS
MONROE, MARILYN (actress) 6 / 1 / 1926 GEMINI
MONROE, VAUGHN (singer) 10 / 7 / 1911 LIBRA
MONTAGU, ASHLEY (novelist) 6 / 28 / 1906 CANCER
MONTAIGNE, MICHEL DE (essayist) 3 / 10 / 1533 PISCES
MONTALBAN, RICARDO (actor) 11 / 25 / 1920 SAGITTARIUS
MONTAND, YVES (actor) 10 / 13 / 1921 LIBRA
MONTESQUIEU, BARON DE (philosopher) 1 / 18 / 1689 CAPRICORN
MONTESSORI, MARIA (educator) 8 / 30 / 1870 VIRGO
MONTEUX, PIERRE (conductor) 4 / 4 / 1875 ARIES
MONTEZ, LOLA (adventuress) 8 / 25 / 1818 VIRGO

MONTEZ, MARIA (actress) 6 / 6 / 1920 GEMINI
MONTGOMERY, ELIZABETH (actress) 4 / 15 / 1933 ARIES
MONTGOMERY, GEORGE (actor) 8 / 29 / 1916 VIRGO
MONTGOMERY, ROBERT (actor) 5 / 21 / 1904 GEMINI
MONTHERLANT, HENRY DE (playwright) 4 / 21 / 1896 TAURUS
MONTOYA, CARLOS (guitarist) 12 / 13 / 1903 SAGITTARIUS
MONTRESOR, BENI (artist) 3 / 31 / 1926 ARIES
MOODY, RALPH (novelist) 12 / 16 / 1898 SAGITTARIUS
MOON, KEITH (rock musician) 8 / 23 / 1947 LEO/VIRGO
MOON, SUN MYUNG (evangelist) 1 / 6 / 1920 CAPRICORN
MOORE, ARCHIE (boxer) 12 / 13 / 1916 SAGITTARIUS
MOORE, DICK (actor) 9 / 12 / 1925 VIRGO
MOORE, DOUGLAS (composer) 8 / 10 / 1893 LEO
MOORE, DUDLEY (comedian) 4 / 19 / 1935 ARIES
MOORE, GARRY (TV personality) 1 / 31 / 1915 AQUARIUS
MOORE, GERALD (pianist) 7 / 30 / 1899 LEO
MOORE, GRACE (soprano) 12 / 5 / 1901 SAGITTARIUS
MOORE, HENRY (sculptor) 7 / 30 / 1898 LEO
MOORE, MARIANNE (poet) 11 / 15 / 1887 SCORPIO
MOORE, MARY TYLER (actress) 12 / 29 / 1937 CAPRICORN
MOORE, MELBA (singer) 10 / 27 / 1945 SCORPIO
MOORE, ROGER (actor) 10 / 14 / 1927 LIBRA
MOORE, SONIA (acting teacher) 12 / 4 / 1902 SAGITTARIUS
MOORE, TERRY (actress) 1 / 7 / 1929 CAPRICORN
MOOREHEAD, AGNES (actress) 12 / 6 / 1906 SAGITTARIUS
MORAVEC, IVAN (pianist) 11 / 9 / 1930 SCORPIO
MORAVIA, ALBERTO (writer) 11 / 28 / 1907 SAGITTARIUS
MORE, KENNETH (actor) 9 / 20 / 1914 VIRGO
MORE, THOMAS (humanist) 2 / 16 / 1478 AQUARIUS
MOREAU, JEANNE (actress) 1 / 23 / 1928 AQUARIUS
MORENO, RITA (actress) 12 / 11 / 1931 SAGITTARIUS
MORGAN, HELEN (singer) 8 / 2 / 1900 LEO
MORGAN, HENRY (TV personality) 4 / 1 / 1915 ARIES
MORGAN, J. P. (financier) 4 / 17 / 1837 ARIES
MORGAN, MICHELE (actress) 2 / 29 / 1920 PISCES
MORI, MASAYUKI (actor) 1 / 13 / 1911 CAPRICORN
MORIARTY, MICHAEL (actor) 4 / 5 / 1941 ARIES
MORINI, ERICA (violinist) 5 / 26 / 1906 GEMINI
MORISON, PATRICIA (actress) 3 / 19 / 1915 PISCES
MORISON, SAMUEL ELIOT (historian) 7 / 9 / 1887 CANCER

MORISOT, BERTHE (painter) 1 / 14 / 1841 CAPRICORN

MORLEY, ROBERT (actor) 5 / 26 / 1908 GEMINI

MORRIS, DESMOND (ethologist) 1 / 24 / 1928 AQUARIUS

MORRIS, ROBERT (sculptor) 2 / 9 / 1931 AQUARIUS

MORRISON, JIM (singer) 12 / 8 / 1945 SAGITTARIUS

MORRISON, VAN (singer) 8 / 31 / 1945 VIRGO

MORROW, VIC (actor) 2 / 14 / 1932 AQUARIUS

MORSE, ROBERT (actor) 5 / 18 / 1931 TAURUS

MORSE, SAMUEL (inventor) 4 / 27 / 1791 TAURUS

MORSE, WAYNE (politician) 10 / 20 / 1900 LIBRA

MORTIMER, JOHN (playwright) 4 / 21 / 1923 TAURUS

MORTON, ROGERS C. B. (government official) 9 / 19 / 1914 VIRGO

MOSCONA, NICOLA (basso) 9 / 23 / 1907 VIRGO/LIBRA

MOSCONI, WILLIE (billiard player) 6 / 27 / 1913 CANCER

MOSES, GRANDMA (painter) 9 / 7 / 1860 VIRGO

MOSES, ROBERT (public official) 12 / 18 / 1888 SAGITTARIUS

MOSS, STERLING (auto racer) 10 / 17 / 1929 LIBRA

MOSTEL, ZERO (comedian) 2 / 28 / 1915 PISCES

MOTHERWELL, ROBERT (painter) 1 / 24 / 1915 AQUARIUS

MOTT, LUCRETIA (feminist) 1 / 3 / 1793 CAPRICORN

MOYERS, BILL (government official) 6 / 5 / 1934 GEMINI

MOZART, LEOPOLD (musician) 11 / 14 / 1719 SCORPIO

MOZART, WOLFGANG AMADEUS (composer) 1 / 27 / 1756 AQUARIUS

MUELLER, MARIA (soprano) 1 / 29 / 1898 AQUARIUS

MUGGERIDGE, MALCOLM (writer) 3 / 24 / 1903 ARIES

MUHAMMAD, ELIJAH (Black Muslim leader) 10 / 7 / 1897 LIBRA

MUIR, JOHN (naturalist) 4 / 21 / 1838 TAURUS

MULDAUR, MARIA (singer) 9 / 12 / 1942 VIRGO

MULHOLLAND, JOHN (magician) 6 / 8 / 1898 GEMINI

MULLIGAN, GERRY (jazz musician) 4 / 6 / 1927 ARIES

MUMFORD, LEWIS (sociologist) 10 / 19 / 1895 LIBRA

MUNCH, CHARLES (conductor) 9 / 26 / 1891 LIBRA

MUNCH, EDVARD (painter) 12 / 12 / 1863 SAGITTARIUS

MUNCHAUSEN, BARON VON (raconteur) 5 / 11 / 1720 TAURUS

MUNI, PAUL (actor) 9 / 22 / 1897 VIRGO

MUNSEL, PATRICE (soprano) 5 / 14 / 1925 TAURUS

MUNSHIN, JULES (comedian) 2 / 22 / 1915 PISCES

MURDOCH, IRIS (novelist) 7 / 15 / 1919 CANCER

MURNAU, F. W. (film director) 12 / 28 / 1888 CAPRICORN

MURPHY, AUDIE (actor) 6 / 20 / 1924 GEMINI

MURPHY, GEORGE (actor and politician) 7 / 4 / 1902 CANCER
MURPHY, PATRICK (public official) 5 / 15 / 1920 TAURUS
MURPHY, ROSEMARY (actress) 1 / 13 / 1927 CAPRICORN
MURRAY, ARTHUR (dance instructor) 4 / 4 / 1895 ARIES
MURRAY, DON (actor) 7 / 31 / 1929 LEO
MURROW, EDWARD R. (newsman) 4 / 25 / 1908 TAURUS
MURTAUGH, DANIEL (baseball manager) 10 / 8 / 1917 LIBRA
MUSIAL, STAN (baseball player) 11 / 21 / 1920 SCORPIO
MUSKIE, EDMUND (politician) 3 / 28 / 1914 ARIES
MUSSET, ALFRED DE (writer) 12 / 11 / 1810 SAGITTARIUS
MUSSOLINI, BENITO (dictator) 7 / 29 / 1883 LEO
MUSSORGSKY, MODEST (composer) 3 / 21 / 1839 PISCES/ARIES
MUSTE, A. J. (pacifist) 1 / 8 / 1885 CAPRICORN
MUZIO, CLAUDIA (soprano) 2 / 7 / 1889 AQUARIUS
MYERSON, BESS (TV personality and consumer advocate)
    7 / 16 / 1924 CANCER

NABOKOV, VLADIMIR (writer) 4 / 23 / 1899 TAURUS
NABORS, JIM (TV personality) 6 / 12 / 1933 GEMINI
NADER, GEORGE (actor) 10 / 19 / 1921 LIBRA
NADER, RALPH (consumer advocate) 2 / 27 / 1934 PISCES
NADJARI, MAURICE (public official) 6 / 17 / 1924 GEMINI
NAGY, IVAN (ballet dancer) 4 / 28 / 1943 TAURUS
NAISH, J. CARROL (actor) 1 / 21 / 1900 CAPRICORN/AQUARIUS
NAMATH, JOE (football player) 5 / 31 / 1943 GEMINI
NAPOLEON BONAPARTE OF FRANCE, EMPEROR 8 / 15 / 1769 LEO
NAPOLEON III OF FRANCE, EMPEROR 4 / 20 / 1808 TAURUS
NASH, GRAHAM (rock musician) 2 / 2 / ? AQUARIUS
NASH, OGDEN (humorist) 8 / 19 / 1902 LEO
NASSER, GAMAL ABDEL (Arab leader) 1 / 15 / 1918 CAPRICORN
NASTASE, ILIE (tennis player) 7 / 19 / 1946 CANCER
NATHAN, ROBERT (writer) 1 / 2 / 1894 CAPRICORN
NATION, CARRY (reformer) 11 / 25 / 1846 SAGITTARIUS
NATWICK, MILDRED (actress) 6 / 19 / 1908 GEMINI
NAZIMOVA, ALLA (actress) 6 / 4 / 1879 GEMINI
NEAL, JAMES F. (lawyer) 9 / 7 / 1929 VIRGO
NEAL, PATRICIA (actress) 1 / 20 / 1926 AQUARIUS
NEARING, SCOTT (farmer) 8 / 6 / 1883 LEO
NECKER, JACQUES (economist) 9 / 30 / 1732 LIBRA

NEFF, HILDEGARDE (actress) 12 / 28 / 1925 CAPRICORN
NEGRI, POLA (actress) 1 / 3 / 1897 CAPRICORN
NEHRU, JAWAHARLAL (Indian politician) 11 / 14 / 1889 SCORPIO
NEILL, A. S. (educator) 10 / 17 / 1883 LIBRA
NELSON, DAVID (actor) 10 / 24 / 1936 LIBRA/SCORPIO
NELSON, HARRIET HILLIARD (actress) 7 / 18 / 1912 CANCER
NELSON, HORATIO (British naval officer) 9 / 29 / 1758 LIBRA
NELSON, KENNETH (actor) 3 / 24 / 1930 ARIES
NELSON, OZZIE (actor) 3 / 20 / 1907 PISCES/ARIES
NELSON, RICK (singer) 5 / 8 / 1940 TAURUS
NERO OF ROME, EMPEROR 12 / 13 / A.D. 37 SAGITTARIUS
NERO, PETER (pianist) 5 / 24 / 1934 GEMINI
NERUDA, PABLO (poet) 7 / 12 / 1904 CANCER
NERVAL, GERARD DE (poet) 5 / 22 / 1808 TAURUS/GEMINI
NERVI, PIER LUIGI (architect) 6 / 21 / 1891 GEMINI/CANCER
NESBIT, E. (writer) 8 / 19 / 1858 LEO
NESBITT, CATHLEEN (actress) 11 / 24 / 1889 SAGITTARIUS
NESSEN, RON (press secretary) 5 / 25 / 1934 GEMINI
NEUTRA, RICHARD J. (architect) 4 / 8 / 1892 ARIES
NEVELSON, LOUISE (sculptor) 9 / 23 / 1900 VIRGO/LIBRA
NEVILLE, JOHN (actor) 5 / 2 / 1925 TAURUS
NEWCOMBE, DON (baseball player) 6 / 14 / 1926 GEMINI
NEWHART, BOB (comedian) 9 / 5 / 1929 VIRGO
NEWLEY, ANTHONY (actor) 9 / 24 / 1931 LIBRA
NEWMAN, BARNETT (artist) 1 / 29 / 1905 AQUARIUS
NEWMAN, EDWIN (newsman) 1 / 25 / 1919 AQUARIUS
NEWMAN, ERNEST (music critic) 11 / 30 / 1868 SAGITTARIUS
NEWMAN, PAUL (actor and film director) 1 / 26 / 1925 AQUARIUS
NEWMAN, PHYLLIS (actress) 3 / 19 / 1935 PISCES
NEWMAN, RANDY (singer) 11 / 28 / 1943 SAGITTARIUS
NEWMAR, JULIE (actress) 8 / 16 / 1935 LEO
NEWTON, ISAAC (physicist) 1 / 4 / 1643 CAPRICORN
NEWTON, WAYNE (singer) 4 / 3 / 1944 ARIES
NIARCHOS, STAVROS (tycoon) 7 / 3 / 1909 CANCER
NICHOLAS II OF RUSSIA, CZAR 5 / 18 / 1868 TAURUS
NICHOLS, MIKE (director) 11 / 6 / 1931 SCORPIO
NICHOLSON, BEN (painter) 4 / 10 / 1894 ARIES
NICHOLSON, JACK (actor) 4 / 22 / 1937 TAURUS
NICKLAUS, JACK (golfer) 1 / 21 / 1940 CAPRICORN/AQUARIUS
NICOLAI, OTTO (composer) 6 / 9 / 1810 GEMINI

NIDETCH, JEAN (weight-watching adviser) 10 / 12 / 1923 LIBRA
NIEBUHR, REINHOLD (theologian) 6 / 21 / 1892 GEMINI/CANCER
NIELSEN, ARTHUR (marketing research engineer) 9 / 5 / 1897
     VIRGO
NIELSEN, CARL (composer) 6 / 9 / 1865 GEMINI
NIEMAYER, OSCAR (architect) 12 / 15 / 1907 SAGITTARIUS
NIETZSCHE, FRIEDRICH WILHELM (philosopher) 10 / 15 / 1844
     LIBRA
NIGHTINGALE, FLORENCE (nurse) 5 / 12 / 1820 TAURUS
NIJINSKY, VASLAW (ballet dancer) 2 / 28 / 1890 PISCES
NILES, JOHN JACOB (folk singer) 4 / 28 / 1892 TAURUS
NILSSON, BIRGIT (soprano) 5 / 17 / 1918 TAURUS
NILSSON, CHRISTINE (soprano) 8 / 20 / 1843 LEO
NILSSON, HARRY (singer) 6 / 15 / 1942 GEMINI
NIMOY, LEONARD (actor) 3 / 26 / 1931 ARIES
NIN, ANAIS (diarist) 2 / 21 / 1903 PISCES
NIVEN, DAVID (actor) 3 / 1 / 1910 PISCES
NIXON, MARNI (singer) 2 / 22 / 1931 PISCES
NIXON, PAT (first lady) 3 / 16 / 1912 PISCES
NIXON, RICHARD M. (politician) 1 / 9 / 1913 CAPRICORN
NOBEL, ALFRED (philanthropist) 10 / 31 / 1833 SCORPIO
NOGUCHI, ISAMU (sculptor) 11 / 17 / 1904 SCORPIO
NOLAN, LLOYD (actor) 8 / 11 / 1902 LEO
NOLDE, EMIL (painter) 8 / 7 / 1867 LEO
NONO, LUIGI (composer) 1 / 27 / 1924 AQUARIUS
NORDICA, LILLIAN (soprano) 5 / 12 / 1857 TAURUS
NORELL, NORMAN (fashion designer) 4 / 20 / 1900 ARIES/TAURUS
NORMAN, JESSYE (soprano) 9 / 15 / 1945 VIRGO
NORRIS, FRANK (novelist) 3 / 5 / 1870 PISCES
NORTH, ALEX (composer) 12 / 4 / 1910 SAGITTARIUS
NORTH, JAY (actor) 8 / 3 / 1952 LEO
NORTH, JOHN RINGLING (circus executive) 8 / 14 / 1903 LEO
NORTH, SHEREE (actress) 1 / 17 / 1933 CAPRICORN
NOSTRADAMUS, MICHEL DE (astrologer) 12 / 23 / 1503 CAPRICORN
NOTO, LORE (producer) 6 / 9 / 1923 GEMINI
NOURRIT, ADOLPHE (tenor) 3 / 3 / 1802 PISCES
NOVAES, GUIOMAR (pianist) 2 / 28 / 1895 PISCES
NOVAK, KIM (actress) 2 / 13 / 1933 AQUARIUS
NOVAK, ROBERT (columnist) 2 / 26 / 1931 PISCES

NUGENT, LUCI BAINES JOHNSON (politician's daughter) 7 / 2 / 1947
   CANCER
NUREYEV, RUDOLF (ballet dancer) 3 / 17 / 1938 PISCES
NUYEN, FRANCE (actress) 7 / 31 / 1939 LEO
NYRO, LAURA (singer) 10 / 18 / 1947 LIBRA

OAKLEY, ANNIE (sharpshooter) 8 / 13 / 1860 LEO
OATES, JOYCE CAROL (novelist) 6 / 16 / 1938 GEMINI
OBERLIN, RUSSELL (countertenor) 10 / 11 / 1928 LIBRA
OBERON, MERLE (actress) 2 / 19 / 1911 AQUARIUS
O'BRIAN, HUGH (actor) 4 / 19 / 1930 ARIES
O'BRIEN, CONOR CRUISE (writer) 11 / 3 / 1917 SCORPIO
O'BRIEN, EDMOND (actor) 9 / 10 / 1915 VIRGO
O'BRIEN, MARGARET (actress) 1 / 15 / 1937 CAPRICORN
O'BRIEN, PAT (actor) 11 / 11 / 1899 SCORPIO
O'CASEY, SEAN (playwright) 3 / 30 / 1880 ARIES
OCHS, PHIL (singer) 12 / 19 / 1940 SAGITTARIUS
O'CONNELL, ARTHUR (actor) 3 / 29 / 1908 ARIES
O'CONNOR, CARROLL (actor) 8 / 2 / 1924 LEO
O'CONNOR, DONALD (actor) 8 / 28 / 1925 VIRGO
O'CONNOR, EDWIN (writer) 7 / 29 / 1918 LEO
O'CONNOR, FLANNERY (writer) 3 / 25 / 1925 ARIES
O'DAY, ANITA (jazz singer) 12 / 18 / 1919 SAGITTARIUS
ODETS, CLIFFORD (playwright) 7 / 18 / 1906 CANCER
ODETTA (folk singer) 12 / 31 / 1930 CAPRICORN
OENSLAGER, DONALD (stage designer) 3 / 7 / 1902 PISCES
O'FAOLAIN, SEAN (writer) 2 / 22 / 1900 PISCES
OFFENBACH, JACQUES (composer) 6 / 20 / 1819 GEMINI
OGDON, JOHN (pianist) 1 / 26 / 1937 AQUARIUS
OGLETHORPE, JAMES (colonizer) 1 / 1 / 1697 CAPRICORN
O'HARA, JOHN (novelist) 1 / 31 / 1905 AQUARIUS
O'HARA, MAUREEN (actress) 8 / 17 / 1921 LEO
O'HEARN, ROBERT (stage designer) 7 / 19 / 1921 CANCER
OHM, GEORG SIMON (physicist) 3 / 16 / 1787 PISCES
O'HORGAN, TOM (director) 5 / 3 / 1926 TAURUS
OISTRAKH, DAVID (violinist) 10 / 30 / 1908 SCORPIO
OISTRAKH, IGOR (violinist) 4 / 27 / 1931 TAURUS
O'KEEFE, DENNIS (actor) 3 / 29 / 1908 ARIES
O'KEEFFE, GEORGIA (painter) 11 / 15 / 1887 SCORPIO

OLAV V OF NORWAY, KING 4 / 2 / 1903 ARIES
OLD, SIDNEY GEORGE (astrologer) 10 / 2 / 1901 LIBRA
OLDENBURG, CLAES (painter) 1 / 28 / 1929 AQUARIUS
OLITSKY, JULES (artist) 3 / 27 / 1923 ARIES
OLIVER, EDNA MAY (actress) 11 / 9 / 1883 SCORPIO
OLIVERO, MAGDA (soprano) 3 / 25 / 1912 ARIES
OLIVIER, LAURENCE (actor) 5 / 22 / 1907 GEMINI
OLMEDO, ALEX (tennis player) 3 / 24 / 1936 ARIES
OLMSTED, FREDERICK LAW (landscape architect) 4 / 26 / 1822
    TAURUS
OLSON, NANCY (actress) 7 / 14 / 1928 CANCER
ONASSIS, ARISTOTLE (tycoon) 1 / 15 / 1906 CAPRICORN
ONASSIS, JACQUELINE KENNEDY (first lady and tycoon's wife)
    7 / 28 / 1929 LEO
O'NEAL, PATRICK (actor) 9 / 26 / 1927 LIBRA
O'NEAL, RYAN (actor) 4 / 20 / 1941 ARIES/TAURUS
O'NEAL, TATUM (actress) 11 / 5 / 1963 SCORPIO
ONEGIN, SIGRID (contralto) 6 / 1 / 1891 GEMINI
O'NEILL, EUGENE (playwright) 10 / 16 / 1888 LIBRA
ONO, YOKO (artist) 2 / 18 / 1933 AQUARIUS
OPHULS, MAX (film director) 5 / 6 / 1902 TAURUS
OPPENHEIMER, J. ROBERT (physicist) 4 / 22 / 1904 TAURUS
ORAGE, A. R. (writer) 1 / 22 / 1873 AQUARIUS
ORBACH, JERRY (actor) 10 / 20 / 1935 LIBRA
ORBISON, ROY (singer) 4 / 23 / 1936 TAURUS
ORFF, CARL (composer) 7 / 10 / 1895 CANCER
ORMANDY, EUGENE (conductor) 11 / 18 / 1899 SCORPIO
OROZCO, JOSE (painter) 11 / 23 / 1883 SCORPIO/SAGITTARIUS
ORR, BOBBY (hockey player) 3 / 20 / 1948 PISCES/ARIES
ORR, MARY (writer) 12 / 21 / 1920 SAGITTARIUS/CAPRICORN
ORTEGA Y GASSET, JOSE (writer) 5 / 9 / 1883 TAURUS
ORWELL, GEORGE (novelist) 6 / 25 / 1903 CANCER
OSBORNE, JOHN (playwright) 12 / 12 / 1929 SAGITTARIUS
OSCARSSON, PER (actor) 1 / 28 / 1927 AQUARIUS
O'SHEA, MILO (actor) 6 / 2 / 1926 GEMINI
OSMOND, DONNY (singer) 12 / 9 / 1957 SAGITTARIUS
OSTERWALD, BIBI (actress) 2 / 3 / 1920 AQUARIUS
O'SULLIVAN, GILBERT (singer) 12 / 1 / 1946 SAGITTARIUS
O'SULLIVAN, MAUREEN (actress) 5 / 17 / 1911 TAURUS
OSWALD, LEE HARVEY (assassin) 10 / 18 / 1939 LIBRA

O'TOOLE, PETER (actor) 8 / 2 / 1933 LEO
OTT, MEL (baseball player and manager) 3 / 2 / 1909 PISCES
OUIMET, FRANCIS D. (golfer) 5 / 8 / 1893 TAURUS
OUSPENSKAYA, MARIA (actress) 7 / 29 / 1876 LEO
OVID (poet) 3 / 18 / 43 B.C. PISCES
OWEN, REGINALD (actor) 8 / 5 / 1887 LEO
OWEN, STEVE (football coach) 4 / 21 / 1898 TAURUS
OWEN, WILFRED (poet) 3 / 18 / 1893 PISCES
OWENS, BUCK (country singer) 8/ 12 / 1929 LEO
OWENS, JESSE (runner) 9 / 12 / 1913 VIRGO
OWENS, ROCHELLE (playwright) 4 / 2 / 1936 ARIES
OWINGS, NATHANIEL (architect) 2 / 5 / 1903 AQUARIUS
OZAWA, SEIJI (conductor) 9 / 1 / 1935 VIRGO
OZU, YASUJIRO (film maker) 12 / 15 / 1903 SAGITTARIUS

PAAR, JACK (TV personality) 5 / 1 / 1918 TAURUS
PABST, G. W. (film director) 8 / 27 / 1885 VIRGO
PACINO, AL (actor) 4 / 25 / 1940 TAURUS
PACKARD, VANCE (writer) 5 / 22 / 1914 GEMINI
PADEREWSKI, IGNACE (pianist) 11 / 18 / 1860 SCORPIO
PAGANINI, NICCOLO (violinist) 10 / 27 / 1782 SCORPIO
PAGE, GENEVIEVE (actress) 12 / 13 / 1931 SAGITTARIUS
PAGE, GERALDINE (actress) 11 / 22 / 1924 SAGITTARIUS
PAGE, PATTI (singer) 11 / 8 / 1927 SCORPIO
PAGET, DEBRA (actress) 8 / 19 / 1933 LEO
PAGNOL, MARCEL (playwright) 2 / 25 / 1895 PISCES
PAIGE, JANIS (actress) 9 / 16 / 1923 VIRGO
PAINE, THOMAS (pamphleteer) 2 / 9 / 1737 AQUARIUS
PAISIELLO, GIOVANNI (composer) 5 / 9 / 1741 TAURUS
PALANCE, JACK (actor) 2 / 18 / 1919 AQUARIUS
PALESTRINA, GIOVANNI DA (composer) 1 / 6 / 1526 CAPRICORN
PALEY, WILLIAM S. (broadcasting executive) 9 / 28 / 1901 LIBRA
PALLADIO, ANDREA (architect) 12 / 10 / 1508 SAGITTARIUS
PALMER, ARNOLD (golfer) 9 / 10 / 1929 VIRGO
PALMER, BETSY (actress) 11 / 1 / 1926 SCORPIO
PALMER, BUD (public official) 9 / 14 / 1923 VIRGO
PALMER, CARL (rock musician) 3 / 20 / 1950 PISCES/ARIES
PALMER, LILLI (actress) 5 / 24 / 1914 GEMINI
PALMER, PETER (actor) 9 / 20 / 1931 VIRGO

PANERAI, ROLANDO (baritone) 10 / 17 / 1924 LIBRA
PANIZZA, ETTORE (conductor) 8 / 12 / 1875 LEO
PANKHURST, EMMELINE (feminist) 7 / 14 / 1858 CANCER
PANOV, VALERY (ballet dancer) 3 / 12 / 1939 PISCES
PAPANDREOU, ANDREAS (Greek politician) 2 / 5 / 1919 AQUARIUS
PAPAS, IRENE (actress) 9 / 3 / 1926 VIRGO
PAPP, JOSEPH (producer) 6 / 22 / 1921 GEMINI/CANCER
PARACELSUS (alchemist) 12 / 27 / 1493 CAPRICORN
PARAY, PAUL (conductor) 5 / 24 / 1886 GEMINI
PARK, MERLE (ballet dancer) 10 / 8 / 1937 LIBRA
PARK, MUNGO (explorer) 9 / 10 / 1771 VIRGO
PARKER, BONNIE (outlaw) 10 / 1 / 1910 LIBRA
PARKER, BUDDY (football coach) 12 / 16 / 1913 SAGITTARIUS
PARKER, CHARLIE (jazz musician) 8 / 29 / 1920 VIRGO
PARKER, DOROTHY (writer) 8 / 22 / 1893 LEO
PARKER, ELEANOR (actress) 6 / 26 / 1922 CANCER
PARKER, FESS (actor) 8 / 16 / 1927 LEO
PARKER, SUZY (actress) 10 / 28 / 1933 SCORPIO
PARKINS, BARBARA (actress) 5 / 22 / 1945 TAURUS/GEMINI
PARKMAN, FRANCIS (historian) 9 / 16 / 1823 VIRGO
PARKS, BERT (TV personality) 12 / 30 / 1914 CAPRICORN
PARMIGIANINO (painter) 1 / 21 / 1503 CAPRICORN/AQUARIUS
PARRISH, MAXFIELD (painter) 7 / 25 / 1870 LEO
PARSEGHIAN, ARA (football coach) 5 / 21 / 1923 TAURUS/GEMINI
PARSONS, ESTELLE (actress) 11 / 20 / 1927 SCORPIO
PARSONS, LOUELLA (columnist) 8 / 6 / 1893 LEO
PARTRIDGE, ERIC (etymologist) 2 / 6 / 1894 AQUARIUS
PASCAL, BLAISE (philosopher) 6 / 19 / 1623 GEMINI
PASOLINI, PIER PAOLO (poet and film maker) 3 / 5 / 1922 PISCES
PASTA, GIUDITTA (soprano) 4 / 9 / 1798 ARIES
PASTERNAK, BORIS (writer) 2 / 10 / 1890 AQUARIUS
PASTEUR, LOUIS (bacteriologist) 12 / 27 / 1822 CAPRICORN
PATCHETT, JEAN (model) 2 / 16 / ? AQUARIUS
PATER, WALTER (writer) 8 / 4 / 1839 LEO
PATON, ALAN (novelist) 1 / 11 / 1903 CAPRICORN
PATRICK, JOHN (playwright) 5 / 17 / 1905 TAURUS
PATTERSON, ELIZABETH (actress) 11 / 22 / 1874 SAGITTARIUS
PATTERSON, FLOYD (boxer) 1 / 4 / 1935 CAPRICORN
PATTI, ADELINA (soprano) 2 / 10 / 1843 AQUARIUS

PERON, ISABEL (Argentine politician) 2 / 4 / 1931 AQUARIUS
PERON, JUAN (Argentine politician) 10 / 8 / 1895 LIBRA
PERRAULT, CHARLES (writer) 1 / 12 / 1628 CAPRICORN
PERRY, MATTHEW (naval officer) 4 / 10 / 1794 ARIES
PERSHING, JOHN JOSEPH (army officer) 9 / 13 / 1860 VIRGO
PERTILE, AURELIANO (tenor) 11 / 9 / 1885 SCORPIO
PETER THE GREAT OF RUSSIA, CZAR 6 / 9 / 1682 GEMINI
PETERS, BERNADETTE (actress) 2 / 28 / 1948 PISCES
PETERS, BROCK (actor) 7 / 2 / 1927 CANCER
PETERS, JEAN (actress) 10 / 15 / 1926 LIBRA
PETERS, ROBERTA (soprano) 5 / 4 / 1930 TAURUS
PETERSON, ROGER TORY (ornithologist) 8 / 28 / 1908 VIRGO
PETINA, IRRA (singer) 4 / 18 / 1914 ARIES
PETIT, ROLAND (choreographer) 1 / 13 / 1924 CAPRICORN
PETRARCH (poet) 7 / 28 / 1304 LEO
PETTIT, ROBERT (basketball player) 12 / 2 / 1932 SAGITTARIUS
PEUGEOT, ROLAND (automobile executive) 3 / 20 / 1926 PISCES/
    ARIES
PEVSNER, ANTOINE (artist) 1 / 18 / 1886 CAPRICORN
PHILIP, PRINCE (royal consort) 6 / 10 / 1921 GEMINI
PHILIP II OF SPAIN, KING 5 / 31 / 1527 GEMINI
PHILIPE, GERARD (actor) 12 / 4 / 1922 SAGITTARIUS
PHILLIPS, MARK (princess' husband) 9 / 22 / 1948 VIRGO
PIAF, EDITH (singer) 12 / 19 / 1915 SAGITTARIUS
PIAGET, JEAN (child psychologist) 8 / 9 / 1896 LEO
PIATIGORSKY, GREGOR (cellist) 4 / 20 / 1903 ARIES/TAURUS
PIAVE, FRANCESCO MARIA (librettist) 5 /18 / 1810 TAURUS
PIAZZA, BEN (actor) 7 / 30 / 1934 LEO
PICASSO, PABLO (artist) 10 / 25 / 1881 SCORPIO
PICCAVER, ALFRED (tenor) 2 / 5 / 1897 AQUARIUS
PICCINNI, NICOLA (composer) 1 / 16 / 1728 CAPRICORN
PICERNI, PAUL (actor) 12 / 1 / 1922 SAGITTARIUS
PICKENS, SLIM (actor) 6 / 29 / 1919 CANCER
PICKETT, WILSON (singer) 3 / 18 / 1941 PISCES
PICKFORD, MARY (actress) 4 / 9 / 1894 ARIES
PICO DELLA MIRANDOLA (writer) 3 / 5 / 1463 PISCES
PICON, MOLLY (actress) 2 / 28 / 1898 PISCES
PIDGEON, WALTER (actor) 9 / 23 / 1898 LIBRA
PIERCE, FRANKLIN (politician) 11 / 23 / 1804 SAGITTARIUS
PIERCE, WEBB (country singer) 8 / 8 / 1926 LEO

PIKE, JAMES (clergyman) 2 / 14 / 1913 AQUARIUS
PIKE, ZEBULON (explorer) 1 / 5 / 1779 CAPRICORN
PILLSBURY, PHILIP WINSTON (flour merchant) 4 / 16 / 1903 ARIES
PINCUS, GREGORY (biologist) 4 / 9 / 1903 ARIES
PINKERTON, ALLAN (detective) 8 / 25 / 1819 VIRGO
PINTER, HAROLD (playwright) 10 / 10 / 1930 LIBRA
PINZA, EZIO (basso) 5 / 18 / 1895 TAURUS
PIRANDELLO, LUIGI (writer) 6 / 28 / 1867 CANCER
PIRANESI, GIOVANNI BATTISTA (architect) 10 / 4 / 1720 LIBRA
PISSARRO, CAMILLE (painter) 7 / 10 / 1830 CANCER
PISTON, WALTER (composer) 1 / 20 / 1894 CAPRICORN/AQUARIUS
PITT, WILLIAM (British statesman) 5 / 28 / 1759 GEMINI
PITTS, ZASU (actress) 1 / 3 / 1898 CAPRICORN
PIUS XII, POPE 3 / 2 / 1876 PISCES
PLANCON, POL (baritone) 6 / 12 / 1854 GEMINI
PLATH, SYLVIA (writer) 10 / 27 / 1932 SCORPIO
PLAYER, GARY (golfer) 11 / 1 / 1935 SCORPIO
PLAYTEN, ALICE (actress) 8 / 28 / 1947 VIRGO
PLEASENCE, DONALD (actor) 10 / 5 / 1919 LIBRA
PLESHETTE, SUZANNE (actress) 1 / 31 / 1937 AQUARIUS
PLEYEL, IGNACE (piano manufacturer) 6 / 1 / 1757 GEMINI
PLIMPTON, GEORGE (playboy) 3 / 18 / 1927 PISCES
PLISETSKAYA, MAYA (ballet dancer) 11 / 20 / 1925 SCORPIO
PLOWRIGHT, JOAN (actress) 10 / 28 / 1929 SCORPIO
PLUMMER, CHRISTOPHER (actor) 12 / 13 / 1929 SAGITTARIUS
PLUNKETT, JIM (football player) 12 / 5 / 1947 SAGITTARIUS
PODGORNY, NIKOLAI (Soviet politician) 2 / 18 / 1903 AQUARIUS/
    PISCES
PODHORETZ, NORMAN (writer) 1 / 16 / 1930 CAPRICORN
POE, EDGAR ALLAN (writer) 1 / 19 / 1809 CAPRICORN
POITIER, SIDNEY (actor) 2 / 20 / 1927 PISCES
POLANSKI, ROMAN (film maker) 8 / 18 / 1933 LEO
POLK, JAMES KNOX (politician) 11 / 2 / 1795 SCORPIO
POLLARD, MICHAEL J. (actor) 5 / 30 / 1939 GEMINI
POLLOCK, JACKSON (painter) 1 / 28 / 1912 AQUARIUS
POMPADOUR, MARQUISE DE (courtesan) 12 / 29 / 1721 CAPRICORN
POMPIDOU, GEORGES (French politician) 7 / 5 / 1911 CANCER
PONCHIELLI, AMILCARE (composer) 8 / 31 / 1834 VIRGO
PONS, LILY (soprano) 4 / 16 / 1904 ARIES
PONSELLE, CARMELA (mezzo-soprano) 6 / 7 / 1892 GEMINI

PONSELLE, ROSA (soprano) 1 / 22 / 1897 AQUARIUS
PONTI, CARLO (film producer) 12 / 11 / 1913 SAGITTARIUS
PONTORMO, JACOPO DA (painter) 6 / 2 / 1494 GEMINI
POPE, ALEXANDER (poet) 5 / 31 / 1688 GEMINI
POPP, LUCIA (soprano) 11 / 12 / 1939 SCORPIO
PORTER, COLE (composer) 6 / 9 / 1893 GEMINI
PORTER, ERIC (actor) 4 / 8 / 1928 ARIES
PORTER, KATHERINE ANNE (writer) 5 / 15 / 1890 TAURUS
PORTER, SYLVIA (columnist) 6 / 18 / 1913 GEMINI
PORTMAN, ERIC (actor) 7 / 13 / 1903 CANCER
POST, EMILY (etiquette adviser) 10 / 27 / 1872 SCORPIO
POST, MRS. MARJORIE MERRIWEATHER (philanthropist) 3 / 15 / 1887
    PISCES
POSTON, TOM (actor) 10 / 17 / 1927 LIBRA
POTTER, BEATRIX (children's writer) 7 / 28 / 1866 LEO
POULENC, FRANCIS (composer) 1 / 7 / 1899 CAPRICORN
POUND, EZRA (poet) 10 / 30 / 1885 SCORPIO
POWELL, ADAM CLAYTON, JR. (politician) 11 / 29 / 1908
    SAGITTARIUS
POWELL, DICK (actor) 11 / 14 / 1904 SCORPIO
POWELL, ELEANOR (dancer) 11 / 21 / 1912 SCORPIO
POWELL, JANE (actress) 4 / 1 / 1929 ARIES
POWELL, WILLIAM (actor) 7 / 29 / 1892 LEO
POWER, TYRONE (actor) 5 / 11 / 1913 TAURUS
POWERS, FRANCIS GARY (spy) 8 / 17 / 1929 LEO
POWERS, LEONA (actress) 3 / 13 / 1896 PISCES
PREMINGER, OTTO (film producer) 12 / 5 / 1906 SAGITTARIUS
PRENTISS, PAULA (actress) 3 / 4 / 1939 PISCES
PRESCOTT, ORVILLE (literary critic) 9 / 8 / 1906 VIRGO
PRESCOTT, WILLIAM HICKLING (historian) 5 / 4 / 1796 TAURUS
PRESLEY, ELVIS (singer) 1 / 8 / 1935 CAPRICORN
PRESTON, ROBERT (actor) 6 / 8 / 1918 GEMINI
PRESTOPINO, GREGORIO (painter) 6 / 21 / 1907 GEMINI/CANCER
PRETRE, GEORGES (conductor) 8 / 14 / 1924 LEO
PREVIN, ANDRE (conductor) 4 / 6 / 1929 ARIES
PREVIN, DORY (composer) 10 / 22 / 1925 LIBRA
PREVITALI, FERNANDO (conductor) 2 / 16 / 1907 AQUARIUS
PREVOST, ABBE (novelist) 4 / 1 / 1697 ARIES
PREY, HERMANN (baritone) 7 / 11 / 1929 CANCER
PRICE, LEONTYNE (soprano) 2 / 10 / 1927 AQUARIUS

PRICE, MARGARET (soprano) 4 / 13 / 1941 ARIES
PRICE, VINCENT (actor) 5 / 27 / 1911 GEMINI
PRIESTLEY, J. B. (writer) 9 / 13 / 1894 VIRGO
PRIMROSE, WILLIAM (violist) 8 / 23 / 1903 LEO/VIRGO
PRIMUS, PEARL (dancer) 11 / 29 / 1921 SAGITTARIUS
PRINCE, HAROLD (producer) 1 / 30 / 1928 AQUARIUS
PRINTEMPS, YVONNE (actress) 7 / 25 / 1895 LEO
PRINZE, FREDDIE (actor) 6 / 22 / 1954 GEMINI/CANCER
PRITCHARD, JOHN (conductor) 2 / 5 / 1921 AQUARIUS
PROFUMO, JOHN (British politician) 1 / 30 / 1915 AQUARIUS
PROKOFIEV, SERGEI (composer) 4 / 23 / 1891 TAURUS
PROUDHON, PIERRE (socialist) 1 / 15 / 1809 CAPRICORN
PROUST, MARCEL (novelist) 7 / 10 / 1871 CANCER
PROVINE, DOROTHY (actress) 1 / 20 / 1937 CAPRICORN/AQUARIUS
PROWSE, JULIET (actress) 9 / 25 / 1936 LIBRA
PRYOR, NICHOLAS (actor) 1 / 28 / 1935 AQUARIUS
PUCCI, EMILIO (fashion designer) 11 / 20 / 1914 SCORPIO
PUCCINI, GIACOMO (composer) 12 / 22 / 1858 SAGITTARIUS/
    CAPRICORN
PULITZER, JOSEPH (publisher) 4 / 10 / 1847 ARIES
PURDY, JAMES (novelist) 7 / 14 / 1923 CANCER
PUSHKIN, ALEXANDER (writer) 6 / 6 / 1799 GEMINI
PUZO, MARIO (novelist) 10 / 15 / 1921 LIBRA

QUANT, MARY (fashion designer) 2 / 11 / 1934 AQUARIUS
QUASIMODO, SALVATORE (poet) 8 / 20 / 1901 LEO
QUAYLE, ANNA (actress) 10 / 6 / 1936 LIBRA
QUAYLE, ANTHONY (actor) 9 / 7 / 1913 VIRGO
QUEEN, ELLERY (writer) 10 / 20 / 1905 LIBRA
QUELER, EVE (conductor) 1 / 1 / 1936 CAPRICORN
QUINN, ANTHONY (actor) 4 / 21 / 1915 TAURUS
QUINTERO, JOSE (director) 10 / 15 / 1924 LIBRA
QUISLING, VIDKUN (Norwegian politician) 7 / 18 / 1887 CANCER

RABB, ELLIS (director) 6 / 20 / 1930 GEMINI
RABE, DAVID (playwright) 3 / 10 / 1940 PISCES
RACHMANINOFF, SERGEI (composer) 4 / 1 / 1873 ARIES

RACINE, JEAN BAPTISTE (playwright) 12 / 22 / 1639 SAGITTARIUS/
  CAPRICORN
RACKHAM, ARTHUR (illustrator) 7 / 19 / 1867 CANCER
RADER, DOTSON (writer) 7 / 25 / 1942 LEO
RADHAKRISHNAN, SARVEPALLI (Indian politician) 9 / 5 / 1888 VIRGO
RADZIWILL, PRINCESS LEE (actress) 3 / 3 / 1933 PISCES
RAE, CHARLOTTE (actress) 4 / 22 / 1926 TAURUS
RAFFERTY, MAX (politician) 5 / 7 / 1917 TAURUS
RAFT, GEORGE (actor) 9 / 24 / 1903 VIRGO/LIBRA
RAGNI, GEROME (actor) 9 / 11 / 1942 VIRGO
RAINER, LUISE (actress) 1 / 12 / 1910 CAPRICORN
RAINES, ELLA (actress) 8 / 6 / 1921 LEO
RAINIER III OF MONACO, PRINCE 5 / 31 / 1923 GEMINI
RAINS, CLAUDE (actor) 11 / 10 / 1889 SCORPIO
RAISA, ROSA (soprano) 5 / 30 / 1893 GEMINI
RAITT, BONNIE (singer) 11 / 8 / 1950 SCORPIO
RAITT, JOHN (actor) 1 / 19 / 1917 CAPRICORN
RALSTON, DENNIS (tennis player) 7 / 27 / 1942 LEO
RALSTON, VERA HRUBA (actress) 6 / 12 / 1921 GEMINI
RAMBEAU, MARJORIE (actress) 7 / 15 / 1889 CANCER
RAMEAU, JEAN PHILIPPE (composer) 9 / 25 / 1683 LIBRA
RAMPAL, JEAN-PIERRE (flutist) 1 / 7 / 1922 CAPRICORN
RAND, AYN (philosopher) 2 / 2 / 1905 AQUARIUS
RANDALL, TONY (actor) 2 / 26 / 1924 PISCES
RANDOLPH, A. PHILIP (labor leader) 4 / 15 / 1889 ARIES
RANK, J. ARTHUR (producer) 12 / 23 / 1888 CAPRICORN
RANSOM, JOHN CROWE (poet) 4 / 30 / 1888 TAURUS
RAPHAEL (painter) 4 / 5 / 1483 ARIES
RASKIN, JUDITH (soprano) 6 / 21 / 1928 GEMINI/CANCER
RATHBONE, BASIL (actor) 6 / 13 / 1892 GEMINI
RATTIGAN, TERENCE (playwright) 6 / 10 / 1911 GEMINI
RAU, SANTHA RAMA (writer) 1 / 24 / 1923 AQUARIUS
RAUSCHENBERG, ROBERT (painter) 10 / 22 / 1925 LIBRA
RAVEL, MAURICE (composer) 3 / 7 / 1875 PISCES
RAWLS, LOU (singer) 12 / 1 / 1935 SAGITTARIUS
RAY, ALDO (actor) 9 / 25 / 1926 LIBRA
RAY, JAMES EARL (assassin) 3 / 10 / 1928 PISCES
RAY, JOHNNIE (singer) 1 / 10 / 1927 CAPRICORN
RAY, MAN (photographer) 8 / 27 / 1890 VIRGO
RAY, SATYAJIT (film maker) 5 / 2 / 1921 TAURUS

RAYBURN, SAM (politician) 1 / 6 / 1882 CAPRICORN
RAYE, MARTHA (singer) 8 / 27 / 1916 VIRGO
RAYMOND, GENE (actor) 8 / 13 / 1908 LEO
READ, HERBERT (art critic) 12 / 4 / 1893 SAGITTARIUS
REAGAN, RONALD (actor and politician) 2 / 6 / 1911 AQUARIUS
REARDON, JOHN (baritone) 4 / 8 / 1930 ARIES
REASON, REX (actor) 11 / 30 / 1928 SAGITTARIUS
REASONER, HARRY (newsman) 4 / 17 / 1923 ARIES
REBOZO, C. G. "BEBE" (banker) 11 / 17 / 1912 SCORPIO
REDDING, OTIS (singer) 9 / 9 / 1941 VIRGO
REDDY, HELEN (singer) 10 / 25 / 1941 SCORPIO
REDFIELD, WILLIAM (actor) 1 / 26 / 1927 AQUARIUS
REDFORD, ROBERT (actor) 8 / 18 / 1937 LEO
REDGRAVE, LYNN (actress) 3 / 8 / 1943 PISCES
REDGRAVE, MICHAEL (actor) 3 / 20 / 1908 PISCES
REDGRAVE, VANESSA (actress) 1 / 30 / 1937 AQUARIUS
REDON, ODILON (artist) 4 / 22 / 1840 TAURUS
REED, CAROL (film director) 12 / 30 / 1906 CAPRICORN
REED, DONNA (actress) 1 / 27 / 1921 AQUARIUS
REED, FLORENCE (actress) 1 / 10 / 1883 CAPRICORN
REED, LOU (singer) 3 / 2 / 1942 PISCES
REED, OLIVER (actor) 2 / 13 / 1938 AQUARIUS
REED, REX (film critic) 10 / 2 / 1940 LIBRA
REED, WALTER (army surgeon) 9 / 13 / 1851 VIRGO
REED, WILLIS (basketball player) 6 / 25 / 1942 CANCER
REEDY, GEORGE (press secretary) 8 / 5 / 1917 LEO
REEMS, HARRY (actor) 8 / 27 / 1947 VIRGO
REESE, DELLA (singer) 7 / 6 / 1932 CANCER
REEVES, STEVE (actor) 12 / 21 / 1926 SAGITTARIUS/CAPRICORN
REGER, MAX (composer) 3 / 19 / 1873 PISCES
REGIOMONTANUS (astronomer) 6 / 15 / 1436 GEMINI
REHNQUIST, WILLIAM H. (jurist) 10 / 1 / 1924 LIBRA
REICH, WILHELM (psychologist) 3 / 24 / 1897 ARIES
REID, BERYL (actress) 6 / 17 / 1920 GEMINI
REID, KATE (actress) 11 / 4 / 1930 SCORPIO
REIK, THEODOR (psychologist) 5 / 12 / 1888 TAURUS
REINER, CARL (comedian) 3 / 20 / 1922 PISCES
REINER, FRITZ (conductor) 12 / 19 / 1888 SAGITTARIUS
REINHARDT, MAX (director) 9 / 9 / 1873 VIRGO
REINING, MARIA (soprano) 8 / 7 / 1905 LEO

REISZ, KAREL (film director) 7 / 21 / 1926 CANCER

REMARQUE, ERICH MARIA (novelist) 6 / 22 / 1898 GEMINI/CANCER

REMBRANDT VAN RIJN (painter) 7 / 15 / 1606 CANCER

REMICK, LEE (actress) 12 / 14 / 1935 SAGITTARIUS

REMINGTON, FREDERIC (painter) 10 / 4 / 1861 LIBRA

RENAUD, MADELEINE (actress) 2 / 21 / 1903 PISCES

RENAULT, MARY (novelist) 9 / 4 / 1905 VIRGO

RENI, GUIDO (painter) 11 / 14 / 1575 SCORPIO

RENNIE, MICHAEL (actor) 8 / 25 / 1909 VIRGO

RENOIR, CLAUDE (photographer) 12 / 4 / 1914 SAGITTARIUS

RENOIR, JEAN (film maker) 9 / 15 / 1894 VIRGO

RENOIR, PIERRE AUGUSTE (painter) 2 / 25 / 1841 PISCES

RESHEVSKY, SAMUEL (chess player) 11 / 26 / 1911 SAGITTARIUS

RESNAIS, ALAIN (film maker) 6 / 3 / 1922 GEMINI

RESNIK, REGINA (mezzo-soprano) 8 / 30 / 1922 VIRGO

RESPIGHI, OTTORINO (composer) 7 / 9 / 1879 CANCER

RESTON, JAMES (journalist) 11 / 3 / 1909 SCORPIO

RETHBERG, ELISABETH (soprano) 9 / 22 / 1894 VIRGO

RETTIG, TOMMY (child actor) 12 / 10 / 1941 SAGITTARIUS

REUBEN, DAVID (physician and author) 11 / 29 / 1933 SAGITTARIUS

REUTHER, WALTER (labor leader) 9 / 1 / 1907 VIRGO

REVERE, ANNE (actress) 6 / 25 / 1903 CANCER

REVERE, PAUL (patriot) 1 / 12 / 1735 CAPRICORN

REVILL, CLIVE (actor) 4 / 18 / 1939 ARIES

REVSON, CHARLES (cosmetics merchant) 10 / 11 / 1906 LIBRA

REYNOLDS, ALLIE (baseball player) 2 / 10 / 1919 AQUARIUS

REYNOLDS, BURT (actor) 2 / 11 / 1936 AQUARIUS

REYNOLDS, DEBBIE (actress) 4 / 1 / 1932 ARIES

REYNOLDS, JOSHUA (painter) 7 / 27 / 1723 LEO

REYNOLDS, MARJORIE (actress) 8 / 12 / 1921 LEO

REYNOLDS, RICK "RICOCHET" (rock musician) 10 / 28 / 1948
    SCORPIO

RHINE, J. B. (parapsychologist) 9 / 29 / 1895 LIBRA

RHODES, CECIL (colonial capitalist) 7 / 5 / 1853 CANCER

RIBERA, JOSE DE (painter) 2 / 17 / 1591 AQUARIUS

RICCI, RUGGIERO (violinist) 7 / 24 / 1918 LEO

RICE, ELMER (playwright) 9 / 28 / 1892 LIBRA

RICE, GRANTLAND (sportswriter) 11 / 1 / 1880 SCORPIO

RICH, ALAN (music critic) 6 / 17 / 1924 GEMINI

RICH, BUDDY (drummer) 6 / 30 / 1917 CANCER

RICHARD THE LION-HEARTED, KING 9 / 15 / 1157 VIRGO

RICHARD II OF ENGLAND, KING 1 / 14 / 1367 CAPRICORN

RICHARD III OF ENGLAND, KING 10 / 11 / 1452 LIBRA

RICHARD, KEITH (rock musician) 12 / 18 / 1943 SAGITTARIUS

RICHARD, LITTLE (singer) 12 / 25 / 1935 CAPRICORN

RICHARD, MAURICE (hockey player) 8 / 4 / 1921 LEO

RICHARDSON, BOBBY (baseball player) 8 / 19 / 1935 LEO

RICHARDSON, ELLIOT (government official) 7 / 20 / 1920 CANCER

RICHARDSON, HENRY HOBSON (architect) 9 / 29 / 1838 LIBRA

RICHARDSON, IAN (actor) 4 / 7 / 1934 ARIES

RICHARDSON, JACK (playwright) 2 / 18 / 1935 AQUARIUS/PISCES

RICHARDSON, LEE (actor) 9 / 11 / 1926 VIRGO

RICHARDSON, RALPH (actor) 12 / 19 / 1902 SAGITTARIUS

RICHARDSON, TONY (director) 6 / 5 / 1928 GEMINI

RICHELIEU, CARDINAL (French statesman) 9 / 9 / 1585 VIRGO

RICHTER, CHARLES F. (seismologist) 4 / 26 / 1900 TAURUS

RICHTER, SVIATOSLAV (pianist) 3 / 20 / 1915 PISCES

RICKENBACKER, EDDIE (aviator) 10 / 8 / 1890 LIBRA

RICORDI, GIULIO (music publisher) 12 / 19 / 1840 SAGITTARIUS

RIDDLE, NELSON (composer) 6 / 1 / 1921 GEMINI

RIEFENSTHAL, LENI (film director) 8 / 22 / 1902 LEO

RIESMAN, DAVID (sociologist) 9 / 22 / 1909 VIRGO

RIGG, DIANA (actress) 7 / 20 / 1938 CANCER

RIGGS, BOBBY (tennis player) 2 / 25 / 1918 PISCES

RIGHTER, CARROLL (astrologer) 2 / 2 / 1900 AQUARIUS

RILEY, JAMES WHITCOMB (poet) 10 / 7 / 1849 LIBRA

RILKE, RAINER MARIA (poet) 12 / 4 / 1875 SAGITTARIUS

RIMBAUD, ARTHUR (poet) 10 / 20 / 1854 LIBRA

RIMSKY-KORSAKOV, NICOLAI (composer) 3 / 18 / 1844 PISCES

RINGLING, CHARLES (circus executive) 12 / 2 / 1863 SAGITTARIUS

RIPLEY, ROBERT (cartoonist) 12 / 25 / 1893 CAPRICORN

RITCHARD, CYRIL (actor) 12 / 1 / 1898 SAGITTARIUS

RITCHIE, JEAN (singer) 12 / 8 / 1922 SAGITTARIUS

RITT, MARTIN (film director) 3 / 2 / 1920 PISCES

RITTER, TEX (country singer) 1 / 12 / 1906 CAPRICORN

RITTER, THELMA (actress) 2 / 14 / 1905 AQUARIUS

RITZ, CESAR (hotelkeeper) 2 / 23 / 1850 PISCES

RIVERA, CHITA (actress) 8 / 17 / 1923 LEO

RIVERA, DIEGO (painter) 12 / 8 / 1886 SAGITTARIUS

RIVERA, GERALDO (TV personality) 7 / 4 / 1943 CANCER
RIVERS, JOHNNY (singer) 11 / 7 / 1942 SCORPIO
RIVERS, LARRY (painter) 8 / 17 / 1923 LEO
RIZZUTO, PHIL (baseball player) 9 / 25 / 1918 LIBRA
ROACH, HAL (film producer) 1 / 14 / 1892 CAPRICORN
ROBARDS, JASON, JR. (actor) 7 / 26 / 1922 LEO
ROBB, LYNDA BIRD JOHNSON (politician's daughter) 3 / 19 / 1944
    PISCES
ROBBE-GRILLET, ALAIN (writer) 8 / 18 / 1922 LEO
ROBBINS, HAROLD (novelist) 5 / 21 / 1916 TAURUS/GEMINI
ROBBINS, JEROME (director) 10 / 11 / 1918 LIBRA
ROBBINS, MARTY (singer) 9 / 26 / 1925 LIBRA
ROBERTS, ORAL (evangelist) 1 / 24 / 1918 AQUARIUS
ROBERTS, RACHEL (actress) 9 / 20 / 1927 VIRGO
ROBERTSON, CLIFF (actor) 9 / 9 / 1925 VIRGO
ROBERTSON, DALE (actor) 7 / 14 / 1923 CANCER
ROBERTSON, OSCAR (basketball player) 11 / 24 / 1938 SAGITTARIUS
ROBERTSON, WARREN (acting teacher) 11 / 6 / 1935 SCORPIO
ROBESON, PAUL (singer) 4 / 9 / 1898 ARIES
ROBESPIERRE, MAXIMILIEN DE (revolutionary leader) 5 / 6 / 1758
    TAURUS
ROBIN, LEO (lyricist) 4 / 6 / 1899 ARIES
ROBINSON, BROOKS (baseball player) 5 / 18 / 1937 TAURUS
ROBINSON, EDWARD G. (actor) 12 / 12 / 1893 SAGITTARIUS
ROBINSON, EDWIN ARLINGTON (poet) 12 / 22 / 1869 CAPRICORN
ROBINSON, FRANK (baseball coach) 8 / 31 / 1935 VIRGO
ROBINSON, JACKIE (baseball player) 1 / 31 / 1919 AQUARIUS
ROBINSON, SUGAR RAY (boxer) 5 / 3 / 1921 TAURUS
ROBSON, FLORA (actress) 3 / 28 / 1902 ARIES
ROBSON, VIVIAN (astrologer) 5 / 26 / 1890 GEMINI
ROBUS, HUGO (sculptor) 5 / 10 / 1885 TAURUS
ROCKEFELLER, DAVID (financier) 6 / 12 / 1915 GEMINI
ROCKEFELLER, HAPPY (politician's wife) 6 / 9 / 1926 GEMINI
ROCKEFELLER, JOHN D. (tycoon) 7 / 8 / 1839 CANCER
ROCKEFELLER, JOHN D., JR. (tycoon) 1 / 29 / 1874 AQUARIUS
ROCKEFELLER, JOHN D., III (tycoon) 3 / 21 / 1906 PISCES/ARIES
ROCKEFELLER, NELSON (politician) 7 / 8 / 1908 CANCER
ROCKEFELLER, WINTHROP (politician) 5 / 1 / 1912 TAURUS
ROCKNE, KNUTE (football coach) 3 / 4 / 1888 PISCES

ROCKWELL, GEORGE LINCOLN (American Nazi) 3 / 9 / 1918 PISCES
ROCKWELL, NORMAN (illustrator) 2 / 3 / 1894 AQUARIUS
RODALE, J. I. (horticulturist) 8 / 16 / 1898 LEO
RODGERS, JIMMIE (country singer) 9 / 8 / 1897 VIRGO
RODGERS, MARY (composer) 1 / 11 / 1931 CAPRICORN
RODGERS, RICHARD (composer) 6 / 28 / 1902 CANCER
RODIN, AUGUSTE (sculptor) 11 / 12 / 1840 SCORPIO
RODRIGUEZ, CHI CHI (golfer) 10 / 23 / 1935 LIBRA/SCORPIO
ROENTGEN, WILHELM (physicist) 3 / 27 / 1845 ARIES
ROETHKE, THEODORE (poet) 5 / 25 / 1908 GEMINI
ROGERS, FRED (TV producer) 3 / 20 / 1928 PISCES/ARIES
ROGERS, GINGER (actress) 7 / 16 / 1911 CANCER
ROGERS, PAUL (actor) 3 / 22 / 1917 ARIES
ROGERS, ROY (actor) 11 / 5 / 1912 SCORPIO
ROGERS, WILL (humorist) 11 / 4 / 1879 SCORPIO
ROGERS, WILLIAM P. (government official) 6 / 23 / 1913 CANCER
ROLAND, GILBERT (actor) 12 / 11 / 1905 SAGITTARIUS
ROLLAND, ROMAIN (writer) 1 / 29 / 1866 AQUARIUS
ROMAN, RUTH (actress) 12 / 23 / 1924 CAPRICORN
ROMANI, FELICE (librettist) 1 / 31 / 1788 AQUARIUS
ROMBERG, SIGMUND (composer) 7 / 29 / 1887 LEO
ROMERO, CESAR (actor) 2 / 15 / 1907 AQUARIUS
ROMM, MIKHAIL ILYICH (film director) 1 / 24 / 1901 AQUARIUS
ROMMEL, ERWIN (German army officer) 11 / 15 / 1891 SCORPIO
ROMNEY, GEORGE (painter) 12 / 26 / 1734 CAPRICORN
ROMNEY, GEORGE (politician) 7 / 8 / 1907 CANCER
RONSARD, PIERRE DE (poet) 9 / 21 / 1524 VIRGO
RONSTADT, LINDA (singer) 7 / 15 / 1945 CANCER
ROONEY, MICKEY (actor) 9 / 23 / 1920 LIBRA
ROOSEVELT, ELEANOR (first lady) 10 / 11 / 1884 LIBRA
ROOSEVELT, FRANKLIN D. (politician) 1 / 30 / 1882 AQUARIUS
ROOSEVELT, THEODORE (politician) 10 / 27 / 1858 SCORPIO
ROREM, NED (composer) 10 / 23 / 1923 LIBRA/SCORPIO
RORSCHACH, HERMANN (psychologist) 11 / 8 / 1884 SCORPIO
ROSAY, FRANÇOISE (actress) 4 / 19 / 1891 ARIES
ROSBAUD, HANS (conductor) 7 / 22 / 1895 CANCER/LEO
ROSE, BILLY (producer) 9 / 6 / 1899 VIRGO
ROSE, DAVID (composer) 6 / 24 / 1910 CANCER
ROSE, GEORGE (actor) 2 / 19 / 1920 AQUARIUS/PISCES

RUBIN, JERRY (revolutionary) 7 / 14 / 1938 CANCER
RUBINI, GIOVANNI-BATTISTA (tenor) 4 / 7 / 1795 ARIES
RUBINSTEIN, ANTON (composer) 11 / 28 / 1829 SAGITTARIUS
RUBINSTEIN, ARTHUR (pianist) 1 / 28 / 1886 AQUARIUS
RUBINSTEIN, HELENA (cosmetics merchant) 12 / 25 / 1870
    CAPRICORN
RUDEL, JULIUS (conductor) 3 / 6 / 1921 PISCES
RUDHYAR, DANE (astrologer) 3 / 23 / 1895 ARIES
RUDOLF, MAX (conductor) 6 / 15 / 1902 GEMINI
RUDOLPH, PAUL (architect) 10 / 23 / 1918 LIBRA/SCORPIO
RUDOLPH, WILMA (athlete) 6 / 23 / 1940 CANCER
RUFFIN, CLOVIS (fashion designer) 7 / 14 / 1942 CANCER
RUFFO, TITTA (baritone) 6 / 9 / 1877 GEMINI
RUGGLES, CHARLES (actor) 2 / 8 / 1892 AQUARIUS
RULE, JANICE (actress) 8 / 15 / 1931 LEO
RUSH, BARBARA (actress) 1 / 4 / 1927 CAPRICORN
RUSH, OTIS (blues musician) 4 / 29 / 1934 TAURUS
RUSH, TOM (singer) 2 / 8 / 1941 AQUARIUS
RUSK, DEAN (government official) 2 / 9 / 1909 AQUARIUS
RUSKIN, JOHN (writer) 2 / 8 / 1819 AQUARIUS
RUSS, GIANNINA (soprano) 3 / 27 / 1873 ARIES
RUSSELL, ANNA (comedienne) 12 / 27 / 1911 CAPRICORN
RUSSELL, BERTRAND (philosopher) 5 / 18 / 1872 TAURUS
RUSSELL, JANE (actress) 6 / 21 / 1921 CANCER
RUSSELL, JOHN (actor) 1 / 3 / 1921 CAPRICORN
RUSSELL, KEN (film maker) 7 / 3 / 1927 CANCER
RUSSELL, KURT (actor) 3 / 17 / 1951 PISCES
RUSSELL, LEON (singer) 4 / 2 / 1942 ARIES
RUSSELL, LILLIAN (actress) 12 / 4 / 1861 SAGITTARIUS
RUSSELL, ROSALIND (actress) 6 / 5 / 1912 GEMINI
RUSSELL, TINA (actress) 9 / 23 / 1948 VIRGO/LIBRA
RUSTIN, BAYARD (civil rights leader) 3 / 17 / 1910 PISCES
RUTH, BABE (baseball player) 2 / 6 / 1895 AQUARIUS
RUTHERFORD, ANN (actress) 11 / 2 / 1917 SCORPIO
RUTHERFORD, MARGARET (actress) 5 / 11 / 1892 TAURUS
RYAN, NOLAN (baseball player) 1 / 31 / 1947 AQUARIUS
RYAN, ROBERT (actor) 11 / 11 / 1909 SCORPIO
RYDELL, BOBBY (singer) 4 / 26 / 1942 TAURUS
RYDER, ALBERT PINKHAM (painter) 3 / 19 / 1847 PISCES
RYDER, ALFRED (actor) 1 / 5 / 1919 CAPRICORN

RYSANEK, LEONIE (soprano) 11 / 14 / 1928 SCORPIO
RYUN, JIM (runner) 4 / 29 / 1947 TAURUS

SAARINEN, EERO (architect) 8 / 20 / 1910 LEO
SABU (actor) 3 / 15 / 1924 PISCES
SACHS, HANS (Meistersinger) 11 / 14 / 1494 SCORPIO
SADAT, ANWAR (Egyptian politician) 12 / 25 / 1918 CAPRICORN
SADE, MARQUIS DE (writer) 6 / 2 / 1740 GEMINI
SAGAN, FRANÇOISE (writer) 6 / 21 / 1935 CANCER
SAHL, MORT (comedian) 5 / 11 / 1927 TAURUS
SAINT, EVA MARIE (actress) 7 / 4 / 1924 CANCER
ST. CLAIR, JAMES D. (lawyer) 4 / 14 / 1920 ARIES
SAINT-EXUPERY, ANTOINE DE (writer) 6 / 29 / 1900 CANCER
ST. JOHN, JILL (actress) 4 / 19 / 1940 ARIES
SAINT LAURENT, YVES (fashion designer) 8 / 1 / 1936 LEO
SAINT-SAENS, CAMILLE (composer) 10 / 9 / 1835 LIBRA
SAINT-SIMON, DUC DE (courtier) 1 / 15 / 1675 CAPRICORN
SAINT-SUBBER, ARNOLD (producer) 2 / 18 / 1918 AQUARIUS/PISCES
SAINTE-MARIE, BUFFY (singer) 2 / 20 / 1941 PISCES
SAKI (writer) 12 / 18 / 1870 SAGITTARIUS
SAKS, GENE (director) 11 / 8 / 1921 SCORPIO
SALES, SOUPY (TV personality) 1 / 8 / 1926 CAPRICORN
SALIERI, ANTONIO (composer) 8 / 18 / 1750 LEO
SALINGER, J. D. (writer) 1 / 1 / 1919 CAPRICORN
SALINGER, PIERRE (government official) 6 / 14 / 1925 GEMINI
SALK, JONAS (epidemiologist) 10 / 28 / 1914 SCORPIO
SALT, JENNIFER (actress) 9 / 4 / 1944 VIRGO
SALWITZ, DAVID "MAGIC DICK" (rock musician) 5 / 13 / 1945
    TAURUS
SALZEDO, CARLOS (harpist) 4 / 6 / 1885 ARIES
SAMARAS, LUCAS (artist) 9 / 14 / 1936 VIRGO
SAND, GEORGE (writer) 7 / 1 / 1804 CANCER
SANDBURG, CARL (writer) 1 / 6 / 1878 CAPRICORN
SANDEAU, JULES (writer) 2 / 19 / 1811 AQUARIUS/PISCES
SANDERS, "COLONEL" HARLAND (restaurateur) 9 / 19 / 1890 VIRGO
SANDERS, GEORGE (actor) 7 / 3 / 1906 CANCER
SANDS, DIANA (actress) 8 / 22 / 1934 LEO
SANDS, DOROTHY (actress) 3 / 5 / 1893 PISCES
SANDS, TOMMY (singer) 8 / 27 / 1937 VIRGO

SCHWARTZ, STEPHEN (composer and lyricist) 3 / 6 / 1948 PISCES
SCHWARZKOPF, ELISABETH (soprano) 12 / 9 / 1915 SAGITTARIUS
SCHWEITZER, ALBERT (humanitarian) 1 / 14 / 1875 CAPRICORN
SCIUTTI, GRAZIELLA (soprano) 4 / 17 / 1932 ARIES
SCOFIELD, PAUL (actor) 1 / 21 / 1922 AQUARIUS
SCOPES, JOHN THOMAS (teacher) 8 / 3 / 1900 LEO
SCOTT, DAVID R. (astronaut) 6 / 6 / 1932 GEMINI
SCOTT, GEORGE C. (actor) 10 / 18 / 1927 LIBRA
SCOTT, GORDON (actor) 8 / 3 / 1927 LEO
SCOTT, HAROLD (actor) 9 / 6 / 1935 VIRGO
SCOTT, HUGH (politician) 11 / 11 / 1900 SCORPIO
SCOTT, LIZABETH (actress) 9 / 29 / 1922 LIBRA
SCOTT, MARTHA (actress) 9 / 22 / 1914 VIRGO
SCOTT, RANDOLPH (actor) 1 / 23 / 1903 AQUARIUS
SCOTT, WALTER (novelist) 8 / 15 / 1771 LEO
SCOTT, ZACHARY (actor) 2 / 21 / 1914 PISCES
SCOTT-MONCRIEFF, C. K. M. (translator) 9 / 25 / 1889 LIBRA
SCOTTI, ANTONIO (baritone) 1 / 25 / 1866 AQUARIUS
SCOTTO, RENATA (soprano) 2 / 24 / 1934 PISCES
SCOURBY, ALEXANDER (actor) 11 / 13 / 1913 SCORPIO
SCRANTON, WILLIAM (politician) 7 / 19 / 1917 CANCER
SCRIABIN, ALEXANDER (composer) 1 / 10 / 1872 CAPRICORN
SCRIBE, EUGENE (playwright) 12 / 24 / 1791 CAPRICORN
SCRIBNER, CHARLES, JR. (publisher) 7 / 13 / 1921 CANCER
SCRUGGS, EARL (country singer) 1 / 6 / 1924 CAPRICORN
SEARS, RICHARD WARREN (merchant) 12 / 7 / 1863 SAGITTARIUS
SEAVER, TOM (baseball player) 11 / 17 / 1944 SCORPIO
SEBERG, JEAN (actress) 11 / 13 / 1938 SCORPIO
SEEFRIED, IRMGARD (soprano) 10 / 9 / 1919 LIBRA
SEEGER, PEGGY (folk singer) 6 / 17 / 1935 GEMINI
SEEGER, PETE (folk singer) 5 / 3 / 1919 TAURUS
SEGAL, ERICH (writer) 6 / 16 / 1937 GEMINI
SEGAL, GEORGE (actor) 2 / 13 / 1934 AQUARIUS
SEGAL, GEORGE (sculptor) 11 / 26 / 1924 SAGITTARIUS
SEGOVIA, ANDRES (guitarist) 2 / 18 / 1894 AQUARIUS/PISCES
SEIDL, ANTON (conductor) 5 / 7 / 1850 TAURUS
SELDES, MARIAN (actress) 8 / 23 / 1928 LEO/VIRGO
SELLERS, PETER (actor) 9 / 8 / 1925 VIRGO
SELWYN-CLARKE, SELWYN (physician) 12 / 17 / 1893 SAGITTARIUS
SELZNICK, DAVID O. (producer) 5 / 10 / 1902 TAURUS

SEMBRICH, MARCELLA (soprano) 2 / 15 / 1858 AQUARIUS
SENDAK, MAURICE (illustrator) 6 / 10 / 1928 GEMINI
SENNETT, MACK (film director and producer) 1 / 17 / 1880
    CAPRICORN
SEPHARIAL (astrologer) 3 / 20 / 1864 PISCES
SERAFIN, TULLIO (conductor) 12 / 8 / 1878 SAGITTARIUS
SERKIN, RUDOLF (pianist) 3 / 28 / 1903 ARIES
SERLING, ROD (writer) 12 / 25 / 1924 CAPRICORN
SERPICO, FRANK (plainclothesman) 4 / 14 / 1936 ARIES
SERRA, JUNIPERO (missionary) 11 / 24 / 1713 SAGITTARIUS
SERRANO, LUPE (ballet dancer) 12 / 7 / 1930 SAGITTARIUS
SERVICE, ROBERT WILLIAM (writer) 1 / 16 / 1874 CAPRICORN
SESSIONS, ROGER (composer) 12 / 28 / 1896 CAPRICORN
SETON, ERNEST THOMPSON (writer) 8 / 14 / 1860 LEO
SEURAT, GEORGES (painter) 12 / 2 / 1859 SAGITTARIUS
SEUSS, DR. (children's humorist) 3 / 2 / 1904 PISCES
SEVAREID, ERIC (writer) 11 / 26 / 1912 SAGITTARIUS
SEVIGNE, MARQUISE DE (writer) 2 / 5 / 1626 AQUARIUS
SEWARD, WILLIAM HENRY (government official) 5 / 16 / 1801
    TAURUS
SEYLER, ATHENE (actress) 5 / 31 / 1889 GEMINI
SEYMOUR, ANNE (actress) 9 / 11 / 1909 VIRGO
SHAFFER, ELAINE (flutist) 10 / 22 / 1925 LIBRA
SHAFFER, PETER (playwright) 5 / 15 / 1926 TAURUS
SHAHN, BEN (painter) 9 / 12 / 1898 VIRGO
SHAKESPEARE, WILLIAM (playwright) 5 / 3 / 1564 (baptismal date)
    TAURUS
SHANKAR, RAVI (sitarist) 4 / 7 / 1920 ARIES
SHARIF, OMAR (actor) 4 / 10 / 1932 ARIES
SHATNER, WILLIAM (actor) 3 / 22 / 1931 ARIES
SHAW, ARTIE (bandleader) 5 / 26 / 1910 GEMINI
SHAW, GEORGE BERNARD (writer) 7 / 26 / 1856 LEO
SHAW, IRWIN (writer) 2 / 27 / 1913 PISCES
SHAW, ROBERT (actor) 8 / 9 / 1927 LEO
SHAW, ROBERT (choral conductor) 4 / 30 / 1916 TAURUS
SHAW, WILBUR (auto racer) 10 / 31 / 1902 SCORPIO
SHAWN, DICK (comedian) 12 / 1 / 1929 SAGITTARIUS
SHAWN, TED (choreographer) 10 / 21 / 1891 LIBRA
SHAZAR, ZALMAN (Israeli politician) 10 / 6 / 1889 LIBRA
SHEARER, MOIRA (ballet dancer) 1 / 17 / 1926 CAPRICORN

SHEARER, NORMA (actress) 8 / 10 / 1904 LEO
SHEARING, GEORGE (jazz musician) 8 / 13 / 1919 LEO
SHEEN, FULTON (clergyman) 5 / 8 / 1895 TAURUS
SHEEN, MARTIN (actor) 8 / 3 / 1940 LEO
SHEFFIELD, JOHNNY (child actor) 4 / 11 / 1931 ARIES
SHELLEY, MARY (writer) 8 / 30 / 1797 VIRGO
SHELLEY, PERCY BYSSHE (poet) 8 / 4 / 1792 LEO
SHEPARD, ALAN (astronaut) 11 / 18 / 1923 SCORPIO
SHEPARD, E. H. (illustrator) 12 / 10 / 1879 SAGITTARIUS
SHEPHERD, JEAN (radio personality) 7 / 26 / 1923 LEO
SHERIDAN, ANN (actress) 2 / 21 / 1915 PISCES
SHERIDAN, RICHARD BRINSLEY (playwright) 11 / 4 / 1751 SCORPIO
SHERMAN, ALLAN (comedian) 11 / 30 / 1924 SAGITTARIUS
SHERMAN, WILLIAM (army officer) 2 / 8 / 1820 AQUARIUS
SHERWOOD, MADELEINE (actress) 11 / 13 / 1926 SCORPIO
SHERWOOD, ROBERT (playwright) 4 / 4 / 1896 ARIES
SHIRLEY, GEORGE (tenor) 4 / 18 / 1934 ARIES
SHOEMAKER, WILLIE (jockey) 8 / 19 / 1931 LEO
SHOLOKHOF, MIKHAIL (novelist) 5 / 24 / 1905 GEMINI
SHOR, TOOTS (restaurateur) 5 / 6 / 1905 TAURUS
SHORE, DINAH (singer) 3 / 1 / 1917 PISCES
SHORT, BOBBY (singer) 9 / 15 / 1924 VIRGO
SHOSTAKOVICH, DMITRI (composer) 9 / 26 / 1906 LIBRA
SHRINER, HERB (humorist) 5 / 29 / 1918 GEMINI
SHRIVER, SARGENT (politician) 11 / 9 / 1915 SCORPIO
SHULA, DON (football coach) 1 / 4 / 1930 CAPRICORN
SHULMAN, MAX (humorist) 3 / 14 / 1919 PISCES
SIBELIUS, JEAN (composer) 12 / 8 / 1865 SAGITTARIUS
SIBLEY, ANTOINETTE (ballet dancer) 2 / 27 / 1939 PISCES
SIDDONS, SARAH (actress) 7 / 5 / 1755 CANCER
SIDNEY, PHILIP (poet) 12 / 10 / 1554 SAGITTARIUS
SIDNEY, SYLVIA (actress) 8 / 8 / 1910 LEO
SIEGEL, BENJAMIN "BUGSY" (mobster) 2 / 28 / 1906 PISCES
SIEPI, CESARE (basso) 2 / 10 / 1923 AQUARIUS
SIGNORET, SIMONE (actress) 3 / 25 / 1921 ARIES
SIHANOUK OF CAMBODIA, KING 10 / 31 / 1922 SCORPIO
SILJA, ANJA (soprano) 4 / 7 / 1940 ARIES
SILLITOE, ALAN (writer) 3 / 4 / 1928 PISCES
SILLS, BEVERLY (soprano) 5 / 25 / 1929 GEMINI
SILVERA, FRANK (actor) 7 / 24 / 1914 LEO

SILVERS, PHIL (comedian) 5 / 11 / 1912 TAURUS
SIMENON, GEORGES (writer) 2 / 13 / 1903 AQUARIUS
SIMIONATO, GIULIETTA (mezzo-soprano) 12 / 15 / 1910 SAGITTARIUS
SIMMONS, "BUCKETFOOT" AL (baseball player) 5 / 22 / 1902
       TAURUS/GEMINI
SIMMONS, JEAN (actress) 1 / 31 / 1929 AQUARIUS
SIMON, CARLY (singer) 6 / 25 / 1945 CANCER
SIMON, JOHN (critic) 5 / 12 / 1925 TAURUS
SIMON, MICHEL (actor) 4 / 9 / 1895 ARIES
SIMON, NEIL (playwright) 7 / 4 / 1927 CANCER
SIMON, PAUL (singer) 11 / 15 / 1942 SCORPIO
SIMONE, NINA (singer) 2 / 21 / 1935 PISCES
SIMPSON, ADELE (fashion designer) 12 / 8 / 1903 SAGITTARIUS
SIMPSON, O. J. (football player) 7 / 9 / 1947 CANCER
SIMS, NAOMI (model and author) 3 / 30 / 1949 ARIES
SINATRA, FRANK (singer) 12 / 12 / 1917 SAGITTARIUS
SINATRA, NANCY (singer) 6 / 9 / 1940 GEMINI
SINCLAIR, UPTON (novelist) 9 / 20 / 1878 VIRGO
SINGER, ISAAC (inventor) 10 / 27 / 1811 SCORPIO
SINGER, ISAAC BASHEVIS (writer) 7 / 14 / 1904 CANCER
SIQUEIROS, DAVID ALFARO (painter) 12 / 29 / 1896 CAPRICORN
SIRICA, JOHN J. (jurist) 3 / 19 / 1904 PISCES
SITWELL, EDITH (writer) 9 / 7 / 1887 VIRGO
SITWELL, OSBERT (writer) 12 / 6 / 1892 SAGITTARIUS
SJOESTROEM, VICTOR (film director) 9 / 20 / 1879 VIRGO
SKELTON, RED (comedian) 7 / 18 / 1913 CANCER
SKIDMORE, LOUIS (architect) 4 / 8 / 1897 ARIES
SKINNER, B. F. (psychologist) 3 / 20 / 1904 PISCES
SKINNER, CORNELIA OTIS (actress) 5 / 30 / 1901 GEMINI
SLENCZYNSKA, RUTH (pianist) 1 / 15 / 1925 CAPRICORN
SLEZAK, LEO (tenor) 8 / 18 / 1875 LEO
SLEZAK, WALTER (actor) 5 / 3 / 1902 TAURUS
SLICK, GRACE (singer) 10 / 30 / 1939 SCORPIO
SLOAN, JOHN FRENCH (painter) 8 / 2 / 1871 LEO
SLOANE, EVERETT (actor) 10 / 1 / 1909 LIBRA
SMART, CHRISTOPHER (poet) 5 / 3 / 1722 TAURUS
SMETANA, BEDRICH (composer) 3 / 2 / 1824 PISCES
SMITH, ADAM (economist) 6 / 16 / 1723 GEMINI
SMITH, AL (politician) 12 / 30 / 1873 CAPRICORN
SMITH, ALEXIS (actress) 6 / 8 / 1921 GEMINI

SMITH, BESSIE (blues singer) 4 / 15 / 1898 ARIES
SMITH, BETTY (novelist) 12 / 15 / 1906 SAGITTARIUS
SMITH, CONNIE (singer) 8 / 14 / 1941 LEO
SMITH, DAVID (sculptor) 3 / 9 / 1906 PISCES
SMITH, HOWARD K. (newsman) 5 / 12 / 1914 TAURUS
SMITH, IAN DOUGLAS (Rhodesian politician) 4 / 8 / 1919 ARIES
SMITH, JOHN (actor) 3 / 6 / 1931 PISCES
SMITH, JOSEPH (Mormon leader) 12 / 23 / 1805 CAPRICORN
SMITH, KATE (singer) 5 / 1 / 1909 TAURUS
SMITH, KEELY (singer) 3 / 9 / 1935 PISCES
SMITH, KENT (actor) 3 / 19 / 1907 PISCES
SMITH, MAGGIE (actress) 12 / 28 / 1934 CAPRICORN
SMITH, MARGARET CHASE (politician) 12 / 14 / 1897 SAGITTARIUS
SMITH, OLIVER (stage designer) 2 / 13 / 1918 AQUARIUS
SMITH, RED (sportswriter) 9 / 25 / 1905 LIBRA
SMITH, ROGER (actor) 12 / 18 / 1932 SAGITTARIUS
SMOTHERS, DICK (comedian) 11 / 20 / 1938 SCORPIO
SMOTHERS, TOMMY (comedian) 2 / 2 / 1937 AQUARIUS
SNEAD, SAM (golfer) 5 / 27 / 1912 GEMINI
SNIDER, DUKE (baseball player) 9 / 19 / 1926 VIRGO
SNOW, C. P. (writer) 10 / 15 / 1905 LIBRA
SOCRATES (philosopher) 5 / 12 / 467 B.C. TAURUS
SOEDERSTROEM, ELISABETH (soprano) 5 / 7 / 1927 TAURUS
SOKOLOW, ANNA (choreographer) 2 / 9 / 1915 AQUARIUS
SOLERI, PAOLO (architect and urban planner) 6 / 21 / 1919
    GEMINI/CANCER
SOLOMON (pianist) 8 / 9 / 1902 LEO
SOLTI, GEORG (conductor) 10 / 21 / 1912 LIBRA
SOLZHENITSYN, ALEXANDER (writer) 12 / 11 / 1918 SAGITTARIUS
SOMMER, ELKE (actress) 11 / 5 / 1941 SCORPIO
SONDHEIM, STEPHEN (lyricist) 3 / 22 / 1930 ARIES
SONTAG, HENRIETTE (soprano) 1 / 3 / 1806 CAPRICORN
SONTAG, SUSAN (writer) 1 / 28 / 1933 AQUARIUS
SORENSON, THEODORE (historian) 5 / 8 / 1928 TAURUS
SOTHERN, ANN (actress) 1 / 22 / 1909 AQUARIUS
SOUEZ, INA (soprano) 5 / 12 / 1908 TAURUS
SOULAGES, PIERRE (painter) 12 / 24 / 1919 CAPRICORN
SOUSA, JOHN PHILIP (composer) 11 / 6 / 1854 SCORPIO
SOUTHERN, TERRY (writer) 5 / 1 / 1928 TAURUS
SOUZAY, GERARD (baritone) 12 / 8 / 1920 SAGITTARIUS

SOYER, RAPHAEL (painter) 12 / 25 / 1899 CAPRICORN
SPAAK, PAUL HENRI (Belgian statesman) 1 / 25 / 1899 AQUARIUS
SPAETH, SIGMUND (music critic) 4 / 10 / 1885 ARIES
SPAHN, WARREN (baseball player) 4 / 23 / 1921 TAURUS
SPASSKY, BORIS (chess player) 1 / 30 / 1937 AQUARIUS
SPECK, RICHARD (mass murderer) 12 / 6 / 1941 SAGITTARIUS
SPELLMAN, FRANCIS (clergyman) 5 / 4 / 1889 TAURUS
SPENCER, HERBERT (philosopher) 4 / 27 / 1820 TAURUS
SPENDER, STEPHEN (writer) 3 / 28 / 1909 ARIES
SPIEGEL, MOCHE JOSEPH, JR. (mail order merchant) 1 / 29 / 1901
     AQUARIUS
SPIEGEL, SAM (producer) 11 / 11 / 1904 SCORPIO
SPILLANE, MICKEY (writer) 3 / 9 / 1918 PISCES
SPINETTI, VICTOR (actor) 9 / 2 / 1933 VIRGO
SPINOZA, BARUCH (philosopher) 11 / 24 / 1632 SAGITTARIUS
SPITZ, MARK (swimmer) 2 / 10 / 1950 AQUARIUS
SPOCK, BENJAMIN (pediatrician) 5 / 2 / 1903 TAURUS
SPONTINI, GASPARO (composer) 11 / 14 / 1774 SCORPIO
SPRINGER, AXEL (publisher) 2 / 2 / 1912 AQUARIUS
SPYROPOULOS, JANNIS (artist) 3 / 12 / 1912 PISCES
SRI CHIMOY (guru) 8 / 27 / 1932 VIRGO
STACK, ROBERT (actor) 1 / 13 / 1919 CAPRICORN
STAEL, MME. DE (writer) 4 / 22 / 1766 TAURUS
STALIN, JOSEPH (dictator) 1 / 2 / 1880 CAPRICORN
STAMOS, THEODOROS (painter) 12 / 31 / 1922 CAPRICORN
STANISLAVSKY, KONSTANTIN (acting teacher) 1 / 17 / 1863
     CAPRICORN
STANKIEWICZ, RICHARD (sculptor) 10 / 18 / 1922 LIBRA
STANLEY, KIM (actress) 2 / 11 / 1925 AQUARIUS
STANS, MAURICE (government official) 3 / 22 / 1908 ARIES
STANTON, ELIZABETH CADY (feminist) 11 / 12 / 1815 SCORPIO
STANTON, FRANK (broadcasting executive) 3 / 20 / 1908 PISCES /
     ARIES
STANWYCK, BARBARA (actress) 7 / 16 / 1907 CANCER
STAPLETON, JEAN (actress) 1 / 19 / 1923 CAPRICORN
STAPLETON, MAUREEN (actress) 6 / 21 / 1925 GEMINI/CANCER
STARKER, JANOS (cellist) 7 / 5 / 1924 CANCER
STARKIE, WALTER (writer) 8 / 9 / 1894 LEO
STARR, BART (football player) 1 / 9 / 1934 CAPRICORN
STARR, BELLE (horse thief and fence) 2 / 5 / 1848 AQUARIUS

STARR, KAY (singer) 7 / 21 / 1922 CANCER
STARR, RINGO (rock musician) 7 / 7 / 1940 CANCER
STAUBACH, ROGER (football player) 2 / 5 / 1942 AQUARIUS
STEADMAN, CRAIG (music critic) 3 / 9 / 1946 PISCES
STEBER, ELEANOR (soprano) 7 / 17 / 1919 CANCER
STEELE, TOMMY (actor) 12 / 17 / 1936 SAGITTARIUS
STEEN, MARGUERITE (writer) 5 / 12 / 1894 TAURUS
STEFFENS, LINCOLN (writer) 4 / 6 / 1866 ARIES
STEICHEN, EDWARD (photographer) 3 / 27 / 1879 ARIES
STEIG, WILLIAM (cartoonist) 11 / 14 / 1925 SCORPIO
STEIGER, ROD (actor) 4 / 14 / 1925 ARIES
STEIN, GERTRUDE (writer) 2 / 3 / 1874 AQUARIUS
STEINBECK, JOHN (writer) 2 / 27 / 1902 PISCES
STEINBERG, DAVID (comedian) 8 / 9 / 1942 LEO
STEINBERG, SAUL (artist) 6 / 15 / 1914 GEMINI
STEINBERG, WILLIAM (conductor) 8 / 1 / 1899 LEO
STEINEM, GLORIA (feminist) 3 / 25 / 1935 ARIES
STEINER, MAX (composer) 5 / 10 / 1888 TAURUS
STELLA, ANTONIETTA (soprano) 3 / 15 / 1929 PISCES
STELLA, FRANK (painter) 5 / 12 / 1936 TAURUS
STENDHAL (writer) 1 / 23 / 1783 AQUARIUS
STENGEL, CASEY (baseball manager) 7 / 31 / 1891 LEO
STERLING, JAN (actress) 4 / 3 / 1923 ARIES
STERN, ISAAC (violinist) 7 / 21 / 1920 CANCER
STERNBERG, JOSEF VON (film director) 5 / 29 / 1894 GEMINI
STERNE, LAWRENCE (novelist) 12 / 5 / 1713 SAGITTARIUS
STEUBEN, FRIEDRICH VON (army officer) 9 / 17 / 1730 VIRGO
STEVENS, CAT (singer) 7 / 21 / 1948 CANCER
STEVENS, CONNIE (actress) 8 / 8 / 1938 LEO
STEVENS, GEORGE (film director) 12 / 18 / 1904 SAGITTARIUS
STEVENS, MARC (producer) 9 / 2 / 1945 VIRGO
STEVENS, MARK (actor) 12 / 13 / 1922 SAGITTARIUS
STEVENS, RISE (mezzo-soprano) 6 / 11 / 1913 GEMINI
STEVENS, WALLACE (poet) 10 / 2 / 1879 LIBRA
STEVENSON, ADLAI (politician) 2 / 5 / 1900 AQUARIUS
STEVENSON, ADLAI, III (politician) 10 / 10 / 1930 LIBRA
STEVENSON, ROBERT LOUIS (writer) 11 / 13 / 1850 SCORPIO
STEWART, ELLEN (producer) 10 / 7 / 1931 LIBRA
STEWART, JAMES (actor) 5 / 20 / 1908 TAURUS
STEWART, ROD (singer) 1 / 10 / 1945 CAPRICORN

STEWART, THOMAS (baritone) 8 / 29 / 1928 VIRGO
STICH-RANDALL, TERESA (soprano) 12 / 24 / 1927 CAPRICORN
STICKNEY, DOROTHY (actress) 6 / 21 / 1900 GEMINI/CANCER
STIEDRY, FRITZ (conductor) 10 / 11 / 1883 LIBRA
STIEGLITZ, ALFRED (photographer) 1 / 1 / 1864 CAPRICORN
STIGNANI, EBE (mezzo-soprano) 7 / 10 / 1907 CANCER
STILLS, STEPHEN (rock musician) 1 / 3 / 1945 CAPRICORN
STOCKHAUSEN, KARLHEINZ (composer) 8 / 22 / 1928 LEO
STOCKTON, FRANK R. (writer) 4 / 5 / 1834 ARIES
STOCKWELL, DEAN (actor) 3 / 5 / 1936 PISCES
STOKES, CARL (politician) 6 / 21 / 1927 GEMINI/CANCER
STOKOWSKI, LEOPOLD (conductor) 4 / 18 / 1882 ARIES
STOLZ, TERESA (soprano) 6 / 2 / 1834 GEMINI
STONE, EDWARD DURELL (architect) 3 / 9 / 1902 PISCES
STONE, I. F. (journalist) 12 / 24 / 1907 CAPRICORN
STONE, IRVING (writer) 7 / 14 / 1903 CANCER
STONE, LUCY (feminist) 8 / 13 / 1818 LEO
STONE, MILBURN (actor) 7 / 5 / 1904 CANCER
STONE, SLY (rock musician) 3 / 15 / 1944 PISCES
STOOKEY, PAUL (singer) 11 / 30 / 1937 SAGITTARIUS
STOPPARD, TOM (playwright) 7 / 3 / 1937 CANCER
STOREY, DAVID (writer) 7 / 13 / 1933 CANCER
STORM, GALE (actress) 4 / 5 / 1922 ARIES
STOUT, REX (writer) 12 / 1 / 1886 SAGITTARIUS
STOWE, HARRIET BEECHER (novelist) 6 / 14 / 1811 GEMINI
STRACCIARI, RICCARDO (baritone) 6 / 26 / 1875 CANCER
STRACHEY, LYTTON (writer) 3 / 1 / 1880 PISCES
STRAND, PAUL (photographer) 10 / 16 / 1890 LIBRA
STRASBERG, LEE (acting teacher) 11 / 17 / 1901 SCORPIO
STRASBERG, SUSAN (actress) 5 / 22 / 1938 GEMINI
STRAUSS, JOHANN, JR. (composer) 10 / 25 / 1825 SCORPIO
STRAUSS, RICHARD (composer) 6 / 11 / 1864 GEMINI
STRAVINSKY, IGOR (composer) 6 / 17 / 1882 GEMINI
STREICH, RITA (soprano) 12 / 18 / 1926 SAGITTARIUS
STREISAND, BARBRA (singer) 4 / 24 / 1942 TAURUS
STREPPONI, GIUSEPPINA (soprano) 9 / 8 / 1815 VIRGO
STRINDBERG, AUGUST (playwright) 1 / 22 / 1849 AQUARIUS
STRITCH, ELAINE (actress) 2 / 2 / 1925 AQUARIUS
STROHEIM, ERICH VON (actor and film director) 9 / 22 / 1885 VIRGO
STRONG, ANNA LOUISE (journalist) 11 / 24 / 1885 SAGITTARIUS

STROUSE, CHARLES (composer) 6 / 7 / 1928 GEMINI
STRUDWICK, SHEPPERD (actor) 9 / 22 / 1907 VIRGO
STRUTHERS, SALLY (actress) 7 / 28 / 1948 LEO
STUART, CHARLES (pretender) 1 / 11 / 1721 CAPRICORN
STUART, GILBERT (painter) 12 / 3 / 1755 SAGITTARIUS
STUART, JESSE (writer) 8 / 8 / 1907 LEO
STUART, LYLE (publisher) 8 / 11 / 1922 LEO
STUBBS, GEORGE (painter) 9 / 4 / 1724 VIRGO
STURGES, PRESTON (playwright and film director) 8 / 29 / 1898
    VIRGO
STYNE, JULE (composer) 12 / 31 / 1905 CAPRICORN
STYRON, WILLIAM (novelist) 6 / 11 / 1925 GEMINI
SUGGS, LOUISE (golfer) 9 / 7 / 1923 VIRGO
SULIOTIS, ELENA (soprano) 5 / 12 / 1943 TAURUS
SULLAVAN, MARGARET (actress) 5 / 16 / 1911 TAURUS
SULLIVAN, ANNIE (teacher) 4 / 14 / 1866 ARIES
SULLIVAN, ARTHUR (composer) 5 / 13 / 1842 TAURUS
SULLIVAN, BARRY (actor) 8 / 29 / 1912 VIRGO
SULLIVAN, ED (TV personality) 9 / 28 / 1902 LIBRA
SULLIVAN, JOHN L. (boxer) 10 / 15 / 1858 LIBRA
SULLIVAN, LOUIS (architect) 9 / 3 / 1856 VIRGO
SULZBERGER, ARTHUR OCHS (publisher) 2 / 5 / 1926 AQUARIUS
SUMAC, YMA (singer) 9 / 10 / 1927 VIRGO
SUN YAT-SEN (revolutionary leader) 11 / 12 / 1866 SCORPIO
SUNDAY, BILLY (evangelist) 11 / 18 / 1862 SCORPIO
SUPERVIA, CONCHITA (mezzo-soprano) 12 / 9/ 1895 SAGITTARIUS
SUPPE, FRANZ VON (composer) 4 / 18 / 1819 ARIES
SUSANN, JACQUELINE (actress and novelist) 8 / 20 / 1921 LEO
SUSSKIND, DAVID (producer) 12 / 19 / 1920 SAGITTARIUS
SUTHERLAND, DONALD (actor) 7 / 17 / 1934 CANCER
SUTHERLAND, GRAHAM VIVIAN (painter) 8 / 24 / 1903 LEO/VIRGO
SUTHERLAND, JOAN (soprano) 11 / 7 / 1926 SCORPIO
SUZUKI, D. T. (Buddhist scholar) 10 / 18 / 1870 LIBRA
SUZUKI, PAT (singer) 9 / 23 / 1934 VIRGO/LIBRA
SVANHOLM, SET (tenor) 9 / 2 / 1904 VIRGO
SVOBODA, LUDWIK (Czech politician) 11 / 25 / 1895 SAGITTARIUS
SWANN, DONALD (comedian) 9 / 30 / 1923 LIBRA
SWANSON, GLORIA (actress) 3 / 27 / 1899 ARIES
SWARTHOUT, GLADYS (mezzo-soprano) 12 / 25 / 1904 CAPRICORN
SWEDENBORG, EMANUEL (philosopher) 2 / 8 / 1688 AQUARIUS

SWENSON, INGA (actress) 12 / 29 / 1934 CAPRICORN
SWIFT, JONATHAN (writer) 12 / 10 / 1667 SAGITTARIUS
SWINBURNE, ALGERNON (poet) 4 / 5 / 1837 ARIES
SYDOW, MAX VON (actor) 4 / 10 / 1929 ARIES
SYLVESTER, WILLIAM (actor) 1 / 31 / 1922 AQUARIUS
SYMINGTON, STUART (politician) 6 / 26 / 1901 CANCER
SYNGE, J. M. (playwright) 4 / 16 / 1871 ARIES
SZELL, GEORGE (conductor) 6 / 7 / 1897 GEMINI
SZERYNG, HENRYK (violinist) 9 / 22 / 1921 VIRGO
SZIGETI, JOSEPH (violinist) 9 / 5 / 1892 VIRGO

TABORI, KRISTOFFER (actor) 8 / 4 / 1952 LEO
TADDEI, GIUSEPPE (baritone) 6 / 26 / 1916 CANCER
TAFT, ROBERT, JR. (politician) 3 / 26 / 1917 ARIES
TAFT, WILLIAM HOWARD (politician) 9 / 15 / 1857 VIRGO
TAGORE, RABINDRANATH (poet) 5 / 7 / 1861 TAURUS
TALBOT, LYLE (actor) 2 / 8 / 1904 AQUARIUS
TALLCHIEF, MARIA (ballet dancer) 1 / 24 / 1925 AQUARIUS
TALLEYRAND, CHARLES DE (French statesman) 2 / 2 / 1754
     AQUARIUS
TALMADGE, HERMAN E. (politician) 8 / 9 / 1913 LEO
TAMAGNO, FRANCESCO (tenor) 12 / 28 / 1850 CAPRICORN
TAMBLYN, RUSS (actor) 12 / 30 / 1934 CAPRICORN
TANDY, JESSICA (actress) 6 / 7 / 1909 GEMINI
TARKENTON, FRAN (football player) 2 / 3 / 1940 AQUARIUS
TARKINGTON, BOOTH (writer) 7 / 29 / 1869 LEO
TASSO, TORQUATO (poet) 3 / 21 / 1544 PISCES/ARIES
TATE, SHARON (actress) 1 / 24 / 1943 AQUARIUS
TATI, JACQUES (film maker) 10 / 9 / 1908 LIBRA
TAUBER, RICHARD (tenor) 5 / 16 / 1892 TAURUS
TAUBMAN, HOWARD (critic) 7 / 4 / 1907 CANCER
TAVEL, RONALD (writer) 5 / 17 / 1941 TAURUS
TAYLOR, DEEMS (composer) 12 / 22 / 1885 SAGITTARIUS/CAPRICORN
TAYLOR, ELIZABETH (actress) 2 / 27 / 1932 PISCES
TAYLOR, JAMES (singer) 3 / 12 / 1948 PISCES
TAYLOR, KENT (actor) 5 / 11 / 1907 TAURUS
TAYLOR, LAURETTE (actress) 4 / 1 / 1884 ARIES
TAYLOR, MAXWELL (army officer) 8 / 26 / 1901 VIRGO
TAYLOR, MICK (rock musician) 1 / 17 / 1948 CAPRICORN

TAYLOR, PAUL (choreographer) 7 / 29 / 1930 LEO

TAYLOR, ROBERT (actor) 8 / 5 / 1911 LEO

TAYLOR, ROD (actor) 1 / 11 / 1930 CAPRICORN

TAYLOR, ZACHARY (politician) 11 / 24 / 1784 SAGITTARIUS

TAYLOR-YOUNG, LEIGH (actress) 1 / 25 / 1945 AQUARIUS

TCHAIKOVSKY, PETER ILYICH (composer) 5 / 7 / 1840 TAURUS

TCHERINA, LUDMILA (ballet dancer) 10 / 10 / 1924 LIBRA

TEAGARDEN, JACK (jazz musician) 8 / 20 / 1905 LEO

TEALE, EDWIN WAY (naturalist) 6 / 2 / 1899 GEMINI

TEASDALE, SARA (poet) 8 / 8 / 1884 LEO

TEBALDI, RENATA (soprano) 1 / 2 / 1922 CAPRICORN

TEILHARD DE CHARDIN, PIERRE (philosopher) 5 / 1 / 1881 TAURUS

TELEMANN, GEORG PHILIPP (composer) 3 / 14 / 1681 PISCES

TELLER, EDWARD (physicist) 1 / 15 / 1908 CAPRICORN

TENNIEL, JOHN (illustrator) 2 / 28 / 1820 PISCES

TENNYSON, ALFRED, LORD (poet) 8 / 6 / 1809 LEO

TER-ARUTUNIAN, ROUBEN (stage designer) 7 / 24 / 1920 LEO

TERESA OF AVILA, ST. (mystic) 4 / 7 / 1515 ARIES

TERESHKOVA, VALENTINA (cosmonaut) 3 / 6 / 1937 PISCES

TERHORST, JERALD F. (journalist) 7 / 11 / 1922 CANCER

TERKEL, STUDS (interviewer) 5 / 16 / 1912 TAURUS

TERRY, ELLEN (actress) 2 / 27 / 1848 PISCES

TERRY, SONNY (blues musician) 10 / 24 / 1911 LIBRA/SCORPIO

TERRY-THOMAS (actor) 7 / 14 / 1911 CANCER

TESLA, NICOLA (inventor) 7 / 10 / 1856 CANCER

TETLEY, GLEN (choreographer) 2 / 3 / 1926 AQUARIUS

TETRAZZINI, LUISA (soprano) 6 / 29 / 1871 CANCER

TEYTE, MAGGIE (soprano) 4 / 17 / 1889 ARIES

THACKERAY, WILLIAM MAKEPEACE (writer) 7 / 18 / 1811 CANCER

THANT, U (UN official) 1 / 22 / 1909 AQUARIUS

THEBOM, BLANCHE (mezzo-soprano) 9 / 19 / 1919 VIRGO

THEODORAKIS, MIKIS (composer) 7 / 29 / 1925 LEO

THIEU, NGUYEN VAN (Vietnamese politician) 4 / 5 / 1923 ARIES

THOMAS, AMBROISE (composer) 8 / 5 / 1811 LEO

THOMAS, DANNY (comedian) 1 / 6 / 1914 CAPRICORN

THOMAS, DYLAN (poet) 10 / 27 / 1914 SCORPIO

THOMAS, JESS (tenor) 4 / 8 / 1927 ARIES

THOMAS, LOWELL (commentator) 4 / 6 / 1892 ARIES

THOMAS, MARLO (actress) 11 / 21 / 1938 SCORPIO

THOMAS, MICHAEL TILSON (conductor) 12 / 21 / 1944 SAGITTARIUS/ CAPRICORN

THOMAS, NORMAN (socialist) 11 / 20 / 1884 SCORPIO

THOMAS, RAY (rock musician) 12 / 29 / ? CAPRICORN

THOMAS, RICHARD (actor) 6 / 13 / 1951 GEMINI

THOMPSON, HANK (singer) 9 / 3 / 1925 VIRGO

THOMPSON, MARSHALL (actor) 11 / 27 / 1925 SAGITTARIUS

THOMPSON, SADA (actress) 9 / 27 / 1929 LIBRA

THOMSON, VIRGIL (composer) 11 / 25 / 1896 SAGITTARIUS

THORBORG, KERSTIN (contralto) 5 / 19 / 1896 TAURUS

THOREAU, HENRY DAVID (writer) 7 / 12 / 1817 CANCER

THORNDIKE, SYBIL (actress) 10 / 24 / 1882 LIBRA/SCORPIO

THORPE, JIM (football player) 5 / 28 / 1888 GEMINI

THULIN, INGRID (actress) 1 / 27 / 1929 AQUARIUS

THURBER, JAMES (humorist) 12 / 8 / 1894 SAGITTARIUS

THURMOND, STROM (politician) 12 / 5 / 1902 SAGITTARIUS

TIBBETT, LAWRENCE (baritone) 11 / 16 / 1896 SCORPIO

TIBERIUS OF ROME, EMPEROR 11 / 14 / 42 B.C. SCORPIO

TIEPOLO, GIAMBATTISTA (painter) 3 / 5 / 1696 PISCES

TIERNEY, GENE (actress) 11 / 20 / 1920 SCORPIO

TIFFANY, LOUIS C. (jeweler) 2 / 18 / 1848 AQUARIUS/PISCES

TIFFIN, PAMELA (actress) 10 / 13 / 1942 LIBRA

TIJERINA, REIES LOPEZ (Chicano leader) 9 / 21 / 1926 VIRGO

TILDEN, BILL (tennis player) 2 / 10 / 1893 AQUARIUS

TILLICH, PAUL (theologian) 8 / 20 / 1886 LEO

TILLIS, MEL (country singer) 8 / 8 / 1932 LEO

TILLSTROM, BURR (puppeteer) 10 / 13 / 1917 LIBRA

TIM, TINY (singer) 4 / 12 / 1930 ARIES

TINTORETTO (painter) 9 / 26 / 1518 LIBRA

TIOMKIN, DMITRI (composer) 5 / 10 / 1899 TAURUS

TIPPETT, MICHAEL (composer) 1 / 2 / 1905 CAPRICORN

TITO, MARSHAL (Yugoslavian politician) 5 / 25 / 1892 GEMINI

TITTLE, Y. A. (football player) 10 / 24 / 1926 LIBRA/SCORPIO

TOBEY, MARK (artist) 12 / 11 / 1890 SAGITTARIUS

TOCQUEVILLE, ALEXIS DE (writer) 7 / 29 / 1805 LEO

TODD, MIKE, JR. (producer) 10 / 18 / 1929 LIBRA

TODD, RICHARD (actor) 6 / 11 / 1919 GEMINI

TODD, THELMA (actress) 7 / 29 / 1905 LEO

TOKLAS, ALICE B. (cook) 4 / 30 / 1877 TAURUS

TOKYO ROSE (propagandist) 7 / 4 / 1916 CANCER
TOLKEIN, J. R. R. (writer) 1 / 3 / 1892 CAPRICORN
TOLSTOY, LEO (writer) 9 / 9 / 1828 VIRGO
TOMLIN, LILY (comedienne) 9 / 1 / 1936 VIRGO
TONE, FRANCHOT (actor) 2 / 27 / 1903 PISCES
TOPOLSKI, FELIKS (painter) 8 / 14 / 1907 LEO
TORME, MEL (singer) 9 / 13 / 1925 VIRGO
TORN, RIP (actor) 2 / 6 / 1931 AQUARIUS
TORRE, JOE (baseball player) 7 / 18 / 1940 CANCER
TOSCANINI, ARTURO (conductor) 3 / 25 / 1867 ARIES
TOULOUSE-LAUTREC, HENRI DE (painter) 11 / 24 / 1864 SAGITTARIUS
TOUREL, JENNIE (mezzo-soprano) 6 / 22 / 1910 GEMINI/CANCER
TOWER, JOHN (politician) 9 / 29 / 1925 LIBRA
TOWNSHEND, PETER (rock musician) 5 / 19 / 1945 TAURUS
TOYNBEE, ARNOLD (historian) 4 / 14 / 1889 ARIES
TOZZI, GIORGIO (basso) 1 / 8 / 1923 CAPRICORN
TRACY, SPENCER (actor) 4 / 5 / 1900 ARIES
TRAPP, MARIA (folk singer) 1 / 26 / 1905 AQUARIUS
TRAUBEL, HELEN (soprano) 6 / 20 / 1899 GEMINI
TRAVELL, JANET (physician) 12 / 17 / 1901 SAGITTARIUS
TRAVERS, BILL (actor) 1 / 3 / 1922 CAPRICORN
TRAVERS, MARY (singer) 11 / 9 / 1936 SCORPIO
TREE, MARIETTA (political worker) 4 / 12 / 1917 ARIES
TREVINO, LEE (golfer) 12 / 1 / 1939 SAGITTARIUS
TREVOR, CLAIRE (actress) 3 / 8 / 1912 PISCES
TRIGERE, PAULINE (fashion designer) 11 / 4 / 1912 SCORPIO
TRILLING, LIONEL (writer) 7 / 4 / 1905 CANCER
TRINTIGNANT, JEAN-LOUIS (actor) 12 / 11 / 1930 SAGITTARIUS
TROLLOPE, ANTHONY (novelist) 4 / 24 / 1815 TAURUS
TROTSKY, LEON (revolutionary) 11 / 7 / 1879 SCORPIO
TROUT, ROBERT (newsman) 10 / 15 / 1908 LIBRA
TRUCKS, BUTCH (rock musician) 5 / 11 / 1947 TAURUS
TRUDEAU, PIERRE ELLIOTT (Canadian politician) 10 / 18 / 1919
    LIBRA
TRUEX, ERNEST (actor) 9 / 19 / 1890 VIRGO
TRUFFAUT, FRANÇOIS (film maker) 2 / 6 / 1932 AQUARIUS
TRUMAN, BESS (first lady) 2 / 13 / 1885 AQUARIUS
TRUMAN, HARRY S (politician) 5 / 8 / 1884 TAURUS
TRUMAN, MARGARET (soprano) 2 / 17 / 1924 AQUARIUS
TRUMBO, DALTON (screenwriter) 12 / 9 / 1905 SAGITTARIUS

TRUNGPA, CHOEGYAM (lama) 2 / 4 / 1939 AQUARIUS
TRYON, TOM (actor) 1 / 14 / 1926 CAPRICORN
TUBB, ERNEST (country singer) 2 / 9 / 1914 AQUARIUS
TUCHMAN, BARBARA (historian) 1 / 30 / 1912 AQUARIUS
TUCKER, FORREST (actor) 2 / 12 / 1919 AQUARIUS
TUCKER, RICHARD (tenor) 8 / 28 / 1913 VIRGO
TUCKER, SOPHIE (actress) 1 / 13 / 1884 CAPRICORN
TUNE, TOMMY (actor) 2 / 28 / 1939 PISCES
TUNNEY, GENE (boxer) 5 / 25 / 1897 GEMINI
TURCOTTE, RON (jockey) 7 / 22 / 1941 CANCER/LEO
TURECK, ROSALYN (pianist) 12 / 14 / 1914 SAGITTARIUS
TURGENEV, IVAN (novelist) 11 / 9 / 1818 SCORPIO
TURINA, JOAQUIN (composer) 12 / 9 / 1882 SAGITTARIUS
TURNER, IKE (singer) 11 / 5 / 1931 SCORPIO
TURNER, J. M. W. (painter) 4 / 23 / 1775 TAURUS
TURNER, LANA (actress) 2 / 8 / 1920 AQUARIUS
TURNER, TINA (singer) 11 / 26 / 1939 SAGITTARIUS
TUSHINGHAM, RITA (actress) 3 / 14 / 1942 PISCES
TUTIN, DOROTHY (actress) 4 / 8 / 1930 ARIES
TWAIN, MARK (writer) 11 / 30 / 1835 SAGITTARIUS
TWEED, WILLIAM MARCY "BOSS" (politician) 4 / 3 / 1823 ARIES
TWIGGY (model) 9 / 19 / 1949 VIRGO
TYLER, JOHN (politician) 3 / 29 / 1790 ARIES
TYNAN, KENNETH (critic) 4 / 2 / 1927 ARIES
TYSON, CICELY (actress) 12 / 19 / 1938 SAGITTARIUS
TYSON, IAN (singer) 9 / 25 / 1933 LIBRA
TYSON, SYLVIA (singer) 9 / 19 / 1940 VIRGO

UDALL, STEWART (government official) 1 / 31 / 1920 AQUARIUS
UGGAMS, LESLIE (singer) 5 / 25 / 1943 GEMINI
UHDE, HERMANN (baritone) 7 / 20 / 1914 CANCER
ULANOVA, GALINA (ballet dancer) 1 / 10 / 1910 CAPRICORN
ULBRICHT, WALTER (German politician) 6 / 30 / 1893 CANCER
ULLMANN, LIV (actress) 12 / 19 / 1938 SAGITTARIUS
UMEKO, MIYOSHI (actress) 4 / 3 / 1929 ARIES
UNAMUNO Y JUGO, MIGUEL DE (philosopher) 9 / 29 / 1864 LIBRA
UNDSET, SIGRID (novelist) 5 / 20 / 1882 TAURUS
UNITAS, JOHNNY (football player) 5 / 7 / 1933 TAURUS
UNRUH, JESSE (politician) 9 / 30 / 1922 LIBRA

UNTERMEYER, LOUIS (writer) 10 / 1 / 1885 LIBRA
UPDIKE, JOHN (novelist) 3 / 18 / 1932 PISCES
URIS, LEON (novelist) 8 / 3 / 1924 LEO
USTINOV, PETER (actor) 4 / 16 / 1921 ARIES
UTRILLO, MAURICE (painter) 12 / 25 / 1883 CAPRICORN

VACCARO, BRENDA (actress) 11 / 18 / 1939 SCORPIO
VADIM, ROGER (film director) 1 / 26 / 1928 AQUARIUS
VALACHI, JOSEPH (mobster) 9 / 22 / 1904 VIRGO
VALENTI, JACK (film executive) 9 / 5 / 1921 VIRGO
VALENTINO (fashion designer) 5 / 11 / 1932 TAURUS
VALENTINO, RUDOLPH (actor) 5 / 6 / 1895 TAURUS
VALERY, PAUL (poet) 10 / 30 / 1871 SCORPIO
VALLEE, RUDY (singer) 7 / 28 / 1901 LEO
VALLETTI, CESARE (tenor) 12 / 18 / 1922 SAGITTARIUS
VALLI, ALIDA (actress) 5 / 31 / 1921 GEMINI
VAN ALLEN, JAMES (physicist) 9 / 7 / 1914 VIRGO
VAN BUREN, ABIGAIL (advice columnist) 7 / 4 / 1918 CANCER
VAN BUREN, MARTIN (politician) 12 / 5 / 1782 SAGITTARIUS
VANCE, NINA (director) 10 / 22 / 1915 LIBRA
VAN DE GRAAFF, ROBERT (physicist) 12 / 20 / 1901 SAGITTARIUS
VANDERBILT, AMY (etiquette adviser) 7 / 22 / 1908 CANCER
VANDERBILT, CORNELIUS (financier) 5 / 27 / 1794 GEMINI
VANDERBILT, GLORIA (artist and socialite) 2 / 20 / 1924 PISCES
VAN DEVERE, TRISH (actress) 3 / 9 / 1945 PISCES
VAN DOREN, CHARLES (academician) 2 / 12 / 1926 AQUARIUS
VAN DOREN, MAMIE (actress) 2 / 6 / 1933 AQUARIUS
VAN DOREN, MARK (writer) 6 / 13 / 1894 GEMINI
VAN DYCK, ANTHONY (painter) 3 / 22 / 1599 ARIES
VAN DYKE, DICK (actor) 12 / 13 / 1925 SAGITTARIUS
VAN FLEET, JO (actress) 12 / 30 / 1919 CAPRICORN
VAN GOGH, VINCENT (painter) 3 / 30 / 1853 ARIES
VAN HORNE, HARRIET (columnist) 5 / 17 / 1920 TAURUS
VAN LOEN, ALFRED (sculptor) 9 / 11 / 1924 VIRGO
VAN PATTEN, JOYCE (actress) 3 / 9 / 1934 PISCES
VAN PEEBLES, MELVIN (writer and producer) 8 / 21 / 1932 LEO
VAN RONK, DAVE (jazz musician) 6 / 30 / 1936 CANCER
VAN VOOREN, MONIQUE (actress) 3 / 17 / 1938 PISCES
VARDA, AGNES (film director) 5 / 30 / 1928 GEMINI

VARESE, EDGARD (composer) 12 / 22 / 1885
SAGITTARIUS/CAPRICORN
VARNAY, ASTRID (soprano) 4 / 25 / 1918 TAURUS
VASARI, GIORGIO (artist) 8 / 9 / 1511 LEO
VASARY, TAMAS (pianist) 8 / 11 / 1933 LEO
VAUGHAN, HENRY (poet) 4 / 27 / 1622 TAURUS
VAUGHAN, SAMUEL S. (publisher) 8 / 3 / 1928 LEO
VAUGHAN, SARAH (jazz singer) 3 / 27 / 1924 ARIES
VAUGHAN WILLIAMS, RALPH (composer) 10 / 12 / 1872 LIBRA
VAUGHN, ROBERT (actor) 11 / 22 / 1932 SCORPIO/SAGITTARIUS
VEASEY, JOSEPHINE (mezzo-soprano) 7 / 10 / 1930 CANCER
VEBLEN, THORSTEIN (economist) 7 / 30 / 1857 LEO
VEE, BOBBY (singer) 4 / 30 / 1943 TAURUS
VEECK, BILL (baseball team president) 2 / 9 / 1914 AQUARIUS
VEGA, LOPE DE (playwright) 12 / 5 / 1562 SAGITTARIUS
VELAZQUEZ (painter) 6 / 6 / 1599 GEMINI
VELIKOVSKY, IMMANUEL (writer) 6 / 10 / 1895 GEMINI
VENTURI, KEN (golfer) 5 / 15 / 1931 TAURUS
VERA-ELLEN (actress) 2 / 16 / 1926 AQUARIUS
VERDI, GIUSEPPE (composer) 10 / 10 / 1813 LIBRA
VERDON, GWEN (actress) 1 / 13 / 1925 CAPRICORN
VERDY, VIOLETTE (ballet dancer) 12 / 1 / 1933 SAGITTARIUS
VERGA, GIOVANNI (writer) 8 / 31 / 1840 VIRGO
VERLAINE, PAUL (poet) 3 / 30 / 1844 ARIES
VERMEER, JAN (painter) 11 / 10 / 1632 SCORPIO
VERNE, JULES (writer) 2 / 8 / 1828 AQUARIUS
VERRETT, SHIRLEY (mezzo-soprano) 5 / 31 / 1931 GEMINI
VESALIUS, ANDREAS (anatomist) 1 / 10 / 1515 CAPRICORN
VESCO, ROBERT (financier) 12 / 4 / 1935 SAGITTARIUS
VESPUCCI, AMERIGO (explorer) 3 / 18 / 1454 PISCES
VIARDOT-GARCIA, PAULINE (mezzo-soprano) 7 / 18 / 1821 CANCER
VICKERS, JON (tenor) 10 / 29 / 1926 SCORPIO
VICTORIA OF ENGLAND, QUEEN 5 / 24 / 1819 GEMINI
VIDAL, GORE (writer) 10 / 3 / 1925 LIBRA
VIDOR, KING WALLIS (film maker) 2 / 8 / 1894 AQUARIUS
VIEIRA DA SILVA (painter) 6 / 13 / 1908 GEMINI
VIGO, JEAN (film maker) 4 / 26 / 1905 TAURUS
VILLA, PANCHO (Mexican rebel) 10 / 4 / 1877 LIBRA
VILLA-LOBOS, HEITOR (composer) 3 / 5 / 1881 PISCES
VILLELLA, EDWARD (ballet dancer) 10 / 1 / 1936 LIBRA

VILLEMURE, GILLES (hockey player) 5 / 30 / 1940 GEMINI
VINCENT, GENE (singer) 2 / 11 / 1935 AQUARIUS
VINCENT, JAN-MICHAEL (actor) 7 / 15 / 1945 CANCER
VINCENT DE PAUL, ST. (religious reformer) 5 / 4 / 1576 TAURUS
VINTON, BOBBY (singer) 4 / 16 / 1941 ARIES
VIRGIL (poet) 10 / 13 / 70 B.C. LIBRA
VISCONTI, LUCHINO (director and film maker) 11 / 2 / 1906 SCORPIO
VISHNEVSKAYA, GALINA (soprano) 10 / 25 / 1926 SCORPIO
VITTI, MONICA (actress) 11 / 3 / 1933 SCORPIO
VIVA (actress) 8 / 23 / 1941 LEO/VIRGO
VIVALDI, ANTONIO (composer) 3 / 4 / 1678 PISCES
VIVEKANANDA, SWAMI (Vedantist) 1 / 12 / 1863 CAPRICORN
VOIGHT, JON (actor) 12 / 29 / 1938 CAPRICORN
VOLTAIRE (philosopher) 11 / 21 / 1694 SCORPIO
VON BRAUN, WERNHER (engineer) 3 / 23 / 1912 ARIES
VON FURSTENBERG, BETSY (actress) 8 / 16 / 1931 LEO
VON KARAJAN, HERBERT (conductor) 4 / 5 / 1908 ARIES
VONNEGUT, KURT (writer) 11 / 11 / 1922 SCORPIO
VOSKOVEC, GEORGE (actor) 6 / 19 / 1905 GEMINI
VOTTO, ANTONINO (conductor) 10 / 30 / 1896 SCORPIO
VUKOVICH, WILLIAM (auto racer) 12 / 13 / 1918 SAGITTARIUS

WAGNER, COSIMA (composer's wife) 12 / 25 / 1837 CAPRICORN
WAGNER, HONUS (baseball player) 2 / 24 / 1874 PISCES
WAGNER, RICHARD (composer) 5 / 22 / 1813 GEMINI
WAGNER, ROBERT (actor) 2 / 10 / 1930 AQUARIUS
WAGNER, ROBERT F. (politician) 4 / 20 / 1910 ARIES/TAURUS
WAGNER, WIELAND (director) 1 / 5 / 1917 CAPRICORN
WAGNER, WOLFGANG (director) 8 / 30 / 1919 VIRGO
WAITE, GENEVIEVE (actress) 2 / 13 / 1949 AQUARIUS
WAKELY, JIMMY (singer) 2 / 16 / 1914 AQUARIUS
WALCOTT, JOE (boxer) 1 / 31 / 1914 AQUARIUS
WALDTEUFEL, EMIL (composer) 12 / 9 / 1837 SAGITTARIUS
WALGREEN, CHARLES RUDOLPH, JR. (druggist) 3 / 4 / 1906 PISCES
WALKER, CLINT (actor) 5 / 30 / 1927 GEMINI
WALKER, MICKEY (boxer) 6 / 13 / 1901 GEMINI
WALKER, NANCY (actress) 5 / 10 / 1922 TAURUS
WALKER, ROBERT (actor) 10 / 13 / 1914 LIBRA
WALLACE, DEWITT (publisher) 11 / 12 / 1889 SCORPIO

WALLACE, GEORGE (politician) 8 / 25 / 1919 VIRGO
WALLACE, IRVING (novelist) 3 / 19 / 1916 PISCES
WALLACE, LURLEEN (politician) 9 / 19 / 1926 VIRGO
WALLACE, MIKE (TV personality) 5 / 19 / 1918 TAURUS
WALLACH, ELI (actor) 12 / 7 / 1915 SAGITTARIUS
WALLENSTEIN, ALBRECHT VON (Austrian army officer) 9 / 24 / 1583
  LIBRA
WALLER, FATS (jazz musician) 5 / 21 / 1904 TAURUS/GEMINI
WALLIS, HAL (producer) 9 / 14 / 1899 VIRGO
WALPOLE, HORACE (writer) 10 / 16 / 1717 LIBRA
WALSH, RAOUL (film director) 3 / 11 / 1889 PISCES
WALSTON, RAY (actor) 11 / 2 / 1918 SCORPIO
WALTER, BRUNO (conductor) 9 / 15 / 1876 VIRGO
WALTERS, BARBARA (TV personality) 9 / 25 / 1931 LIBRA
WALTON, IZAAK (writer) 8 / 19 / 1593 LEO
WALTON, WILLIAM (composer) 3 / 29 / 1902 ARIES
WANAMAKER, JOHN (merchant) 7 / 11 / 1838 CANCER
WANAMAKER, SAM (actor) 6 / 14 / 1919 GEMINI
WARD, MONTGOMERY (merchant) 2 / 17 / 1843 AQUARIUS
WARDEN, JACK (actor) 9 / 18 / 1920 VIRGO
WARFIELD, WILLIAM (singer) 1 / 22 / 1920 AQUARIUS
WARHOL, ANDY (artist) 8 / 6 / 1927 LEO
WARING, FRED (choral conductor) 6 / 9 / 1900 GEMINI
WARNECKE, JOHN CARL (architect) 2 / 24 / 1919 PISCES
WARNER, DAVID (actor) 7 / 29 / 1941 LEO
WARNER, JACK L. (film executive) 8 / 2 / 1892 LEO
WARREN, EARL (jurist) 3 / 19 / 1891 PISCES
WARREN, LEONARD (baritone) 4 / 21 / 1911 TAURUS
WARREN, LESLEY ANN (actress) 8 / 16 / 1946 LEO
WARREN, ROBERT PENN (writer) 4 / 24 / 1905 TAURUS
WARWICK, DIONNE (singer) 12 /12 / 1940 SAGITTARIUS
WASHBOURNE, MONA (actress) 11 / 27 / 1903 SAGITTARIUS
WASHINGTON, DINAH (singer) 8 / 29 / 1924 VIRGO
WASHINGTON, GEORGE (army officer) 2 / 22 / 1732 PISCES
WASHINGTON, MARTHA (first lady) 6 / 21 / 1731 GEMINI/CANCER
WASSERMAN, DALE (playwright) 11 / 2 / 1917 SCORPIO
WASSERMANN, AUGUST VON (bacteriologist) 2 / 21 / 1866 PISCES
WATERS, ETHEL (singer) 10 / 31 / 1900 SCORPIO
WATERS, MUDDY (blues singer) 4 / 4 / 1915 ARIES
WATERS, ROGER (rock musician) 9 / 6 / ? VIRGO

WATERSTON, SAM (actor) 11 / 15 / 1940 SCORPIO

WATSON, JAMES (biochemist) 4 / 6 / 1928 ARIES

WATSON, THOMAS J. (computer executive) 2 / 17 / 1874 AQUARIUS

WATT, JAMES (inventor) 1 / 30 / 1736 AQUARIUS

WATTEAU, JEAN ANTOINE (painter) 10 / 10 / 1684 LIBRA

WATTS, ALAN (writer) 1 / 6 / 1915 CAPRICORN

WATTS, ANDRE (pianist) 6 / 20 / 1946 GEMINI

WATTS, CHARLIE (rock musician) 6 / 2 / 1941 GEMINI

WATTS, ISAAC (hymnist) 7 / 27 / 1674 LEO

WATTS, RICHARD (drama critic) 1 / 12 / 1898 CAPRICORN

WAUGH, ALEC (novelist) 7 / 8 / 1898 CANCER

WAUGH, EVELYN (novelist) 10 / 28 / 1903 SCORPIO

WAYNE, ANTHONY (army officer) 1 / 12 / 1745 CAPRICORN

WAYNE, DAVID (actor) 1 / 30 / 1914 AQUARIUS

WAYNE, JOHN (actor) 5 / 26 / 1907 GEMINI

WEAVER, ANDREW (author) 3 / 5 / 1946 PISCES

WEAVER, DENNIS (actor) 6 / 4 / 1924 GEMINI

WEAVER, FRITZ (actor) 1 / 19 / 1926 CAPRICORN

WEBB, ALAN (actor) 7 / 2 / 1906 CANCER

WEBB, CLIFTON (actor) 11 / 19 / 1891 SCORPIO

WEBB, JACK (actor) 4 / 2 / 1920 ARIES

WEBER, CARL MARIA VON (composer) 11 / 18 / 1786 SCORPIO

WEBER, MAX (sociologist) 4 / 21 / 1864 TAURUS

WEBERN, ANTON VON (composer) 12 / 3 / 1883 SAGITTARIUS

WEBSTER, DANIEL (orator) 1 / 18 / 1782 CAPRICORN

WEBSTER, MARGARET (director) 3 / 15 / 1905 PISCES

WEBSTER, NOAH (lexicographer) 10 / 16 / 1785 LIBRA

WEDEKIND, FRANK (playwright) 7 / 24 / 1864 LEO

WEEDE, ROBERT (baritone) 2 / 22 / 1903 PISCES

WEICKER, LOWELL P. (politician) 5 / 16 / 1931 TAURUS

WEILL, KURT (composer) 3 / 2 / 1900 PISCES

WEISKOPF, TOM (golfer) 11 / 9 / 1942 SCORPIO

WEISS, PETER (writer) 11 / 8 / 1916 SCORPIO

WEISSMULLER, JOHNNY (actor) 6 / 2 / 1907 GEMINI

WELCH, JOSEPH (lawyer) 10 / 22 / 1890 LIBRA

WELCH, RAQUEL (actress) 9 / 5 / 1940 VIRGO

WELCH, ROBERT (John Bircher) 12 / 1 / 1899 SAGITTARIUS

WELD, TUESDAY (actress) 8 / 27 / 1943 VIRGO

WELITSCH, LJUBA (soprano) 7 / 10 / 1913 CANCER

WELK, LAWRENCE (bandleader) 3 / 11 / 1903 PISCES

WELLES, ORSON (actor and film director) 5 / 6 / 1915 TAURUS
WELLINGTON, DUKE OF (British army officer) 5 / 1 / 1769 TAURUS
WELLS, H. G. (writer) 9 / 21 / 1866 VIRGO
WELTY, EUDORA (writer) 4 / 13 / 1909 ARIES
WERFEL, FRANZ (writer) 9 / 10 / 1890 VIRGO
WERNER, OSKAR (actor) 11 / 13 / 1922 SCORPIO
WESKER, ARNOLD (playwright) 5 / 24 / 1932 GEMINI
WESLEY, JOHN (Methodist) 6 / 28 / 1703 CANCER
WEST, BENJAMIN (painter) 10 / 21 / 1738 LIBRA
WEST, MAE (actress) 8 / 17 / 1892 LEO
WEST, NATHANAEL (novelist) 10 / 17 / 1904 LIBRA
WEST, REBECCA (writer) 12 / 21 / 1892 SAGITTARIUS/CAPRICORN
WESTINGHOUSE, G. (inventor) 10 / 6 / 1846 LIBRA
WESTMORELAND, WILLIAM C. (army officer) 3 / 26 / 1914 ARIES
WHARTON, EDITH (novelist) 1 / 24 / 1862 AQUARIUS
WHEELER, MORTIMER (archaeologist) 9 / 10 / 1890 VIRGO
WHIPPLE, FRED LAWRENCE (astronomer) 11 / 5 / 1906 SCORPIO
WHISTLER, JAMES (painter) 7 / 10 / 1834 CANCER
WHITE, E. B. (writer) 7 / 11 / 1899 CANCER
WHITE, EDWARD H. (astronaut) 11 / 14 / 1930 SCORPIO
WHITE, JOSH (folk singer) 2 / 11 / 1908 AQUARIUS
WHITE, PAUL DUDLEY (physician) 6 / 6 / 1886 GEMINI
WHITE, STANFORD (architect) 11 / 9 / 1853 SCORPIO
WHITE, T. H. (writer) 5 / 6 / 1915 TAURUS
WHITEHEAD, ALFRED NORTH (philosopher) 2 / 15 / 1861 AQUARIUS
WHITEHEAD, "COMMANDER" EDWARD (soft-drink executive)
     5 / 20 / 1908 TAURUS
WHITEMAN, PAUL (conductor) 3 / 28 / 1891 ARIES
WHITING, MARGARET (singer) 7 / 22 / 1924 CANCER/LEO
WHITMAN, STUART (actor) 2 / 1 / 1929 AQUARIUS
WHITMAN, WALT (poet) 5 / 31 / 1819 GEMINI
WHITMORE, JAMES (actor) 10 / 1 / 1921 LIBRA
WHITNEY, ELI (inventor) 12 / 8 / 1765 SAGITTARIUS
WHITNEY, JOHN HAY (publisher) 8 / 17 / 1904 LEO
WHITTIER, JOHN GREENLEAF (poet) 12 / 17 / 1807 SAGITTARIUS
WHORF, RICHARD (actor) 6 / 4 / 1906 GEMINI
WICKER, TOM (journalist) 6 / 18 / 1926 GEMINI
WIDDOES, KATHLEEN (actress) 3 / 21 / 1939 PISCES/ARIES
WIDERBERG, BO (film maker) 6 / 8 / 1930 GEMINI
WIDMARK, RICHARD (actor) 12 / 26 / 1914 CAPRICORN

WILSON, FLIP (comedian) 12 / 8 / 1935 SAGITTARIUS
WILSON, HAROLD (British politician) 3 / 11 / 1916 PISCES
WILSON, MALCOLM (politician) 2 / 26 / 1914 PISCES
WILSON, MARGARET BUSH (black leader) 1 / 30 / 1919 AQUARIUS
WILSON, MARIE (actress) 12 / 30 / 1917 CAPRICORN
WILSON, MARY (singer) 3 / 6 / 1944 PISCES
WILSON, NANCY (singer) 2 / 20 / 1937 PISCES
WILSON, SLOAN (writer) 5 / 8 / 1920 TAURUS
WILSON, WOODROW (politician) 12 / 28 / 1856 CAPRICORN
WINCHELL, WALTER (columnist) 4 / 7 / 1897 ARIES
WINDGASSEN, WOLFGANG (tenor) 6 / 26 / 1914 CANCER
WINDSOR, DUCHESS OF (socialite) 6 / 19 / 1896 GEMINI
WINDSOR, DUKE OF (socialite) 6 / 23 / 1894 CANCER
WINDSOR, MARIE (actress) 12 / 11 / 1924 SAGITTARIUS
WINSTON, HARRY (jeweler) 3 / 1 / 1896 PISCES
WINTERS, JONATHAN (comedian) 11 / 11 / 1925 SCORPIO
WINTERS, SHELLEY (actress) 8 / 18 / 1922 LEO
WINTERS, YVOR (writer) 10 / 17 / 1900 LIBRA
WINTHROP, JOHN (colonist) 1 / 22 / 1588 AQUARIUS
WINWOOD, ESTELLE (actress) 1 / 24 / 1883 AQUARIUS
WINWOOD, STEVE (rock musician) 5 / 12 / 1948 TAURUS
WISDOM, NORMAN (actor) 2 / 4 / 1920 AQUARIUS
WISE, ROBERT (film director) 9 / 10 / 1914 VIRGO
WITHERS, JANE (actress) 4 / 12 / 1926 ARIES
WITTGENSTEIN, LUDWIG (philosopher) 4 / 26 / 1889 TAURUS
WODEHOUSE, P. G. (writer) 10 / 15 / 1881 LIBRA
WOLF, HUGO (composer) 3 / 13 / 1860 PISCES
WOLF, PETER (singer) 3 / 7 / 1946 PISCES
WOLF-FERRARI, ERMANNO (composer) 1 / 12 / 1876 CAPRICORN
WOLFE, THOMAS (novelist) 10 / 3 / 1900 LIBRA
WOLFE, TOM (writer) 3 / 2 / 1931 PISCES
WOLFIT, DONALD (actor) 4 / 20 / 1902 ARIES/TAURUS
WOLFSON, MARTIN (actor) 4 / 4 / 1904 ARIES
WONDER, STEVIE (singer) 5 / 13 / 1950 TAURUS
WONG, ANNA MAY (actress) 1 / 3 / 1907 CAPRICORN
WOOD, GRANT (painter) 2 / 13 / 1892 AQUARIUS
WOOD, NATALIE (actress) 7 / 20 / 1938 CANCER
WOOD, PEGGY (actress) 2 / 9 / 1892 AQUARIUS
WOODLAWN, HOLLY (actress) 10 / 26 / 1946 SCORPIO
WOODS, ROSE MARY (secretary) 12 / 26 / 1917 CAPRICORN

WOODWARD, BOB (reporter) 5 / 5 / 1943 TAURUS
WOODWARD, JOANNE (actress) 2 / 27 / 1930 PISCES
WOOLF, VIRGINIA (writer) 1 / 25 / 1882 AQUARIUS
WOOLLEY, LEONARD (archaeologist) 4 / 17 / 1880 ARIES
WOOLWORTH, FRANK WINFIELD (merchant) 4 / 13 / 1852 ARIES
WORDSWORTH, WILLIAM (poet) 4 / 7 / 1770 ARIES
WORTH, IRENE (actress) 6 / 23 / 1916 CANCER
WOUK, HERMAN (writer) 5 / 27 / 1915 GEMINI
WRAY, FAY (actress) 9 / 10 / 1907 VIRGO
WREN, CHRISTOPHER (architect) 10 / 31 / 1632 SCORPIO
WRIGHT, FRANK LLOYD (architect) 6 / 8 / 1869 GEMINI
WRIGHT, MICKEY (golfer) 2 / 14 / 1935 AQUARIUS
WRIGHT, ORVILLE (inventor) 8 / 19 / 1871 LEO
WRIGHT, RICHARD (novelist) 9 / 4 / 1908 VIRGO
WRIGHT, RICHARD (rock musician) 1 / 28 / ? AQUARIUS
WRIGHT, TERESA (actress) 10 / 27 / 1918 SCORPIO
WRIGHT, WILBUR (inventor) 4 / 16 / 1867 ARIES
WRIGLEY, PHILIP K. (gum manufacturer) 12 / 5 / 1894 SAGITTARIUS
WUNDERLICH, FRITZ (tenor) 9 / 26 / 1930 LIBRA
WUORINEN, CHARLES (composer) 6 / 9 / 1938 GEMINI
WYATT, JANE (actress) 8 / 10 / 1912 LEO
WYETH, ANDREW (painter) 7 / 12 / 1917 CANCER
WYETH, JAMES (painter) 7 / 6 / 1946 CANCER
WYETH, N. C. (illustrator) 10 / 22 / 1882 LIBRA
WYLER, WILLIAM (film director) 7 / 1 / 1902 CANCER
WYLIE, ELINOR (poet) 9 / 7 / 1885 VIRGO
WYLIE, PHILIP (writer) 5 / 12 / 1902 TAURUS
WYMAN, BILL (rock musician) 10 / 24 / 1941 LIBRA/SCORPIO
WYMAN, JANE (actress) 1 / 4 / 1914 CAPRICORN
WYNN, EARLY (baseball player) 1 / 6 / 1920 CAPRICORN
WYNN, ED (comedian) 11 / 9 / 1886 SCORPIO
WYNN, KEENAN (actor) 7 / 27 / 1916 LEO

XAVIER, ST. FRANCIS (Jesuit) 4 / 17 / 1506 ARIES
XENAKIS, IANNIS (composer) 5 / 29 / 1922 GEMINI

YAHYA KHAN, AGHA MUHAMMED (Pakistani army officer)
2 / 4 / 1917 AQUARIUS

YAMASAKI, MINORU (architect) 12 / 1 / 1912 SAGITTARIUS
YARBOROUGH, RALPH (politician) 6 / 8 / 1903 GEMINI
YARBROUGH, GLENN (singer) 1 / 12 / 1930 CAPRICORN
YARROW, PETER (singer) 5 / 31 / 1938 GEMINI
YASTRZEMSKI, CARL (baseball player) 8 / 22 / 1939 LEO
YEATS, WILLIAM BUTLER (writer) 6 / 13 / 1865 GEMINI
YERBY, FRANK (novelist) 9 / 5 / 1916 VIRGO
YEVTUSHENKO, YEVGENY (poet) 7 / 18 / 1933 CANCER
YORK, MICHAEL (actor) 3 / 27 / 1942 ARIES
YORK, SUSANNAH (actress) 1 / 9 / 1941 CAPRICORN
YORTY, SAM (politician) 10 / 1 / 1908 LIBRA
YOSHIDA, ISOYA (architect) 12 / 19 / 1894 SAGITTARIUS
YOUNG, ALAN (comedian) 11 / 19 / 1919 SCORPIO
YOUNG, BRIGHAM (Mormon leader) 6 / 1 / 1801 GEMINI
YOUNG, CHIC (cartoonist) 1 / 9 / 1901 CAPRICORN
YOUNG, GIG (actor) 11 / 4 / 1913 SCORPIO
YOUNG, JOHN W. (astronaut) 9 / 24 / 1930 LIBRA
YOUNG, LORETTA (actress) 1 / 6 / 1913 CAPRICORN
YOUNG, NEIL (rock musician) 11 / 11 / 1945 SCORPIO
YOUNG, ROBERT (actor) 2 / 22 / 1907 PISCES
YOUNG, WHITNEY, JR. (social worker) 7 / 31 / 1921 LEO
YOUSKEVITCH, IGOR (ballet dancer) 3 / 13 / 1912 PISCES
YURIKO (dancer) 2 / 2 / 1920 AQUARIUS
YURKA, BLANCHE (actress) 6 / 19 / 1893 GEMINI

ZABALETA, NICANOR (harpist) 1 / 7 / 1907 CAPRICORN
ZAHARIAS, BABE (golfer) 6 / 26 / 1914 CANCER
ZANDONAI, RICCARDO (composer) 5 / 28 / 1883 GEMINI
ZANUCK, DARRYL F. (film producer) 9 / 5 / 1902 VIRGO
ZAPPA, FRANK (singer) 12 / 21 / 1940 SAGITTARIUS/CAPRICORN
ZEFFIRELLI, FRANCO (stage designer and director) 2 / 12 / 1923
          AQUARIUS
ZENATELLO, GIOVANNI (tenor) 2 / 22 / 1879 PISCES
ZEPPELIN, FERDINAND VON (aeronaut) 7 / 8 / 1838 CANCER
ZETTERLING, MAI (film director) 5 / 24 / 1925 GEMINI
ZIEGFELD, FLORENZ (producer) 3 / 21 / 1869 PISCES/ARIES
ZIEGLER, RONALD (press secretary) 5 / 12 / 1939 TAURUS
ZIMBALIST, EFRAM, JR. (actor) 11 / 30 / 1923 SAGITTARIUS
ZINDEL, PAUL (playwright) 5 / 15 / 1936 TAURUS

ARIES

Element: Fire / Quality: Cardinal

Fire, with its meaning of warmth and outgoing vitality, appears in Aries in its primary manifestation, as it is first revealed when a flame bursts into blaze, or in any spontaneous release of energy directed toward starting something. Arians are initiators, taking the lead when energetic beginnings have to be made, and where directness and singleness of purpose are required. The Arian way to self-realization lies in pure action; caught up in the performance of an action, without much reflection or regard for consequences, Arians are able to move with abrupt force, at least until the original impetus to act burns itself out, with business sometimes left unfinished. The absorption in their own deeds which allows them freedom to operate unconditioned by secondary considerations may also make them oblivious to the viewpoints of other individuals, so that they are better suited to forging ahead alone than in cooperative arrangements. Their symbol is the ram, because he batters his way headfirst. The planetary ruler is Mars, the indicator of physical energy and bravery, ruler of combat and warfare, and of aggressive sexuality. The typical Aries appropriately is vigorous, bold, enthusiastic, and ready for battle, whether in the war between the sexes or on other fields less perilous.

Giovanni Casanova was an Aries whose name came to stand for amorousness and adventuring, a reputation well deserved by his checkered history. Engaged in studies for the priesthood, he was expelled for immorality, and began to make his living by gambling, spying, writing, and most notably by his power to seduce women; in his retirement, not content with idleness, he relived the events of his life once again through his memoirs. The Casanova myth is perpetuated today by Aries Hugh Hefner of *Playboy* magazine, and incarnated in the public's fantasy images of such Aries film stars as Marlon Brando, Gregory Peck, Steve McQueen, Jean-Paul Belmondo, Omar Sharif, and Warren Beatty. The Martian qualities of forceful aggressiveness and assertive individuality projected by an audience onto these movie idols make them embodiments of a popular ideal of virility; in female stars the same traits have lent themselves in the past to the portrayal of "bitch" types on the screen, as in many roles of Arians Gloria Swanson, Joan Crawford, and Bette Davis.

Other Arians have led lives of exemplary saintliness, devoting their abounding energy to the service of God and humanity. Two of the very greatest of Christian mystics, St. Catherine of Siena and St. Teresa of Avila, far from retreating from the outer world in contemplative quietism or visionary ecstasies, were impelled by the force of their inspiration into extremely active Arian careers. St. Catherine labored tirelessly for the poor and sick, and as papal ambassador she played a major part in church politics at the time of the Great Schism of the fourteenth century. Nearly everywhere she went she started a spiritual revival, kindling her fire in the hearts of devoted followers. Two centuries later, during the Catholic Reformation in Spain, St. Teresa also brought about a great reawakening of religious fervor; she inspired others by the example of her inner strength and by her devotional writings, and she founded reformed convents for nuns and friars who continued her work. In the same period another Aries, St. Francis Xavier, having associated with Ignatius Loyola in the establishment of the Jesuit Society, carried his mission to the Far East; he had great success preaching and converting in the East Indies, Ceylon, India and Japan, and was on his way to China when he died, an Aries activist to the end.

Charlemagne's activist way of converting pagans was to subdue them with force, and in setting up Frankish institutions and creating the Frankish empire he took a similarly direct, decisive Arian approach. The empire, however, in spite of the good beginnings he had made, did not survive long, a fate common to many Aries projects when the founder's initial spark has died. Aries Thomas Jefferson's individualist ideals of liberty, set forth by him in the Declaration of Independence when the United States was conceived, proved to be unrealized for many citizens as American society proceeded to develop in directions not foreseen by Jefferson. The agrarian democracy which he had envisioned failed to mature in an age of industrialism, although the original principles, always the Arian's strongest

point, had seemed sound. Nor did the second German Reich long out-
live its aggressive Aries creator Otto von Bismarck, who by promoting
Prussian (not to say Martian) militarism laid the foundations for
its eventual demise.

In artistic works, which perpetuate indefinitely the impulse felt by
their creator, the Arian heat of initial inspiration finds lasting life.
Irrepressible Aries energy is the source of the vital, ongoing drive in
the music of J. S. Bach, and of the vigorous, extroverted style of
Joseph Haydn. In painting, the Arian appreciation of personal selfhood is evident in the works that made the fame of Anthony van Dyck,
his numerous portraits, in which the sitters' unique individualities in-
sist on coming to life. Another Aries also renowned in portraiture,
Francisco Goya, turned to depicting the horrors of war and other
scenes of savage violence, subjects that are eminently Martian and
Arian; a similarly mad sense of violence, even in still life and landscape, pervades the later work of Aries Vincent van Gogh. On film,
mayhem runs rampant in the Samurai sagas directed by Akira Kurosawa and starring Toshiro Mifune, both Aries.

The true spirit of Aries, however, is better expressed in Arian
René Descartes' formulation, *"Cogito ergo sum"* (I think, therefore
I am), which deduces merely from the evidence of intelligent consciousness the existence of a personal ego. Most Arians unconsciously
make the same assumption.

MARCH 21

Torquato Tasso (poet)	1544
Benito Juarez (Mexican politician)	1806
Modest Mussorgsky (composer)	1839
Albert Kahn (architect)	1869
Florenz Ziegfeld (producer)	1869
Hans Hoffmann (painter)	1880
Phyllis McGinley (writer)	1905
John D. Rockefeller III (tycoon)	1906
Peter Brook (director)	1925
James Coco (actor)	1929
Kathleen Widdoes (actress)	1939

MARCH 22

Anthony Van Dyck (painter)	1599
Chico Marx (comedian)	1891
Joseph Schildkraut (actor)	1895
Maurice Stans (government official)	1908
Martha Moedl (opera singer)	1912
Karl Malden (actor)	1914
Paul Rogers (actor)	1917
James Brown (actor)	1920
Marcel Marceau (mime)	1923
Stephen Sondheim (lyricist)	1930
William Shatner (actor)	1931
May Britt (actress)	1936

MARCH 23

Dane Rudhyar (astrologer)	1895
Erich Fromm (psychologist)	1900
Joan Crawford (actress)	1908
Akira Kurosawa (film maker)	1910
Wernher von Braun (engineer)	1912
Regine Crespin (opera singer)	1927
Roger Bannister (runner)	1929
Craig Breedlove (auto racer)	1938
Lee May (baseball player)	1943

MARCH 24

Maria Malibran (opera singer)	1808
Mathilde Marchesi (singing teacher)	1821
Fatty Arbuckle (actor)	1887

March 24 (*continued*)
Wilhelm Reich
  (psychologist)   1897
Thomas E. Dewey
  (politician)   1902
Malcolm Muggeridge
  (writer)   1903
Dwight MacDonald (writer)   1906
Clyde Barrow (outlaw)   1909
Enrique Jorda (composer)   1911
Richard Conte (actor)   1914
Lawrence Ferlinghetti (poet)   1919
Byron Janis (pianist)   1928
Steve McQueen (actor)   1930
Kenneth Nelson (actor)   1930
Alex Olmedo (tennis player)   1936

MARCH 25

Arturo Toscanini
  (conductor)   1867
Bela Bartok (composer)   1881
Ed Begley (actor)   1901
David Lean (film director)   1908
Magda Olivero (opera
  singer)   1912
Robert Rounseville (actor)   1914
Jeanne Cagney (actress)   1919
Howard Cosell (sportscaster)   1920
Nancy Kelly (actress)   1921
Simone Signoret (actress)   1921
Eileen Ford (modeling
  agent)   1922
Machiko Kyo (actress)   1924
Flannery O'Connor (writer)   1925
James A. Lovell, Jr.
  (astronaut)   1928
Gloria Steinem (feminist)   1935
Anita Bryant (singer)   1940
Aretha Franklin (singer)   1942
Elton John (singer)   1947

MARCH 26

Robert Frost (poet)   1875
Duncan Hines (merchant)   1880
Wilhelm Backhaus (pianist)   1884
Joseph Campbell (writer)   1904
Andre Cluytens (conductor)   1905
William C. Westmoreland
  (army officer)   1914
Tennessee Williams
  (playwright)   1914
Sterling Hayden (actor)   1916
Robert Taft, Jr. (politician)   1917
Bob Elliott (comedian)   1923
Pierre Boulez (conductor)   1925
Leonard Nimoy (actor)   1931
Alan Arkin (actor)   1934
James Caan (actor)   1939
Erica Jong (novelist)   1942
Diana Ross (singer)   1944

MARCH 27

Wilhelm Roentgen
  (physicist)   1845
Vincent d'Indy (composer)   1851
Edward Steichen
  (photographer)   1879
Ludwig Mies van der Rohe
  (architect)   1886
Ferde Grofe (composer)   1892
Gloria Swanson (actress)   1899
Jules Olitski (artist)   1923
Sarah Vaughan (jazz singer)   1924
David Janssen (actor)   1930
Arthur Mitchell
  (choreographer)   1934
Michael York (actor)   1942
Maria Schneider (actress)   1952

MARCH 28

Maxim Gorky (writer) 1868
Paul Whiteman (conductor) 1891
Christian Herter
(government official) 1895
Flora Robson (actress) 1902
Rudolf Serkin (pianist) 1903
Nelson Algren (writer) 1909
Stephen Spender (writer) 1909
Frank Lovejoy (actor) 1914
Edmund Muskie (politician) 1914
Dirk Bogarde (actor) 1921
Grace Hartigan (artist) 1922
Freddie Bartholomew (child
actor) 1924
Rick Barry (basketball
player) 1944

MARCH 29

John Tyler (politician) 1790
Rosina Lhevinne (piano
teacher) 1880
William Walton (composer) 1902
E. Power Biggs (organist) 1906
Arthur O'Connell (actor) 1908
Dennis O'Keefe (actor) 1908
Eugene McCarthy
(politician) 1916
Pearl Bailey (singer) 1918
Eileen Heckart (actress) 1919
Dennis McLain (baseball
player) 1944
Walt Frazier (basketball
player) 1945

MARCH 30

Francisco de Goya (painter) 1746
Paul Verlaine (poet) 1844

Vincent van Gogh (painter) 1853
Sean O'Casey (playwright) 1880
John A. Burns (politician) 1909
Richard Helms (government
official) 1913
Frankie Laine (singer) 1913
McGeorge Bundy
(government official) 1919
Warren Beatty (actor) 1937
Jerry Lucas (basketball
player) 1940
Eric Clapton (rock musician) 1945
Jim "Dandy" Mangrum
(rock musician) 1948
Naomi Sims (model and
author) 1949

MARCH 31

Rene Descartes
(philosopher) 1596
Johann Sebastian Bach
(composer) 1685
Franz Josef Haydn
(composer) 1732
Nikolai Gogol (writer) 1809
Andrew Lang (fairy tale
collector) 1844
Jack Johnson (boxer) 1878
Richard Kiley (actor) 1922
Sydney Chaplin (actor) 1926
John Fowles (novelist) 1926
Beni Montresor (artist) 1926
Cesar Chavez (labor
reformer) 1927
Gordie Howe (hockey
player) 1928
Shirley Jones (actress) 1934
Herb Alpert (bandleader) 1935
Richard Chamberlain (actor) 1935
David Eisenhower
(politician's grandson) 1948

APRIL 1

Abbe Prevost (writer)	1697
Otto von Bismarck (German statesman)	1815
Ferruccio Busoni (composer)	1866
Edmond Rostand (playwright)	1868
Sergei Rachmaninoff (composer)	1873
Lon Chaney (actor)	1883
Laurette Taylor (actress)	1884
Eddy Duchin (pianist)	1909
Henry Morgan (TV personality)	1915
Toshiro Mifune (actor)	1920
William Manchester (writer)	1922
Brendan Byrne (politician)	1924
George Grizzard (actor)	1928
Jane Powell (actress)	1929
Debbie Reynolds (actress)	1932
Ali MacGraw (actress)	1939

APRIL 2

Giovanni Casanova (adventurer)	1725
Hans Christian Andersen (writer)	1805
Emile Zola (novelist)	1840
Max Ernst (painter)	1891
King Olav V of Norway	1903
Arnie Herber (football player)	1910
Alec Guinness (actor)	1914
Jack Webb (actor)	1920
Kenneth Tynan (critic)	1927
Rita Gam (actress)	1928
Rochelle Owens (playwright)	1936
Marvin Gaye (singer)	1939
Leon Russell (singer)	1942

APRIL 3

St. Catherine of Siena (mystic)	1347
Washington Irving (writer)	1783
William Marcy "Boss" Tweed (politician)	1823
Leslie Howard (actor)	1893
George Jessel (actor)	1898
Henry Luce (publisher)	1898
Herb Caen (columnist)	1916
Jan Sterling (actress)	1923
Marlon Brando (actor)	1924
Doris Day (actress)	1924
Virgil Grissom (astronaut)	1926
Johnny Horton (actor)	1929
Miyoshi Umeko (actress)	1929
Wayne Newton (singer)	1944

APRIL 4

Dorothea Dix (prison reformer)	1802
Pierre Monteux (conductor)	1875
Arthur Murray (dance instructor)	1895
Robert Sherwood (playwright)	1896
Martin Wolfson (actor)	1904
Marguerite Duras (writer)	1914
Muddy Waters (blues singer)	1915
Robert Abplanalp (financier)	1922
Elmer Bernstein (composer)	1922
Gil Hodges (baseball player)	1924
Maya Angelou (writer)	1929
Anthony Perkins (actor)	1932

APRIL 5

Raphael (painter)	1483

April 5 (*continued*)

Adrienne Lecouvreur (actress)	1692
Jean Honore Fragonard (painter)	1732
Joseph Lister (surgeon)	1827
Frank R. Stockton (writer)	1834
Algernon Swinburne (poet)	1837
Albert Roussel (composer)	1869
David Burpee (horticulturist)	1893
Spencer Tracy (actor)	1900
Chester Bowles (politician)	1901
Melvyn Douglas (actor)	1901
Richard Eberhart (poet)	1904
Bette Davis (actress)	1908
Mary Hemingway (writer's wife)	1908
Herbert von Karajan (conductor)	1908
Gregory Peck (actor)	1916
Arthur Hailey (novelist)	1920
Gale Storm (actress)	1922
Nguyen Van Thieu (Vietnamese politician)	1923
Roger Corman (film director)	1926
Merle Haggard (country singer)	1937
Michael Moriarty (actor)	1941

APRIL 6

Emperor Charlemagne	742
Moses Maimonides (rabbi)	1135
Butch Cassidy (outlaw)	1866
Lincoln Steffens (writer)	1866
Harry Houdini (magician)	1874
Walter Huston (actor)	1884
Carlos Salzedo (harpist)	1885
Lowell Thomas (commentator)	1892
Gerry Mulligan (jazz musician)	1927

James Watson (biochemist)	1928
Andre Previn (conductor)	1929
Richard Alpert (drug experimenter)	1931

APRIL 7

St. Teresa of Avila (mystic)	1515
William Wordsworth (poet)	1770
Giovanni-Battista Rubini (opera singer)	1795
Bronislaw Malinowsky (anthropologist)	1884
Walter Winchell (columnist)	1897
Robert Casadesus (pianist)	1899
Percy Faith (bandleader)	1908
Billie Holiday (jazz singer)	1915
Ravi Shankar (sitarist)	1920
James Garner (actor)	1928
Daniel Ellsberg (economist)	1931
Ian Richardson (actor)	1934
Edmund Brown, Jr. (politician)	1938
Francis Ford Coppola (film director)	1939
David Frost (TV personality)	1939
Janis Ian (singer)	1951

APRIL 8

Adrian Boult (conductor)	1889
Richard J. Neutra (architect)	1892
Louis Skidmore (architect)	1897
Josef Krips (conductor)	1902
Ilka Chase (actress)	1905
Sonja Henie (skater)	1912
Betty Ford (first lady)	1918
Ian Douglas Smith (Rhodesian politician)	1919
Franco Corelli (opera singer)	1923

April 8 (*continued*)

Jess Thomas (opera singer)	1927
John Gavin (actor)	1928
Eric Porter (actor)	1928
Walter Berry (opera singer)	1929
Jacques Brel (composer)	1929
John Reardon (opera singer)	1930
Dorothy Tutin (actress)	1930
Jim "Catfish" Hunter (baseball player)	1946

APRIL 9

Michael "Captain Lightfoot" Martin (highwayman)	1775
Giuditta Pasta (opera singer)	1798
Charles Baudelaire (poet)	1821
Sol Hurok (impresario)	1888
Charles Burchfield (artist)	1893
Mary Pickford (actress)	1894
Mance Lipscomb (blues musician)	1895
Michel Simon (actor)	1895
Paul Robeson (singer)	1898
Gregory Pincus (biologist)	1903
Ward Bond (actor)	1905
J. William Fulbright (politician)	1905
Antal Dorati (conductor)	1906
Robert Helpmann (ballet dancer)	1909
Bill Leonard (newsman)	1916
Hugh Hefner (publisher)	1926
Jean-Paul Belmondo (actor)	1933
Brandon de Wilde (actor)	1942

APRIL 10

Andrew Marvell (poet)	1621
William Hazlitt (writer)	1778

Matthew Perry (naval officer)	1794
Joseph Pulitzer (publisher)	1847
Bernard F. Gimbel (merchant)	1885
Victor de Sabata (conductor)	1892
Ben Nicholson (painter)	1894
Herbert Graf (director)	1903
Clare Boothe Luce (playwright)	1903
Roy Hofheinz (entrepreneur)	1912
Martin Denny (composer)	1915
Chuck Connors (actor)	1921
Max von Sydow (actor)	1929
Omar Sharif (actor)	1932

APRIL 11

William Harvey (physician)	1578
Dean Acheson (government official)	1893
Oleg Cassini (fashion designer)	1913
Alberto Ginastera (composer)	1916
Hugh Carey (politician)	1919
Ethel Kennedy (politician's widow)	1928
Johnny Sheffield (child actor)	1931
Joel Grey (actor)	1932

APRIL 12

Henry Clay (statesman)	1777
Joseph Lapchick (basketball coach)	1900
Marietta Tree (political worker)	1917

April 12 (*continued*)
Maurice Girodias (publisher)   1919
Ann Miller (dancer)   1919
Jane Withers (actress)   1926
Hardy Kruger (actor)   1928
Tiny Tim (singer)   1930
Jack Gelber (playwright)   1932
Montserrat Caballe (opera
  singer)   1933
John Kay (rock musician)   1944
David Cassidy (singer)   1950

APRIL 13

George Herbert (poet)   1593
Thomas Jefferson (politician) 1743
Frank Winfield Woolworth
  (merchant)   1852
James Ensor (painter)   1860
Samuel Beckett (writer)   1906
Eudora Welty (writer)   1909
Howard Keel (actor)   1917
Stanley Donen (film director) 1924
Margaret Price (opera singer) 1941
Jack Casady (rock musician)   1944

APRIL 14

Annie Sullivan (teacher)   1866
Arnold Toynbee (historian)   1889
John Gielgud (actor)   1904
François Duvalier (dictator)   1907
Mary Healy (TV personality)   1918
James D. St. Clair (lawyer)   1920
Rod Steiger (actor)   1925
Gloria Jean (actress)   1928
Bradford Dillman (actor)   1930
Loretta Lynn (singer)   1932
Frank Serpico
  (plainclothesman)   1936
Julie Christie (actress)   1941

APRIL 15

Thomas Hobbes
  (philosopher)   1588
Henry James (novelist)   1843
A. Philip Randolph (labor
  leader)   1889
Bessie Smith (blues singer)   1898
William Congdon (painter)   1912
Al Bloomingdale (merchant)   1916
Elizabeth Montgomery
  (actress)   1933
Claudia Cardinale (actress)   1938

APRIL 16

Anatole France (writer)   1844
Wilbur Wright (inventor)   1867
J. M. Synge (playwright)   1871
Charlie Chaplin (comedian)   1889
Milton Cross (radio
  commentator)   1897
Polly Adler (procuress)   1900
Philip Winston Pillsbury
  (flour merchant)   1903
Clifford P. Case (politician) 1904
Lily Pons (opera singer)   1904
Merce Cunningham
  (choreographer)   1919
Peter Ustinov (actor)   1921
Kingsley Amis (writer)   1922
Henry Mancini (composer)   1924
Herbie Mann (jazz musician)   1930
Edie Adams (singer)   1931
Bobby Vinton (singer)   1941
Lew Alcindor (basketball
  player)   1947

APRIL 17

St. Francis Xavier (Jesuit)   1506

April 17 (*continued*)

J. P. Morgan (financier)	1837
Cap Anson (baseball player)	1851
Leonard Woolley (archaeologist)	1880
Artur Schnabel (pianist)	1882
Maggie Teyte (singer)	1889
Nikita Khrushchev (Soviet politician)	1894
Thornton Wilder (writer)	1897
Rebekah Harkness (composer and patron of dance)	1915
Sirimavo Bandaranaike (Ceylonese politician)	1916
William Holden (actor)	1918
Harry Reasoner (newsman)	1923

APRIL 18

Franz von Suppe (composer)	1819
Clarence Darrow (lawyer)	1857

Leopold Stokowski (conductor)	1882
Frida Leider (opera singer)	1888
Huntington Hartford (art patron)	1911
Irra Petina (singer)	1914
Queen Frederika of Greece	1917
Barbara Hale (actress)	1922
Robert Hooks (actor)	1937
Clive Revill (actor)	1939
Hayley Mills (actress)	1946

APRIL 19

Françoise Rosay (actress)	1891
Kenneth (hairdresser)	1927
Hugh O'Brian (actor)	1930
Jayne Mansfield (actress)	1933
Dudley Moore (comedian)	1935
Jill St. John (actress)	1940

TAURUS

Element: Earth / Quality: Fixed

The idea of materiality which earth represents is realized in Taurus in its most stable form, as solid, concentrated substance, such as the planet Earth itself, for example. The power of Taurus is the force of inertia, the energy which keeps something from moving or changing, unless it is acted upon by an outside force; Taureans, therefore, are inclined not to budge from a set position, and stubbornly resist being disturbed. Instead of spending their efforts in diffuse activity, they conserve their resources of energy, and their material productions and possessions, for the purpose of maintaining their stability. Deliberate and slow to arouse, they may, however, be goaded to anger, like their animal the bucolic bull, whose dangerous temper is everywhere respected. This beast is also in some way symbolic of manifest materiality, the realm of Mother Nature, because the bull was inseparably associated at sites all over the neolithic Near East with the worship of the great mother-goddess. This is the same deity who as Venus (represented by the planet Venus) presides over Taurus, the original earth-mother in her aspect of love-goddess, proprietress of beauty and sensual satisfactions. Her rulership points up the affectionate nature, the love of beautiful things and of comforts, and the ultimate reliance on sensory perception, which are common among Taureans.

Two Taurus empresses whose reigns were roughly parallel, Maria Theresa of Austria and Catherine the Great of Russia, present a picture of contrasts and similarities which is an instructive illustration. The two ladies in their private lives were very different from each other, but both Taurean; Maria Theresa, a staunch Catholic, head of the court that took the most moral tone in Europe, was decidedly domestic, a devoted wife and fond mother to the large family she produced, while Catherine was notorious for her gross sensuality and the number of lovers she kept (one of whom, incidentally, was the murderer of her husband). Each extreme is an expression of one of the several faces of Venus, revealed in a Taurean manner, fixedly determined in its earthiness. Similarly Taurean in politics, both rulers were primarily concerned with the consolidation of their power, and reorganized the administration of their lands to increase centralization of control over rural districts, which they well understood to be the basis of their wealth and strength. Both dabbled a little in fashionable liberal social reform but remained conservative at heart, property-minded Tauruses who had no real inclination to tamper with the feudal system which placed property in the hands of their own class; they stood rather for the self-complacent entrenchment of the Old Regime.

Marx and Lenin, Tauruses likewise concerned with the ownership of property, but representing the interests of the working class, maintained that ownership should be shared equally by all members of society. This idea was the conclusion drawn from Marx's interpretation of history, which is emphatically Taurean in its strict materialism, holding that all human institutions are created solely in response to economic needs; that people are divided into classes by their relation to the land and capital, the sources of production; and that the ruling classes are inevitably toppled by those beneath them to effect a wider distribution of the wealth, until private property and the social classes based on it shall finally disappear altogether. Such a view of the world, centered entirely around the notion of materiality as the ultimate reality, shows to what lengths a Taurus can carry that idea. Another example is arch-capitalist William Randolph Hearst, who compulsively accumulated money and a collection of art objects which overflowed his home and filled warehouses. In *Citizen Kane,* the movie based on his life, this obsession was fully appreciated by the director and star, Orson Welles, himself a Taurus; he very pointedly shows Kane dwarfed by the overwhelming scale of the magnificent furnishings in his mansion, and at the end he lets the camera dwell on the acres of objects in storage that are the remains of Kane's life, monuments to a Taurean attachment to things.

This attachment may also be felt by Tauruses as a love of the earth, or nature, which is the original, eternal expression of "thingness," or materiality. The energy inherent in matter, revealed in the power of nature's dynamic processes, is a force that the Taurus especially understands and respects, and the beauty of nature provides satisfaction for his visual sense-desires, the eye for color and form for which Tauruses are noted. Translating his emotional and visual experience of nature through painting, Joseph Mallord William Turner conveyed a fascinated awe of the elements in their endless play, particularly the play of light and color. He continually refined his skill at approximating his visual sensations on canvas, and succeeded to the point where pure sensation alone, an almost abstract perception of color, is represented to suggest the scenes depicted. (Turner was also remarkably successful at turning his art back into matter, in the form of money, for which he had a healthy Taurean regard.) In America, two outstanding members of the "Hudson River school" of landscape painting were Tauruses, Frederick Edwin Church and George Inness; they painted beautiful, rolling vistas in which the Earth is celebrated as the great, fertile body that supports life. Wildlife was the preoccupation of Taurus John James Audubon, who combined his absorbing interest in natural history with his aptitude for drawing in a unique series of bird and animal portraits. In the fantastic scenes painted by Taurus Henri Rousseau, wild animals and lush vegetation frequently dominate the picture.

The instinctive feeling for nature that is seen in the work of these artists is also apparent in the life work of John Muir, an early crusader for national parks, and Frederick Law Olmsted, who designed city parks (such as Central Park in New York) that still make life bearable in major urban areas of congestion. The beauty that these Tauruses struggled to preserve a century ago has since become precious to all.

APRIL 20

Emperor Napoleon III of France	1808
Adolf Hitler (dictator)	1889
Joan Miro (painter)	1893
Harold Lloyd (actor)	1894
Norman Norell (fashion designer)	1900
Donald Wolfit (actor)	1902
Gregor Piatigorsky (cellist)	1903
Stanley Marcus (merchant)	1905
Robert F. Wagner (politician)	1910
Lionel Hampton (xylophonist)	1914
Nina Foch (actress)	1924
Ryan O'Neal (actor)	1941
Michael Greer (actor)	1943

APRIL 21

Charlotte Bronte (novelist)	1816
John Muir (naturalist)	1838
Max Weber (sociologist)	1864
Joe McCarthy (baseball manager)	1887
Henry de Montherlant (playwright)	1896
Steve Owen (football coach)	1898
Edmund "Pat" Brown (politician)	1905
Leonard Warren (opera singer)	1911
Anthony Quinn (actor)	1915
John Mortimer (playwright)	1923
Queen Elizabeth II of England	1926
Silvana Mangano (actress)	1930
Elaine May (comedienne)	1932

APRIL 22

Immanuel Kant (philosopher)	1724
Mme. de Stael (writer)	1766
Odilon Redon (artist)	1840
Nikolai Lenin (revolutionary leader)	1870
Alexander Kerensky (revolutionary leader)	1881
J. Robert Oppenheimer (physicist)	1904
Eddie Albert (actor)	1908
Kathleen Ferrier (singer)	1912
Yehudi Menuhin (violinist)	1916
Hal March (quizmaster)	1920
Janet Blair (actress)	1921
Richard Diebenkorn (artist)	1922

April 22 (*continued*)

Charlie Mingus (jazz musician)	1922
Charlotte Rae (actress)	1926
Kenneth Jay Lane (fashion designer)	1932
Fiorenza Cossotto (opera singer)	1936
Jack Nicholson (actor)	1937
Glen Campbell (singer)	1938
Jason Miller (actor and playwright)	1939

APRIL 23

Queen Elizabeth of Valois	1545
J. M. W. Turner (painter)	1775
James Buchanan (politician)	1791
Stephen A. Douglas (politician)	1813
Sergei Prokofiev (composer)	1891
Lucius D. Clay (army officer)	1897
Lester Pearson (Canadian politician)	1897
Vladimir Nabokov (writer)	1899
Warren Spahn (baseball player)	1921
Shirley Temple Black (actress and politician)	1928
Roy Orbison (singer)	1936
Sandra Dee (actress)	1942
Delano Meriwether (sprinter)	1943
Bernadette Devlin (Irish politician)	1947

APRIL 24
St. V. de Paul

Leonardo da Vinci (artist and inventor)	1452

Anthony Trollope (novelist)	1815
Willem de Kooning (painter)	1904
Robert Penn Warren (writer)	1905
Shirley MacLaine (actress)	1934
John Williams (guitarist)	1941
Barbra Streisand (singer)	1942

APRIL 25

Walter de la Mare (poet)	1873
Guglielmo Marconi (inventor)	1874
Fred Haney (baseball player)	1898
William Brennan (jurist)	1906
Edward R. Murrow (newsman)	1908
Jerry Barber (golfer)	1916
Ella Fitzgerald (jazz singer)	1918
Astrid Varnay (opera singer)	1918
Albert King (blues musician)	1925
Melissa Hayden (ballet dancer)	1928
Al Pacino (actor)	1940

APRIL 26

Emperor Marcus Aurelius of Rome	A.D. 121
Charles Willson Peale (painter)	1741
Lady Emma Hamilton (naval officer's mistress)	1763
John James Audubon (naturalist)	1785
Ferdinand Delacroix (painter)	1799
Friedrich von Flotow (composer)	1812
Frederick Law Olmsted (landscape architect)	1822
Michel Fokine (choreographer)	1880

April 26 (*continued*)
Ludwig Wittgenstein
 (philosopher) 1889
Anita Loos (writer) 1893
Rudolf Hess (Nazi official) 1894
Charles F. Richter
 (seismologist) 1900
Jean Vigo (film maker) 1905
Bernard Malamud (novelist) 1914
I. M. Pei (architect) 1917
Bruce Jay Friedman (writer) 1930
Carol Burnett (comedienne) 1934
Bobby Rydell (singer) 1942

APRIL 27

Henry Vaughan (poet) 1622
Edward Gibbon (historian) 1737
Samuel Morse (inventor) 1791
Herbert Spencer
 (philosopher) 1820
Ulysses S. Grant (politician) 1822
Norman Bel Geddes
 (producer and stage
 designer) 1893
Rogers Hornsby (baseball
 manager) 1896
Ludwig Bemelmans (writer) 1898
Walter Lantz (cartoonist) 1900
Snooky Lanson (singer) 1914
Coretta Scott King (civil
 rights leader) 1927
Igor Oistrakh (violinist) 1931
Anouk Aimee (actress) 1932
Sandy Dennis (actress) 1937

APRIL 28

James Monroe (politician) 1758
Louise Homer (opera singer) 1871
Joseph "Diamond Joe"
 Esposito (mobster) 1872

Lionel Barrymore (actor) 1878
John Jacob Niles (folk
 singer) 1892
Dunninger (magician) 1896
Tony "Big Tuna" Accardo
 (mobster) 1906
Robert Anderson
 (playwright) 1917
Rowland Evans, Jr.
 (columnist) 1921
Harper Lee (novelist) 1926
Carolyn Jones (actress) 1933
Ann-Margret (actress) 1941
Ivan Nagy (ballet dancer) 1943

APRIL 29

William Randolph Hearst
 (publisher) 1863
Thomas Beecham
 (conductor) 1879
Duke Ellington (jazz
 musician) 1899
Emperor Hirohito of Japan 1901
Fred Zinnemann (film
 director) 1907
Tom Ewell (actor) 1909
Celeste Holm (actress) 1919
Rod McKuen (poet and
 singer) 1933
Otis Rush (blues musician) 1934
Zubin Mehta (conductor) 1936
Johnny Miller (golfer) 1947
Jim Ryun (runner) 1947

APRIL 30

Franz Lehar (composer) 1870
Alice B. Toklas (cook) 1877
John Crowe Ransom (poet) 1888
Herbert Ferber (sculptor) 1906
Queen Juliana of the

April 30 (*continued*)

Netherlands	1909
Eve Arden (actress)	1912
Robert Shaw (choral conductor)	1916
Sheldon Harnick (lyricist)	1924
Corinne Calvet (actress)	1925
Cloris Leachman (actress)	1930
Bobby Vee (singer)	1943
King Carl XVI Gustavus of Sweden	1946
Don Schollander (swimmer)	1946

MAY 1

Queen Isabella of Castile	1451
Duke of Wellington (British army officer)	1769
George Inness (painter)	1825
Pierre Teilhard de Chardin (philosopher)	1881
Mark Clark (army officer)	1896
Theodore Roszak (artist)	1907
Kate Smith (singer)	1909
Winthrop Rockefeller (politician)	1912
Glenn Ford (actor)	1916
Danielle Darrieux (actress)	1917
Jack Paar (TV personality)	1918
Joseph Heller (novelist)	1923
Scott Carpenter (astronaut)	1925
Terry Southern (writer)	1928
Frank Beard (golfer)	1939
Judy Collins (folk singer)	1939

MAY 2

Alessandro Scarlatti (composer)	1660
Empress Catherine the Great of Russia	1729
Lorenz Hart (lyricist)	1895

Brian Aherne (actor)	1902
Benjamin Spock (pediatrician)	1903
Bing Crosby (singer)	1904
Philippe Halsman (photographer)	1906
Satyajit Ray (film maker)	1921
Theodore Bikel (folk singer)	1924
John Neville (actor)	1925
Lesley Gore (singer)	1946

MAY 3

King Edward II of England	1284
William Shakespeare (playwright) (baptismal date)	1564
Henry Fielding (novelist)	1707
Christopher Smart (poet)	1722
Marcel Dupre (organist)	1886
Golda Meir (Israeli politician)	1898
Walter Slezak (actor)	1902
Mary Astor (actress)	1906
Earl Wilson (columnist)	1907
Virgil Fox (organist)	1912
William Inge (playwright)	1913
Betty Comden (lyricist)	1915
Pete Seeger (folk singer)	1919
John Lewis (jazz musician)	1920
Sugar Ray Robinson (boxer)	1921
Tom O'Horgan (director)	1926
Joe Layton (choreographer)	1931
Engelbert Humperdinck (singer)	1937

MAY 4

St. Vincent de Paul (religious reformer)	1576
Horace Mann (educational reformer)	1796

May 4 (*continued*)

William Hickling Prescott (historian)	1796
Thomas Huxley (biologist)	1825
Frederick Edwin Church (painter)	1826
Francis Spellman (clergyman)	1889
Mary Ellis Peltz (journalist)	1896
Howard Da Silva (actor)	1909
Audrey Hepburn (actress)	1929
Roberta Peters (opera singer)	1930
El Cordobes (bullfighter)	1936

MAY 5

Oliver Cromwell (Puritan statesman)	1599
Soren Kierkegaard (philosopher)	1813
Karl Marx (philosopher)	1818
James Beard (gourmet)	1903
Ursula Jeans (actress)	1906
Alice Faye (actress)	1915
Pat Carroll (actress)	1927
Bob Woodward (reporter)	1943

MAY 6

Queen Marie de Medicis of France	1573
Andre Massena (army officer)	1758
Maximilien de Robespierre (revolutionary leader)	1758
Sigmund Freud (psychologist)	1856
Robert Peary (explorer)	1856
Rudolph Valentino (actor)	1895
Harry Golden (writer)	1902

Max Ophuls (film director)	1902
Toots Shor (restaurateur)	1905
Weeb Ewbank (football coach)	1907
Stewart Granger (actor)	1913
Orson Welles (actor and film director)	1915
T. H. White (writer)	1915
Ross Hunter (producer)	1924
Willie Mays (baseball player)	1931

MAY 7

David Hume (philosopher)	1711
Robert Browning (poet)	1812
Johannes Brahms (composer)	1833
Peter Ilyich Tchaikovsky (composer)	1840
Rabindranath Tagore (poet)	1861
Gabby Hayes (actor)	1885
Archibald MacLeish (writer)	1892
Gary Cooper (actor)	1901
Max Rafferty (politician)	1917
Eva Peron (Argentine politician)	1919
Darren McGavin (actor)	1922
Anne Baxter (actress)	1923
Dick Williams (baseball manager)	1929
Teresa Brewer (singer)	1931
Johnny Unitas (football player)	1933

MAY 8

Oscar Hammerstein (impresario)	1846
Harry S Truman (politician)	1884
Thomas B. Costain (writer)	1885
Francis D. Ouimet (golfer)	1893

May 8 (*continued*)

Fulton Sheen (clergyman)	1895
Edmund Wilson (critic)	1895
Fernandel (comedian)	1903
Roberto Rossellini (film director)	1906
Mary Lou Williams (jazz musician)	1910
Carmen Mathews (singer)	1918
Lex Barker (actor)	1919
Sloan Wilson (writer)	1920
Theodore Sorenson (historian)	1928
Sonny Liston (boxer)	1932
Salome Jens (actress)	1935
Rick Nelson (singer)	1940
Gary Glitter (singer)	1944

MAY 9

Giovanni Paisiello (composer)	1741
John Brown (abolitionist)	1800
James Barrie (writer)	1860
Henry J. Kaiser (industrialist)	1882
Jose Ortega y Gasset (writer)	1883
Carlo Maria Giulini (conductor)	1914
Daniel Berrigan (clergyman)	1921
Pancho Gonzales (tennis player)	1928
Geraldine McEwan (actress)	1932
Albert Finney (actor)	1936
Glenda Jackson (actress)	1936

MAY 10

John Wilkes Booth (assassin)	1838
Benito Perez Galdos (writer)	1843

Hugo Robus (sculptor)	1885
Max Steiner (composer)	1888
Fred Astaire (dancer)	1899
Dmitri Tiomkin (composer)	1899
David O. Selznick (producer)	1902
Carl Albert (politician)	1908
Ella Grasso (politician)	1919
Margo (actress)	1920
Nancy Walker (actress)	1922
Françoise Fabian (actress)	1935
Arthur Kopit (playwright)	1937
Manuel Santana (tennis player)	1938
Judith Jamison (dancer)	1944

MAY 11

William Lilly (astrologer)	1602
Joseph Addison (writer)	1672
Baron von Munchausen (raconteur)	1720
Alma Gluck (opera singer)	1866
Irving Berlin (composer)	1888
Margaret Rutherford (actress)	1892
Martha Graham (dancer and choreographer)	1894
Bidu Sayao (opera singer)	1902
Salvador Dali (painter)	1904
Kent Taylor (actor)	1907
Phil Silvers (comedian)	1912
Tyrone Power (actor)	1913
Mort Sahl (comedian)	1927
Valentino (fashion designer)	1932
Doug McClure (actor)	1938
Nancy Greene (skier)	1943

MAY 12

Socrates (philosopher)	467 B.C.
Emperor Justinian of Rome	A.D. 483

May 12 (*continued*)
Niccolo Machiavelli (Italian
statesman)   1469
Edward Lear (humorist)   1812
Florence Nightingale (nurse) 1820
Dante Gabriel Rossetti (poet
and painter)   1828
Jules Massenet (composer)   1842
Theodor Reik (psychologist)   1888
Marguerite Steen (writer)   1894
Jiddu Krishnamurti
(lecturer)   1895
Philip Wylie (writer)   1902
Wilfrid Hyde-White (actor)   1903
Howard K. Smith (newsman)   1914
Julius Rosenberg (alleged
spy)   1918
Yogi Berra (baseball player)   1925
John Simon (critic)   1925
Burt Bacharach (composer)   1929
Frank Stella (painter)   1936
George Carlin (comedian)   1937
Ronald Ziegler (press
secretary)   1939
Susan Hampshire (actress)   1941
Steve Winwood (rock
musician)   1948

MAY 13

Carolus Linnaeus (botanist)   1707
Empress Maria Theresa of
Austria   1717
Alphonse Daudet (poet)   1840
Arthur Sullivan (composer)   1842
Gabriel Faure (composer)   1845
Georges Braque (painter)   1882
Daphne du Maurier (writer)   1907
Joe Louis (boxer)   1914
Richard Avedon
(photographer)   1923
Theodore Mann (director)   1924

Beatrice Arthur (actress)   1926
Clive Barnes (critic)   1927
Mike Gravel (politician)   1930
Zohra Lampert (actress)   1936
Stevie Wonder (singer)   1950

MAY 14

Gabriel Fahrenheit
(physicist)   1686
Otto Klemperer (conductor)   1885
Norman Luboff (choral
conductor)   1917
Patrice Munsel (singer)   1925
Bobby Darin (singer)   1936
Jack Bruce (rock musician)   1943

MAY 15

Klemens von Metternich
(Austrian statesman)   1773
L. Frank Baum (writer)   1856
Pierre Curie (physicist)   1859
Arthur Schnitzler
(playwright)   1862
Otto Dibelius (Lutheran
leader)   1880
Katherine Anne Porter
(writer)   1890
Arletty (actress)   1898
Richard Daley (politician)   1902
Clifton Fadiman (literary
critic)   1904
Joseph Cotten (actor)   1905
Thomas C. Dodd (politician) 1907
James Mason (actor)   1909
Constance Cummings
(actress)   1910
Max Frisch (writer)   1911

May 15 (*continued*)

Eddy Arnold (country
   singer)   1918
Patrick Murphy (public
   official)   1920
Peter Shaffer (playwright)   1926
Jasper Johns (artist)   1930
Ken Venturi (golfer)   1931
Anna Maria Alberghetti
   (actress)   1936
Paul Zindel (playwright)   1936
Trini Lopez (bandleader)   1937

MAY 16

William Henry Seward
   (government official)   1801
Richard Tauber (opera
   singer)   1892
Kenji Mizoguchi (film
   maker)   1898
Henry Fonda (actor)   1905
Margaret Sullavan (actress)   1911
Studs Terkel (interviewer)   1912
Woody Herman
   (bandleader)   1913
Ephraim Katzir (Israeli
   politician)   1916
Liberace (pianist)   1920
Lowell P. Weicker
   (politician)   1931
Lainie Kazan (singer)   1940
Olga Korbut (gymnast)   1955

MAY 17

Erik Satie (composer)   1866
Fausto Cleva (conductor)   1902
Jean Gabin (actor)   1904

Carl McIntire (evangelist)   1906
Zinka Milanov (opera singer)   1906
Clark Kerr (university
   official)   1911
Maureen O'Sullivan (actress)   1911
Archibald Cox (lawyer)   1912
Stewart Alsop (newsman)   1914
Birgit Nilsson (opera singer)   1918
Bob Merrill (songwriter)   1920
Harriet Van Horne
   (columnist)   1920
Dennis Hopper (actor)   1936
Paolo Bortoluzzi (ballet
   dancer)   1938
Ronald Tavel (writer)   1941

MAY 18

Louis Gottschalk (composer)   1829
Karl Goldmark (composer)   1830
Czar Nicholas II of Russia   1868
Bertrand Russell
   (philosopher)   1872
Walter Gropius (architect)   1883
Ezio Pinza (opera singer)   1895
Frank Capra (film maker)   1897
Kenneth Keating (politician)   1900
Meredith Willson
   (composer)   1902
Jacob Javits (politician)   1904
Clifford Curzon (pianist)   1907
John Crosby (TV critic)   1912
Perry Como (singer)   1913
Boris Christoff (opera singer)   1919
Margot Fonteyn (ballet
   dancer)   1919
Patrick Dennis (novelist)   1921
Robert Morse (actor)   1931
Dwayne Hickman (actor)   1934
Brooks Robinson (baseball
   player)   1937

May 18 (*continued*)
Reggie Jackson (baseball
  player)   1946

MAY 19

Nellie Melba (opera singer)   1861
Lady Nancy Astor
  (politician)   1879
Ho Chi Minh (Vietnamese
  politician)   1890
Mike Wallace (TV
  personality) *LITTLE*   1918
Malcolm X. (black leader)   1925
Harvey Cox (clergyman)   1929
Lorraine Hansberry
  (playwright)   1930
Nancy Kwan (actress)   1939
Peter Townshend (rock
  musician)   1945
John Paul II   *1920*

MAY 20

Dolley Madison (first lady)   1768
Honore de Balzac (novelist)   1799
John Stuart Mill
  (philosopher)   1806
Sigrid Undset (novelist)   1882
James Stewart (actor)   1908
"Commander" Edward
  Whitehead (soft-drink
  executive)   1908
Mary-Margaret Gibb
  (Siamese twins)   1912
Moshe Dayan (Israeli army
  officer)   1915
George Gobel (comedian)   1920
David Hedison (actor)   1929
Ken Boyer (baseball player)   1931
Stan Mikita (hockey player)   1940
Joe Cocker (singer)   1944
Cher (entertainer)   1946
Jimmy Henderson (rock
  musician)   1954

GEMINI

Element: Air / Quality: Mutable

Moving air, the inconstant wind, serves as a figure for the meaning of Gemini. In this changeable form air signifies human relations and communications established in all possible directions, first in one quarter and then in another, but not steadily maintained for a long time. Geminis are people whose minds are quick, curious, and restless for novelty, who make brief contacts for conversation and exchange of information with a wide variety of people, always moving from one encounter to a new one. In some way, even if only in a superficial, verbal fashion, they are able to relate to nearly everyone they meet, but are not so likely to form deep, intensely emotional attachments, being easily distracted and somewhat flighty. Their strength lies in the adaptability of the Gemini mind, which has inspired the imagery of a pair of twins; the Gemini has a sense of a dual or multiple self, which takes on one aspect or another as required by mood, circumstances, and the surrounding personalities, so that two or more fairly distinct persons may be seen to inhabit one versatile individual. The sign is ruled by Mercury, the planet named after the fleet-footed messenger of the gods, significator of verbal communication and cleverness of wit.

The Geminian facility with handling words and mental constructions is particularly noticeable, of course, in writers and thinkers. Ralph Waldo Emerson, who considered himself to be first a poet, is best known as author of the *Essays,* exercises purely of linguistic style and intellect such as especially suited his Gemini talents; even his poems, containing pithy thoughts or bits of philosophy, rather than sentiment or fantasy, are themselves like little essays in verse. In Emerson's horoscope his Gemini sun occupies the "house" that represents the expansion of intellectual horizons, philosophical understanding, metaphysics, and religion; this indicates a Geminian will (which is one inclined to reveal itself variously in mental activity, speaking, and writing) exercised in the area of higher thought, which would include the transcendentalist beliefs that Emerson expressed. By contrast, Walt Whitman's Gemini sun, in the "house" of ideals and hopes for society, shows his inner drive (again demonstrated verbally, and in numerous and varied contacts with others) directed toward cultural progress and the advancement of his fellow men. Thus, his Geminian skill with words was often used to extol American democracy, and during the Civil War, to promote the cause of preserving the Union; his belief in his society's great potential was based on acquaintance with many individuals of all sorts whom he met around the country and amid the bustle of city life (which he particularly enjoyed). The range of human conditions that he observed around him he also saw included in dual aspects of himself:

> I am of old as much as of young,
> Regardless of others, ever regardful of others,
> Maternal as well as paternal, a child as well as a man,
> Stuff'd with the stuff that is coarse and stuff'd with the stuff that is
> fine . . .
> A Southerner soon as a Northerner . . .

A highly developed Gemini intellect motivates the writings of Thomas Mann, a thinker whose ideas are represented by fictional characters, a novelist whose plots outline theories on such subjects as art, politics, and cultural mythology. His presence is felt as an intelligence in the background behind his characters, manipulating through them patterns of ideas, as he manipulates words in extremely complex sentence structures. The same sense of the artist standing behind his work as a thinker or theorist is felt in the music dramas of Gemini Richard Wagner, whom Mann greatly admired. The personages created by Wagner, like those of Mann, are figurations of mental concepts, acting out plays of ideas; the creator's head guides his heart. Working out intellectually his method of composition, Wagner perfected the Geminian technique of employing a system of short musical motifs, each associated with a specific character, thing, emotion, or idea, together constituting a whole musical vocabulary which could be arranged in endless combinations and modifications to convey meaning, like the words of language. Richard Strauss, a Gemini opera composer of lesser genius, borrowed from Wagner's technique, but lacked the compelling conviction of Wagner's mind; his Gemini tendencies are exhibited in extraordinary cleverness in composition, and in a talent for mentally calculated effects. In the music of Igor Stravinsky the Geminian cerebral approach results in a quality of clear objectivity, brilliant but cold. Another example of the Gemini mind directing creative impulses is seen in the graphic art of M. C. Escher, who devised ingenious visual patterns and puzzles that trick the perceptions and demand to be analyzed by thought processes.

A knack for intricate logic, often characteristic of Geminis, is the stock in trade of the super-rationalist Sherlock Holmes, created by a Gemini, Arthur Conan Doyle. Another Gemini master of detective fiction was Dashiell Hammett. His "Thin Man" Nick Charles and Nick's wife Nora, a pair noted for Geminian qualities including intelligence, wit, skill at fast repartee, and fondness for convivial socializing, were partly modeled on Hammett himself and his companion Lillian Hellman, also a Gemini.

The life of a socialite, with a large circle of acquaintances and frequent opportunities to meet new people, seems suited to Gemini inclinations, as in the case of Elsa Maxwell or the Duchess of Windsor. The ability to deal with many different people is used in another way by Gemini Henry Kissinger, expert at "shuttle diplomacy," which constantly requires adaptability to varying situations and personalities.

One more Gemini, Christine Jorgensen, the pioneer of sex changes, affords the most striking example of Gemini's essential quality, the duality of the twins.

MAY 21

Henri Rousseau (painter)	1844
Robert Montgomery (actor)	1904
Fats Waller (jazz musician)	1904
Gina Bachauer (pianist)	1913
Harold Robbins (novelist)	1916
Raymond Burr (actor)	1917
Dennis Day (singer)	1917
Ara Parseghian (football coach)	1923
Peggy Cass (actress)	1925

MAY 22

Dante Alighieri (poet)	1265
Gerard de Nerval (poet)	1808
Richard Wagner (composer)	1813
Mary Cassatt (painter)	1845
Arthur Conan Doyle (writer)	1859
Marcel Breuer (architect)	1902
"Bucketfoot" Al Simmons (baseball player)	1902
Laurence Olivier (actor)	1907
Vance Packard (writer)	1914
Judith Crist (film critic)	1922
Charles Aznavour (singer)	1924
Marisol (artist)	1930
Richard Benjamin (actor)	1938

Susan Strasberg (actress)	1938
Michael Sarrazin (actor)	1940
Barbara Parkins (actress)	1945

MAY 23

Anton Mesmer (hypnotist)	1733
Douglas Fairbanks (actor)	1883
Herbert Marshall (actor)	1890
Max Abramovitz (architect)	1908
Alicia de Larrocha (pianist)	1923
Rosemary Clooney (singer)	1928
Barbara Barrie (actress)	1931
John Browning (pianist)	1933
Joan Collins (actress)	1933
Daniel Klein (rock musician)	1946

MAY 24

Jean Paul Marat (revolutionary leader)	1744
Queen Victoria of England	1819
George Washington Carver (scientist)	1864
Harry Emerson Fosdick (preacher)	1878
Elsa Maxwell (socialite)	1883
Mikhail Sholokhof (novelist)	1905

May 24 (*continued*)

Lilli Palmer (actress)	1914
Siobhan McKenna (actress)	1923
Mai Zetterling (film director)	1925
Arnold Wesker (playwright)	1932
Peter Nero (pianist)	1934
Chong (comedian)	1939
Bob Dylan (singer)	1941
Patti LaBelle (singer)	1947

MAY 25

Thomas Gainsborough (painter)	1727
Ralph Waldo Emerson (writer)	1803
Marshal Tito (Yugoslavian politician)	1892
Gene Tunney (boxer)	1897
Bennett Cerf (publisher)	1898
Theodore Roethke (poet)	1908
Steve Cochran (actor)	1917
Dorothy Sarnoff (actress)	1919
Jeanne Crain (actress)	1925
Miles Davis (jazz musician)	1926
Beverly Sills (opera singer)	1929
Ron Nessen (press secretary)	1934
Leslie Uggams (singer)	1943

MAY 26

John Wesley Hardin (outlaw)	1853
A. E. Housman (poet)	1859
Al Jolson (singer)	1886
Vivian Robson (astrologer)	1890
Mrs. Miller (TV personality)	1897
Erica Morini (violinist)	1906
John Wayne (actor)	1907
Robert Morley (actor)	1908
Aldo Gucci (shoe merchant)	1909

Artie Shaw (bandleader)	1910
Peter Cushing (actor)	1913
Inge Borkh (opera singer)	1917
Peggy Lee (singer)	1920
James Arness (actor)	1923
Alec McCowen (actor)	1925

MAY 27

Cornelius Vanderbilt (financier)	1794
Fromental Halevy (composer)	1799
Amelia Bloomer (feminist)	1818
Julia Ward Howe (writer)	1819
Jay Gould (financier)	1836
Wild Bill Hickok (frontiersman)	1837
Arnold Bennett (novelist)	1867
Georges Rouault (painter)	1871
Isadora Duncan (dancer)	1878
Dashiell Hammett (writer)	1894
Peter Marshall (chaplin)	1902
Rachel Carson (naturalist)	1907
Hubert Humphrey (politician)	1911
Vincent Price (actor)	1911
John Cheever (novelist)	1912
Sam Snead (golfer)	1912
Herman Wouk (writer)	1915
Christopher Lee (actor)	1922
Henry Kissinger (government official)	1923
John Barth (novelist)	1930
Cilla Black (singer)	1943

MAY 28

Edward Jenner (physician)	1749
William Pitt (British statesman)	1759

May 28 (*continued*)

Riccardo Zandonai (composer)	1883
Jim Thorpe (football player)	1888
Ian Fleming (novelist)	1908
Dietrich Fischer-Dieskau (opera singer)	1925
Carroll Baker (actress)	1931
Yvonne Dionne (quintuplet)	1934
Madeleine Le Roux (actress)	1946

Christine Jorgensen (transsexual)	1926
Clint Walker (actor)	1927
Agnes Varda (film director)	1928
Keir Dullea (actor)	1936
Michael J. Pollard (actor)	1939
Gilles Villemure (hockey player)	1940
Gayle Sayers (football player)	1943

MAY 29

Isaac Albeniz (composer)	1860
Josef von Sternberg (film director)	1894
Beatrice Lillie (comedienne)	1898
Bob Hope (comedian)	1904
John F. Kennedy (politician)	1917
Herb Shriner (humorist)	1918
Pearl Lang (dancer)	1922
Iannis Xenakis (composer)	1922
Paul Ehrlich (environmentalist)	1932

MAY 30

Albrecht Duerer (painter)	1471
Michael Bakunin (Russian revolutionary)	1814
Alexander Archipenko (sculptor)	1887
Howard Hawks (film director)	1896
Cornelia Otis Skinner (actress)	1901
Benny Goodman (clarinetist)	1909
Hugh Griffith (actor)	1912
Frank Blair (newscaster)	1915
George London (opera singer)	1920

MAY 31

King Philip II of Spain	1527
Alexander Pope (poet)	1688
Walt Whitman (poet)	1819
Fred Allen (comedian)	1894
Norman Vincent Peale (clergyman)	1898
Don Ameche (actor)	1908
Alfred Deller (singer)	1912
Henry Jackson (politician)	1912
Alida Valli (actress)	1921
Ellsworth Kelly (painter)	1923
Prince Rainier III of Monaco	1923
Julian Beck (actor)	1925
Clint Eastwood (actor)	1931
Shirley Verrett (opera singer)	1931
Peter Yarrow (singer)	1938
Joe Namath (football player)	1943

JUNE 1

Ignace Pleyel (piano manufacturer)	1757
Brigham Young (Mormon leader)	1801
John Masefield (poet)	1878
Ely Kahn (architect)	1884
Nelson Riddle (composer)	1921
Joan Caulfield (actress)	1922

June 1 (*continued*)
Andy Griffith (actor)   1926
Marilyn Monroe (actress)   1926
Pat Boone (singer)   1934
Cleavon Little (actor)   1939
Dean Chance (baseball
    player)   1941

JUNE 2

Jacopo da Pontormo
    (painter)   1494
Marquis de Sade (writer)   1740
Mikhail Glinka (composer)   1804
Thomas Hardy (novelist)   1840
Edward Elgar (composer)   1857
Hedda Hopper (columnist)   1890
Edwin Way Teale
    (naturalist)   1899
Johnny Weissmuller (actor)   1907
Ben Grauer (newscaster)   1908
Milo O'Shea (actor)   1926
Charles Conrad, Jr.
    (astronaut)   1930
Sally Kellerman (actress)   1938
King Constantine II of
    Greece   1940
Stacy Keach (actor)   1941
Charlie Watts (rock
    musician)   1941

JUNE 3

Jefferson Davis (Confederate
    politician)   1808
King George V of England   1865
Raoul Dufy (painter)   1877
Maurice Evans (actor)   1901
Jan Peerce (opera singer)   1904
Josephine Baker (dancer)   1906
Paulette Goddard (actress)   1911

Alain Resnais (film maker)   1922
Tony Curtis (actor)   1925
Colleen Dewhurst (actress)   1926
Allen Ginsberg (poet)   1926

JUNE 4

Alla Nazimova (actress)   1879
Mme. Chiang Kai-shek
    (sociologist)   1899
Richard Whorf (actor)   1906
Fedora Barbieri (opera
    singer)   1919
Robert Merrill (opera singer)   1919
Dennis Weaver (actor)   1924
Judith Malina (actress)   1926

JUNE 5

John Maynard Keynes
    (economist)   1883
Ruth Benedict
    (anthropologist)   1887
William Boyd (actor)   1898
Federico Garcia Lorca
    (writer)   1899
Jean-Paul Sartre
    (philosopher)   1905
Rosalind Russell (actress)   1912
Conrad Marca-Relli (artist)   1913
Tony Richardson (director)   1928
Bill Moyers (government
    official)   1934

JUNE 6

Velazquez (painter)   1599
Pierre Corneille (playwright)   1606
Nathan Hale (patriot)   1755
Alexander Pushkin (writer)   1799

June 6 (*continued*)

Empress Alexandra of Russia	1872
Thomas Mann (writer)	1875
Paul Dudley White (physician)	1886
Ninette de Valois (choreographer)	1898
Aram Khachaturian (composer)	1903
Maria Montez (actress)	1920
David R. Scott (astronaut)	1932
Philippe Entremont (pianist)	1934
Roy Innis (black leader)	1934
Dalai Lama XIV (Buddhist leader)	1935
Edward Giacomin (hockey player)	1939

JUNE 7

Beau Brummell (dandy)	1778
Empress Carlota of Mexico	1840
Paul Gauguin (painter)	1848
Carmela Ponselle (singer)	1892
George Szell (conductor)	1897
Elizabeth Bowen (novelist)	1899
Jessica Tandy (actress)	1909
Dolores Gray (actress)	1924
Charles Strouse (composer)	1928
Virginia McKenna (actress)	1931
Tom Jones (singer)	1940

JUNE 8

Robert Schumann (composer)	1810
J. E. Millais (painter)	1829
Frank Lloyd Wright (architect)	1869
John Mulholland (magician)	1898
Grant Lewi (astrologer)	1902
Ralph Yarborough (politician)	1903
Robert Preston (actor)	1918
Alexis Smith (actress)	1921
Malcolm Boyd (clergyman)	1923
Bo Widerberg (film maker)	1930
William L. Calley, Jr. (army officer)	1943

JUNE 9

Czar Peter the Great of Russia	1682
Patrick Henry (patriot)	1735
Otto Nicolai (composer)	1810
Carl Nielsen (composer)	1865
Titta Ruffo (opera singer)	1877
Cole Porter (composer)	1893
Fred Waring (choral conductor)	1900
Marcia Davenport (writer)	1903
Robert Cummings (actor)	1910
Robert McNamara (government official)	1916
Les Paul (singer)	1916
Lore Noto (producer)	1923
Mona Freeman (actress)	1926
Happy Rockefeller (politician's wife)	1926
Charles Wuorinen (composer)	1938
Nancy Sinatra (singer)	1940

JUNE 10

King Charles II of England	1630
Gustave Courbet (painter)	1819
Sessue Hayakawa (actor)	1890
Hattie McDaniel (actress)	1895
Immanuel Velikovsky (writer)	1895
Frederick Loewe (composer)	1904
Chester A. Burnett (blues singer)	1910

June 10 (*continued*)
Ralph Kirkpatrick
  (harpsichordist) 1911
Terence Rattigan
  (playwright) 1911
Saul Bellow (novelist) 1915
Prince Philip (royal consort) 1921
Judy Garland (singer) 1922
Maurice Sendak (illustrator) 1928
James McDivitt (astronaut) 1929
Gardner McKay (actor) 1932
F. Lee Bailey (lawyer) 1933

JUNE 11

John Constable (painter) 1776
Gerard Manley Hopkins
  (poet) 1844
Richard Strauss (composer) 1864
Richard Loeb (murderer) 1905
Jacques-Yves Cousteau
  (oceanographer) 1910
Vince Lombardi (football
  coach) 1913
Rise Stevens (opera singer) 1913
Richard Todd (actor) 1919
Michael Cacoyannis
  (director) 1922
William Styron (novelist) 1925
Carlisle Floyd (composer) 1926
Gene Wilder (actor) 1934
Chad Everett (actor) 1936
Joey Dee (actor) 1940

JUNE 12

Djuna Barnes (writer) 1892
Anthony Eden (British
  politician) 1897
William Lundigan (actor) 1914
David Rockefeller (financier) 1915
Uta Hagen (actress) 1919

Vera Hruba Ralston (actress) 1921
George Bush (government
  official) 1924
Vic Damone (singer) 1928
Brigid Brophy (writer) 1929
Jim Nabors (TV personality) 1933

JUNE 13

Fanny Burney (novelist) 1752
William Butler Yeats (writer) 1865
Elisabeth Schumann (singer) 1891
Basil Rathbone (actor) 1892
Mark Van Doren (writer) 1894
Carlos Chavez (composer) 1899
Ian Hunter (actor) 1900
Mickey Walker (boxer) 1901
Red Grange (football player) 1903
Luis Alvarez (physicist) 1906
Vieira da Silva (painter) 1908
Prince Aly Khan (playboy) 1911
Ralph Edwards (TV
  personality) 1913
Paul Lynde (actor) 1926
Michel Jazy (runner) 1936
Billy Cunningham
  (basketball player) 1943
Richard Thomas (actor) 1951

JUNE 14

Harriet Beecher Stowe
  (novelist) 1811
Carter the Great (magician) 1874
John McCormack (singer) 1884
Burl Ives (folk singer and
  actor) 1909
Dorothy McGuire (actress) 1918
Sam Wanamaker (actor) 1919
Gene Barry (actor) 1922
Pierre Salinger (government
  official) 1925

June 14 (*continued*)

Don Newcombe (baseball
player)   1926
Che Guevara (revolutionary
leader)   1928

JUNE 15

Regiomontanus (astronomer)   1436
King George III of England   1738
Edvard Grieg (composer)   1843
Ernestine Schumann-Heink
(opera singer)   1861
Harry Langdon (actor)   1884
Malvina Hoffman
(sculptress)   1887
Robert Russell Bennett
(composer)   1894
Erik H. Erikson
(psychologist)   1902
Max Rudolf (conductor)   1902
Saul Steinberg (artist)   1914
Erroll Garner (jazz
musician)   1921
Harry Nilsson (singer)   1942
Xaviera Hollander
(procuress)   1943
Aron Kinkaid (actor)   1943

JUNE 16

Adam Smith (economist)   1723
Alice Bailey (theosophist)   1880
Stan Laurel (comedian)   1895
Gerhard A. Gesell (jurist)   1910
Katharine Graham
(publisher)   1917
Desmond Doyle (ballet
dancer)   1932
Jim Dine (painter)   1935

Erich Segal (writer)   1937
Joyce Carol Oates (novelist) 1938

JUNE 17

Paul Delaroche (painter)   1797
Charles Gounod (composer)   1818
Igor Stravinsky (composer)   1882
Ralph Bellamy (actor)   1904
Red Foley (country singer)   1910
John Hersey (writer)   1914
Dean Martin (singer)   1917
Beryl Reid (actress)   1920
Maurice Nadjari (public
official)   1924
Alan Rich (music critic)   1924
Peggy Seeger (folk singer)   1935

JUNE 18

Ivan Goncharov (novelist)   1812
M. C. Escher (graphic artist) 1898
Grand Duchess Anastasia of
Russia   1901
Kay Kyser (bandleader)   1906
Jeanette MacDonald
(actress)   1907
E. G. Marshall (actor)   1910
Sammy Cahn (songwriter)   1913
Sylvia Porter (columnist)   1913
Richard Boone (actor)   1917
Louis Jourdan (actor)   1921
Tom Wicker (journalist)   1926
Paul McCartney (rock
musician)   1942

JUNE 19

Blaise Pascal (philosopher)   1623
Charles Coburn (actor)   1877

June 19 (*continued*)
Blanche Yurka (actress)   1893
Duchess of Windsor
   (socialite)   1896
Guy Lombardo (bandleader) 1902
Lou Gehrig (baseball player) 1903
George Voskovec (actor)   1905
Mildred Natwick (actress)   1908
Abe Fortas (jurist)   1910
Martin Gabel (actor)   1912
Alan Cranston (politician)   1914
Pauline Kael (film critic)   1919
Nancy Marchand (actress)   1928
Pier Angeli (actress)   1932
Gena Rowlands (actress)   1936

Malcolm McDowell (actor)   1943

JUNE 20

Jacques Offenbach
   (composer)   1819
Helen Traubel (opera singer) 1899
Lillian Hellman (playwright) 1905
Errol Flynn (actor)   1909
Chet Atkins (guitarist)   1924
Audie Murphy (actor)   1924
Ellis Rabb (director)   1930
Brian Wilson (singer)   1942
Andre Watts (pianist)   1946

CANCER

Element: Water / Quality: Cardinal

Cancer represents the source of the waters of the emotions, the spring where the feelings well up with an irresistible initial force. Feeling is the motivating energy in Cancers, in accordance with the principle of subjectivity symbolized by their ruler the moon, and the moods by which they are governed fluctuate like the moon's changing phases. As the moon influences plant and animal growth in a way that is imagined to be maternal, so Cancers have an urge to nourish, protect, and provide tender care for living things; at their best they are sympathetic and responsive to the needs of those close to them. For their own spiritual nourishment they put down deep roots grounded in home, family, and tradition, often clinging to relics and familiar usages honored in the past, or to the comfort and security of the household they establish, a warm and sheltered environment in which they can lead their all-important private lives. Like their namesake the crab they are intent upon self-protection, for although the Cancerian shell appears tough, it is brittle and readily cracked to expose a soft and vulnerable inside. Cancers are also as keenly sensitive to all kinds of emotional nuances as they are to being hurt.

The sensitivity and depth of spirituality associated with Cancer are evident in the appreciation of the human soul that makes the paintings of Rembrandt van Rijn memorable. Finely attuned to the most subtle feelings, Rembrandt explored a whole range of psychological complexities in his narrative pictures and portraits, treating his subjects (especially women and old people) with a loving tenderness that is exemplary of the sympathetic nature of Cancers. In a series of self-portraits from youth to old age his own soul is laid bare, undiminished, as this Cancerian was instinctively aware, by the limitations of the flesh.

Delight in full-bodied flesh, however, is outstandingly characteristic of the work of Peter Paul Rubens, also a Cancer. Unlike Rembrandt, Rubens was not inclined to view the body as a rather pitiable encumbrance to spirituality, nor did he suffer the reverses of fortune that made Rembrandt more than ever conscious of the transience of material forms; his huge appetite for life unabated, Rubens preferred to express his own deeply felt response to the human soul in a celebration of its splendid vehicle, the human body in a state of robust health and vigor. This did not prevent his penetrating eye from revealing in portraits the inner life of his subjects; further, it enabled him to immortalize in painting his love for the two women he married, as Rembrandt did in the paintings of his beloved Saskia and Hendrickje. Both men showed in this way how dear to the hearts of Cancers their home lives can be.

The complicated domestic affairs of King Henry VIII of England are the dominant feature in his personal history, which records obsessively repeated attempts at establishing a family that would satisfy his Cancerian need for security. With more lasting success he also established the Church of England; although his motive in this was political rather than religious, in setting himself up as head of a church he showed a resemblance to a number of other Cancers who initiated religious movements.

The most prominent of these is John Calvin, one of the founding fathers of Protestantism, who believed (as Henry VIII, a reigning monarch, could not) in the subordination of the state to the church, an ideal achieved in his Geneva theocracy and in Puritan New England; this accords with a Cancerian leaning toward the personal and private rather than the public aspects of life, or the spiritual rather than the temporal. Two other Cancers whose religious convictions led them to start major churches of their own were John Wesley, founder of the Methodist Church, and Mary Baker Eddy of the Christian Scientists.

A preoccupation with personal moral issues (as opposed to social morality) runs through the entire work of Cancer Nathaniel Hawthorne. He came naturally by this concern, being descended from old Salem Puritans and having spent twelve years after his graduation from college as a semi-recluse in the Salem home of his childhood, in a Cancerian retreat to the ancestral past. There he absorbed local history and legend, which provided him with much of the material for his later stories. A contemporary Cancer, Henry David Thoreau, is known for pitting the demands of individual conscience against those of the state (in the essay "On the Duty of Civil Disobedience"), and even better known for his retreat to a home in the woods, back to Mother Nature herself, whom he dearly loved.

The sentiments are usually well developed in Cancers, and in some cases sentimentality as well. Stephen Foster had a genius for both, which made his songs very successful in an era noted for particularly mawkish popular taste. More recently, the musical comedies of Frank Loesser, Richard Rodgers, Oscar Hammerstein II, and Jerry Herman, all Cancers, make a similar appeal to the sentimentality of modern audiences.

This emphasis on the soft-hearted emotions is related to the Cancerian mothering instinct, which takes various forms. It is altruistic in a saint such as Mother Cabrini, who instituted hospitals, orphanages, nurseries and schools for the poor, or in the case of Father Flanagan of Boys' Town, for example. Art Linkletter and Captain Kangaroo have made television careers out of their rapport with children, and Ann Landers and Abigail Van Buren, twin Cancers, have semi-officially established themselves in the image of everybody's American Mom. What is operating in all these cases is the responsive function symbolized in astrology by Cancer and its ruler, the moon.

JUNE 21

Cosimo de Medici (Italian statesman)	1519
Ben Jonson (playwright)	1572
Martha Washington (first lady)	1731
Rockwell Kent (painter)	1882
Pier Luigi Nervi (architect)	1891
Hermann Scherchen (conductor)	1891
Reinhold Niebuhr (theologian)	1892
Dorothy Stickney (actress)	1900
Percy Forman (lawyer)	1902
Al Hirschfeld (caricaturist)	1903
Gregorio Prestopino (painter)	1907
Mary McCarthy (writer)	1912
Paolo Soleri (architect)	1919
Jane Russell (actress)	1921
Judy Holliday (actress)	1922
Maureen Stapleton (actress)	1925
Carl Stokes (politician)	1927
Françoise Sagan (writer)	1935
Ron Ely (actor)	1938

JUNE 22

Henry Rider Haggard (writer)	1856

Julian Huxley (biologist)	1887
Erich Maria Remarque (novelist)	1898
David Burns (actor)	1902
John Dillinger (outlaw)	1903
Billy Wilder (film director)	1906
Anne Morrow Lindbergh (writer)	1906
Katherine Dunham (choreographer)	1910
Peter Pears (singer)	1910
Jennie Tourel (singer)	1910
Gower Champion (choreographer)	1921
Joseph Papp (producer)	1921
Bill Blass (fashion designer)	1922
Kris Kristofferson (singer)	1936
Pete Maravich (basketball player)	1948
Freddie Prinze (actor)	1954

JUNE 23

Empress Josephine of France	1763
Duke of Windsor (socialite)	1894
Alfred Kinsey (sexologist)	1894
Jean Anouilh (playwright)	1910
William P. Rogers (government official)	1913
Irene Worth (actress)	1916
Larry Blyden (actor)	1925

June 23 (*continued*)
Bob Fosse (director)   1927
Richard Bach (writer and
  aviator)   1936
Wilma Rudolph (athlete)   1940
James Levine (conductor)   1943

JUNE 24

King Edward I of England   1239
Henry Ward Beecher
  (preacher)   1813
Ambrose Bierce (writer)   1842
Jack Dempsey (boxer)   1895
Pierre Fournier (cellist)   1906
Phil Harris (actor)   1906
David Rose (composer)   1910
Norman Cousins (publisher)   1915
John Ciardi (poet)   1916
Jimmy Ernst (artist)   1920
Claude Chabrol (film maker)   1930
Pete Hamill (columnist)   1935
Jeff Beck (rock musician)   19—

JUNE 25

Antonio Gaudi (architect)   1852
Gustave Charpentier
  (composer)   1860
George Abbott (playwright
  and producer)   1887
Walter Brennan (actor)   1894
Moses Hadas (classicist)   1900
George Orwell (novelist)   1903
Anne Revere (actress)   1903
William Cahill (politician)   1912
Peter Lind Hayes (TV
  personality)   1915
Sidney Lumet (film director)   1924
June Lockhart (actress)   1925

James Meredith (civil rights
  leader)   1933
Willis Reed (basketball
  player)   1942
Carly Simon (singer)   1945

JUNE 26

George Catlin (painter)   1796
Baron Kelvin (physicist)   1824
Bernard Berenson (art critic)   1865
Riccardo Stracciari (opera
  singer)   1875
Jeanne Eagels (actress)   1890
Pearl S. Buck (writer)   1892
Stuart Symington (politician)   1901
Peter Lorre (actor)   1904
Wolfgang Windgassen (opera
  singer)   1914
Babe Zaharias (golfer)   1914
Giuseppe Taddei (opera
  singer)   1916
Eleanor Parker (actress)   1922
John Turner Sargent
  (publisher)   1924
Colin Wilson (writer)   1931
Claudio Abbado (conductor)   1933
Anna Moffo (opera singer)   1935

JUNE 27

W. T. Grant (merchant)   1876
Helen Keller (lecturer)   1880
Toti Dal Monte (opera
  singer)   1893
Philip Guston (painter)   1913
Willie Mosconi (billiard
  player)   1913
Captain Kangaroo (TV
  personality)   1927
Gary Crosby (singer)   1933

JUNE 28

John Wesley (Methodist)   1703
Jean-Jacques Rousseau
    (philosopher)   1712
Luigi Pirandello (writer)   1867
Richard Rodgers (composer)   1902
Ashley Montagu (novelist)   1906
Lester Flatt (country singer) 1914

JUNE 29

King James I of England   1566
Giacomo Leopardi (poet)   1798
George Washington Goethals
    (engineer)   1858
William Mayo (surgeon)   1861
Luisa Tetrazzini (opera
    singer)   1871
Paul G. Clancy (astrologer)   1897
Antoine de Saint-Exupery
    (writer)   1900
Nelson Eddy (actor)   1901
Joan Davis (comedienne)   1907
Leroy Anderson (composer)   1908
Frank Loesser (composer)   1910
Rafael Kubelik (conductor)   1914
Slim Pickens (actor)   1919
Harmon Killebrew (baseball
    player)   1936
Stokely Carmichael (black
    militant)   1941

JUNE 30

Walter Ulbricht (German
    politician)   1893
Francisco da Costa Gomes
    (Portuguese politician)   1914
Lena Horne (singer)   1917

Buddy Rich (drummer)   1917
Susan Hayward (actress)   1919
Dave Van Ronk (jazz
    musician)   1936

JULY 1

Increase Mather (clergyman)   1639
Gottfried Wilhelm von
    Leibnitz (philosopher)   1646
George Sand (writer)   1804
Charles Laughton (actor)   1899
William Wyler (film director) 1902
Mary Calderone (sex
    educator)   1904
Olivia deHavilland (actress)   1916
Farley Granger (actor)   1925
Hans Werner Henze
    (composer)   1926
Leslie Caron (actress)   1931
Rod Gilbert (hockey player)   1941
Karen Black (actress)   1942
Delaney Bramlett (singer)   19—

JULY 2

St. John of Capistrano
    (preacher)   1386
Christoph Willibald von
    Gluck (composer)   1714
Friedrich Gottlieb Klopstock
    (poet)   1724
Hermann Hesse (novelist)   1877
Tyrone Guthrie (director)   1900
Alan Webb (actor)   1906
Robert Sarnoff (broadcasting
    executive)   1918
Dan Rowan (comedian)   1922
Medgar W. Evers (black
    leader)   1925

July 2 (*continued*)

Patrice Lumumba (Congolese
  politician)   1925
Brock Peters (actor)   1927
Ahmad Jamal (jazz musician)   1930
Luci Baines Johnson Nugent
  (politician's daughter)   1947

J U L Y 3

Leos Janacek (composer)   1854
Franz Kafka (writer)   1883
George Sanders (actor)   1906
Earl Butz (government
  official)   1909
Stavros Niarchos (tycoon)   1909
Dorothy Kilgallen
  (journalist)   1913
Ken Russell (film maker)   1927
Pete Fountain (jazz
  musician)   1930
Carlos Kleiber (conductor)   1930
Tom Stoppard (playwright)   1937
Jean-Claude Duvalier
  (dictator)   1951

J U L Y 4

St. John of the Cross (mystic)   1542
Nathaniel Hawthorne
  (writer)   1804
Giuseppe Garibaldi (Italian
  patriot)   1807
Stephen Foster (composer)   1826
Calvin Coolidge (politician)   1872
George M. Cohan (producer)   1878
Louis Armstrong (jazz
  musician)   1900
Gertrude Lawrence (actress)   1901
Meyer Lansky (mobster)   1902

George Murphy (actor and
  politician)   1902
Lionel Trilling (writer)   1905
Howard Taubman (critic)   1907
Mitch Miller (musician)   1911
Francesco Molinari-Pradelli
  (conductor)   1911
Virginia Graham (TV
  personality)   1913
Baruch M. Korff (rabbi)   1914
Tokyo Rose (propagandist)   1916
Ann Landers (advice
  columnist)   1918
Abigail Van Buren (advice
  columnist)   1918
Eva Marie Saint (actress)   1924
Neil Simon (playwright)   1927
Stephen Boyd (actor)   1928
Gina Lollobrigida (actress)   1928
Geraldo Rivera (TV
  personality)   1943

J U L Y 5

Sarah Siddons (actress)   1755
David Farragut (naval
  officer)   1801
P. T. Barnum (showman)   1810
Cecil Rhodes (colonial
  capitalist)   1853
Wanda Landowska
  (harpsichordist)   1877
Jean Cocteau (writer)   1891
Henry Cabot Lodge, Jr.
  (government official)   1902
Milburn Stone (actor)   1904
Georges Pompidou (French
  politician)   1911
Janos Starker (cellist)   1924
Shirley Knight (actress)   1937

July 5 (*continued*)
Julie Nixon Eisenhower
   (politician's daughter)   1948

Mary Ford (singer)   1924
Vince Edwards (actor)   1928
Ringo Starr (rock musician)   1940

JULY 6

Emperor Maximilian of
   Mexico   1832
Andrei Gromyko (Soviet
   official)   1909
Laverne Andrews (singer)   1915
Dorothy Kirsten (opera
   singer)   1917
Merv Griffin (TV
   personality)   1925
Janet Leigh (actress)   1927
Donald McKayle
   (choreographer)   1930
Della Reese (singer)   1932
Vladimir Ashkenazy (pianist)   1937
James Wyeth (painter)   1946
Susan Ford (politician's
   daughter)   1957

JULY 7

King Henry VIII of England   1491
Gustav Mahler (composer)   1860
Marc Chagall (painter)   1887
George Cukor (film director)   1899
Julius Hoffman (jurist)   1895
Vittorio De Sica (film
   director)   1901
Robert A. Heinlein (writer)   1907
Gian Carlo Menotti
   (composer)   1911
William Kunstler (lawyer)   1919
Clinton Wilder (producer)   1920
Ezzard Charles (boxer)   1921
Pierre Cardin (fashion
   designer)   1922

JULY 8

Emperor Julius Caesar   102 B.C.
Jean de La Fontaine (poet
   and fabulist)   1621
Ferdinand von Zeppelin
   (aeronaut)   1838
John D. Rockefeller
   (tycoon)   1839
Percy Grainger (composer)   1882
Alec Waugh (novelist)   1898
Philip Johnson (architect)   1906
George Romney (politician)   1907
Nelson Rockefeller
   (politician)   1908
Walter Kerr (drama critic)   1913
Billy Eckstine (singer)   1914
Pamela Brown (actress)   1917
Faye Emerson (actress)   1917
Steve Lawrence (singer)   1935
Barbara Loden (actress and
   director)   1937
Cynthia Gregory (ballet
   dancer)   1945
Kim Darby (actress)   1948

JULY 9

Peter Paul Rubens (painter)   1577
Elias Howe (inventor)   1819
Ottorino Respighi
   (composer)   1879
Samuel Eliot Morison
   (historian)   1887
Edward Heath (British
   politician)   1916
Leonard Pennario (pianist)   1924

July 9 (*continued*)

David Hockney (artist)	1937
O. J. Simpson (football player)	1947

JULY 10

Camille Pissarro (painter)	1830
James Whistler (painter)	1834
Nicola Tesla (inventor)	1856
Marcel Proust (novelist)	1871
Giorgio de Chirico (painter)	1888
Carl Orff (composer)	1895
Legs Diamond (mobster)	1897
Ebe Stignani (opera singer)	1907
Thurgood Marshall (jurist)	1908
Ljuba Welitsch (opera singer)	1913
David Brinkley (newsman)	1920
Jean Kerr (writer)	1923
Bernard Buffet (painter)	1928
Jerry Herman (composer)	1933
Arthur Ashe (tennis player)	1943
Sue Lyon (actress)	1946
Arlo Guthrie (singer)	1947

JULY 11

Thomas Cranmer (clergyman)	1489
Thomas Bowdler (editor)	1754
John Quincy Adams (politician)	1767
John Wanamaker (merchant)	1838
Thomas Mitchell (actor)	1892
E. B. White (writer)	1899
Yul Brynner (actor)	1920
Jerald F. terHorst (journalist)	1922
Nicolai Gedda (opera singer)	1925
Herman Prey (opera singer)	1929
Tab Hunter (actor)	1931
Mark Lester (actor)	1958

JULY 12

Henry David Thoreau (writer)	1817
George Eastman (inventor and industrialist)	1854
Amedeo Modigliani (painter)	1884
Beatrice Fenton (sculptress)	1887
Kirsten Flagstad (opera singer)	1895
Buckminster Fuller (engineer and writer)	1895
Oscar Hammerstein II (lyricist)	1895
Pablo Neruda (poet)	1904
Milton Berle (comedian)	1908
Andrew Wyeth (painter)	1917
Mark Hatfield (politician)	1922
Van Cliburn (pianist)	1934
Bill Cosby (comedian)	1937

JULY 13

Father Flanagan (clergyman)	1886
Sidney Blackmer (actor)	1898
Kenneth Clark (art historian)	1903
Eric Portman (actor)	1903
Bosley Crowther (film critic)	1905
Dave Garroway (TV personality)	1913
Charles Scribner, Jr. (publisher)	1921
Carlo Bergonzi (opera singer)	1924
David Storey (writer)	1933
Cheech (comedian)	1946

JULY 14

John Singleton Copley (painter)	1738

July 14 (*continued*)

Emmeline Pankhurst (feminist)	1858
Irving Stone (writer)	1903
Isaac Bashevis Singer (writer)	1904
Terry-Thomas (actor)	1911
Woody Guthrie (folk singer)	1912
Gerald R. Ford (politician)	1913
Jerome Lawrence (playwright)	1915
Douglas Edwards (newscaster)	1917
Ingmar Bergman (film maker)	1918
Arthur Laurents (playwright)	1920
Dale Robertson (actor)	1923
John Chancellor (TV personality)	1927
Nancy Olson (actress)	1928
Polly Bergen (actress)	1930
Jerry Rubin (revolutionary)	1938
Clovis Ruffin (fashion designer)	1942

JULY 15

Rembrandt van Rijn (painter)	1606
Mother Cabrini (nun)	1850
Marjorie Rambeau (actress)	1889
Dorothy Fields (lyricist)	1905
Iris Murdoch (novelist)	1919
Julian Bream (guitarist)	1933
Linda Ronstadt (singer)	1945
Jan-Michael Vincent (actor)	1945

JULY 16

Alexander the Great (conqueror)	356 B.C.

Andrea del Sarto (painter)	1486
Mary Baker Eddy (Christian Scientist)	1821
Roald Amundsen (explorer)	1872
Barbara Stanwyck (actress)	1907
Ginger Rogers (actress)	1911
Bess Myerson (TV personality and consumer advocate)	1924
Patricia Wilde (ballet dancer)	1928
Margaret Court (tennis player)	1942

JULY 17

John Paul Jones (naval officer)	1747
John Jacob Astor (fur merchant)	1763
Erle Stanley Gardner (novelist)	1889
James Cagney (actor)	1904
Hardy Amies (fashion designer)	1909
Art Linkletter (TV personality)	1912
Lou Boudreau (baseball player)	1917
Phyllis Diller (comedienne)	1917
Eleanor Steber (opera singer)	1919
Donald Sutherland (actor)	1934
Diahann Carroll (singer)	1935

JULY 18

William Makepeace Thackeray (writer)	1811
Pauline Viardot-Garcia (opera singer)	1821
Edward Dent (musicologist)	1876
Vidkun Quisling (Norwegian politician)	1887

July 18 (*continued*)

Gene Lockhart (actor)	1891
S. I. Hayakawa (philologist)	1906
Clifford Odets (playwright)	1906
Hume Cronyn (actor)	1911
Harriet Hilliard Nelson (actress)	1912
Red Skelton (comedian)	1913
Kenneth Armitage (sculptor)	1916
L. Patrick Gray III (government official)	1916
John Glenn (astronaut)	1921
Yevgeny Yevtushenko (poet)	1933
Dion DiMucci (singer)	1939
Joe Torre (baseball player)	1940

JULY 19

Samuel Colt (inventor)	1814
Hilaire Degas (painter)	1834
Charles Mayo (surgeon)	1865
Arthur Rackham (illustrator)	1867
Herbert Marcuse (philosopher)	1898
William Scranton (politician)	1917
Robert O'Hearn (stage designer)	1921
George McGovern (politician)	1922
Patricia Medina (actress)	1923
Pat Hingle (actor)	1924
Helen Gallagher (actress)	1926
Ilie Nastase (tennis player)	1946

JULY 20

Hermann Uhde (opera singer)	1914
Edmund Hillary (explorer)	1919
Elliot Richardson (government official)	1920
Lola Albright (actress)	1925

Sally Ann Howes (actress)	1930
Nelson Doubleday (publisher)	1933
Diana Rigg (actress)	1938
Natalie Wood (actress)	1938

JULY 21

John Calvin (theologian)	1509
Frances Parkinson Keyes (writer)	1885
Hart Crane (poet)	1899
Ernest Hemingway (writer)	1899
Marshall McLuhan (writer)	1911
Isaac Stern (violinist)	1920
Kay Starr (singer)	1922
Anne Meacham (actress)	1925
Karel Reisz (film director)	1926
Jonathan Miller (comedian)	1934
Cat Stevens (singer)	1948

JULY 22

Gregor Johann Mendel (biologist)	1822
Edward Hopper (painter)	1882
Rose Kennedy (politicians' mother)	1890
Karl Menninger (psychiatrist)	1893
Hans Rosbaud (conductor)	1895
Stephen Vincent Benet (writer)	1898
Alexander Calder (sculptor)	1898
Amy Vanderbilt (etiquette adviser)	1908
Licia Albanese (opera singer)	1913
Margaret Whiting (singer)	1924
Orson Bean (actor)	1928
Vivien Merchant (actress)	1929
Oscar de la Renta (fashion designer)	1932

LEO

Element: Fire / Quality: Fixed

The fire of Leo is concentrated, intense solar fire, which stands for the vital energy that burns steadily at the heart of things. The desire to be the central point of a sphere, like Leo's ruler the sun, radiating heat and light outward in all directions, dominates the will of the Leo individual; the energy which he projects is his own cherished sense of personality, a conception dramatized and constantly re-enacted in personal and social encounters, or in public performance or creative endeavors. He gives generously of himself, and requires of others in return their admiration and respect for his dignity. If he feels sufficiently appreciated he is generally cheery and good-humored, fond of jokes, games, amusements, and recreations, the company of convivial friends, and spending money (if he can) on presents, personal indulgences, and entertainment. His outgoing, affable disposition usually brightens any gathering and wins him popularity, if his tendency to dominate does not become overbearing. He is at his best in a position where he can rightfully command, like the stereotype of the regal lion, his zodiacal beast, whose anthropomorphic qualities of nobility, pride, and magnanimity have always been associated with the sign.

Attaining to a position where unconditional power may be centralized around his own person, a Leo shines forth magnificently, delighting in his own splendor and in the sense of events revolving around himself. His flair for dramatic leadership is likely to inspire popular enthusiasm, but in his pride and eagerness to increase his power he invites the envious attacks of enemies. One example is Napoleon Bonaparte, a conqueror hailed in the name of liberalism, who made himself master of Europe and had himself proclaimed Emperor (taking the crown from the hands of the Pope and setting it on his own head). He loved the pompous trappings of royalty, and proceeded to create about himself an imperial court and satellite nobility, and set up his brothers and close allies as kings in all the states surrounding him. His ambition for glory, still not satisfied, tempted him to further enlarge his sphere of influence until he extended his forces too far, and eventually met defeat and disgrace.

Similarly Leonine was the career of Simon Bolivar, who achieved the position of most powerful man on the South American continent, unrivaled after San Martin's mysterious retirement from the field following a secret meeting with Bolivar (in which the Leo probably maintained that there should be only one king of the mountain—himself—and persuaded the more self-effacing Pisces to agree). As president of Greater Colombia, Bolivar's methods were highhanded, and he was widely accused of imperial designs; he did declare himself dictator, but was later forced to resign. Another dictator, Benito Mussolini, displayed his Leonine tendencies in grandstanding public performances and in his show of trumpery Roman grandeur and public works designed to please the crowds and glorify himself. Like Napoleon and Bolivar, he pushed his luck too far, and came to an ignominious end.

Haile Selassie of Ethiopia, styled "The Lion of Judah," was a long-surviving specimen of imperial Leonine grandiosity that seems anachronistic today. Fidel Castro, a Leo dictating absolutely in more modern fashion, has made a show of his guerrilla's costume and uninhibited proletarian exuberance instead of gold and purple robes and noble posturing, but he basks as happily as any king in the adulation of his people.

The role of graciously accepting public admiration, especially gratifying to the Leonine ego, is one not easily given up. Leo Henry Ford cultivated the image of a paternalistic benefactor beloved of his employees, ostentatiously paying them higher wages than any other industrial workers then received. However, when the trade union movement ungratefully threatened to take away management's lead as the guiding light of labor, Ford balked, suddenly no longer the solicitous guardian of his workers' welfare if it meant sharing with them the central command.

A Leonine talent for putting on a good show with an emphasis on plenty of color is the hallmark of Cecil B. DeMille's Hollywood spectaculars, as of Mick Jagger's personal performances with the Rolling Stones. Less overtly, it crops up in literary guise in Walter Scott's his-

torical romances such as *Ivanhoe,* in the swashbuckling adventure
novels (*The Three Musketeers, The Count of Monte Cristo*) of Alexandre Dumas the elder, and in accounts of true adventures, such as
The Seven Pillars of Wisdom by T. E. Lawrence (of Arabia).

A famous Leo adventuress, Mata Hari, apparently also had a liking
for color and excitement in her life; in her short but brilliant career
as a spy she put to practical use her Leonine self-assuredness and
fondness for taking risks. She illustrates the bold quality that is played
up as a kind of brassiness in her Leo sisters Mae West, Lucille Ball,
and Shelley Winters, and which has enabled Jacqueline Onassis to live
as she pleases in defiance of gossip and criticism. Its sustaining source
is the Leo's well-developed sense of self, which demands expression.

A science of selfhood was the life work of Carl Jung, who went
further than any other psychologist to include the depths of the unconscious in his view of the totality of self; that Jung never quite took
the next further step, beyond conscious and unconscious notions of
self altogether, is due to his resistance as a Leo to any psychology that
would dispense with a central "person" (as does Buddhist psychology,
for example). Madame Helena Blavatsky, an imposing Leo lady and
a founder of the Theosophical Society, borrowed from Buddhists and
others what she liked; she was content to acquire supernormal powers
which she often showed off, revealing in her spiritual pride that she
too was far from having disposed of the powerful Leonine conception
of self.

JULY 23

Max Heindel (occultist)	1865
Emil Jannings (actor)	1886
Raymond Chandler (writer)	1888
Emperor Haile Selassie of Ethiopia	1891
Michael Wilding (actor)	1912
Coral Browne (actress)	1913
Gloria DeHaven (actress)	1925
Leon Fleischer (pianist)	1928
Bert Convy (actor)	1935
Don Drysdale (baseball player)	1936

JULY 24

Simon Bolivar (liberator)	1783
Alexandre Dumas (*père*) (writer)	1802
Adolphe Adam (composer)	1803
Frank Wedekind (playwright)	1864
Ernest Bloch (composer)	1880
Amelia Earhart (aviatrix)	1898
Zelda Fitzgerald (novelist)	1900
Frank Silvera (actor)	1914

Ruggiero Ricci (violinist)	1918
Bella Abzug (politician)	1920
Alexander H. Cohen (producer)	1920
Rouben Ter-Arutunian (stage designer)	1920
Giuseppe di Stefano (opera singer)	1921
Ruth Buzzi (comedienne)	1936

JULY 25

Inigo Jones (architect and stage designer)	1573
Maxfield Parrish (painter)	1870
Yvonne Printemps (actress)	1895
Eric Hoffer (writer)	1902
Gianandrea Gavazzeni (conductor)	1909
Jack Gilford (actor)	1913
Frank Church (politician)	1924
Stanley Dancer (harness racing driver)	1927
Al Carmines (clergyman and composer)	1936
Dotson Rader (writer)	1942
Janet Margolin (actress)	1943

JULY 26

George Bernard Shaw
  (writer)   1856
Serge Koussevitzky
  (conductor)   1874
Carl Jung (psychologist)   1875
Andre Maurois (writer)   1885
Aldous Huxley (writer)   1894
Robert Graves (writer)   1895
Gracie Allen (comedienne)   1905
Salvador Allende (Chilean
  politician)   1908
Jason Robards, Jr. (actor)   1922
Jean Shepherd (radio
  personality)   1923
Stanley Kubrick (film maker)   1928
Mary Jo Kopechne
  (secretary)   1940
Mick Jagger (singer)   1943

JULY 27

Isaac Watts (hymnist)   1674
Joshua Reynolds (painter)   1723
Charlotte Corday (assassin)   1768
Alexandre Dumas (*fils*)
  (writer)   1824
Enrique Granados
  (composer)   1867
Ernst von Dohnanyi
  (composer)   1877
Anton Dolin (ballet dancer)   1904
Leo Durocher (baseball
  manager)   1906
Igor Markevitch (conductor)   1912
Mario Del Monaco (opera
  singer)   1915
Keenan Wynn (actor)   1916
Homer (country singer)   1920
David Blair (ballet dancer)   1932
Dennis Ralston (tennis
  player)   1942

Bobbie Gentry (singer)   1944
Peggy Fleming (skater)   1948

JULY 28

Petrarch (poet)   1304
Jean Baptiste Corot (painter)   1796
Giuditta Grisi (opera singer)   1805
Giulia Grisi (opera singer)   1811
Beatrix Potter (children's
  writer)   1866
Marcel Duchamp (artist)   1887
Joe E. Brown (comedian)   1892
Harry Bridges (labor leader)   1901
Rudy Vallee (singer)   1901
Gottlob Frick (opera singer)   1906
Malcolm Lowry (writer)   1909
Jacqueline Kennedy Onassis
  (first lady and tycoon's
  wife)   1929
Darryl Hickman (actor)   1933
Jacques D'Amboise (ballet
  dancer)   1934
Peter Duchin (bandleader)   1937
Mike Bloomfield (blues
  musician)   1943
Bill Bradley (basketball
  player)   1943
Sally Struthers (actress)   1948
Vida Blue (baseball player)   1949

JULY 29

Alexis de Tocqueville
  (writer)   1805
Francesco Cilea (composer)   1866
Booth Tarkington (writer)   1869
Maria Ouspenskaya (actress)   1876
Benito Mussolini (dictator)   1883
Sigmund Romberg
  (composer)   1887

July 29 (*continued*)

William Powell (actor)	1892
Clara Bow (actress)	1905
Dag Hammarskjoeld (UN official)	1905
Thelma Todd (actress)	1905
Melvin Belli (lawyer)	1907
Edwin O'Connor (writer)	1918
Richard Egan (actor)	1923
Robert Horton (actor)	1924
Mikis Theodorakis (composer)	1925
Don Carter (bowler)	1926
Paul Taylor (choreographer)	1930
David Warner (actor)	1941

JULY 30

Emperor Claudius I of Rome	10 B.C.
Emily Bronte (novelist)	1818
Thorstein Veblen (economist)	1857
Henry Ford (automobile manufacturer)	1863
Henry Moore (sculptor)	1898
Gerald Moore (pianist)	1899
Ben Piazza (actor)	1934
Buddy Guy (blues musician)	1936
Peter Bogdanovich (film director)	1939
Paul Anka (singer)	1941

JULY 31

S. S. Kresge (merchant)	1867
Casey Stengel (baseball manager)	1891
Jean Dubuffet (painter)	1901
Whitney Young, Jr. (social worker)	1921

Hank Bauer (baseball manager)	1922
Don Murray (actor)	1929
France Nuyen (actress)	1939
Geraldine Chaplin (actress)	1944
Evonne Goolagong (tennis player)	1951

AUGUST 1

William Clark (explorer)	1770
Francis Scott Key (lawyer)	1779
Richard Henry Dana (writer)	1815
Herman Melville (novelist)	1819
Jack Kramer (tennis player)	1921
Lionel Bart (composer)	1930
Julie Bovasso (playwright and director)	1930
Tally Brown (singer)	1934
Yves Saint Laurent (fashion designer)	1936
Jerry Garcia (rock musician)	1941

AUGUST 2

John French Sloan (painter)	1871
Arthur Dove (artist)	1880
Arthur Bliss (composer)	1891
Jack L. Warner (film executive)	1892
Helen Morgan (singer)	1900
Myrna Loy (actress)	1905
Gary Merrill (actor)	1915
Ike Williams (boxer)	1923
James Baldwin (writer)	1924
Carroll O'Connor (actor)	1924
Peter O'Toole (actor)	1933
Gundula Janowitz (opera singer)	1937
Marvin David Levy (composer)	1937
Kathy Lennon Clark (singer)	1943

AUGUST 3

John Thomas Scopes
(teacher)   1900
Dolores Del Rio (actress)   1905
Richard Adler (composer and
producer)   1921
Marilyn Maxwell (actress)   1922
Leon Uris (novelist)   1924
Billy James Hargis
(evangelist)   1925
Tony Bennett (singer)   1926
Bethel Leslie (actress)   1929
Egil "Bud" Krogh (lawyer)   1939
Martin Sheen (actor)   1940
Jay North (actor)   1952

AUGUST 4

Percy Bysshe Shelley (poet)   1792
Walter Pater (writer)   1839
William Henry Hudson
(writer)   1841
William Schuman
(composer)   1910
Maurice Richard (hockey
player)   1921
Kristoffer Tabori (actor)   1952

AUGUST 5

Ambroise Thomas
(composer)   1811
Guy de Maupassant (writer) 1850
Reginald Owen (actor)   1887
Conrad Aiken (poet)   1889
Naum Gabo (sculptor)   1890
Erich Kleiber (conductor)   1890
John Huston (film director)   1906
Robert Taylor (actor)   1911
George Reedy (press
secretary)   1917

Richard Kleindienst
(government official)   1923
Neil Armstrong (astronaut)   1930
John Saxon (actor)   1935
Gary Beban (football player) 1946

AUGUST 6

Alfred, Lord Tennyson
(poet)   1809
Scott Nearing (farmer)   1883
Louella Parsons (columnist) 1893
Dutch Schultz (mobster)   1902
Lucille Ball (comedienne)   1911
Michael Burke (baseball
executive)   1916
Robert Mitchum (actor)   1917
Ella Raines (actress)   1921
Andy Warhol (artist)   1927

AUGUST 7

Alan Leo (astrologer)   1860
Emil Nolde (painter)   1867
Gustav Krupp (industrialist) 1870
Mata Hari (spy)   1876
Billie Burke (actress)   1885
Ralph Bunche (government
official)   1904
Anjanette Comer (actress)   1942
Lana Cantrell (singer)   1944

AUGUST 8

Sara Teasdale (poet)   1884
Ernest Lawrence (physicist)   1901
Jesse Stuart (writer)   1907
Arthur Goldberg (jurist)   1908
Sylvia Sidney (actress)   1910
Daniel Mann (film director) 1912

August 8 (*continued*)

Dino De Laurentiis (film producer)	1919
Rory Calhoun (actor)	1922
Rudi Gernreich (fashion designer)	1922
Esther Williams (actress)	1923
Webb Pierce (country singer)	1926
Mel Tillis (country singer)	1932
Frank Howard (baseball player)	1936
Dustin Hoffman (actor)	1937
Connie Stevens (actress)	1938
Keith Carradine (actor)	1949

AUGUST 9

Giorgio Vasari (artist)	1511
Edouard Rothschild (financier)	1845
Reynaldo Hahn (composer)	1875
Walter Starkie (writer)	1894
Leonide Massine (choreographer)	1896
Jean Piaget (child psychologist)	1896
Solomon (pianist)	1902
Zino Francescatti (violinist)	1905
Herman E. Talmadge (politician)	1913
Ferenc Fricsay (conductor)	1914
Ralph Houk (baseball manager)	1919
Robert Shaw (actor)	1927
Bob Cousy (basketball player)	1928
David Steinberg (comedian)	1942

AUGUST 10

Camillo di Cavour (Italian statesman)	1810

Alexander Glazunov (composer)	1865
Herbert Hoover (politician)	1874
Douglas Moore (composer)	1893
John Ogden Merrill (architect)	1896
Norma Shearer (actress)	1904
Jane Wyatt (actress)	1912
Witold Malcuzynski (pianist)	1914
Rhonda Fleming (actress)	1923
Jimmy Dean (country singer)	1928
Eddie Fisher (singer)	1928
Martha Hyer (actress)	1934
Robert La Tourneaux (actor)	1946

AUGUST 11

Carrie Jacobs Bond (composer)	1862
Louise Bogan (sculptress)	1897
Lloyd Nolan (actor)	1902
Lyle Stuart (publisher)	1922
Mike Douglas (TV personality)	1925
Arlene Dahl (actress)	1927
Fernando Arrabal (playwright)	1932
Jerzy Grotowski (director)	1933
Tamas Vasary (pianist)	1933
Allegra Kent (ballet dancer)	1938

AUGUST 12

Mme. Helena Blavatsky (theosophist)	1831
Diamond Jim Brady (financier)	1856
Edith Hamilton (classicist)	1867
Christy Mathewson (baseball player)	1880

August 12 (*continued*)
Cecil B. DeMille (film
    producer)   1881
Oscar Homolka (actor)   1898
Czarevitch Alexis of Russia   1904
Cantinflas (comedian)   1911
Kurt Kasznar (actor)   1913
Marjorie Reynolds (actress)   1921
Cynthia Gooding (folk
    singer)   1924
John Derek (actor)   1926
Buck Owens (country
    singer)   1929
George Hamilton (actor)   1939

AUGUST 13

Lucy Stone (feminist)   1818
Annie Oakley (sharpshooter)   1860
Bert Lahr (comedian)   1895
Alfred Hitchcock (film
    director)   1899
Alfred Krupp (industrialist)   1907
Gene Raymond (actor)   1908
Ben Hogan (golfer)   1912
Archbishop Makarios III
    (Greek Orthodox prelate)   1913
Claudia McNeil (actress)   1917
George Shearing (jazz
    musician)   1919
Fidel Castro (dictator)   1927
Jim Buckley (publisher)   1944

AUGUST 14

Ernest Thompson Seton
    (writer)   1860
John Galsworthy (novelist)   1867
John Ringling North (circus
    executive)   1903

Feliks Topolski (painter)   1907
Georges Pretre (conductor)   1924
Russell Baker (journalist)   1925
David Crosby (rock
    musician)   1941
Connie Smith (singer)   1941
Debbie Meyer (swimmer)   1952

AUGUST 15

Emperor Napoleon Bonaparte
    of France   1769
Walter Scott (novelist)   1771
Thomas De Quincey (writer)   1785
Emma Calve (opera singer)   1858
Sri Aurobindo (mystic)   1872
Ethel Barrymore (actress)   1879
Edna Ferber (novelist)   1887
T. E. Lawrence (adventurer)   1888
Jacques Ibert (composer)   1890
Bill Baird (puppeteer)   1904
Julia Child (cook)   1912
Wendy Hiller (actress)   1912
Jack Lynch (Irish politician)   1917
Lukas Foss (composer)   1922
Robert Bolt (playwright)   1924
Janice Rule (actress)   1931
Princess Anne of England   1950

AUGUST 16

Antoine Lavoisier (chemist)   1743
Otto Harbach (lyricist)   1873
George Meany (labor leader)   1894
J. I. Rodale (horticulturist)   1898
Mae Clark (actress)   1910
Fess Parker (actor)   1927
Anne Blyth (actress)   1928
Robert Culp (actor)   1930
Frank Gifford (sportscaster)   1930

August 16 (*continued*)

Betsy von Furstenberg
(actress)   1931
Eydie Gorme (singer)   1932
Julie Newmar (actress)   1935
Suzanne Farrell (ballet
dancer)   1945
Lesley Ann Warren
(actress)   1946

AUGUST 17

King Henry V of England   1387
Davy Crockett
(frontiersman)   1786
Llewellyn George
(astrologer)   1876
Mae West (actress)   1892
John Hay Whitney
(publisher)   1904
Maureen O'Hara (actress)   1921
Chita Rivera (actress)   1923
Larry Rivers (painter)   1923
Francis Gary Powers (spy)   1929
Robert De Niro (actor)   1943

AUGUST 18

Meriwether Lewis (explorer)   1774
Emperor Franz Josef of
Austria   1830
Marshall Field (merchant)   1834
Pietro Belluschi (architect)   1899
Marcel Carne (film maker)   1906
John Koch (artist)   1909
Cisco Houston (singer)   1918
Walter J. Hickel
(government official)   1919
Jean Eckart (stage designer)   1921
Alain Robbe-Grillet (writer)   1922
Shelley Winters (actress)   1922

Grant Williams (actor)   1930
Roman Polanski (film maker)   1933
Roberto Clemente (baseball
player)   1934
Rafer Johnson (athlete)   1935
Robert Redford (actor)   1937
Ginger Baker (rock
musician)   1939
Christopher Jones (actor)   1941
Sarah Dash (singer)   1948

AUGUST 19

Izaak Walton (writer)   1593
John Dryden (writer)   1631
Mme. du Barry (courtesan)   1746
E. Nesbit (writer)   1858
Bernard Baruch (financier)   1870
Orville Wright (inventor)   1871
Georges Enesco (composer)   1881
Coco Chanel (fashion
designer)   1883
Alfred Lunt (actor)   1893
Ogden Nash (humorist)   1902
James Gould Cozzens
(novelist)   1903
Willie Shoemaker (jockey)   1931
Debra Paget (actress)   1933
Bobby Richardson (baseball
player)   1935

AUGUST 20

Benjamin Harrison
(politician)   1833
Edgar A. Guest (poet)   1881
Rudolph Bultmann
(theologian)   1884
Paul Tillich (theologian)   1886
Salvatore Quasimodo (poet)   1901

August 20 (*continued*)
Jack Teagarden (jazz
   musician) 1905
Al Lopez (baseball manager) 1908
Eero Saarinen (architect) 1910
Van Johnson (actor) 1916
Jacqueline Susann (actress
   and novelist) 1921
Carla Fracci (ballet dancer) 1938
Isaac Hayes (composer) 1942

AUGUST 21

Jean Greuze (painter) 1725
Jules Michelet (historian) 1798
Count Basie (jazz musician) 1906
Princess Margaret of
   England 1930
Melvin Van Peebles (writer
   and producer) 1932
Janet Baker (singer) 1933
Wilt Chamberlain (basketball
   player) 1936
Mart Crowley (playwright) 1936
Patty McCormack (actress) 1945

AUGUST 22

St. Anthony of Padua
   (monk) 1195
Claude Debussy (composer) 1862
Edward Johnson (operatic
   impresario) 1881
Jeff Davis (hobo king) 1883
Jacques Lipchitz (sculptor) 1891
Dorothy Parker (writer) 1893
Leni Riefensthal (film
   director) 1902
Henri Cartier-Bresson
   (photographer) 1908
John Lee Hooker (blues
   musician) 1917
Ray Bradbury (writer) 1920
Karlheinz Stockhausen
   (composer) 1928
Diana Sands (actress) 1934
Donald MacLeary (ballet
   dancer) 1937
Carl Yastrzemski (baseball
   player) 1939
Valerie Harper (actress) 1940

VIRGO

Element: Earth / Quality: Mutable

Virgo's element is earth metamorphosized, like ore smelted and refined into metal, or rock broken down by weathering and transformed by the addition of organic matter into soil. The process represented is that of adaptation to serve the requirements of utility, in which the unnecessary or impure is carefully eliminated, and the unmanageable reduced to small, workable units. The imperfections which Virgos recognize in themselves as undesirable elements they conscientiously strive to remove, especially such faults as laziness, silliness, sloppiness, and inefficiency, which they despise. Realistic and practical, they have an ability to analyze large, complicated problems or tasks into particularized components, and to deal with the separate details in turn. At work they are painstaking and persevering, being motivated by a sense of duty or by a desire to be of service to others. Virgo is ruled by Mercury, the planet associated with intelligence and craft. The Virgoan mind is acutely discriminating and analytical, and Virgos are often mercurially adept at small, detailed jobs, excelling at neat, careful work. The emblem of the sign is a young girl who is supposed to symbolize fastidiousness and caution, impeccable correctness and spotlessness, whether or not she is actually a virgin.

The question "whether or not . . ." has been asked about Queen Elizabeth I of England, who in any case was called "The Virgin Queen" because she put off all suitors for her hand, motivated partly by very practical political considerations. Awareness of her responsibility as a ruler ruled her life, so that with an instinctive Virgoan sense of duty she subordinated her personal affairs to the service of her high calling. As qualifications for her work she had all the diligence, caution, and calculating shrewdness associated with her sign—

qualities that also characterized another great Virgo monarch, Louis XIV of France, who did extremely properly the job of being king. Virgo Lyndon B. Johnson, himself no slouch at hard work and shrewd political maneuvering, wanted to be remembered in history for his great services to the "Great Society" he would perfect, but was prevented from realizing that Virgoan dream by a foreign war which his imagination failed to comprehend.

General Maxwell Taylor likewise misunderstood the Vietnam War, assuming that the conflict, which was political, could be resolved by military means; he was so blindly devoted to the military because it gave him the opportunity to satisfy his personal Virgoan desire to serve, service being his Virgoan ideal. A similar attitude led to renown for other efficient, organized Virgo generals, among them General John Joseph Pershing, Baron von Steuben, and the Marquis de Lafayette.

Social service is another vocation in which Virgos have typically distinguished themselves. One example is Jane Addams, founder of Hull House, a community settlement established to meet the educational, recreational, and medical needs of poor immigrants. Another Virgo, Margaret Sanger, who began her work as a public health nurse, went on to become a pioneer promoter of birth control. New techniques in the education of young children were the contribution of Maria Montessori, who determined that in order to train a young child's mind, his body and his faculties of sense perception must first be trained, through games and exercises that develop muscular coordination and sensory discrimination. This clear-sighted emphasis on the basic, concrete facts of experience is characteristic of the Virgoan approach to life.

Virgo Samuel Johnson was an outstanding exponent of the virtue of good sense gained through concrete experience; his ideal was a mind cleared of rubbish, a product of Virgoan selectivity and elimination of the useless. Johnson's great labor of "beating the track of the alphabet with sluggish resolution" (as he put it) resulted in the famous dictionary, which stands as a model of the Virgoan ability to categorize and analyze details. Johann Wolfgang von Goethe, another Virgo with an all-encompassing intellect, applied his brain not only to poetry but also to detailed analyses of scientific subjects, in an attempt to evolve theories based on the careful study of observable natural phenomena, instead of on pure mathematical abstraction. Equally opposed to impersonal abstractness in art, he once said, "I think nothing of poetry that is not rooted in the real."

The novels of Leo Tolstoy, based on acute observation of behavior, were a means of presenting in orderly fashion the chaotic material of the author's life, but Tolstoy demanded even more of art—that it be useful; in a late essay entitled "What Is Art?" he depreciated the value of his own fiction, declaring that *Uncle Tom's Cabin* was a more important work than *War and Peace* because it served a social purpose. Perhaps only a double Virgo could be so concerned with usefulness, and so self-critical. Tolstoy's Virgo sun and moon, situated in the horoscopic "house" that shows the private or inner spiritual life, indicate meticulous soul-searching, which resulted in a conversion to a religion of humility, symbolized by the adoption of peasant dress and a life of simplicity.

The longing for simplicity and return to nature may also be seen in the writings of other Virgos, such as Edgar Rice Burroughs, author of the Tarzan stories, or D. H. Lawrence, a relentless critic of modern industrial society. Walt Kelly, creator of *Pogo,* and R. Crumb of *Zap Comix* fame are two Virgos of recent times whose criticism of society has been voiced through simple, "natural" or very earthy characters.

What member of this sign might be taken to represent the figure of the Virgo herself? She is somewhere between the extremes of Twiggy on the one hand, and Sophia Loren and Raquel Welch on the other; Greta Garbo and Ingrid Bergman fall nicely in the middle, possibly best epitomizing the spirit of that cool, collected young woman.

AUGUST 23

King Louis XVI of France 1754
Edgar Lee Masters (poet) 1869
William Primrose (violist) 1903
Gene Kelly (dancer) 1912
Tex Williams (singer) 1917
Marian Seldes (actress) 1928
Vera Miles (actress) 1930
Viva (actress) 1941
Patricia McBride (ballet
  dancer) 1942
Keith Moon (rock musician) 1947

AUGUST 24

Aubrey Beardsley (artist) 1872
Max Beerbohm (writer) 1872
Richard Cushing
  (clergyman) 1895
Jorge Luis Borges (writer) 1899
Graham Vivian Sutherland
  (painter) 1903

AUGUST 25

King Ludwig I of Bavaria 1786
Lola Montez (adventuress) 1818

Allan Pinkerton (detective) 1819
Bret Harte (writer) 1839
Thomas Eakins (painter) 1844
King Ludwig II of Bavaria 1845
Bruno Bettelheim
  (sociologist) 1903
Ruby Keeler (dancer) 1909
Michael Rennie (actor) 1909
Walt Kelly (cartoonist) 1913
Mel Ferrer (actor) 1917
Leonard Bernstein
  (conductor) 1918
Richard Greene (actor) 1918
George Wallace (politician) 1919
Althea Gibson (tennis
  player) 1927
Sean Connery (actor) 1930

AUGUST 26

Prince Albert (royal consort) 1819
Guillaume Apollinaire
  (writer) 1880
Earl Long (politician) 1895
Peggy Guggenheim (art
  collector) 1898
Maxwell Taylor (army
  officer) 1901

August 26 (*continued*)

Christopher Isherwood
(writer) 1904

Wolfgang Sawallisch
(conductor) 1923

AUGUST 27

Georg Wilhelm Friedrich
Hegel (philosopher) 1770

Umberto Giordano
(composer) 1867

Theodore Dreiser (novelist) 1871

Samuel Goldwyn (film
executive) 1882

Man Ray (photographer) 1890

Lyndon Baines Johnson
(politician) 1908

Martha Raye (singer) 1916

Ira Levin (novelist) 1929

Sri Chimoy (guru) 1932

Tommy Sands (singer) 1937

Tuesday Weld (actress) 1943

Harry Reems (actor) 1947

AUGUST 28

Johann Wolfgang von Goethe
(poet) 1749

Karl Boehm (conductor) 1894

Charles Boyer (actor) 1899

Roger Tory Peterson
(ornithologist) 1908

Richard Tucker (opera
singer) 1913

Donald O'Connor (actor) 1925

Istvan Kertesz (conductor) 1929

Ben Gazzara (actor) 1930

Tito Capobianco (director) 1931

Andy Bathgate (hockey
player) 1932

Alice Playten (actress) 1947

AUGUST 29

Jean Auguste Ingres (painter) 1780

Oliver Wendell Holmes
(jurist) 1809

Maurice Maeterlinck
(playwright) 1862

Preston Sturges (playwright
and film director) 1898

Barry Sullivan (actor) 1912

Ingrid Bergman (actress) 1916

George Montgomery (actor) 1916

Charlie Parker (jazz
musician) 1920

Richard Attenborough
(actor) 1923

Dinah Washington (singer) 1924

Thomas Stewart (opera
singer) 1928

Elliott Gould (actor) 1938

AUGUST 30

Emperor Caligula of Rome A.D. 12

Jacques Louis David
(painter) 1748

Mary Shelley (writer) 1797

Maria Montessori (educator) 1870

Huey P. Long (politician) 1893

Raymond Massey (actor) 1896

John Gunther (writer) 1901

Roy Wilkins (black leader) 1901

Shirley Booth (actress) 1907

Fred MacMurray (actor) 1908

Joan Blondell (actress) 1909

Wolfgang Wagner (director) 1919

Regina Resnik (opera singer) 1922

August 30 (*continued*)

Elizabeth Ashley (actress)	1941
R. Crumb (cartoonist)	1943
Jean-Claude Killy (skier)	1943

AUGUST 31

Hermann Ludwig von Helmholtz (physicist)	1821
Amilcare Ponchielli (composer)	1834
Giovanni Verga (poet)	1840
Fredric March (actor)	1897
Arthur Godfrey (radio and TV personality)	1903
Dore Schary (playwright and producer)	1905
William Saroyan (writer)	1908
Richard Basehart (actor)	1914
Alan Jay Lerner (lyricist)	1918
Ted Williams (baseball player)	1918
Buddy Hackett (comedian)	1924
James Coburn (actor)	1928
Eldridge Cleaver (writer)	1935
Frank Robinson (baseball coach)	1935
Van Morrison (singer)	1945

SEPTEMBER 1

Emanuel Schikaneder (librettist)	1751
Engelbert Humperdinck (composer)	1854
Gentleman Jim Corbett (boxer)	1866
Edgar Rice Burroughs (novelist)	1875
Don Wilson (radio and TV personality)	1900

Walter Reuther (labor leader)	1907
Yvonne de Carlo (actress)	1922
Vittorio Gassman (actor)	1922
Melvin Laird (government official)	1922
Rocky Marciano (boxer)	1924
George Maharis (actor)	1933
Seiji Ozawa (conductor)	1935
Lily Tomlin (comedienne)	1936

SEPTEMBER 2

Queen Liliuokalani of Hawaii	1838
Eugene Field (poet)	1850
Friedrich Schorr (opera singer)	1888
Jean Dalrymple (producer and director)	1910
Romare Bearden (artist)	1914
Cleveland Amory (TV critic)	1917
Allen Drury (novelist)	1918
Martha Mitchell (public figure)	1918
Marge Champion (dancer)	1923
Victor Spinetti (actor)	1933
Mary Jo Catlett (actress)	1938
Jimmy Connors (tennis player)	1952

SEPTEMBER 3

Sarah Orne Jewett (writer)	1849
Louis Sullivan (architect)	1856
Loren Eiseley (anthropologist)	1907
Alan Ladd (actor)	1913
Kitty Carlisle (actress)	1914
Hank Thompson (singer)	1925
Anne Jackson (actress)	1926
Irene Papas (actress)	1926

SEPTEMBER 4

Czar Ivan the Terrible of Russia	1530
George Stubbs (painter)	1724
François Rene Chateaubriand (writer)	1768
Anton Bruckner (composer)	1824
Darius Milhaud (composer)	1892
Mary Renault (novelist)	1905
Richard Wright (novelist)	1908
Henry Ford II (automobile executive)	1917
Craig Claiborne (gourmet)	1920
Thomas Eagleton (politician)	1929
Mitzi Gaynor (actress)	1931
Richard Castellano (actor)	1933
Ken Harrelson (baseball player)	1941
Jennifer Salt (actress)	1944

SEPTEMBER 5

King Louis XIV of France	1638
Johann Christian Bach (composer)	1735
Giacomo Meyerbeer (composer)	1791
Jesse James (outlaw)	1847
Sarvepalli Radhakrishnan (Indian politician)	1888
B. Iden Payne (producer)	1891
Joseph Szigeti (violinist)	1892
Arthur Nielsen (marketing research engineer)	1897
Florence Eldridge (actress)	1901
Darryl F. Zanuck (film producer)	1902
Arthur Koestler (novelist)	1905
John Cage (composer)	1912
Frank Yerby (novelist)	1916

Jack Valenti (film executive)	1921
Bob Newhart (comedian)	1929
Carol Lawrence (actress)	1934
Joan Kennedy (politician's wife)	1936
Jonathan Kozol (writer)	1936
Raquel Welch (actress)	1940

SEPTEMBER 6

Marquis de Lafayette (army officer)	1757
Jane Addams (social worker)	1860
Joseph Kennedy (financier)	1888
Billy Rose (producer)	1899
Harold Scott (actor)	1935

SEPTEMBER 7

Victorien Sardou (playwright)	1831
Grandma Moses (painter)	1860
Elinor Wylie (poet)	1885
Edith Sitwell (writer)	1887
Taylor Caldwell (novelist)	1900
Michael DeBakey (surgeon)	1908
Elia Kazan (director)	1909
Anthony Quayle (actor)	1913
James Van Allen (physicist)	1914
Jacob Lawrence (painter)	1917
Peter Lawford (actor)	1923
Louise Suggs (golfer)	1923
Daniel Inouye (politician)	1924
James F. Neal (lawyer)	1929
Buddy Holly (singer)	1936
John Phillip Law (actor)	1937

SEPTEMBER 8

John Locke (philosopher)	1632
Antonin Dvorak (composer)	1841

September 8 (*continued*)

Jimmie Rodgers (country
singer)   1897
Orville Prescott (literary
critic)   1906
Jean-Louis Barrault (actor)   1910
Sid Caesar (comedian)   1922
Grace Metalious (novelist)   1924
Peter Sellers (actor)   1925
Nguyen Cao Ky (Vietnamese
politician)   1930
Patsy Cline (country singer)   1932
Frankie Avalon (singer)   1940

SEPTEMBER 9

Cardinal Richelieu (French
statesman)   1585
William Bligh (British naval
officer)   1754
Leo Tolstoy (writer)   1828
Max Reinhardt (director)   1873
Granville Hicks (writer)   1901
Paul Goodman (writer)   1911
Cliff Robertson (actor)   1925
Sylvia Miles (actress)   1932
Otis Redding (singer)   1941

SEPTEMBER 10

Mungo Park (explorer)   1771
Franz Werfel (writer)   1890
Mortimer Wheeler
(archaeologist)   1890
Leonard Lyons (columnist)   1906
Fay Wray (actress)   1907
Robert Wise (film director)   1914
Edmond O'Brien (actor)   1915
Yma Sumac (singer)   1927
Arnold Palmer (golfer)   1929
Roger Maris (baseball
player)   1934
Jose Feliciano (singer)   1945

SEPTEMBER 11

Edward Alleyn (actor)   1566
O. Henry (writer)   1862
D. H. Lawrence (writer)   1885
Alexander Dovzhenko (film
maker)   1894
Anne Seymour (actress)   1909
Jessica Mitford (writer)   1917
Charles Evers (black leader)   1922
Tom Landry (baseball
player)   1924
Alfred van Loen (sculptor)   1924
Lee Richardson (actor)   1926
Reubin Askew (politician)   1928
Ken Kesey (novelist)   1935
Gerome Ragni (actor)   1942

SEPTEMBER 12

H. L. Mencken (writer)   1880
Maurice Chevalier (actor)   1888
Alfred A. Knopf (publisher)   1892
Lewis Hershey (government
official)   1893
Ben Shahn (painter)   1898
Jesse Owens (runner)   1913
Irene Dailey (actress)   1920
Frank McGee (newsman)   1921
Dick Moore (actor)   1925
Harvey Schmidt (composer)   1929
Maria Muldaur (singer)   1942

SEPTEMBER 13

Diane de Poitiers (king's
mistress)   1499
Clara Schumann (pianist)   1819
Walter Reed (army surgeon)   1851
John Joseph Pershing (army
officer)   1860
Arnold Schoenberg
(composer)   1874

September 13 (*continued*)

Sherwood Anderson
  (novelist)   1876
J. B. Priestley (writer)   1894
Ruth McDevitt (actress)   1895
Leland Hayward (producer)   1902
Claudette Colbert (actress)   1905
Herbert Berghof (acting
  teacher)   1909
Roald Dahl (writer)   1916
Scott Brady (actor)   1924
Mel Torme (singer)   1925
Robert Indiana (painter)   1928
Nicolai Ghiaurov (opera
  singer)   1929
Jacqueline Bisset (actress)   1944

William Howard Taft
  (politician)   1857
Bruno Walter (conductor)   1876
Agatha Christie (writer)   1890
Jean Renoir (film maker)   1894
Milton Eisenhower
  (government official)   1899
John Mitchell
  (government official)   1913
Margaret Lockwood (actress)   1916
Jackie Cooper (actor)   1922
Bobby Short (singer)   1924
Cannonball Adderley (jazz
  musician)   1928
Rafael Fruehbeck de Burgos
  (conductor)   1933

SEPTEMBER 14

Luigi Cherubini (composer)   1760
Margaret Sanger (birth
  control advocate)   1883
Vittorio Gui (conductor)   1885
Hal Wallis (producer)   1899
Jack Hawkins (actor)   1910
Rolf Liebermann
  (impresario)   1910
Kay Medford (actress)   1920
Bud Palmer (public official)   1923
Zoe Caldwell (actress)   1933
Kate Millett (feminist)   1934
Lucas Samaras (artist)   1936
Nicol Williamson (actor)   1938

SEPTEMBER 15

King Richard the
  Lion-Hearted   1157
Duc de La Rochefoucauld
  (epigrammatist)   1613
James Fenimore Cooper
  (novelist)   1789

SEPTEMBER 16

Mikhail Kutuzov (Russian
  army officer)   1745
Nathan Meyer Rothschild
  (financier)   1777
Francis Parkman (historian)   1823
J. C. Penney (merchant)   1875
Jean Arp (artist)   1887
Nadia Boulanger (music
  teacher)   1887
Allen Funt (TV personality)   1914
Janis Paige (actress)   1923
Lauren Bacall (actress)   1924
Charlie Byrd (guitarist)   1925
B. B. King (blues musician)   1925
Peter Falk (actor)   1927
Anne Francis (actress)   1932
George Chakiris (actor)   1933
Rosemary Casals (tennis
  player)   1948

SEPTEMBER 17

Lodovico Ariosto (poet)   1474

September 17 (*continued*)
Queen Elizabeth I of England 1533
Friedrich von Steuben
    (army officer)   1730
William Carlos Williams
    (writer)   1883
Frederick Ashton
    (choreographer)   1906
Warren Burger (jurist)   1907
Hank Williams (country
    singer)   1923
George Blanda (football
    player)   1927
Roddy McDowall (actor)   1928
Anne Bancroft (actress)   1931
Orlando Cepeda (baseball
    player)   1937

SEPTEMBER 18

Samuel Johnson (writer)   1709
John Diefenbaker (Canadian
    politician)   1895
Harold Clurman (drama
    critic)   1901
Eddie Anderson (comedian)   1905
Greta Garbo (actress)   1905
Rossano Brazzi (actor)   1916
Jack Warden (actor)   1920

SEPTEMBER 19

Emperor Augustus Caesar
    of Rome   63 B.C.
"Colonel" Harland Sanders
    (restaurateur)   1890
Ernest Truex (actor)   1890
Bergen Evans (etymologist)   1904
Leon Jaworski (lawyer)   1905
William Golding (novelist)   1911
Clifton Daniel (newsman)   1912

Rogers C. B. Morton
    (government official)   1914
Charles Conerly (football
    player)   1922
Duke Snider (baseball
    player)   1926
Lurleen Wallace (politician)   1926
Rosemary Harris (actress)   1930
David McCallum (actor)   1933
Brian Epstein (rock
    musicians' agent)   1934
Sylvia Tyson (singer)   1940
Larry Brown (football
    player)   1947
Twiggy (model)   1949

SEPTEMBER 20

Upton Sinclair (novelist)   1878
Victor Sjoestroem (film
    director)   1879
Chuck Dressen (baseball
    manager)   1898
Kenneth More (actor)   1914
Arnold Auerbach (basketball
    executive)   1917
Goeran Gentele (operatic
    impresario)   1917
James Galanos (fashion
    designer)   1924
Rachel Roberts (actress)   1927
Peter Palmer (actor)   1931
Sophia Loren (actress)   1934

SEPTEMBER 21

King Francis I of France   1494
Pierre de Ronsard (poet)   1524
H. G. Wells (writer)   1866
Gustav Holst (composer)   1874

September 21 (*continued*)
Faber Birren (color theorist)   1900
Umberto Mastroianni
  (sculptor)   1910
Chico Hamilton (guitarist)   1921
Reies Lopez Tijerina
  (Chicano leader)   1926
Leonard Cohen (poet)   1934

SEPTEMBER 22

Michael Faraday (physicist)   1791
Erich von Stroheim (actor

and film director)   1885
Elisabeth Rethberg (opera
  singer)   1894
Paul Muni (actor)   1897
Joseph Valachi (mobster)   1904
Shepperd Strudwick (actor)   1907
David Riesman (sociologist)   1909
Martha Scott (actress)   1914
Henryk Szeryng (violinist)   1921
Joni James (singer)   1930
Ingemar Johansson (boxer)   1932
Mark Phillips (princess'
  husband)   1948

LIBRA

Element: Air / Quality: Cardinal

Communication and relatedness among people, represented in the zodiac by the element air, have their beginnings in the Libran impulse to establish connections with others, to reconcile opposites and bring about concord. The kind of tie that Libras are inclined to form is direct and personal, between one individual and another, as in a co-operative partnership involving two equals. This is the significance of the scales, an instrument used to balance one weight against another. The Libran appreciates the fact that one side of an equation is meaningless without the relationship to its opposite number that the scales imply, and accordingly he defines his central sense of "I" as it stands in relation to a "thou." Always seeing two sides to a proposition, he has difficulty making clear-cut choices between alternatives; he prefers instead to make compromises that will harmonize conflicts within his own mind, or between himself and others. The rulership of Venus over Libra emphasizes the desire for harmony and amicable relations, and denotes a love of beauty, of pleasant surroundings and agreeable company; the Libran is usually good-tempered and amiable, exercising the tact and diplomacy of a peacemaker, and the power of a charming smile.

Miguel de Cervantes in his *Don Quixote* used a scheme for tackling the subject of life that shows clearly the two-sidedness of the Libran general view. Idealism, personified in the novel by the knight, is set off against the persistent realism of the squire, both outlooks being presented fairly for just what they are worth, and pitted against each other in continuing arguments that never finally resolve the issue. To the Libran author it was evident that both sides are equally necessary to a unified conception of the total paradoxical truth, or that the truth lies somewhere in the middle between them. This is exactly the teaching of the Buddhist "Middle Way," that neither "the world" nor "release from the world" can be considered as ultimately real by itself, the one polarity requiring the existence of the other. The foremost propounder of this doctrine in the West has been the renowned Buddhist scholar and Libra, D. T. Suzuki, whose sun sign is further revealed in his dedication to achieving a Libran rapprochement between the ideas of East and West.

The philosophies of the idealists and of the realist-pragmatists were both rejected by Friedrich Nietzsche, an iconoclast who formulated his own ideas of truth in opposition to everyone else, including the masters he had once revered. Nietzsche's virulently antagonistic stance toward the rest of the world illustrates a form of the Libran compulsion to come to terms with others in some way—as a dedicated opponent if the possibility of compromise and friendly relations is denied.

Relation between opposites is of course most essentially manifest in the various forms of relation between the sexes. This is the subject that occupied Choderlos de Laclos in his novel *Les Liaisons dangereuses,* which is an examination of the game of seduction as played in late eighteenth-century society, and its tragic consequences of preventing real communion between men and women. The story's drastic, fatal conclusion dramatizes the author's Libran conviction that no good can come from desecrating the altar of Venus.

Unabashed worship of Venus, in the form of countless paintings of the goddess and of other sensuous, sinuous nude ladies, flowed from the studio of Libra Lucas Cranach, a purveyor of sixteenth-century German courtly elegance. Cranach was the most prolific and most accomplished among the northern artists of his time who revived a pagan eroticism at the expense of the Virgin Mary's hitherto unrivaled popularity as a subject for painting. Unchristian sensuality, even lewdness, likewise stand out in many of the works of the Italian Libra Caravaggio, as much in pictures of a wanton young John the Baptist as in those showing a lecherous Bacchus enjoying his refined pleasures.

The Libran dedication to pleasure, beauty and Amor proved stronger than the moral pieties of the Reformation century, but its happiest expression was found later, in an age that cultivated an unequivocally worldly style of amorous gallantry, the age of Antoine Watteau. Although aware that love's magic moments are fleeting, Watteau as a Libra was yet entirely in sympathy with human nature's attempt to catch at those moments. The lovers in his paintings are sometimes haunted by a sad regret, although they are fondly depicted in dress suitable for occasions of fashionable amusement. Later in the same century, François Boucher, a Libra of more superficial sensibilities than Watteau, decorated boudoirs, portrayed Madame de Pompadour in some of her gorgeous gowns, and also painted a great many Venuses and other attractive naked goddesses or royal mistresses (resembling Cranach both in his taste for painting fancy, stylish women's clothes, and in his large output of gracefully stylized female nudes).

Libra women, not surprisingly, are supposed to have a particularly winning manner, the quality that, allied to talent, endeared Jenny Lind, Sarah Bernhardt, Eleanora Duse, and Helen Hayes to large, adoring publics; the ability of Libra men to charm audiences has been most remarkably demonstrated by Ed Sullivan and Johnny Carson. Libran charm also helped Eleanor Roosevelt, Dwight D. Eisenhower, and Pierre Elliott Trudeau to win public affection. Natives of the sign who are not inspired by television or politics might identify instead with Brigitte Bardot or Marcello Mastroianni as examples of the Libran appeal.

SEPTEMBER 23

Euripides (playwright)   480 B.C.
William Holmes McGuffey
   (educator)   1800
Walter Lippmann (journalist) 1889
Walter Pidgeon (actor)   1898
Louise Nevelson (sculptor)   1900
Mickey Rooney (actor)   1920
Ray Charles (singer)   1932
Pat Suzuki (singer)   1934
Romy Schneider (actress)   1938
Tina Russell (actress)   1948

SEPTEMBER 24

Albrecht von Wallenstein
   (Austrian army officer)   1583
John Marshall (jurist)   1755
F. Scott Fitzgerald (novelist) 1896
Cheryl Crawford (producer
   and director)   1902
George Raft (actor)   1903
Jim McKay (sportscaster)   1921
John W. Young (astronaut)   1930
Anthony Newley (actor)   1931
Svetlana Beriosova (ballet
   dancer)   1932

Barbara Birdfeather
   (astrologer)   1940

SEPTEMBER 25

Jean Philippe Rameau
   (composer)   1683
C. K. M. Scott-Moncrieff
   (translator)   1889
William Faulkner (novelist)   1897
Mark Rothko (painter)   1903
Red Smith (sportswriter)   1905
Robert Bresson (film
   director)   1907
Phil Rizzuto (baseball
   player)   1918
Aldo Ray (actor)   1926
Colin Davis (conductor)   1927
Barbara Walters (TV
   personality)   1931
Glenn Gould (pianist)   1932
Ian Tyson (singer)   1933
Juliet Prowse (actress)   1936

SEPTEMBER 26

Tintoretto (painter)   1518
John Gay (composer)   1685

September 26 (*continued*)

Johnny Appleseed (pioneer)	1775
Jean Louis Gericault (painter)	1791
Ivan Pavlov (physiologist)	1849
Edmund Gwenn (actor)	1875
Alfred Cortot (pianist)	1877
T. S. Eliot (poet)	1888
Martin Heidegger (philosopher)	1889
Charles Munch (conductor)	1891
Pope Paul VI	1897
George Gershwin (composer)	1898
Donald Cook (actor)	1901
Dmitri Shostakovich (composer)	1906
Marty Robbins (singer)	1925
Julie London (singer)	1926
Patrick O'Neal (actor)	1927
Fritz Wunderlich (opera singer)	1930

SEPTEMBER 27

King Louis XIII of France	1601
George Cruikshank (illustrator)	1792
Sam Ervin, Jr. (politician)	1896
Albert Ellis (sexologist)	1913
Catherine Marshall (writer)	1914
Charles Percy (politician)	1919
Arthur Penn (film director)	1922
Jayne Meadows (actress)	1923
Sada Thompson (actress)	1929
Claude Jarman, Jr. (actor)	1934

SEPTEMBER 28

Prosper Merimee (writer)	1803
Friedrich Engels (socialist)	1820

Georges Clemenceau (French statesman)	1841
Elmer Rice (playwright)	1892
William S. Paley (broadcasting executive)	1901
Ed Sullivan (TV personality)	1902
Al Capp (cartoonist)	1909
Ethel Rosenberg (alleged spy)	1915
Peter Finch (actor)	1916
Marcello Mastroianni (actor)	1924
Brigitte Bardot (actress)	1934

SEPTEMBER 29

François Boucher (painter)	1703
Horatio Nelson (British naval officer)	1758
Elizabeth Gaskell (novelist)	1810
Henry Hobson Richardson (architect)	1838
Miguel de Unamuno y Jugo (philosopher)	1864
J. B. Rhine (parapsychologist)	1895
Enrico Fermi (physicist)	1901
Gene Autry (actor)	1907
Greer Garson (actress)	1908
Michelangelo Antonioni (film maker)	1912
Stanley Kramer (film producer)	1913
Trevor Howard (actor)	1916
John Butler (choreographer)	1920
Lizabeth Scott (actress)	1922
John Tower (politician)	1925
Anita Ekberg (actress)	1931
Richard Bonynge (conductor)	1930
Jerry Lee Lewis (singer)	1935
Madeline Kahn (actress)	1942

SEPTEMBER 30

Girolamo Savonarola
(reformer)   1452
Jacques Necker (economist)   1732
Hans Geiger (physicist)   1882
Lester Maddox (politician)   1915
Deborah Kerr (actress)   1921
Jesse Unruh (politician)   1922
Donald Swann (comedian)   1923
Truman Capote (writer)   1924
Angie Dickinson (actress)   1931
Johnny Mathis (singer)   1935
Marc Bolan (singer)   1947

OCTOBER 1

Annie Besant (theosophist)   1847
Paul Dukas (composer)   1865
Louis Untermeyer (writer)   1885
Oskar Kokoschka (painter)   1886
Marc Edmund Jones
(astrologer)   1888
Stanley Holloway (actor)   1890
Faith Baldwin (novelist)   1893
Vladimir Horowitz (pianist)   1904
Sam Yorty (politician)   1908
Everett Sloane (actor)   1909
Bonnie Parker (outlaw)   1910
Rudy Bond (actor)   1915
Walter Matthau (actor)   1920
James Whitmore (actor)   1921
William H. Rehnquist (jurist)   1924
Roger Williams (pianist)   1926
Tom Bosley (actor)   1927
Laurence Harvey (actor)   1928
Richard Harris (actor)   1930
George Peppard (actor)   1933
Julie Andrews (actress)   1935
Edward Villella (ballet
dancer)   1936

OCTOBER 2

Lord Chesterfield (writer)   1694
Paul von Hindenburg
(German statesman)   1847
Mohandas K. Gandhi
(Hindu leader)   1869
Wallace Stevens (poet)   1879
Groucho Marx (comedian)   1895
Bud Abbott (comedian)   1898
Sidney George Old
(astrologer)   1901
Graham Greene (novelist)   1904
Shirley Clarke (film maker)   1927
Moses Gunn (actor)   1929
Maury Wills (baseball player) 1932
Rex Reed (film critic)   1940
Don McLean (singer)   1945
Edward F. Cox (politician's
son-in-law)   1946

OCTOBER 3

William Crawford Gorgas
(epidemiologist)   1854
Eleanora Duse (actress)   1859
Pierre Bonnard (painter)   1867
Paul Foster Case (occultist)   1874
Karinska (costume designer)   1886
Louis Aragon (writer)   1897
Leo McCarey (film director)   1898
Gertrude Berg (actress)   1899
Thomas Wolfe (novelist)   1900
Jack LaLanne (physical
culturist)   1914
Gore Vidal (writer)   1925
Erik Bruhn (ballet dancer)   1928
Ming Cho Lee (stage
designer)   1930
Chubby Checker (singer)   1941

OCTOBER 4

Lucas Cranach (painter)	1472
Cesare Borgia (Italian politician)	1478
Giovanni Battista Piranese (architect)	1720
Jean Millet (painter)	1814
Rutherford B. Hayes (politician)	1822
Frederic Remington (painter)	1861
Pancho Villa (Mexican rebel)	1877
Buster Keaton (comedian)	1895
Frank Crosetti (baseball coach)	1910
Charlton Heston (actor)	1924
Felicia Farr (actress)	1932
H. Rap Brown (black militant)	1943

OCTOBER 5

Francesco Guardi (painter)	1712
Denis Diderot (philosopher)	1713
Chester Alan Arthur (politician)	1829
Louis Jean Lumiere (film maker)	1864
Karl Barth (theologian)	1886
Georges Bidault (French politician)	1899
Joshua Logan (director)	1908
Donald Pleasence (actor)	1919
Philip Berrigan (clergyman)	1923
Glynis Johns (actress)	1923
Diane Cilento (actress)	1933
Steve Miller (rock musician)	1943

OCTOBER 6

Jenny Lind (opera singer)	1820
G. Westinghouse (inventor)	1846

Edwin Fischer (pianist)	1886
Maria Jeritza (opera singer)	1887
Le Corbusier (architect)	1887
Zalman Shazar (Israeli politician)	1889
Janet Gaynor (actress)	1906
Carole Lombard (actress)	1908
Richard Dyer-Bennet (folk singer)	1913
Thor Heyerdahl (ethnologist)	1914
Paul Badura-Skoda (pianist)	1927
Anna Quayle (actress)	1936

OCTOBER 7

James Whitcomb Riley (poet)	1849
Niels Bohr (physicist)	1885
Elijah Muhammad (Black Muslim leader)	1897
Heinrich Himmler (Nazi official)	1900
Andy Devine (actor)	1905
Helen MacInnes (novelist)	1907
Alain Rothschild (financier)	1910
Vaughn Monroe (singer)	1911
Sarah Churchill (actress)	1914
Alfred Drake (actor)	1914
June Allyson (actress)	1923
Diana Lynn (actress)	1926
R. D. Laing (psychologist)	1927
Ellen Stewart (producer)	1931
Leroi Jones (writer)	1934

OCTOBER 8

Michelangelo Caravaggio (painter)	1573
Heinrich Schuetz (composer)	1585
Samuel Adams (patriot)	1722
Eddie Rickenbacker (aviator)	1890
Juan Peron (Argentine politician)	1895

October 8 (*continued*)

Daniel Murtaugh (baseball
    manager)   1917
Rona Barrett (columnist)   1936
Merle Park (ballet dancer)   1937

OCTOBER 9

Camille Saint-Saens
    (composer)   1835
Alfred Dreyfus (French
    army officer)   1859
Aimee Semple McPherson
    (evangelist)   1899
Jacques Tati (film maker)   1908
E. Howard Hunt
    (intelligence agent)   1918
John Lennon (rock musician)   1940
Joe Pepitone (baseball
    player)   1940
John Entwistle (rock
    musician)   1944
Nona Hendryx (singer)   1947
Jackson Browne (singer)   1948

OCTOBER 10

Jean Antoine Watteau
    (painter)   1684
Giuseppe Verdi (composer)   1813
Helen Hayes (actress)   1900
Alberto Giacometti
    (sculptor)   1901
Thelonious Monk (jazz
    musician)   1918
Ludmila Tcherina (ballet
    dancer)   1924
Harold Pinter (playwright)   1930
Adlai Stevenson III
    (politician)   1930

Daniel Massey (actor)   1933
Greg Lake (rock musician)   1947

OCTOBER 11

King Richard III of England   1452
Fernando De Lucia (opera
    singer)   1860
Fritz Stiedry (conductor)   1883
Eleanor Roosevelt (first lady) 1884
François Mauriac (writer)   1885
Charles Revson (cosmetics
    merchant)   1906
Joseph Alsop (newsman)   1910
Jerome Robbins (director)   1918
Russell Oberlin (singer)   1928
Ron Leibman (actor)   1937

OCTOBER 12

Helena Modjeska (actress)   1844
Ralph Vaughan Williams
    (composer)   1872
Aleister Crowley (occultist)   1875
Perle Mesta (hostess)   1891
Grayson Kirk (university
    official)   1903
Joe Cronin (sports executive) 1906
Jean Nidetch (weight-
    watching adviser)   1923
Dick Gregory (comedian)   1932
Luciano Pavarotti (opera
    singer)   1935

OCTOBER 13

Virgil (poet)   70 B.C.
Lillie Langtry (actress)   1852
Herblock (cartoonist)   1909
Robert Walker (actor)   1914

October 13 (*continued*)

Cornel Wilde (actor)	1915
Burr Tillstrom (puppeteer)	1917
Jack MacGowran (actor)	1918
Laraine Day (actress)	1920
Yves Montand (actor)	1921
Lennie Bruce (comedian)	1925
Frank D. Gilroy (playwright)	1925
Eddie Mathews (baseball player)	1931
Cliff Gorman (actor)	1936
Melinda Dillon (actress)	1939
Pamela Tiffin (actress)	1942

OCTOBER 14

Katherine Mansfield (writer)	1888
Dwight David Eisenhower (politician)	1890
e. e. cummings (poet)	1894
Lillian Gish (actress)	1896
Hannah Arendt (writer)	1906
Roger Moore (actor)	1927
Gary Graffman (pianist)	1928
John W. Dean III (government official)	1938

OCTOBER 15

Friedrich Wilhelm Nietzsche (philosopher)	1844
John L. Sullivan (boxer)	1858
P. G. Wodehouse (writer)	1881
Ina Claire (actress)	1895
C. P. Snow (writer)	1905
John Kenneth Galbraith (economist)	1908
Robert Trout (newsman)	1908
Arthur Schlesinger, Jr. (historian)	1917

Mario Puzo (novelist)	1921
Jose Quintero (director)	1924
Jean Peters (actress)	1926
Linda Lavin (actress)	1939

OCTOBER 16

Giuseppe Antonio Guarneri (violin maker)	1687
Jonathan Edwards (clergyman)	1703
Horace Walpole (writer)	1717
Noah Webster (lexicographer)	1785
Oscar Wilde (writer)	1854
David Ben-Gurion (Israeli statesman)	1886
Eugene O'Neill (playwright)	1888
Paul Strand (photographer)	1890
William O. Douglas (jurist)	1898
Robert Ardrey (anthropologist)	1908
Alice Pearce (actress)	1917
Linda Darnell (actress)	1923
Angela Lansbury (actress)	1925
Guenter Grass (novelist)	1927
Charles W. Colson (government official)	1931
Henry Lewis (conductor)	1932
Dave DeBusschere (basketball player)	1940

OCTOBER 17

Miguel de Cervantes (writer)	1547
William Laud (clergyman)	1573
Georg Buechner (playwright)	1813
A. S. Neill (educator)	1883
Isak Dinesen (writer)	1885
Spring Byington (actress)	1893

October 17 (*continued*)

Yvor Winters (writer)	1900
Nathanael West (novelist)	1904
Josef Marais (folk singer)	1905
Jean Arthur (actress)	1908
Arthur Miller (playwright)	1915
Marsha Hunt (actress)	1917
Rita Hayworth (actress)	1918
Montgomery Clift (actor)	1920
Rolando Panerai (opera singer)	1924
Tom Poston (actor)	1927
Julie Adams (actress)	1928
Sterling Moss (auto racer)	1929
Robert C. Atkins (physician and author)	1930
Jimmy Breslin (journalist)	1930
Evel Knievel (daredevil)	1938

OCTOBER 18

Canaletto (painter)	1697
Heinrich von Kleist (playwright)	1777
D. T. Suzuki (Buddhist scholar)	1870
Fanny Hurst (novelist)	1889
Lotte Lenya (singer)	1900
Miriam Hopkins (actress)	1902
Pierre Elliott Trudeau (Canadian politician)	1919
Richard Stankiewicz (sculptor)	1922
Melina Mercouri (actress)	1925
Chuck Berry (singer)	1926
George C. Scott (actor)	1927
Mike Todd, Jr. (producer)	1929
Lee Harvey Oswald (assassin)	1939
Laura Nyro (singer)	1947

OCTOBER 19

Choderlos de Laclos (writer)	1741
Lewis Mumford (sociologist)	1895
Emil Gilels (pianist)	1916
Herbert Kalmbach (lawyer)	1921
George Nader (actor)	1921
Jack Anderson (columnist)	1922
John Le Carre (novelist)	1931
Peter Max (artist)	1937

OCTOBER 20

Arthur Rimbaud (poet)	1854
John Dewey (philosopher)	1859
Charles Ives (composer)	1874
Bela Lugosi (actor)	1882
Wayne Morse (politician)	1900
Ellery Queen (writer)	1905
Arlene Francis (TV personality)	1908
Art Buchwald (columnist)	1925
Joyce Brothers (TV personality)	1928
Mickey Mantle (baseball player)	1931
Michael Dunn (actor)	1934
Jerry Orbach (actor)	1935

OCTOBER 21

Benjamin West (painter)	1738
Samuel Taylor Coleridge (poet)	1772
Alphonse de Lamartine (poet)	1790
Ted Shawn (choreographer)	1891
Georg Solti (conductor)	1912
Dizzy Gillespie (jazz musician)	1917

October 21 (*continued*)
Whitey Ford (baseball
  player)   1928
Manfred Mann (jazz
  musician)   1940

OCTOBER 22

Franz Liszt (composer)   1811
N. C. Wyeth (illustrator)   1882
Giovanni Martinelli (opera
  singer)   1885
Joseph Welch (lawyer)   1890

Constance Bennett (actress)   1905
Jimmy Foxx (baseball
  player)   1907
Nina Vance (director)   1915
Joan Fontaine (actress)   1917
Timothy Leary
  (psychedelicist)   1920
Dory Previn (composer)   1925
Robert Rauschenberg
  (painter)   1925
Elaine Shaffer (flutist)   1925
Annette Funicello (actress)   1942
Catherine Deneuve (actress)   1943

SCORPIO

Element: Water / Quality: Fixed

Water appears in Scorpio in a state of fixity, as if retained in a reservoir such as in a subterranean cavern, or behind a dam where its accumulated force may be used to generate energy in a new form. The power of emotion, symbolized by water, is built up by Scorpios in reserves of intense inner passions, violent antipathies and burning desires, which under control provide the source of their driving vitality and air of concealed strength. Motivated by extremist feelings, Scorpios destroy and create with equal fervor; they see these two compulsions reflected in all dynamic processes of growth, subsequent decay, and new growth, and are endlessly fascinated by this wonder of eternal life and death. They seek to plumb its mystery through avid practice of the alchemy of sex, the interlocking of two bodies which miraculously annihilates individual selfhoods in the momentary creation of a being which is only one. In its occult significance this act, symbolic of death and transfiguration, may be referred to Scorpio's ruler Pluto, significator of the principle of total transformation of conditions by cutting away or obliterating, thus clearing the way for regeneration. The scorpion, a secretive and death-dealing creature, less abstractly conveys a similar meaning.

The earliest incident recalled in the *Autobiography* of Benvenuto Cellini is of his taking a childish fancy to a scorpion and holding onto it, surprisingly without being stung. This story may reveal little more than that Cellini was intrigued by his sign's symbolism (of which he was certainly aware), and possibly that he attributed his good luck in surviving throughout a hazardous career to a charmed Scorpionic affinity for the violent and dangerous; in any event, his life was Scorpionic in being devoted equally to the development of his creative genius, and to whoring, brawling, and scheming against his enemies, always with passionate intensity. His propensity for sexual exploits, his easily provoked wrath and murderous vengefulness, his hot-blooded lust for living and his constant sense of the presence of death are all true to zodiacal type.

In other centuries the Scorpionic impulse has been expressed in various different ways, but the basic themes remain the same. William Hogarth, whose chief fame rests on *The Harlot's Progress* and *The Rake's Progress,* two series of pictures plainly drawn from experience, was also typically Scorpionic in his bitter fighting with his enemies, although being an eighteenth-century English Scorpio and not a Renaissance Italian one, he used his skill as a lampoonist instead of a sword. In the nineteenth century, Romantic enthusiasts of the diabolical were enchanted by the scary figure of a Scorpio, Niccolo Paganini, whose reputedly dissolute habits, Mephistophelean appearance, and uncanny ability as a violinist combined to create a legend. Charles Manson, whose name suggests Satanism, sex and murder, is an archetype for today of the terrible, demonic aspect of the Scorpion.

Feodor Dostoyevsky struggled against possession by the Scorpionic devils of violent, destructive passions that beset him, and which he saw inhabiting one part of the split Russian soul, contesting the field with a holy spirit of redeeming power. The drama of guilt and atonement, damnation and salvation, Satan against Christ, is the subject of his novels, which are mostly stories reeking with the smell of murder but also illuminated by a presence of saintliness. Dostoyevsky's obsession with the dualism of evil and good makes clear the persistence of an esoteric ancient symbol (mentioned in the Bible) for the sign known as Scorpio, that of an eagle; astrologers have interpreted its meaning by the image of a bird fierce and rapacious, but with the power of soaring high above the earth to the sky, suggesting the idea of the spirit's rebirth implicit in the death that the scorpion represents.

Martin Luther's Scorpionic aim was to stamp out evils in the Catholic Church so that faith might be reborn, but that goal necessitated extreme Scorpionic measures: a complete surgical removal from the Church. Voltaire, with his slogan *"Écrasez l'infâme!"* (Crush the infamous thing—referring to the Church and the Old Regime in general), was another Scorpio extremist in his deadly animosities, which he expressed in the most caustic terms. Ferreting out hidden evils and eliminating them was the preoccupation of Joseph McCarthy, hunter of Communist witches; other Scorpios have also acquired reputations for exposing corruption—Robert Kennedy on the Senate Labor Rackets Committee, and Senator Howard Baker in the Watergate investigation.

The Scorpio in politics is a formidable figure, cagey, tough and determined, and generally not averse to the use of force. Theodore Roosevelt, sneaking about with his big stick, is one example; Chiang Kai-shek, the indomitable old pirate of Taiwan, is another. Jawaharlal Nehru, in spite of being an advocate of peace, used warfare to drive the Portuguese from Goa and the Pakistanis from Kashmir, thus eliminating dangerous growths in the body of India; his daughter Indira Gandhi, also a strong, decisive Scorpio leader, attacks India's domestic problems as forcefully as she reacted to the civil war in Bangladesh.

As scientists, Scorpios are particularly keen to probe nature's secrets, to uncover what is hidden. Anton van Leeuwenhoek, the pioneer microscopist, and Edmund Halley and William Herschel, discoverers of astronomical bodies, followed the track of the concealed unknown in two different directions. Marie Curie was absorbed in the study of radioactivity, that process of disintegration in certain substances which in "dying" release great energy, a phenomenon that a Scorpio could especially well appreciate. Scorpio Christiaan Barnard was the first to successfully perform heart transplant surgery, a technique also decidedly figurative of Scorpio's meaning, that of life obtained through death.

OCTOBER 23

Sarah Bernhardt (actress)	1844
Paul Rudolph (architect)	1918
Ned Rorem (composer)	1923
Johnny Carson (TV personality)	1925
Diana Dors (actress)	1931
Chi Chi Rodriguez (golfer)	1935
Jordan Christopher (actor)	1940
Pele (soccer player)	1940
Michael Crichton (novelist)	1942

OCTOBER 24

Anton van Leeuwenhoek (microscopist)	1632
William Penn (colonist)	1644
Sybil Thorndike (actress)	1882
Moss Hart (playwright)	1904
Sonny Terry (blues musician)	1911
Tito Gobbi (opera singer)	1915
Sena Jurinac (opera singer)	1921
Y. A. Tittle (football player)	1926
David Nelson (actor)	1936
Bill Wyman (rock musician)	1941

OCTOBER 25

Johann Strauss, Jr. (composer)	1825
Georges Bizet (composer)	1838
Pablo Picasso (artist)	1881
Richard E. Byrd (explorer)	1888
Micheal Mac Liammoir (actor)	1899
Henry Steele Commager (historian)	1902
Paul Draper (dancer)	1909
Minnie Pearl (country singer)	1912
Norman O. Brown (writer)	1913
Barbara Cook (singer)	1927
Tony Franciosa (actor)	1928
Helen Reddy (singer)	1941

OCTOBER 26

King James II of England	1633
Domenico Scarlatti (composer)	1685
Philip Evergood (painter)	1901
Mahalia Jackson (gospel singer)	1911
Jackie Coogan (actor)	1914

October 26 (*continued*)
Lynn Anderson (singer)   1945
Holly Woodlawn (actress)   1946

OCTOBER 27

Niccolo Paganini (violinist)   1782
Isaac Singer (inventor)   1811
Theodore Roosevelt
    (politician)   1858
Emily Post (etiquette adviser)   1872
Alexei, Patriarch of Russia
    (Russian Orthodox leader)   1877
Jack Carson (actor)   1910
Jan Kott (literary critic)   1914
Dylan Thomas (poet)   1914
Teresa Wright (actress)   1918
Nanette Fabray (actress)   1922
Roy Lichtenstein (painter)   1923
Ruby Dee (actress)   1924
H. R. Haldeman
    (government official)   1926
Roberto Iglesias (dancer)   1927
Kyle Rote (sportscaster)   1928
Sylvia Plath (writer)   1932
Melba Moore (singer)   1945

OCTOBER 28

Georges Jacques Danton
    (revolutionary leader)   1759
Howard Hanson (composer)   1896
Elsa Lanchester (actress)   1902
Evelyn Waugh (novelist)   1903
Edith Head (costume
    designer)   1907
Jonas Salk (epidemiologist)   1914
Cleo Laine (singer)   1927
Joan Plowright (actress)   1929
Suzy Parker (actress)   1933

Jim Beatty (runner)   1934
Jane Alexander (actress)   1939

OCTOBER 29

John Keats (poet)   1795
Jean Giraudoux (playwright)   1882
Fanny Brice (comedienne)   1891
Paul Joseph Goebbels
    (Nazi official)   1897
Bill Mauldin (cartoonist)   1921
Jon Vickers (opera singer)   1926

OCTOBER 30

Christopher Columbus
    (explorer)   1451
John Adams (politician)   1735
Andre Chenier (poet)   1762
Paul Valery (poet)   1871
Ezra Pound (poet)   1885
Charles Atlas (bodybuilder)   1893
Ruth Gordon (actress)   1896
Antonino Votto (conductor)   1896
David Oistrakh (violinist)   1908
Fred W. Friendly (TV
    producer)   1915
Ruth Hussey (actress)   1917
Louis Malle (film maker)   1932
Grace Slick (singer)   1939

OCTOBER 31

Christopher Wren (architect)   1632
Alfred Nobel
    (philanthropist)   1833
Chiang Kai-shek (army
    officer)   1886
Ethel Waters (singer)   1900
Wilbur Shaw (auto racer)   1902

October 31 (*continued*)

Dale Evans (actress)   1912
Barbara Bel Geddes (actress) 1922
King Sihanouk of Cambodia   1922
Andrew Sarris (film critic)   1928
Lee Grant (actress)   1927
Michael Collins (astronaut)   1930
Tom Paxton (singer)   1937
Sally Kirkland (actress)   1944

NOVEMBER 1

Antonio Canova (sculptor)   1757
Stephen Crane (writer)   1871
Grantland Rice
  (sportswriter)   1880
Eugen Jochum (conductor)   1902
Victoria de los Angeles
  (singer)   1923
Betsy Palmer (actress)   1926
Gary Player (golfer)   1935
Jeannie Berlin (actress)   1949

NOVEMBER 2

Jean Baptiste Chardin
  (painter)   1699
Daniel Boone (frontiersman)   1734
Queen Marie Antoinette
  of France   1755
James Knox Polk (politician)   1795
Warren G. Harding
  (politician)   1865
Paul Ford (actor)   1901
Luchino Visconti (director
  and film maker)   1906
Burt Lancaster (actor)   1913
Ann Rutherford (actress)   1917
Ray Walston (actor)   1918
Keith Emerson (rock
  musician)   1944

NOVEMBER 3

William Cullen Bryant (poet)   1794
Vincenzo Bellini (composer)   1801
Andre Malraux (writer)   1901
Walker Evans
  (photographer)   1903
James Reston (journalist)   1909
Conor Cruise O'Brien
  (writer)   1917
Bob Feller (baseball player)   1918
Charles Bronson (actor)   1922
Monica Vitti (actress)   1933
Roy Emerson (tennis player)   1936
Terrence McNally
  (playwright)   1939

NOVEMBER 4

Richard Brinsley Sheridan
  (playwright)   1751
Will Rogers (humorist)   1879
Eugene Berman (artist)   1899
Ida Kaminska (actress)   1899
Paul Douglas (actor)   1907
Pauline Trigere (fashion
  designer)   1912
Gig Young (actor)   1913
Walter Cronkite (newsman)   1916
Art Carney (actor)   1918
Cameron Mitchell (actor)   1918
Martin Balsam (actor)   1919
Dick Groat (baseball player)   1930
Kate Reid (actress)   1930
Clark Graebner (tennis
  player)   1943

NOVEMBER 5

Eugene Debs (labor leader)   1855
Will Durant (writer)   1885

November 5 (*continued*)

Walter Gieseking (pianist)	1895
Joel McCrea (actor)	1905
Fred Lawrence Whipple (astronomer)	1906
Roy Rogers (actor)	1912
Vivien Leigh (actress)	1913
John McGiver (actor)	1913
Clifford Irving (writer)	1930
Ike Turner (singer)	1931
Donald Madden (actor)	1933
Jeb Stuart Magruder (government official)	1935
Art Garfunkel (singer)	1941
Elke Sommer (actress)	1941
Tatum O'Neal (actress)	1963

NOVEMBER 6

Desiderius Erasmus (humanist)	1467
John Philip Sousa (composer)	1854
Gus Kahn (composer)	1886
Walter P. Johnson (baseball player)	1887
Edsel Ford (automobile executive)	1893
Seymour Lipton (sculptor)	1903
Ray Conniff (bandleader)	1916
James Jones (novelist)	1921
Mike Nichols (director)	1931
Agustin Anievas (pianist)	1934
Warren Robertson (acting teacher)	1935
Sally Field (actress)	1946

NOVEMBER 7

Francisco de Zurbaran (painter)	1598

Captain James Cook (explorer)	1728
Marie Curie (physicist)	1867
Leon Trotsky (revolutionary)	1879
Dean Jagger (actor)	1903
Albert Camus (writer)	1913
Billy Graham (evangelist)	1918
Al Hirt (jazz musician)	1922
Joan Sutherland (opera singer)	1926
Johnny Rivers (singer)	1942
Joni Mitchell (singer)	1943

NOVEMBER 8

Hermann Rorschach (psychologist)	1884
Bucky Harris (baseball manager)	1896
Margaret Mitchell (novelist)	1900
Katharine Hepburn (actress)	1909
June Havoc (actress)	1916
Peter Weiss (writer)	1916
Gene Saks (director)	1921
Christiaan Barnard (surgeon)	1922
Patti Page (singer)	1927
Alain Delon (actor)	1935
Bonnie Raitt (singer)	1950

NOVEMBER 9

James Boswell (writer)	1740
Ivan Turgenev (novelist)	1818
Charubel (seer)	1826
King Edward VII of England	1841
Stanford White (architect)	1853
Marie Dressler (actress)	1871
Edna May Oliver (actress)	1883
Aureliano Pertile (opera singer)	1885
Ed Wynn (comedian)	1886

November 9 (*continued*)
Hedy Lamarr (actress)   1913
Sargent Shriver (politician)   1915
Spiro Agnew (politician)   1918
Florence Chadwick
  (swimmer)   1918
Ivan Moravec (pianist)   1930
Robert Gibson (baseball
  player)   1935
Mary Travers (singer)   1936
Tom Weiskopf (golfer)   1942

NOVEMBER 10

Jan Vermeer (painter)   1632
François Couperin
  (composer)   1668
Friedrich von Schiller
  (writer)   1759
Claude Rains (actor)   1889
J. P. Marquand (novelist)   1893
Tommy Dorsey (bandleader)   1905
Harry Andrews (actor)   1911
Jane Froman (singer)   1917
Richard Burton (actor)   1925

NOVEMBER 11

Feodor Dostoyevsky
  (novelist)   1821
King Gustavus VI of Sweden   1882
Ernest Ansermet (conductor)   1883
George Patton (army
  officer)   1885
Rabbit Maranville (baseball
  player)   1891
Lucky Luciano (mobster)   1897
Rene Clair (film maker)   1898
Pat O'Brien (actor)   1899
Hugh Scott (politician)   1900
Alger Hiss (public official)   1904

Sam Spiegel (producer)   1904
Robert Ryan (actor)   1909
Howard Fast (novelist)   1914
Kurt Vonnegut (writer)   1922
Jonathan Winters
  (comedian)   1925
LaVern Baker (singer)   1929
Bibi Andersson (actress)   1935
Susan Kohner (actress)   1936
Neil Young (rock musician)   1945

NOVEMBER 12

Benvenuto Cellini (artist)   1500
Elizabeth Cady Stanton
  (feminist)   1815
Alexander Borodin
  (composer)   1834
Auguste Rodin (sculptor)   1840
Sun Yat-sen (revolutionary
  leader)   1866
Dewitt Wallace (publisher)   1889
Al Schacht (baseball
  comedian)   1894
Harry Blackmun (jurist)   1908
Kim Hunter (actress)   1922
Grace Kelly (actress)   1929
Charles Manson (criminal)   1934
Ina Balin (actress)   1937

NOVEMBER 13

Edwin Booth (actor)   1833
Robert Louis Stevenson
  (writer)   1850
Mary Wigman (dancer)   1886
Hermione Baddeley (actress)   1908
Gunnar Bjoernstrand (actor)   1909
Eugene Ionesco (playwright)   1912
Oskar Werner (actor)   1922

November 13 (*continued*)

Linda Christian (actress)	1923
Madeleine Sherwood (actress)	1926
Jean Seberg (actress)	1938

NOVEMBER 14

Emperor Tiberius of Rome	42 B.C.
St. Augustine (theologian)	A.D. 354
Hans Sachs (Meistersinger)	1494
Guido Reni (painter)	1575
William of Orange	1650
Leopold Mozart (musician)	1719
Robert Fulton (inventor)	1765
Claude Monet (painter)	1840
Minnie Hauk (opera singer)	1852
Jawaharlal Nehru (Indian politician)	1889
Mamie Eisenhower (first lady)	1896
Aaron Copland (composer)	1900
Morton Downey (singer)	1902
Marya Mannes (writer)	1904
Dick Powell (actor)	1904
Louise Brooks (actress)	1906
Joseph McCarthy (politician)	1909
Barbara Hutton (heiress)	1912
Veronica Lake (actress)	1919
Brian Keith (actor)	1921
William Steig (cartoonist)	1925
Leonie Rysanek (opera singer)	1928
Edward H. White (astronaut)	1930
King Hussein of Jordan	1935
Prince Charles of England	1948

NOVEMBER 15

William Herschel (astronomer)	1738

Gerhart Hauptmann (playwright)	1862
Felix Frankfurter (jurist)	1882
Marianne Moore (poet)	1887
Georgia O'Keeffe (painter)	1887
Averell Harriman (government official)	1891
Erwin Rommel (German army officer)	1891
Mantovani (orchestra leader)	1905
Curtis LeMay (air force officer)	1906
Howard Baker (politician)	1925
John Kerr (actor)	1931
Petula Clark (singer)	1932
Sam Waterston (actor)	1940
Daniel Barenboim (conductor)	1942
Paul Simon (singer)	1942

NOVEMBER 16

W. C. Handy (composer)	1873
George S. Kaufman (playwright)	1889
Paul Hindemith (composer)	1895
Lawrence Tibbett (opera singer)	1896
Mary Margaret McBride (radio commentator)	1899
Eddie Condon (jazz musician)	1905
Burgess Meredith (actor)	1908
Bob Gibson (singer)	1931
Antonio Gades (dancer)	1936

NOVEMBER 17

Frank Fay (actor)	1897
Lee Strasberg (acting teacher)	1901

November 17 (*continued*)

Isamu Noguchi (sculptor)	1904
C. G. "Bebe" Rebozo (banker)	1912
Rock Hudson (actor)	1925
Charles Mackerras (conductor)	1925
David Amram (composer)	1930
Gordon Lightfoot (singer)	1938
Lauren Hutton (model and actress)	1943
Tom Seaver (baseball player)	1944

NOVEMBER 18

Edmund Halley (astronomer)	1656
Carl Maria von Weber (composer)	1786
Louis Daguerre (inventor)	1789
William Gilbert (librettist)	1836
Ignace Paderewski (pianist)	1860
Billy Sunday (evangelist)	1862
Jacques Maritain (philosopher)	1882
Amelita Galli-Curci (opera singer)	1889
Eugene Ormandy (conductor)	1899
George Gallup (pollster)	1901
Imogene Coca (comedienne)	1908
Johnny Mercer (singer)	1909
Alan Shepard (astronaut)	1923
Dorothy Collins (singer)	1926
Karl Schranz (skier)	1938
Brenda Vaccaro (actress)	1939

NOVEMBER 19

Martin Luther (religious reformer)	1483

George Rogers Clark (soldier)	1752
Ferdinand de Lesseps (engineer)	1805
James Abram Garfield (politician)	1831
Clifton Webb (actor)	1891
Indira Gandhi (Indian politician)	1917
Alan Young (comedian)	1919
Geza Anda (pianist)	1921
Roy Campanella (baseball player)	1921
Dick Cavett (TV personality)	1936
Jose Molina (choreographer)	1937
Bonnie Bramlett (singer)	19—

NOVEMBER 20

William Hogarth (painter)	1697
Selma Lagerloef (writer)	1858
Norman Thomas (socialist)	1884
Chester Gould (cartoonist)	1900
Alexandra Danilova (ballet dancer)	1904
Henri-Georges Clouzot (film director)	1907
Alistair Cooke (journalist)	1908
Emilio Pucci (fashion designer)	1914
Alberta Masiello (vocal coach)	1915
Judy Canova (comedienne)	1916
Corita Kent (artist)	1918
Gene Tierney (actress)	1920
Jim Garrison (public official)	1921
Robert Kennedy (politician)	1925
Maya Plisetskaya (ballet dancer)	1925
Kaye Ballard (comedienne)	1926

November 20 (*continued*)
Estelle Parsons (actress) 1927
Dick Smothers (comedian) 1938
Duane Allman (rock
   musician) 1946

NOVEMBER 21

Voltaire (philosopher) 1694
Oliver Goldsmith (writer) 1728
Abigail Adams (first lady) 1744
Hetty Green (financier) 1835
Vito Genovese (mobster) 1897
Rene Magritte (painter) 1898

Martha Deane (radio
   personality) 1902
Eleanor Powell (dancer) 1912
Ralph Meeker (actor) 1920
Stan Musial (baseball player) 1920
Maria Casares (actress) 1922
Vivian Blaine (actress) 1924
Marlo Thomas (actress) 1938
Natalia Makarova (ballet
   dancer) 1940
David Hemmings (actor) 1941
Juliet Mills (actress) 1941
Larry Mahan (rodeo
   cowboy) 1943
Goldie Hawn (actress) 1945
Barbara Jo Rubin (jockey) 1949

SAGITTARIUS

Element: Fire / Quality: Mutable

The volatility of eager, upward-leaping flames, the blazing release of energy from the confinement of matter, represent fire in its Sagittarius aspect; the spirit of Sagittarians is not to be contained, it breaks free in a burst of outgoing vitality from restrictions imposed on body or mind. The Sagittarius feels an urge to reach outside of himself, beyond the boundaries of immediate surroundings and petty personal concerns, toward goals far off in the distance, whether geographical or metaphysical. His symbol is an archer shooting an arrow at the sky, a centaur with galloping hooves, allied to human wisdom; the Sagittarius resembles him in having high aims and an unbridled fondness for physical activity, travel, exploration and adventure, and for mental excursions in the limitless realms of philosophy and religion. He loves the truth as much as freedom, and is honest, sincere, fair-minded, and straightforward to a fault. His ruler is Jupiter, ruler of the principle of expansion, which denotes the Sagittarian breadth of vision, largeness of spirit, optimism, and open-mindedness. Natives of Jupiter's sign, if they do not feel themselves to be hemmed in by circumstances, may be noted for their joviality and gusto, their generosity and overflowing enthusiasm.

A good example of the Sagittarius type is Ludwig van Beethoven, with both his sun and moon in that sign. He was unruly and independent, despising the restrictions of convention, more at home out of doors than in indoor society, where his blunt Sagittarian honesty and directness seemed brusque and even rude. He was devoted to ideals of human freedom and brotherhood, but not very adroit at dealing with day-to-day personal relations. He cherished his liberty, and never married.

Mozart predicted of the young Beethoven that he would "make a noise in the world," and like a true Sagittarius, Beethoven did. His music communicates the boisterous energy and the profound thought associated with his sign; impetuous or sober, it makes no attempt to charm or seduce, but instead assaults head-on with the force of a blow. Also notably Sagittarian is Beethoven's boldness in ignoring the rules of harmony when it suited him, and his need to define new space for himself by expanding the framework of established musical forms. In this he was followed by another independent Sagittarius composer, Hector Berlioz. The worst fault in Berlioz' music is a tendency toward excessive Jupiterian bombast, but the other side of the same coin is the grand sweep and flamboyant Sagittarian energy that impels it forward. Gaetano Donizetti excelled in Italian Romantic opera, a crudely vigorous and extroverted form which portrayed large-scale emotions larger than life on the stage. Donizetti's music has a directness and thrust and a rousing sort of banginess typical of Sagittarius; it has been most effectively performed by his fellow-Sagittarius, noted for her fiery temperament, Maria Callas.

A rambunctious, bangy quality also prevails in the music of the Rolling Stones, largely composed by Sagittarius Keith Richard. The same quality is illustrated in the lives and personalities of other Sagittarians, including Carry Nation, the hatchet-wielding saloon-buster; Winston Churchill, a brash youth and later a bold, energetic wartime leader; Frank Sinatra, Sammy Davis, Jr., and Jim Morrison, notoriously loud characters even in the flashy world of show business; and Adam Clayton Powell and Abbie Hoffman, who led explosively colorful political careers. The deaths of Sagittarians have also sometimes been attended by a bang, as in the case of Mary Stuart, Queen of Scots, King Charles I of England, and General George Armstrong Custer, all of whom were brought down by their Sagittarian willfulness and recklessness carried too far.

At a more elevated level, Sagittarians make lofty thinkers and distinguished religionists. Pope John XXIII exemplified a Sagittarian forward-looking attitude in religion (as well as epitomizing the hearty, Jupiterian type of personality). John Milton represents the scholarly religious type; he set out in *Paradise Lost* to "justify the ways of God to man," an appropriately Sagittarian pursuit, one that includes the whole of creation, from heaven to hell. William Blake, another Sagittarius poet, explored a spiritual territory equally vast in his writing, and as a painter he chose to illustrate such works as *Paradise Lost,* the book of Job, and Dante's *Inferno,* all dealing with the relation between the divine and the human on the most universal scale possible.

Sagittarius minds turned in other directions are particularly sharp at detecting hypocrisy and small-mindedness, which they despise more than anything else, and love to expose. Harpo Marx as a comedian took special delight in this; Jonathan Swift was more bitter, attacking in *Gulliver's Travels* what he recognized as false and ridiculous values of society, hitting his marks dead-on like a true archer. Mark Twain was another Sagittarius satirist who aimed his barbs at all varieties of pretentiousness and false sentiment.

Jane Austen took something of the same tone in her ridiculing of pompousness and stupidity. She was like many other Sagittarians in never marrying, but unlike the standard Sagittarius type in that she led a quiet life and never moved far from her original home. These circumstances she shared with Sagittarius Emily Dickinson, who (as she says) never saw a moor, or the sea; but elsewhere she writes:

> There is no Frigate like a Book
> To take us Lands away
> Nor any coursers like a page
> Of prancing Poetry.

She and Jane Austen undoubtedly traveled considerably by such means.

Louisa May Alcott's portrait of her Sagittarius self as Jo March in *Little Women* sums up this sign: an exuberant, coltish, tomboyish young woman, generous, good-humored and warm-hearted, frank, blunt, and sometimes unintentionally tactless, and likely to trip over herself at awkward moments; strong and independent, with literary aspirations, only ending up married, as Louisa herself did not.

NOVEMBER 22

Robert de la Salle (explorer)	1643
George Eliot (novelist)	1819
Andre Gide (writer)	1869
Elizabeth Patterson (actress)	1874
Charles de Gaulle (French statesman)	1890
Hoagy Carmichael (composer)	1899
Doris Duke (heiress)	1912
Benjamin Britten (composer)	1913
Orestes Minoso (baseball player)	1922
Geraldine Page (actress)	1924
Gunther Schuller (composer)	1925
Peter Hall (director)	1930
Robert Vaughn (actor)	1932
Billie Jean King (tennis player)	1943

NOVEMBER 23

Franklin Pierce (politician)	1804
Billy the Kid (outlaw)	1859
Manuel de Falla (composer)	1876
Jose Orozco (painter)	1883

Boris Karloff (actor)	1887
Harpo Marx (comedian)	1893
Victor Jory (actor)	1902
Charles Berlitz (educator)	1914
Jerry Bock (composer)	1928
Krzysztof Penderecki (composer)	1933

NOVEMBER 24

Baruch Spinoza (philosopher)	1632
Junipero Serra (missionary)	1713
Zachary Taylor (politician)	1784
Lilli Lehmann (opera singer)	1848
Henri de Toulouse-Lautrec (painter)	1864
Scott Joplin (composer)	1868
Anna Louise Strong (journalist)	1885
Dale Carnegie (writer)	1888
Cathleen Nesbitt (actress)	1889
Garson Kanin (director)	1912
Geraldine Fitzgerald (actress)	1914
Howard Duff (actor)	1917
John V. Lindsay (politician)	1921

November 24 (*continued*)
William F. Buckley, Jr.
   (columnist) 1925
Oscar Robertson (basketball
   player) 1938
Claudia Dreifus (feminist) 1944

NOVEMBER 25

Charles Kemble (actor) 1775
Andrew Carnegie (tycoon) 1835
Carry Nation (reformer) 1846
Joseph Wood Krutch
   (writer) 1893
Wilhelm Kempff (pianist) 1895
Anastas Mikoyan (Soviet
   official) 1895
Ludwik Svoboda (Czech
   politician) 1895
Virgil Thomson (composer) 1896
Jessie Royce Landis (actress) 1904
Joe DiMaggio (baseball
   player) 1914
Ricardo Montalban (actor) 1920
Murray Schisgal
   (playwright) 1926
Jeffrey Hunter (actor) 1927
John Kennedy, Jr.
   (politician's son) 1960

NOVEMBER 26

Norbert Wiener
   (mathematician) 1894
Cyril Cusak (actor) 1910
Samuel Reshevsky (chess
   player) 1911
Eric Sevareid (writer) 1912
Charles Schulz (cartoonist) 1922

George Segal (sculptor) 1924
Michael Butler (producer) 1926
Robert Goulet (singer) 1933
Marian Mercer (singer) 1935
Tina Turner (singer) 1939

NOVEMBER 27

Bronzino (painter) 1503
Pope John XXIII 1881
Mona Washbourne (actress) 1903
James Agee (writer) 1909
David Merrick (producer) 1912
Alexander Dubcek (Czech
   politician) 1921
Marshall Thompson (actor) 1925
Bruce Lee (actor) 1940
Jimi Hendrix (rock
   musician) 1942
Caroline Kennedy
   (politician's daughter) 1957

NOVEMBER 28

William Blake (artist and
   poet) 1757
Anton Rubinstein
   (composer) 1829
Stefan Zweig (writer) 1881
Brooks Atkinson (drama
   critic) 1894
Jose Iturbi (pianist) 1895
James Eastland (politician) 1904
Alberto Moravia (writer) 1907
Claude Levi-Strauss
   (anthropologist) 1908
Gloria Grahame (actress) 1925
Hope Lange (actress) 1933
Randy Newman (singer) 1943

NOVEMBER 29

Robert Devereux (courtier)	1566
Jean Baptiste Lully (composer)	1633
Gaetano Donizetti (composer)	1797
Amos Bronson Alcott (transcendentalist)	1799
Louisa May Alcott (novelist)	1832
Busby Berkeley (film director)	1895
Adam Clayton Powell, Jr. (politician)	1908
Harold C. Schonberg (music critic)	1915
John Gary (singer)	1932
John Mayall (blues singer)	1933
David Reuben (physician and author)	1933
James Rosenquist (painter)	1933

NOVEMBER 30

King Charles I of England	1600
Mark Twain (writer)	1835
Ernest Newman (music critic)	1868
Winston Churchill (British statesman)	1874
Jacques Barzun (writer)	1907
Brownie McGhee (blues musician)	1915
Efram Zimbalist, Jr. (actor)	1923
Shirley Chisholm (politician)	1924
Allan Sherman (comedian)	1924
Rex Reason (actor)	1928
Dick Clark (TV personality)	1929
G. Gordon Liddy (lawyer)	1930
Abbie Hoffman (revolutionary)	1936
Paul Stookey (singer)	1937

DECEMBER 1

Rex Stout (writer)	1886
Cyril Ritchard (actor)	1898
Robert Welch (John Bircher)	1899
W. A. "Tony" Boyle (labor leader)	1904
Alicia Markova (ballet dancer)	1910
Smokey Alston (baseball manager)	1911
Minoru Yamasaki (architect)	1912
Mary Martin (actress)	1913
Paul Picerni (actor)	1922
Keith Michell (actor)	1928
Dick Shawn (comedian)	1929
Woody Allen (comedian)	1935
Lou Rawls (singer)	1935
Lee Trevino (golfer)	1939
Bette Midler (singer)	1944

DECEMBER 2

Georges Seurat (painter)	1859
Charles Ringling (circus executive)	1863
Ruth Draper (monologuist)	1884
Nikos Kazantzakis (writer)	1885
Carlos Merida (painter)	1891
John Barbirolli (conductor)	1899
Adolph Green (lyricist)	1915
Randolph Hearst (publisher)	1915
Alexander Haig (government official)	1924
Julie Harris (actress)	1925
Robert Pettit (basketball player)	1932

DECEMBER 3

Gilbert Stuart (painter)	1755
Joseph Conrad (writer)	1857

December 3 (*continued*)

Josef Lhevinne (pianist)	1874
Anton von Webern (composer)	1883
Anna Freud (psychologist)	1895
Nino Rota (composer)	1911
Tanya Moiseiwitsch (stage designer)	1914
Maria Callas (opera singer)	1923
Jean-Luc Godard (film maker)	1930
Andy Williams (singer)	1930

DECEMBER 4

Thomas Carlyle (writer)	1795
Samuel Butler (novelist)	1835
Lillian Russell (actress)	1861
Rainer Maria Rilke (poet)	1875
Francisco Franco (dictator)	1892
Herbert Read (art critic)	1893
Sonia Moore (acting teacher)	1902
Pappy Boyington (flying ace)	1906
Claude Renoir (photographer)	1914
Deanna Durbin (actress)	1922
Gerard Philipe (actor)	1922
Horst Buchholz (actor)	1933
Robert Vesco (financier)	1935

DECEMBER 5

Lope de Vega (playwright)	1562
Lawrence Sterne (novelist)	1713
Martin Van Buren (politician)	1782
George Custer (army officer)	1839
Wassily Kandinsky (painter)	1866
Fritz Lang (film maker)	1890
Christina Georgina Rossetti (poet)	1893

Philip K. Wrigley (gum manufacturer)	1894
Walt Disney (film producer)	1901
Grace Moore (singer)	1901
Strom Thurmond (politician)	1902
Otto Preminger (film producer)	1906
Larry Kert (actor)	1934
Chad Mitchell (singer)	1936
Jim Plunkett (football player)	1947

DECEMBER 6

Horace (poet)	65 B.C.
Wilhelmina Schroeder-Devrient (opera singer)	1804
Friedrich Max Mueller (Sanskrit scholar)	1823
William S. Hart (actor)	1872
Joyce Kilmer (poet)	1886
Lynn Fontanne (actress)	1887
Ira Gershwin (lyricist)	1896
Agnes Moorehead (actress)	1906
Dave Brubeck (jazz musician)	1920
Wally Cox (actor)	1924
Patsy Mink (politician)	1927
Richard Speck (mass murderer)	1941

DECEMBER 7

Giovanni Bernini (artist)	1598
William Cowper (poet)	1731
Pietro Mascagni (composer)	1863
Richard Warren Sears (merchant)	1863
Willa Cather (novelist)	1873
Joyce Cary (writer)	1888
Stuart Davis (painter)	1894

December 7 (*continued*)

Rod Cameron (actor)	1912
Eli Wallach (actor)	1915
Noam Chomsky (writer)	1928
Harry Chapin (singer)	1942
Johnny Bench (baseball player)	1947

DECEMBER 8

Eli Whitney (inventor)	1765
Georges Melies (film maker)	1861
Georges Feydeau (playwright)	1862
Jean Sibelius (composer)	1865
Tullio Serafin (conductor)	1878
Diego Rivera (painter)	1886
James Thurber (humorist)	1894
Adele Simpson (fashion designer)	1903
Gerard Souzay (singer)	1920
Jean Ritchie (singer)	1922
Sammy Davis, Jr. (singer)	1925
Maximilian Schell (actor and film director)	1930
Flip Wilson (comedian)	1935
James MacArthur (actor)	1937
David Carradine (actor)	1940
Jim Morrison (rock musician)	1945
Greg Allman (rock musician)	19—

DECEMBER 9

King Gustavus Adolphus of Sweden	1594
Joel Chandler Harris (writer)	1848
Conchita Supervia (singer)	1895
Hermione Gingold (actress)	1897
Emmett Kelly (clown)	1898

Margaret Hamilton (actress)	1902
Dalton Trumbo (screenwriter)	1905
Douglas Fairbanks, Jr. (actor)	1909
Lee J. Cobb (actor)	1911
Broderick Crawford (actor)	1911
Elisabeth Schwarzkopf (opera singer)	1915
Kirk Douglas (actor)	1916
Dina Merrill (actress)	1925
Luis Miguel Dominguin (bullfighter)	1926
John Cassavetes (actor and film director)	1929
Willie Hartack (jockey)	1932
Beau Bridges (actor)	1941
Donny Osmond (singer)	1957

DECEMBER 10

Andrea Palladio (architect)	1508
Philip Sidney (poet)	1554
Jonathan Swift (writer)	1667
William Lloyd Garrison (abolitionist)	1805
Cesar Franck (composer)	1822
Emily Dickinson (poet)	1830
Pierre Louys (writer)	1870
E. H. Shepard (illustrator)	1879
Una Merkel (actress)	1903
Olivier Messiaen (composer)	1908
Chet Huntley (newsman)	1911
Morton Gould (composer)	1913
Dorothy Lamour (actress)	1914
Tommy Rettig (child actor)	1941
Maharaj Ji (guru)	1957

DECEMBER 11

Hector Berlioz (composer)	1803
Alfred de Musset (writer)	1810

December 11 (*continued*)
Robert Koch (bacteriologist) 1843
Max Born (physicist) 1882
Fiorello La Guardia (politician) 1882
Mark Tobey (artist) 1890
Gilbert Roland (actor) 1905
Carlos Arias Navarro (Spanish politician) 1908
Elliott Carter (composer) 1908
Jean Marais (actor) 1913
Carlo Ponti (film producer) 1913
Alexander Solzhenitsyn (writer) 1918
Marie Windsor (actress) 1924
Jean-Louis Trintignant (actor) 1930
Rita Moreno (actress) 1931
Anne Heywood (actress) 1933
Brenda Lee (singer) 1944

DECEMBER 12

Gustave Flaubert (novelist) 1821
Edvard Munch (painter) 1863
Edward G. Robinson (actor) 1893
Jules Dassin (film director) 1911
Alan Schneider (director) 1917
Frank Sinatra (singer) 1917
Helen Frankenthaler (painter) 1928
John Osborne (playwright) 1929
Connie Francis (singer) 1938
Dionne Warwick (singer) 1940
Richard Betts (rock musician) 19—

DECEMBER 13

Emperor Nero of Rome A.D. 37
Heinrich Heine (poet) 1797

Mary Todd Lincoln (first lady) 1818
Marc Connelly (writer) 1890
Drew Pearson (columnist) 1897
Carlos Montoya (guitarist) 1903
Van Heflin (actor) 1910
Lillian Roth (singer) 1910
Archie Moore (boxer) 1916
William Vukovich (auto racer) 1918
Mark Stevens (actor) 1922
Dick Van Dyke (actor) 1925
Christopher Plummer (actor) 1929
Genevieve Page (actress) 1931
Aga Khan IV (Muslim leader) 1937

DECEMBER 14

King George VI of England 1895
Margaret Chase Smith (politician) 1897
Spike Jones (comedian) 1911
Rosalyn Tureck (pianist) 1914
Dan Dailey (actor) 1917
Shirley Jackson (writer) 1919
Abbie Lane (actress) 1935
Lee Remick (actress) 1935
Patty Duke (actress) 1946

DECEMBER 15

Baldassare Castiglione (writer) 1478
Alexandre Gustave Eiffel (engineer) 1882
Maxwell Anderson (playwright) 1888
J. Paul Getty (tycoon) 1892
Yasujiro Ozu (film maker) 1903
Betty Smith (novelist) 1906

December 15 (*continued*)

Oscar Niemayer (architect)	1907
Giulietta Simionato (opera singer)	1910
Jeff Chandler (actor)	1918
Alan Freed (disc jockey)	1921

DECEMBER 16

Mary Stuart, Queen of Scots	1542
Ludwig van Beethoven (composer)	1770
Jane Austen (novelist)	1775
George Santayana (philosopher)	1863
Zoltan Kodaly (composer)	1882
Ralph Moody (novelist)	1898
Noel Coward (playwright)	1899
Margaret Mead (anthropologist)	1901
Buddy Parker (football coach)	1913
Arthur C. Clarke (writer)	1917
George Schaefer (TV director)	1920

DECEMBER 17

Domenico Cimarosa (composer)	1749
John Greenleaf Whittier (poet)	1807
Ford Madox Ford (writer)	1873
Arthur Fiedler (conductor)	1894
Janet Travell (physician)	1901
Erskine Caldwell (novelist)	1903
Paul Cadmus (painter)	1904
Martin Landau (actor)	1917
Richard Long (actor)	1927
Julia Meade (actress)	1928
Tommy Steele (actor)	1936

DECEMBER 18

Edward MacDowell (composer)	1861
Archduke Ferdinand of Austria	1863
Saki (writer)	1870
Paul Klee (painter)	1879
Ty Cobb (baseball player)	1886
Gladys Cooper (actress)	1888
Robert Moses (public official)	1888
George Stevens (film director)	1904
Christopher Fry (playwright)	1907
Abe Burrows (producer)	1910
Willy Brandt (German politician)	1913
Betty Grable (actress)	1916
Anita O'Day (jazz singer)	1919
Ramsey Clark (politician)	1927
Roger Smith (actor)	1932
Keith Richard (rock musician)	1943

DECEMBER 19

Giulio Ricordi (music publisher)	1840
Henry Clay Frick (industrialist)	1849
Fritz Reiner (conductor)	1888
Oliver La Farge (writer)	1901
Ralph Richardson (actor)	1902
Leonid Brezhnev (Soviet politician)	1906
Jean Genet (writer)	1910
Edith Piaf (singer)	1915
David Susskind (producer)	1920
Galt MacDermot (composer)	1928
Al Kaline (baseball player)	1934
Cicely Tyson (actress)	1938

December 19 (*continued*)

Liv Ullmann (actress)	1938
Phil Ochs (singer)	1940
Chris Jagger (singer)	1947

DECEMBER 20

John Milton (poet)	1608
Harvey S. Firestone (industrialist)	1868
Susanne Langer (philosopher)	1895
Robert Van de Graaff (physicist)	1901
Sidney Hook (writer)	1902
Max Lerner (columnist)	1902
Irene Dunne (actress)	1904
Bob Hayes (football player)	1942

DECEMBER 21

Benjamin Disraeli (British statesman)	1804
John McCormack (politician)	1891
Walter Hagen (golfer)	1892
Rebecca West (writer)	1892
Luigi Barzini (writer)	1908
Joshua Gibson (baseball player)	1911
Heinrich Boell (writer)	1917
Alicia Alonso (ballet dancer)	1921
Jane Fonda (actress)	1937
Frank Zappa (singer)	1940
Michael Tilson Thomas (conductor)	1944
Chris Evert (tennis player)	1954

CAPRICORN

Element: Earth / Quality: Cardinal

The meaning of Capricorn is taken from the idea of earth in its primary phase, which is rock; Capricorn stands for hardness and durability. It is ruled by Saturn, the planet which governs the crystallization of all forms, the organization of matter as well as of society, and which, in its manifestation as the figure of Father Time, rules processes that take a long time to complete, and solidly based structures that endure. The Capricorn subjects of Saturn have patience and great powers of perseverance, and recognize the importance of long-term achievements arrived at necessarily through toil, trials, and setbacks; they are dependably tough, with firm convictions and determination in the pursuit of their aims. These practical qualities which appear foremost spring from profound depths of character underneath, as indicated by the sign's emblem, a fabulous goat with the tail of a sea monster, or a divinity of the sea. Using the combination of stubbornness, hardiness, and mysterious sagacity which this creature suggests, Capricorns are likely to advance far, and ultimately to attain the goals they set for themselves. They are frequently found occupying positions of power or authority, where skillful and responsible management are required.

Their ability to run things, and an innate understanding of the workings of social institutions are used to advantage by many Capricorns in the field of governmental politics. The Capricorn's conscientiousness and exceptional staying power enable him to survive and move up in a political career, even to the very top of the system, in which position he would exercise firm control, usually with conservative intent. Joseph Stalin, who is remembered for strengthening and maintaining the edifice of Soviet communism using whatever means necessary, is the prototype of the stern, authoritarian Capricorn. Mao Tse-tung is another example, builder of a social system emphasizing complete regimentation and subordination of the individual to the whole of society (a Capricornian ideal taken to its extreme), later to inspire a "cultural revolution" the goal of which was to stamp out creeping revisionism in politics and dangerous softness in the national life. Like Stalin, Mao was able to implement his designs only with the help of a powerful totalitarian machine, which is probably better suited to a Capricornian style of leadership than the less dependable processes of democracy.

Richard Nixon is one Capricorn who came to power through democratic channels (in a manner true to his sign; that is, slowly, with discouraging failures along the way but steadily and with eventual success); as President he sought to appropriate to his own office unprecedented political power, attempting to control the other branches of government, the press and public opinion. His misguided Capricornian efforts to consolidate authority and to insure his security brought him to grief, yet he never lost the tenacity of the goat in maintaining the rightness of his position.

Others of this sort were J. Edgar Hoover and Al Capone (both born just before sunrise, so that they both had Capricorn rising and their Capricorn suns in prominent positions), both outstanding bosses of large, complex, powerful organizations, and arch-enemies besides. It took one double Capricorn to finally get the better of the other—possibly no one else could have done it. (The same could apply to Joe Frazier's defeat of Muhammad Ali, or Ali's defeat of George Foreman: only one Capricorn top dog can beat another.)

Lest it appear from the foregoing that Capricorns all resemble old scoundrels and dictators, it should be pointed out that their sober view of life and interest in the social organism often leads to a serious concern for solving humanitarian problems, for which they are well equipped with their talent for organization and capacity for steady work. Among Capricorns whose labors have benefited society in various ways are Clara Barton, who single-handedly founded the Red Cross; Woodrow Wilson, who might be called the grandfather of the United Nations; Albert Schweitzer, and Martin Luther King, Jr., all of whom succeeded with Capricornian will power and persistence in the face of enormous difficulties.

Capricorns also succeed in the entertainment business, although their style is not normally frivolous. Joan Baez, for instance, is well known for the unrelieved Capricornian seriousness of her material. Janis Joplin had a much more colorful public image, that of a hard-living, hard-loving toughie (with a soft heart, as shown by her moon in Cancer, influencing her private life). Most appropriate to the sign of cardinal earth was the forceful, "earthy" sexuality that she projected. Elvis Presley, another Capricorn, became famous for a similar quality in his performances; Marlene Dietrich and Cary Grant, once celebrated (like Joplin and Presley) as sex symbols, are now both past seventy, still looking well and pursuing successful careers, evidence that aging seems to suit Capricorns better than it does many other people.

There remains to be considered the best known of all Capricorn birthdays, that symbolically assigned to Jesus, Christmas Day. The twenty-fifth of December formerly marked the winter solstice, the moment the sun enters the sign of Capricorn, the darkest day of the year in the northern hemisphere. (The calendar has since shifted, so that now the solstice occurs on the twenty-second.) The esoteric significance of this day lies in the fact that although darkness prevails, from this point on the light increases, and thus hope is born out of despair. The same birthday has also been given in the past to the god Mithra, to Alexander the Great, and to other world-savior figures, which gives Capricorns a great deal to live up to.

DECEMBER 22

Jean Baptiste Racine (playwright)	1639
Giacomo Puccini (composer)	1858
Connie Mack (baseball manager)	1862
Edwin Arlington Robinson (poet)	1869
Andre Kostelanetz (conductor)	1901
Peggy Ashcroft (actress)	1907
Lady Bird Johnson (first lady)	1912
Fernando Corena (opera singer)	1923
Steve Carlton (baseball player)	1944
Robert Blankshine (ballet dancer)	1948

DECEMBER 23

Michel de Nostradamus (astrologer)	1503
King Henri de Navarre	1533
Tycho Brahe (astronomer)	1546
John Jay (jurist)	1745
Joseph Smith (Mormon leader)	1805

Edouard de Reszke (opera singer)	1855
John Marin (painter)	1870
Vincent Sardi (restaurateur)	1885
J. Arthur Rank (producer)	1888
Don McNeill (radio personality)	1907
Barney Ross (boxer)	1909
Jose Greco (dancer)	1918
Helmut Schmidt (German politician)	1918
Ruth Roman (actress)	1924
Harry Guardino (actor)	1925
Akihito (crown prince of Japan)	1933
Paul Hornung (football player)	1935
Jorma Kaukonen (rock musician)	1940
Elizabeth Hartman (actress)	1941

DECEMBER 24

Eugene Scribe (playwright)	1791
Kit Carson (frontiersman)	1809
Matthew Arnold (writer)	1822
Antoine (hairdresser)	1884
Louis Jouvet (actor)	1887

December 24 (*continued*)
Howard Hughes (tycoon)   1905
Cab Calloway (singer)   1907
I. F. Stone (journalist)   1907
Pierre Soulages (painter)   1919
Ava Gardner (actress)   1922
Leadbelly (folk singer)   1922
Robert Joffrey
    (choreographer)   1930

DECEMBER 25

Clara Barton (nurse)   1821
Cosima Wagner (composer's
    wife)   1837
Aristide Maillol (sculptor)   1861
Helena Rubinstein (cosmetics
    merchant)   1870
Giuseppe de Luca (opera
    singer)   1876
Maurice Utrillo (painter)   1883
Conrad Hilton (hotel
    executive)   1887
Robert Ripley (cartoonist)   1893
Humphrey Bogart (actor)   1899
Raphael Soyer (painter)   1899
Clark Clifford (government
    official)   1906
Tony Martin (singer)   1913
Oscar Lewis (sociologist)   1914
Anwar Sadat (Egyptian
    politician)   1918
Rod Serling (writer)   1924
Nellie Fox (baseball player)   1927
Carlos Castaneda
    (anthropologist)   1931
Little Richard (singer)   1935

DECEMBER 26

George Romney (painter)   1734
Henry Miller (novelist)   1891

Mao Tse-tung (revolutionary
    leader)   1893
Albert Gore (politician)   1907
Richard Widmark (actor)   1914
Rose Mary Woods
    (secretary)   1917
Steve Allen (TV personality)   1921
Doris Lilly (writer)   1926
Alan King (comedian)   1927
Donald Moffat (actor)   1930

DECEMBER 27

Paracelsus (alchemist)   1493
Louis Pasteur
    (bacteriologist)   1822
Carl Zuckmayer (writer)   1896
Marlene Dietrich (actress)   1904
Andreas Feininger
    (photographer)   1906
Oscar Levant (pianist)   1906
Anna Russell (comedienne)   1911
William H. Masters
    (sexologist)   1915

DECEMBER 28

Francesco Tamagno (opera
    singer)   1850
Woodrow Wilson (politician)   1856
F. W. Murnau (film director)   1888
Roger Sessions (composer)   1896
Mortimer Adler (educator)   1902
Earl Hines (jazz musician)   1903
Cliff Arquette (actor)   1905
Lew Ayres (actor)   1908
Sam Levenson (TV
    personality)   1911
Lou Jacobi (actor)   1913
Hildegarde Neff (actress)   1925
Maggie Smith (actress)   1934

DECEMBER 29

Marquise de Pompadour
  (courtesan)   1721
Charles Goodyear (inventor) 1800
Andrew Johnson (politician) 1808
William Gladstone (British
  statesman)   1809
Pablo Casals (cellist)   1876
David Alfaro Siqueiros
  (painter)   1896
Viveca Lindfors (actress)   1920
Inga Swenson (actress)   1934
Mary Tyler Moore (actress)   1937
Jon Voight (actor)   1938
Fred Hansen (athlete)   1940

DECEMBER 30

Masaccio (painter)   1401
Rudyard Kipling (writer)   1865
Al Smith (politician)   1873
Reinhold Gliere (composer)   1874
Alfred Einstein
  (musicologist)   1880
Vincent Lopez (bandleader)   1895
Dmitri Kabalevsky
  (composer)   1904
Carol Reed (film director)   1906
Bert Parks (TV personality)   1914
Marie Wilson (actress)   1917
Jo Van Fleet (actress)   1919
Bo Diddley (rock musician)   1928
Jack Lord (actor)   1930
Skeeter Davis (country
  singer)   1931
Russ Tamblyn (actor)   1934
Sandy Koufax (baseball
  player)   1935

DECEMBER 31

King John of England   1167

Henri Matisse (painter)   1869
George Marshall (army
  officer)   1880
Nathan Milstein (violinist)   1904
Jule Styne (composer)   1905
Theodoros Stamos (painter)   1922
Taylor Mead (actor)   1924
Candy Jones (cosmetologist)   1925
Odetta (folk singer)   1930
John Denver (singer)   1943
Sarah Miles (actress)   1943
Joe Dallesandro (actor)   1948

JANUARY 1

Marcus Tullius Cicero
  (Roman statesman)   106 B.C.
James Oglethorpe (colonizer)   1697
Betsy Ross (seamstress)   1752
James Frazer
  (anthropologist)   1854
Alfred Stieglitz
  (photographer)   1864
E. M. Forster (novelist)   1879
William Fox (film executive)   1879
J. Edgar Hoover
  (government official)   1895
Xavier Cugat (bandleader)   1900
Dana Andrews (actor)   1909
Barry Goldwater (politician)   1909
Hank Greenberg (baseball
  player)   1911
J. D. Salinger (writer)   1919
Barbara Baxley (actress)   1927
Maurice Bejart
  (choreographer)   1927
Yuri Grigorovich
  (choreographer)   1927

JANUARY 2

St. Ignatius of Loyola
  (Jesuit)   1492

January 2 (*continued*)

Joseph Stalin (dictator)	1880
Tito Schipa (opera singer)	1889
Robert Nathan (writer)	1894
Michael Tippett (composer)	1905
Vera Zorina (actress)	1917
Isaac Asimov (writer)	1920
Renata Tebaldi (opera singer)	1922
Julius La Rosa (singer)	1930
Roger Miller (country singer)	1936

JANUARY 3

Pietro Metastasio (poet)	1698
Lucretia Mott (feminist)	1793
Henriette Sontag (opera singer)	1806
Josephine Hull (actress)	1886
J. R. R. Tolkein (writer)	1892
Pola Negri (actress)	1897
Zasu Pitts (actress)	1898
Marion Davies (actress)	1900
Anna May Wong (actress)	1907
Ray Milland (actor)	1908
Victor Borge (entertainer)	1909
Betty Furness (TV personality and consumer advocate)	1916
Maxene Andrews (singer)	1918
John Russell (actor)	1921
Bill Travers (actor)	1922
Bobby Hull (hockey player)	1939
Richard Ben-Veniste (lawyer)	1943
Stephen Stills (rock musician)	1945

JANUARY 4

Thomas Beckett (clergyman)	1119
Isaac Newton (physicist)	1643
Giovanni Battista Pergolesi (composer)	1710

Jakob Grimm (folklorist)	1785
Louis Braille (teacher of the blind)	1806
Everett Dirksen (politician)	1896
Jane Wyman (actress)	1914
William E. Colby (government official)	1920
Barbara Rush (actress)	1927
Dyan Cannon (actress)	1929
Don Shula (football coach)	1930
Floyd Patterson (boxer)	1935
Grace Melzia Bumbry (opera singer)	1937

JANUARY 5

Zebulon Pike (explorer)	1779
Konrad Adenauer (German politician)	1876
Wieland Wagner (director)	1917
Alfred Ryder (actor)	1919
Arturo Benedetti Michelangeli (pianist)	1920
Friedrich Duerrenmatt (writer)	1921
Alvin Ailey (choreographer)	1931
Chuck McKinley (tennis player)	1941

JANUARY 6

Giovanni da Palestrina (composer)	1526
Johann Kepler (astronomer)	1572
Thomas Gray (poet)	1717
Heinrich Schliemann (archaeologist)	1822
Gustave Dore (artist)	1832
Max Bruch (composer)	1838
Carl Sandburg (writer)	1878
Tom Mix (actor)	1880
Sam Rayburn (politician)	1882

January 6 (*continued*)

Kahlil Gibran (poet)	1883
Rose N. Franzblau (advice columnist)	1904
Loretta Young (actress)	1913
Danny Thomas (comedian)	1914
Alan Watts (writer)	1915
Sun Myung Moon (evangelist)	1920
Early Wynn (baseball player)	1920
Louis Harris (pollster)	1921
Earl Scruggs (country singer)	1924
Capucine (actress)	1933
Darlene Hard (tennis player)	1936
Murray Rose (swimmer)	1939

JANUARY 7

Millard Fillmore (politician)	1800
Albert Bierstadt (painter)	1830
St. Bernadette of Lourdes (nun)	1844
Clara Haskil (pianist)	1895
Francis Poulenc (composer)	1899
Nicanor Zabaleta (harpist)	1907
Orval Faubus (politician)	1910
Charles Addams (cartoonist)	1912
Jean-Pierre Rampal (flutist)	1922
William Peter Blatty (novelist)	1928
Terry Moore (actress)	1929
Tony Conigliaro (baseball player)	1945

JANUARY 8

Hans von Buelow (conductor)	1830
Frank Nelson Doubleday (publisher)	1862
A. J. Muste (pacifist)	1885
W. M. Kiplinger (writer)	1891

Sherman Adams (government official)	1899
Butterfly McQueen (actress)	1911
Jose Ferrer (actor)	1912
Soupy Sales (TV personality)	1926
Evelyn Lear (opera singer)	1929
Bill Graham (rock impresario)	1931
Elvis Presley (singer)	1935
Shirley Bassey (singer)	1937
Little Anthony (singer)	1940
Yvette Mimieux (actress)	1941
David Bowie (singer)	1948

JANUARY 9

Gracie Fields (singer)	1898
Chic Young (cartoonist)	1901
Rudolf Bing (operatic impresario)	1902
George Balanchine (choreographer)	1904
Simone de Beauvoir (writer)	1908
Miranda Marais (folk singer)	1912
Richard M. Nixon (politician)	1913
Gypsy Rose Lee (stripper)	1914
Fernando Lamas (actor)	1920
Bart Starr (football player)	1934
Joan Baez (singer)	1941
Susannah York (actress)	1941

JANUARY 10

Ulrich Zwingli (Protestant reformer)	1484
Andreas Vesalius (anatomist)	1515
Charles Cornwallis (army officer)	1739
Alexander Scriabin (composer)	1872

January 10 (*continued*)

Francis X. Bushman (actor)	1883
Florence Reed (actress)	1883
Robinson Jeffers (poet)	1887
Ray Bolger (actor)	1904
Paul Henreid (actor)	1908
Galina Ulanova (ballet dancer)	1910
Gisele MacKenzie (singer)	1927
Johnnie Ray (singer)	1927
Donald Brooks (fashion and costume designer)	1928
Sherrill Milnes (opera singer)	1935
Al Goldstein (publisher)	1936
Willie McCovey (baseball player)	1938
Sal Mineo (actor)	1939
Jim Croce (singer)	1943
Rod Stewart (singer)	1945
George Foreman (boxer)	1949

JANUARY 11

Charles Stuart (pretender)	1721
Alexander Hamilton (statesman)	1757
William James (philosopher)	1842
Paddy Driscoll (football coach)	1896
Eva Le Gallienne (actress)	1899
Alan Paton (novelist)	1903
Rod Taylor (actor)	1930
Mary Rodgers (composer)	1931
Bobby Goldsboro (singer)	1941
Christine Kaufmann (actress)	1945

JANUARY 12

Charles Perrault (writer)	1628
Paul Revere (patriot)	1735

Anthony Wayne (army officer)	1745
John Singer Sargent (painter)	1856
Swami Vivekananda (Vedantist)	1863
Jack London (writer)	1876
Ermanno Wolf-Ferrari (composer)	1876
Hermann Wilhelm Goering (Nazi official)	1893
Tex Ritter (country singer)	1906
Jose Limon (choreographer)	1908
Patsy Kelly (actress)	1910
Luise Rainer (actress)	1910
Edward Gurney (politician)	1914
James Farmer (black leader)	1920
Glenn Yarbrough (singer)	1930
Bernardine Dohrn (revolutionary)	1942

JANUARY 13

Horatio Alger (novelist)	1834
G. I. Gurdjieff (philosopher)	1877
Sophie Tucker (actress)	1884
Alfred Fuller (brush manufacturer)	1885
Masayuki Mori (actor)	1911
Robert Stack (actor)	1919
Roland Petit (choreographer)	1924
Gwen Verdon (actress)	1925
Rosemary Murphy (actress)	1927

JANUARY 14

King Richard II of England	1367
Berthe Morisot (painter)	1841
Jean de Reszke (opera singer)	1850
Albert Schweitzer (humanitarian)	1875

January 14 (*continued*)
Hal Roach (film producer) 1892
John Dos Passos (novelist) 1896
Cecil Beaton (stage designer) 1904
William Bendix (actor) 1906
Joseph Losey (film
director) 1909
Yukio Mishima (writer) 1925
Tom Tryon (actor) 1926
Gerald Arpino
(choreographer) 1928
Harriet Andersson (actress) 1932
Jack Jones (singer) 1938
Julian Bond (politician) 1940
Faye Dunaway (actress) 1941
Marjoe Gortner (evangelist) 1944

JANUARY 15

St. Joan of Arc (soldier) 1412
Moliere (playwright) 1622
Duc de Saint-Simon
(courtier) 1675
Franz Grillparzer (poet) 1791
Pierre Proudhon (socialist) 1809
King Saud of Saudi Arabia 1902
Aristotle Onassis (tycoon) 1906
Edward Teller (physicist) 1908
Gene Krupa (drummer) 1909
Lloyd Bridges (actor) 1913
Alan Lomax (folk song
collector) 1915
Gamal Abdel Nasser (Arab
leader) 1918
Maurice Herzog (mountain
climber) 1919
Ulrich Franzen (architect) 1921
Maria Schell (actress) 1926
Martin Luther King, Jr.
(civil rights leader) 1929
Thomas P. F. Hoving (art
museum manager) 1931

Margaret O'Brien (actress) 1937

JANUARY 16

Nicola Piccinni (composer) 1728
Gordon Craig (producer and
stage designer) 1872
Robert William Service
(writer) 1874
Fulgencio Batista (dictator) 1901
Ethel Merman (singer) 1908
Dizzy Dean (sportscaster) 1911
Norman Podhoretz (writer) 1930
Pilar Lorengar (opera singer) 1933
Marilyn Horne (opera singer) 1934
A. J. Foyt (auto racer) 1935

JANUARY 17

Pedro Calderon de la Barca
(playwright) 1600
Benjamin Franklin
(statesman and inventor) 1706
Anne Bronte (novelist) 1820
Anton Chekhov (writer) 1860
David Lloyd George (British
statesman) 1863
Konstantin Stanislavsky
(acting teacher) 1863
Mack Sennett (film director
and producer) 1880
Al Capone (mobster) 1899
Frank Hogan (public
official) 1902
Moira Shearer (ballet
dancer) 1926
Thomas Dooley (physician) 1927
James Earl Jones (actor) 1931
Sheree North (actress) 1933
Shari Lewis (entertainer) 1934
Muhammad Ali (boxer) 1942
Joe Frazier (boxer) 1944

January 17 (*continued*)
Kay Mazzo (ballet dancer)   1947
Mick Taylor (rock musician)   1948

JANUARY 18

Baron de Montesquieu
   (philosopher)   1689
Daniel Webster (orator)   1782
Emmanuel Chabrier
   (composer)   1841
A. A. Milne (writer)   1882
Antoine Pevsner (artist)   1886
Oliver Hardy (comedian)   1892
Cary Grant (actor)   1904
Danny Kaye (comedian)   1913

JANUARY 19

Robert E. Lee (army officer)   1807
Edgar Allan Poe (writer)   1809
Paul Cezanne (painter)   1839
Oveta Culp Hobby (publisher
   and government official)   1905
Hans Hotter (opera singer)   1909
John Raitt (actor)   1917
Guy Madison (actor)   1922
Jean Stapleton (actress)   1923
Fritz Weaver (actor)   1926
Richard Lester (film director)   1932
Phil Everly (singer)   1939
Janis Joplin (singer)   1943
Desi Arnaz, Jr. (actor)   1953

AQUARIUS

Element: Air / Quality: Fixed

Air is the element which stands for communication because it touches and connects all the things on earth; it is represented in Aquarius in its fixed condition, signifying communication and relationships maintained and broadened to their greatest extent. This may be understood in the social sense of universal brotherhood, or else as the function of human intelligence, the common ground which joins minds all over the world. The overall view is what matters to Aquarians, whether of society as a cross-cultural unity, or of ideas, which they are particularly adept at arranging together to form all-encompassing theories. This inclusiveness is the meaning of the Waterbearer, a man or angel dispensing on the earth a gift which flows freely over all alike. With such a benign spirit toward people in general, Aquarians are friendly but rather detached in their dealings with particular individuals, whom they see primarily as parts of larger circles; their dispassionate view of other people enables them to keep clear heads and open minds, which the operation of their intelligence demands. They are independent thinkers and receptive to new and advanced ideas, a progressive attitude inspired by their ruler Uranus, the planet of originality, innovations, revolutions, and sudden and unexpected breakthroughs.

Aquarian Francis Bacon is outstanding among forward-looking thinkers in history for his comprehensive grasp of the knowledge of his time and his realization that this medieval knowledge had to be ordered in an entirely new way to serve what he called "the new philosophy," which we call modern science. The objective, scientific view, associated with Aquarius, which Bacon was the first to propose, came into its own in the Age of Reason and the so-called Enlightenment;

this era's great faith in man's rational capabilities and in the possibility of perfecting human society in accordance with natural laws—decidedly Aquarian ideals—eventually led to Aquarian revolutions, first in America and then in France (accompanied by the discovery in 1781 of Uranus, which symbolized the fact that the Uranian/Aquarian principle of revolution had fully entered into the general human consciousness).

Aquarians representative of the Uranian eighteenth century include Frederick the Great, original type of the "enlightened despot," cool-headed military man, player of the flute, and a great admirer of the rationalist Voltaire; Lessing, Germany's poet of the Enlightenment, who preached tolerance and the universality of religion; and Beaumarchais, who gave considerable material support to the American revolution, and wrote a play, *The Marriage of Figaro,* which heralded the revolution in France. Mozart, another Aquarius, who composed an opera based on *The Marriage of Figaro,* was not interested in revolutions, political or musical, but in the illumination of human life by the power of love. He was attracted to the very Aquarian Society of Freemasons with their idealistic vision of goodness and truth and the joys of the brotherhood, and he found in this brotherhood his chief support in life besides music. His last great opera, *The Magic Flute,* expressed the Masonic conviction that wisdom and virtue, led by love, would triumph over evil and open up a bright new future for mankind—a typically Aquarian tomorrow.

The impulse to construct a perfect society (or "Utopia," as Thomas More, an Aquarius, called it in his famous work) may take the shape of humanistic social reform, of which one of the most notable advocates was Charles Dickens. Dickens saw clearly the misery and injustice suffered by the poor, by industrial workers, prisoners, orphans, and other unfortunates exploited or cast out by society, at a time when most people thought nothing of such conditions. Through his writings he made the public newly aware of social ills, and had a significant influence on the passage of progressive legislation aimed at reform. Dickens' contemporary and fellow Aquarian Abraham Lincoln became the personal instrument of reform in his society by abolishing slavery, while another Aquarius, Susan B. Anthony, was agitating for legal recognition of the rights of women. Franklin D. Roosevelt is a recent example of Aquarian concern for improving the welfare of society and shaping an ideal future through progressive laws.

Aquarian social meliorism, the idea that the development of society should follow a course of progressive improvement, had its scientific parallel in Aquarius Charles Darwin's theory of evolution, which stated that by a continuous process of natural selection, biological species approach ever nearer to a state of perfect attunement to their environment. Such a concept accorded with the Aquarian notion of progress better than the Biblical story of a static creation; it opened up for consideration the possibility of man's future evolution, which was understood by some to lie in the advancement of society as a whole, while others held that mankind adapts himself to the future's requirements by creating technological extensions of himself. The latter way was shown most brilliantly by an Aquarius, Thomas Edison, whose original mind conceived some of the inventions most essential to "progress" in the twentieth century. In fiction, Aquarius Jules Verne described elaborate futuristic mechanisms facilitating undersea and outer-space travel, and many other marvels considered utterly fantastic in his time but actually realized in ours, the Aquarian age.

Beyond technology, man might evolve by developing his psychic abilities, which elude scientific investigation but continue to interest forward-looking researchers. The most widely publicized explorations in this area have been those of an Aquarius, Bishop James Pike, whose open-mindedness on the subject may have been an attitude of faith or merely of credulity, or another example of an Aquarius taking a strikingly unorthodox view ahead of others of his time.

JANUARY 20

Josef Hofmann (pianist)	1876
Walter Piston (composer)	1894
George Burns (comedian)	1896
Joy Adamson (wildlife conservationist)	1910
Federico Fellini (film maker)	1920
Mario Lanza (singer)	1921
Patricia Neal (actress)	1926
Edwin "Buzz" Aldrin (astronaut)	1930
Dorothy Provine (actress)	1937
Carol E. Heiss (skater)	1940

JANUARY 21

Parmigianino (painter)	1503
Ethan Allen (patriot)	1738
John Charles Fremont (explorer)	1813
Stonewall Jackson (army officer)	1824
Henri Duparc (composer)	1848
Mischa Elman (violinist)	1891
J. Carrol Naish (actor)	1900
Christian Dior (fashion designer)	1905

Paul Scofield (actor)	1922
Telly Savalas (actor)	1924
Steve Reeves (actor)	1926
Jack Nicklaus (golfer)	1940
Placido Domingo (opera singer)	1941
Richie Havens (rock musician)	1941

JANUARY 22

Emperor Hadrian of Rome	A.D. 76
John Winthrop (colonist)	1588
Gotthold Ephraim Lessing (writer)	1729
Manuel Garcia (singing teacher)	1775
Lord Byron (poet)	1788
August Strindberg (playwright)	1849
A. R. Orage (writer)	1873
D. W. Griffith (film maker)	1875
Constance Collier (actress)	1880
Rosa Ponselle (opera singer)	1897
Ann Sothern (actress)	1909
U Thant (UN official)	1909
Ray Anthony (bandleader)	1922

January 22 (*continued*)

Piper Laurie (actress) 1932
Linda Blair (actress) 1959

JANUARY 23

Edmund Burke (writer) 1729
John Hancock (patriot) 1737
Muzio Clementi (composer) 1752
Stendhal (writer) 1783
Edouard Manet (painter) 1832
Sergei Eisenstein (film maker) 1898
Randolph Scott (actor) 1903
Dan Duryea (actor) 1907
Ernie Kovacs (comedian) 1919
Jeanne Moreau (actress) 1928

JANUARY 24

Farinelli (castrato) 1705
King Frederick the Great of
  Prussia 1712
Pierre Augustin
  Beaumarchais (playwright) 1732
King Gustavus III
  of Sweden 1746
E. T. A. Hoffmann (writer) 1776
Edith Wharton (novelist) 1862
Estelle Winwood (actress) 1883
Mikhail Ilyich Romm (film
  director) 1901
Robert Motherwell (painter) 1915
Ernest Borgnine (actor) 1917
Oral Roberts (evangelist) 1918
Santha Rama Rau (writer) 1923
Maria Tallchief (ballet
  dancer) 1925
Desmond Morris (ethologist) 1928
Neil Diamond (singer) 1941
Sharon Tate (actress) 1943

JANUARY 25

Benedict Arnold (traitor) 1741
Robert Burns (poet) 1759
Antonio Scotti (opera singer) 1866
W. Somerset Maugham
  (novelist) 1874
Virginia Woolf (writer) 1882
Wilhelm Furtwaengler
  (conductor) 1886
Paul Henri Spaak (Belgian
  statesman) 1899
Mildred Dunnock (actress) 1906
Ewan MacColl (folk singer) 1915
Edwin Newman (newsman) 1919
Dean Jones (actor) 1936
Leigh Taylor-Young (actress) 1945

JANUARY 26

Douglas MacArthur (army
  officer) 1880
Frank Costello (mobster) 1893
Maria Trapp (folk singer) 1905
Cora Baird (puppeteer) 1912
Anne Jeffreys (singer) 1923
Paul Newman (actor and
  film director) 1925
William Redfield (actor) 1927
Eartha Kitt (singer) 1928
Roger Vadim (film director) 1928
Jules Feiffer (humorist) 1929
John Ogdon (pianist) 1937
Angela Davis (black militant) 1944
Jacqueline du Pre (cellist) 1945

JANUARY 27

Wolfgang Amadeus Mozart
  (composer) 1756
Edouard Lalo (composer) 1823

January 27 (*continued*)

Lewis Carroll (writer)   1832
Samuel Gompers (labor
  leader)   1850
Kaiser Wilhelm II
  of Germany   1859
Learned Hand (jurist)   1872
Jerome Kern (composer)   1885
Olin Downes (music critic)   1886
Ilya Ehrenburg (writer)   1891
William Randolph Hearst, Jr.
  (publisher)   1908
Skitch Henderson
  (bandleader)   1918
Donna Reed (actress)   1921
Ingrid Thulin (actress)   1929
Troy Donahue (actor)   1937
Mikhail Baryshnikov (ballet
  dancer)   1948

JANUARY 28

Colette (writer)   1873
Arthur Rubinstein (pianist)   1886
Jackson Pollock (painter)   1912
Claes Oldenburg (painter)   1929
Susan Sontag (writer)   1933
Nicholas Pryor (actor)   1935
Alan Alda (actor)   1936
Corky Laing (rock musician)   1948

JANUARY 29

William McKinley
  (politician)   1843
Frederick Delius (composer)   1862
Romain Rolland (writer)   1866
John D. Rockefeller, Jr.
  (tycoon)   1874
W. C. Fields (comedian)   1880
Ernst Lubitsch (film director)   1892
Moche Joseph Spiegel, Jr.

  (mail-order merchant)   1901
Victor Mature (actor)   1916
John Forsythe (actor)   1918
Paddy Chayefsky
  (playwright)   1923
Noel Harrison (actor)   1936
Germaine Greer (feminist)   1939
Katharine Ross (actress)   1943

JANUARY 30

James Watt (inventor)   1736
Franklin D. Roosevelt
  (politician)   1882
Martita Hunt (actress)   1900
Winnie Ruth Judd
  (murderess)   1905
Hugh Marlowe (actor)   1911
Barbara Tuchman (historian)   1912
John Ireland (actor)   1914
David Wayne (actor)   1914
John Profumo (British
  politician)   1915
Margaret Bush Wilson (black
  leader)   1919
Carol Channing (actress)   1921
Dick Martin (comedian)   1922
Norman Ross (radio
  personality)   1922
Dorothy Malone (actress)   1925
Harold Prince (producer)   1928
Gene Hackman (actor)   1931
Tammy Grimes (actress)   1936
Vanessa Redgrave (actress)   1937
Boris Spassky (chess player)   1937
Marty Balin (singer)   1943

JANUARY 31

Franz Schubert (composer)   1797
Zane Grey (novelist)   1875
Anna Pavlova (ballet dancer)   1882

January 31 (*continued*)

Eddie Cantor (comedian)	1892
Tallulah Bankhead (actress)	1902
John O'Hara (novelist)	1905
Joe Walcott (boxer)	1914
Thomas Merton (writer)	1915
Garry Moore (TV personality)	1915
Jackie Robinson (baseball player)	1919
Stewart Udall (government official)	1920
John Agar (actor)	1921
William Sylvester (actor)	1922
Joanne Dru (actress)	1923
Norman Mailer (writer)	1923
Jean Simmons (actress)	1929
Ernie Banks (baseball player)	1931
Suzanne Pleshette (actress)	1937
Nolan Ryan (baseball player)	1947

FEBRUARY 1

John Philip Kemble (actor)	1757
Victor Herbert (composer)	1859
Hugo von Hofmannsthal (poet)	1874
Alexander Kipnis (basso)	1891
John Ford (film director)	1895
Clark Gable (actor)	1901
Langston Hughes (writer)	1902
S. J. Perelman (humorist)	1904
Hildegarde (singer)	1906
John Canaday (art critic)	1907
Stuart Whitman (actor)	1929
Don Everly (singer)	1937

FEBRUARY 2

Francis Bacon (philosopher)	1561
Charles de Talleyrand (French statesman)	1754

Alphonse Rothschild (financier)	1827
Havelock Ellis (psychologist)	1859
Fritz Kreisler (violinist)	1875
James Joyce (writer)	1882
Carroll Righter (astrologer)	1900
Jascha Heifetz (violinist)	1901
Ayn Rand (philosopher)	1905
Axel Springer (publisher)	1912
Anne Fogarty (fashion designer)	1919
James Dickey (poet)	1923
Red Schoendienst (baseball manager)	1923
Elaine Stritch (actress)	1925
Valery Giscard d'Estaing (French politician)	1926
Stan Getz (jazz musician)	1927
Tommy Smothers (comedian)	1937
Graham Nash (rock musician)	19—

FEBRUARY 3

Felix Mendelssohn (composer)	1809
Horace Greeley (journalist)	1811
Giulio Gatti-Casazza (operatic impresario)	1869
Gertrude Stein (writer)	1874
Carl Dreyer (film maker)	1889
Norman Rockwell (illustrator)	1894
Mabel Mercer (singer)	1900
Duke of Hamilton (British air force officer)	1903
James Michener (novelist)	1907
Joey Bishop (TV personality)	1918
Bibi Osterwald (actress)	1920
Shelley Berman (comedian)	1924
Glen Tetley (choreographer)	1926

February 3 (*continued*)
Jim Hartz (TV personality)   1940
Fran Tarkenton (football
    player)   1940
Melanie (singer)   1947

FEBRUARY 4

Robert Boyle (scientist)   1627
Fernand Leger (artist)   1881
Ugo Betti (writer)   1892
Ludwig Erhard (German
    politician)   1897
Charles A. Lindbergh
    (aviator)   1902
Erich Leinsdorf (conductor)   1912
Agha Muhammed Yahya
    Khan (Pakistani army
    officer)   1917
Ida Lupino (actress and film
    director)   1918
Norman Wisdom (actor)   1920
Betty Friedan (feminist)   1921
Isabel Peron (Argentine
    politician)   1931
Ivan Davis (pianist)   1932
Choegyam Trungpa (lama)   1939
Alice Cooper (rock
    musician)   1948

FEBRUARY 5

Marquise de Sevigne (writer)   1626
Ole Bull (violinist)   1810
Joris Karl Huysmans (writer)   1848
Belle Starr (horse thief and
    fence)   1848
Adlai Stevenson (politician)   1900
Nathaniel Owings (architect)   1903
John Carradine (actor)   1906
Jussi Bjoerling (opera singer)   1911
William Burroughs (writer)   1914

Red Buttons (actor)   1919
Andreas Papandreou (Greek
    politician)   1919
Arthur Ochs Sulzberger
    (publisher)   1926
Hank Aaron (baseball
    player)   1934
Roger Staubach (football
    player)   1942
Al Kooper (singer)   1944

FEBRUARY 6

Aaron Burr (politician)   1756
Henry Irving (actor)   1838
Eric Partridge (etymologist)   1894
Babe Ruth (baseball player)   1895
Claudio Arrau (pianist)   1903
Ronald Reagan (actor and
    politician)   1911
Eva Braun (dictator's
    mistress)   1912
Zsa Zsa Gabor (actress)   1923
Rip Torn (actor)   1931
François Truffaut (film
    maker)   1932
Mamie Van Doren (actress)   1933
Martina Arroyo (opera
    singer)   1939
Fabian (singer)   1943

FEBRUARY 7

John Henry Fuseli (painter)   1741
John Deere (inventor)   1804
Charles Dickens (novelist)   1812
Laura Ingalls Wilder (writer)   1867
Alfred Adler (psychologist)   1870
Eubie Blake (songwriter)   1873
Sinclair Lewis (writer)   1885
Claudia Muzio (opera singer)   1889
Buster Crabbe (actor)   1908
Eddie Bracken (actor)   1920

FEBRUARY 8

Emanuel Swedenborg
  (philosopher)   1688
John Ruskin (writer)   1819
William Sherman (army
  officer)   1820
Jules Verne (writer)   1828
Evangeline Adams
  (astrologer)   1868
Martin Buber (philosopher)   1878
Franz Marc (painter)   1880
Edith Evans (actress)   1888
Charles Ruggles (actor)   1892
King Wallis Vidor (film
  maker)   1894
Lyle Talbot (actor)   1904
Ray Middleton (actor)   1907
Betty Field (actress)   1918
Lana Turner (actress)   1920
Jack Lemmon (actor)   1925
James Dean (actor)   1931
Tom Rush (singer)   1941
Jackie Curtis (actress)   1948

FEBRUARY 9

Thomas Paine (pamphleteer)   1737
William Henry Harrison
  (politician)   1773
Mrs. Patrick Campbell
  (actress)   1865
Amy Lowell (poet)   1874
Alban Berg (composer)   1885
Ronald Colman (actor)   1891
Peggy Wood (actress)   1892
Brian Donlevy (actor)   1903
Dean Rusk (government
  official)   1909
Carmen Miranda (singer)   1914
Ernest Tubb (country singer)   1914
Bill Veeck (baseball team
  president)   1914

Brendan Behan (writer)   1923
Kathryn Grayson (actress)   1923
Carole King (singer)   1941
Mia Farrow (actress)   1945

FEBRUARY 10

Charles Lamb (writer)   1775
Adelina Patti (opera singer)   1843
Boris Pasternak (writer)   1890
Jimmy Durante (comedian)   1893
Bill Tilden (tennis player)   1893
Harold MacMillan (British
  politician)   1894
Judith Anderson (actress)   1898
Bertolt Brecht (playwright)   1898
Lon Chaney, Jr. (actor)   1915
Allie Reynolds (baseball
  player)   1919
Alex Comfort (physician and
  author)   1920
Cesare Siepi (opera singer)   1923
Leontyne Price (opera singer)   1927
Robert Wagner (actor)   1930
Elaine (proprietress)   1939
Roberta Flack (singer)   1940
Donovan (singer)   1946
Mark Spitz (swimmer)   1950

FEBRUARY 11

Thomas Alva Edison
  (inventor)   1847
Vivian Fuchs (geologist)   1908
Josh White (folk singer)   1908
Joseph Mankiewicz (film
  producer)   1909
Florynce Kennedy (feminist)   1916
King Farouk of Egypt   1920
Virginia E. Johnson
  (sexologist)   1925
Kim Stanley (actress)   1925

February 11 (*continued*)
Eva Gabor (actress)   1926
Tina Louise (actress)   1934
Mary Quant (fashion
  designer)   1934
Gene Vincent (singer)   1935
Burt Reynolds (actor)   1936

FEBRUARY 12

Nell Gwyn (courtesan)   1560
Tadeusz Kosciusko (Polish
  patriot)   1746
Peter Cooper (inventor)   1791
Charles Darwin (naturalist)   1809
Abraham Lincoln (politician)   1809
George Meredith (writer)   1828
John L. Lewis (labor leader)   1880
Alice Roosevelt Longworth
  (politician's daughter)   1884
Omar Bradley (army officer)   1893
Roy Harris (composer)   1898
Todd Duncan (actor)   1903
Ted Mack (TV personality)   1904
Lorne Greene (actor)   1915
Joseph Alioto (politician)   1916
Forrest Tucker (actor)   1919
Franco Zeffirelli (stage
  designer and director)   1923
Joe Garagiola (TV
  personality)   1926
Charles Van Doren
  (academician)   1926

FEBRUARY 13

Paul Choisnard (astrologer)   1867
Feodor Chaliapin (opera
  singer)   1873
Bess Truman (first lady)   1885
Grant Wood (painter)   1892

Georges Simenon (writer)   1903
Patty Berg (golfer)   1918
Oliver Smith (stage designer)   1918
Tennessee Ernie Ford
  (singer)   1919
Eileen Farrell (opera singer)   1920
Schuyler G. Chapin (operatic
  impresario)   1923
Kim Novak (actress)   1933
George Segal (actor)   1934
Oliver Reed (actor)   1938
Carol Lynley (actress)   1943
Genevieve Waite (actress)   1949

FEBRUARY 14

Jack Benny (comedian)   1894
Thelma Ritter (actress)   1905
Mel Allen (sportscaster)   1913
Jimmy Hoffa (labor leader)   1913
James Pike (clergyman)   1913
Hugh Downs (TV
  personality)   1921
Vic Morrow (actor)   1932
Florence Henderson (actress)   1934
Mickey Wright (golfer)   1935
Carl Bernstein (reporter)   1944
Tim Buckley (singer)   1947

FEBRUARY 15

King Louis XV of France   1710
Jeremy Bentham
  (philosopher)   1748
Cyrus McCormick (inventor)   1809
Susan B. Anthony (feminist)   1820
Alfred North Whitehead
  (philosopher)   1861
John Barrymore (actor)   1882
Harold Arlen (composer)   1905
Cesar Romero (actor)   1907

February 15 (*continued*)
Kevin McCarthy (actor)   1914
Graham Hill (auto racer)   1929
James R. Schlesinger
    (government official)   1929
Claire Bloom (actress)   1931

FEBRUARY 16

Thomas More (humanist)   1478
Christopher Marlowe
    (playwright)   1564
Queen Anne of England   1665
Henry Adams (writer)   1838
Robert Flaherty (film maker)   1884
Van Wyck Brooks (writer)   1886
Katharine Cornell (actress)   1898
Mario Pei (semanticist)   1901
Edgar Bergen (ventriloquist)   1903
Jimmy Wakely (singer)   1914
Patty Andrews (singer)   1920
John Schlesinger (film
    director)   1926
Vera-Ellen (actress)   1926
Brian Bedford (actor)   1935
Sonny Bono (entertainer)   1935
Jean Patchett (model)   19—
Anthony Dowell (ballet
    dancer)   1943

FEBRUARY 17

Jose de Ribera (painter)   1591
Arcangelo Corelli (composer)   1653

Montgomery Ward
    (merchant)   1843
Thomas J. Watson (computer
    executive)   1874
H. L. Hunt (tycoon)   1889
Red Barber (sportscaster)   1908
Marjorie Lawrence (opera
    singer)   1909
Arthur Kennedy (actor)   1914
Margaret Truman (soprano)   1924
Hal Holbrook (actor)   1925
Alan Bates (actor)   1934
Jim Brown (football player)   1936

FEBRUARY 18

Louis C. Tiffany (jeweler)   1848
Sholom Aleichem (writer)   1859
Adolphe Menjou (actor)   1890
Wendell Willkie (politician)   1892
Andres Segovia (guitarist)   1894
Nikolai Podgorny (Soviet
    politician)   1903
Dane Clark (actor)   1915
Ossie Davis (actor)   1917
Jack Palance (actor)   1919
Bill Cullen (TV personality)   1920
Brian Faulkner (Irish
    politician)   1921
Helen Gurley Brown (writer)   1922
George Kennedy (actor)   1925
Milos Forman (film maker)   1932
Yoko Ono (artist)   1933
Jack Richardson
    (playwright)   1935

PISCES

Element: Water / Quality: Mutable

Pisces is the sign of water in its most variable state, the sea, which adapts its form to fill any space, which is constantly assuming changing colors and moods, flat on the surface, concealing mysteries in its depths. The sea is the common pool into which rivers flow and lose their separate identities, and a similar merging takes place in the Piscean conception of self, which is felt to spring from a multiplicity of indistinct sources. Pisceans recognize themselves in other people and other people in themselves, thus easily sympathizing with others and instinctively adapting to them. They are able to fit with ease into new and unfamiliar circumstances, and to adjust quickly and without surprise to strange news or revelations. Piscean adaptability is symbolized by a pair of fishes swimming in opposite directions, illustrating the ability to follow contrary courses with equal ease. Pisces' ruler is Neptune, lord of dissolving processes, of imagination and intuition, and of glamour, illusion, and deception. The Neptunian spell sometimes draws Pisceans toward the enchantments of music, poetry, or the theater, or into dreaminess and escapism (such as through alcoholism), or religious mysticism; the power that Neptune represents may victimize or transfigure.

Applied to the pursuit of scientific knowledge, as in the work of Nicolaus Copernicus and Galileo Galilei, Pisces minds gifted with the insight of Neptunian intuition may perceive visions of universal reality that transcend accustomed forms of belief. In this way Copernicus developed theories, upheld by Galileo, that brought about the dissolution of the Ptolemaic cosmological system, which had pictured an earth-centered universe of concentric spheres leading by grades ultimately to God. Religious authorities execrated the heretical implication that God and man could be situated anywhere other than at separated points on a scale, but Copernicus and Galileo were able to maintain both scientific theory and religious faith, reconciling apparently contradictory views just as the coupled fishes of their sign swim in two directions at once. The vantage point of man in regard to the universe remained for them the point of view which must be central to a study of man (both serious astrologers, they never disputed this relative truth in the Ptolemaic system), but they pointed up the deceptiveness of man's subjective view when applied to a study of the total universe. The lesson that ordinary perceptions of the world are relative and illusory was once again demonstrated by a Pisces, Albert Einstein, who showed the inadequacy of the traditional Newtonian physics to describe a universe in which matter and energy, space and time, are ultimately identical.

Pisceans able to look past space and time, the phenomenal world of appearances, have been inspired by glimpses of otherworldly eternity that takes on its own heightened reality for them. In the Sistine Chapel fresco of the Last Judgment, the masterpiece of Michelangelo's old age, the end of the world is depicted with the overwhelming conviction of a Pisces who had actually seen an awesome truth beyond that of the world. Arthur Schopenhauer, another Pisces, proposed an end to the world by a negation of the will to live; paradoxically, this annihilation of self would make possible, according to Schopenhauer, an identification with the sufferings of other selves through sympathy or compassion, which is a distinctly Piscean ideal.

Compassion for suffering humanity, or *"les miserables,"* was a prominent trait in Pisces Victor Hugo, as also in another Pisces novelist, John Steinbeck, who identified with laborers and migrants, the poor and dispossessed. George Washington's sympathy with the hard lot of his ragged soldiers is widely reported, an instance of the concern which prompted him to lead the revolt of an oppressed people, like a later Pisces liberator, Jose de San Martin. Other Pisceans popularly identified with the cause of the common man include Andrew Jackson, Edward Kennedy, Ralph Nader, and Johnny Cash.

A sympathetic personality along with a Neptunian air of mystery that escapes definition is a secret of the charm exercised by some Pisceans, which has contributed to the success of movie stars such as Jean Harlow, Anna Magnani, Elizabeth Taylor, Joanne Woodward, and the rather more offbeat Liza Minnelli; these women express a femininity that seems complex, fascinating, and inviting in a peculiarly bewitching way. Such ways are not particularly notable among men in the movies, but in the ballet, where enchanting grace is of the essence, the legendary male stars Vaslaw Nijinsky and Rudolph Nureyev have embodied the Pisces mystique.

The undefinable quality in the Piscean personality is often extended to the Piscean's work or life course, which may follow no discernible pattern, but change with fluid adaptivity in response to outside influences. Pisceans George Frederick Handel and Gioacchino Rossini were both established as the most famous and successful opera composers of their respective times, until the fashion in public taste abruptly shifted to new musical styles less ingratiating than theirs; Handel readily adjusted by abandoning opera and turning to the composition of oratorios, Rossini by quitting composition almost altogether for the last forty years of his life. Lorenzo da Ponte, who wrote for Mozart the greatest of opera librettos, later wandered to America and tried shopkeeping, opera production, and a professorship at Columbia University. "Buffalo Bill" Cody made his name as a scout and hunter in the early days of the Old West; when the buffalo vanished and the West became settled, he organized his "Wild West" troupe and devoted the rest of his career to show business. These Pisces turnabouts illustrate once again the fact that the fishes are not limited to a single course, and may completely change directions at some point in life.

FEBRUARY 19

Luigi Boccherini (composer)	1743
Jules Sandeau (writer)	1811
Cedric Hardwicke (actor)	1893
Andre Breton (writer)	1896
Merle Oberon (actress)	1911
Stan Kenton (jazz musician)	1912
Eddie Arcaro (jockey)	1916
Carson McCullers (novelist)	1917
George Rose (actor)	1920
Lee Marvin (actor)	1924
John Frankenheimer (film director)	1930
Cass Elliot (singer)	1941

FEBRUARY 20

Karl Czerny (pianist)	1791
Honore Daumier (painter)	1808
Mary Garden (opera singer)	1877
Georges Bernanos (writer)	1888
Enzo Ferrari (automobile executive)	1898
Louis I. Kahn (architect)	1901
Alexei Kosygin (Soviet politician)	1904
John Daly (TV personality)	1914

Gloria Vanderbilt (artist and socialite) | 1924
Gloria Vanderbilt (artist and socialite)	1924
Robert Altman (film director)	1925
Roy Cohn (lawyer)	1927
Sidney Poitier (actor)	1927
Amanda Blake (actress)	1931
Nancy Wilson (singer)	1937
Buffy Sainte-Marie (singer)	1941
Phil Esposito (hockey player)	1942
J. Geils (rock musician)	1946
Edward Albert (actor)	1951
Patricia "Tania" Hearst (outlaw)	1954

FEBRUARY 21

Antonio Lopez de Santa Anna (Mexican army officer)	1795
Leo Delibes (composer)	1836
August von Wassermann (bacteriologist)	1866
Constantin Brancusi (sculptor)	1876
Sacha Guitry (actor and playwright)	1885
Anais Nin (diarist)	1903
Madeleine Renaud (actress)	1903
George Mitchell (actor)	1905

February 21 (*continued*)
W. H. Auden (poet) 1907
Zachary Scott (actor) 1914
Ann Sheridan (actress) 1915
J. Fred Buzhardt (lawyer) 1924
Sam Peckinpah (film
  director) 1925
Hubert de Givenchy
  (fashion designer) 1927
Nina Simone (singer) 1935
Barbara Jordan (politician) 1936
Ron Clarke (runner) 1937
Richard Beymer (actor) 1939
Tricia Nixon Cox
  (politician's daughter) 1946

Marni Nixon (singer) 1931
Edward Kennedy (politician) 1932

FEBRUARY 23

George Frederick Handel
  (composer) 1685
Cesar Ritz (hotelkeeper) 1850
Victor Fleming (film
  director) 1883
Elston Howard (baseball
  player) 1930
Peter Fonda (actor) 1939
Louis Abolafia (politician) 1943

FEBRUARY 22

Cotton Mather (clergyman) 1663
George Washington (army
  officer) 1732
Arthur Schopenhauer
  (philosopher) 1788
Frederic Chopin (composer) 1810
James Russell Lowell (writer) 1819
Robert Baden-Powell (Boy
  Scouts founder) 1857
Edna St. Vincent Millay
  (poet) 1892
Luis Bunuel (film maker) 1900
Sean O'Faolain (writer) 1900
Robert Young (actor) 1907
Romulo Betancourt
  (Venezuelan politician) 1908
Irving Kolodin (music critic) 1908
John Mills (actor) 1908
Jules Munshin (comedian) 1915
Charles O. Finley (baseball
  manager) 1918
Giulietta Masina (actress) 1921
Sybil Leek (occultist) 1922

FEBRUARY 24

Wilhelm Grimm (folklorist) 1786
Winslow Homer (painter) 1836
Arrigo Boito (composer and
  poet) 1842
Honus Wagner (baseball
  player) 1874
Marjorie Main (actress) 1890
John Carl Warnecke
  (architect) 1919
Steven Hill (actor) 1922
Michael Harrington
  (socialist) 1928
Barbara Lawrence (actress) 1930
Joan Diener (actress) 1934
Christos Lambrakis
  (journalist) 1934
Renata Scotto (opera singer) 1934

FEBRUARY 25

Galileo Galilei (astronomer) 1564
Carlo Goldoni (playwright) 1707

February 25 (*continued*)

Jose de San Martin (liberator)	1778
Pierre Auguste Renoir (painter)	1841
Benedetto Croce (philosopher)	1866
Enrico Caruso (opera singer)	1873
John Foster Dulles (government official)	1888
Myra Hess (pianist)	1890
Bert Bell (football commissioner)	1894
Meher Baba (mystic)	1894
Zeppo Marx (comedian)	1901
Adelle Davis (nutritionist)	1904
Jim Backus (actor)	1913
Anthony Burgess (writer)	1917
Bobby Riggs (tennis player)	1918
Tom Courtenay (actor)	1937
Diane Baker (actress)	1940
George Harrison (rock musician)	1943

FEBRUARY 26

Victor Hugo (writer)	1802
Buffalo Bill Cody (showman)	1846
Emmy Destinn (opera singer)	1878
Grover Cleveland Alexander (baseball player)	1887
Madeleine Carroll (actress)	1909
Malcolm Wilson (politician)	1914
Jackie Gleason (comedian)	1916
Betty Hutton (actress)	1921
Margaret Leighton (actress)	1922
Tony Randall (actor)	1924
Fats Domino (singer)	1928
Robert Novak (columnist)	1931
Johnny Cash (country singer)	1932
Godfrey Cambridge (comedian)	1933

FEBRUARY 27

Henry Wadsworth Longfellow (poet)	1807
Ellen Terry (actress)	1848
Mattia Battistini (opera singer)	1857
Hugo Black (jurist)	1886
Lotte Lehmann (opera singer)	1888
David Sarnoff (broadcasting executive)	1891
Marian Anderson (singer)	1902
John Steinbeck (writer)	1902
Franchot Tone (actor)	1903
James T. Farrell (novelist)	1904
Joan Bennett (actress)	1910
Peter De Vries (writer)	1910
Lawrence Durrell (writer)	1912
Irwin Shaw (writer)	1913
John Connally (politician)	1917
James Leo Herlihy (novelist)	1927
Joanne Woodward (actress)	1930
Elizabeth Taylor (actress)	1932
Ralph Nader (consumer advocate)	1934
Mirella Freni (opera singer)	1935
Antoinette Sibley (ballet dancer)	1939

FEBRUARY 28

Queen Mary I of England	1516
John Tenniel (illustrator)	1820
Geraldine Farrar (opera singer)	1882
Vaslaw Nijinsky (ballet dancer)	1890
Ben Hecht (writer)	1894
Guiomar Novaes (pianist)	1895
Molly Picon (actress)	1898

February 28 (*continued*)

Linus Pauling (chemist)	1901
Benjamin "Bugsy" Siegel (mobster)	1906
Milton Caniff (cartoonist)	1907
Vincente Minnelli (film director)	1913
Zero Mostel (comedian)	1915
Svetlana Alliluyeva (dictator's daughter)	1926
Tommy Tune (actor)	1939
Mario Andretti (auto racer)	1940
Brian Jones (rock musician)	1942
Bernadette Peters (actress)	1948

FEBRUARY 29

Gioacchino Rossini (composer)	1792
Pepper Martin (baseball player)	1904
James Mitchell (actor)	1920
Michele Morgan (actress)	1920

MARCH 1

Nicolaus Copernicus (astronomer)	1473
William Dean Howells (writer)	1837
Lytton Strachey (writer)	1880
Dmitri Mitropoulos (conductor)	1896
Harry Winston (jeweler)	1896
Glenn Miller (bandleader)	1909
David Niven (actor)	1910
Ralph Ellison (writer)	1914
Robert Lowell (poet)	1917
Dinah Shore (singer)	1917
Michael Flanders (comedian)	1922

Al Rosen (baseball player)	1925
Pete Rozelle (football commissioner)	1926
Harry Belafonte (singer)	1927
Roger Daltrey (rock musician)	1945

MARCH 2

David Garrick (actor)	1717
Sam Houston (soldier and politician)	1793
Bedrich Smetana (composer)	1824
Pope Pius XII	1876
Paul de Kruif (writer)	1890
Kurt Weill (composer)	1900
Dr. Seuss (children's humorist)	1904
Mel Ott (baseball player and manager)	1909
Desi Arnaz (actor)	1917
Jim Konstanty (baseball player)	1917
Jennifer Jones (actress)	1919
Martin Ritt (film director)	1920
Tom Wolfe (writer)	1931
Lou Reed (singer)	1942

MARCH 3

Alexander Graham Bell (inventor)	1847
Wee Willie Keeler (baseball player)	1872
Harry Hanson (actor)	1895
Edna Best (actress)	1900
Jean Harlow (actress)	1911
Julius Boros (golfer)	1920
Princess Lee Radziwill (actress)	1933

March 3 (*continued*)

Gia Scala (actress)	1936
Bobby Driscoll (actor)	1937

MARCH 4

Antonio Vivaldi (composer)	1678
Knute Rockne (football coach)	1888
Charles Goren (bridge player)	1901
Luis Carrero Blanco (Spanish politician)	1903
George Gamow (physicist)	1904
Charles Rudolph Walgreen, Jr. (druggist)	1906
Lili Kraus (pianist)	1908
Joan Greenwood (actress)	1921
Alan Sillitoe (writer)	1928
Miriam Makeba (singer)	1932
Jim Clark (auto racer)	1936
Barbara McNair (singer)	1939
Paula Prentiss (actress)	1939
Chastity Bono (entertainers' daughter)	1969

MARCH 5

Pico della Mirandola (writer)	1463
Samuel Pepys (diarist)	1633
Giambattista Tiepolo (painter)	1696
Frank Norris (novelist)	1870
Heitor Villa-Lobos (composer)	1881
Dorothy Sands (actress)	1893
Rex Harrison (actor)	1908
Pier Paolo Pasolini (poet and film maker)	1922
Jack Cassidy (actor)	1927

Jerrie Cobb (pilot)	1931
Dean Stockwell (actor)	1936
Samantha Eggar (actress)	1939
Randy Matson (athlete)	1945

MARCH 6

Emperor Charles V	1500
Cyrano de Bergerac (soldier and writer)	1620
Elizabeth Barrett Browning (poet)	1806
Nicholas Berdyaev (philosopher)	1874
Ring Lardner (writer)	1885
Barry Jones (actor)	1893
Robert "Lefty" Grove (baseball player)	1900
Hugh Williams (actor)	1904
Lou Costello (comedian)	1908
Julius Rudel (conductor)	1921
Ed McMahon (TV personality)	1923
Gordon Cooper (astronaut)	1927
Lorin Maazel (conductor)	1930
Carmen De Lavallade (dancer)	1931
John Smith (actor)	1931
Valentina Tereshkova (cosmonaut)	1937
Mary Wilson (singer)	1944
Stephen Schwartz (composer and lyricist)	1948

MARCH 7

Alessandro Manzoni (writer)	1785
Luther Burbank (horticulturist)	1849
Piet Mondriaan (painter)	1872

March 7 (*continued*)

Maurice Ravel (composer)	1875
Milton Avery (painter)	1893
Donald Oenslager (stage designer)	1902
Anna Magnani (actress)	1908
Morton DaCosta (producer)	1918
Antony Armstrong-Jones (photographer)	1930
Peter Wolf (singer)	1946

MARCH 8

Carl Philipp Emanuel Bach (composer)	1714
Oliver Wendell Holmes (jurist)	1841
Ruggiero Leoncavallo (composer)	1858
Kenneth Grahame (writer)	1859
Otto Hahn (physicist)	1879
Mississippi John Hurt (folk singer)	1892
Sam Jaffe (actor)	1897
Alan Hovhaness (composer)	1911
Claire Trevor (actress)	1912
Eileen Herlie (actress)	1920
Cyd Charisse (actress)	1923
Jim Bouton (baseball player)	1939
Dick Allen (baseball player)	1942
Lynn Redgrave (actress)	1943

MARCH 9

Vyacheslav Molotov (Soviet official)	1890
Will Geer (actor)	1902
Edward Durell Stone (architect)	1902

David Smith (sculptor)	1906
Samuel Barber (composer)	1910
George Lincoln Rockwell (American Nazi)	1918
Mickey Spillane (writer)	1918
Floyd McKissick (civil rights leader)	1922
James L. Buckley (politician)	1923
Andre Courreges (fashion designer)	1923
Herbert Gold (writer)	1924
Jackie Jensen (baseball player)	1927
Thomas Schippers (conductor)	1930
Yuri Gagarin (cosmonaut)	1934
Joyce Van Patten (actress)	1934
Keely Smith (singer)	1935
Raul Julia (actor)	1940
Bobby Fischer (chess player)	1943
Trish Van Devere (actress)	1945

MARCH 10

Michel de Montaigne (essayist)	1533
Lorenzo Da Ponte (poet and librettist)	1749
Joseph von Eichendorff (poet)	1788
Anna Hyatt Huntingdon (sculptress)	1876
Barry Fitzgerald (actor)	1888
Arthur Honegger (composer)	1892
Pamela Mason (actress)	1918
Jethro (country singer)	1920
James Earl Ray (assassin)	1928
David Rabe (playwright)	1940
Katharine Houghton (actress)	1945

MARCH 11

Francesco Lamperti (singing teacher)	1811
Raoul Walsh (film director)	1889
Henry Cowell (composer)	1897
Dorothy Gish (actress)	1898
King Frederik IX of Denmark	1899
Dorothy Schiff (publisher)	1903
Lawrence Welk (bandleader)	1903
Howard Mitchell (actor)	1911
Harold Wilson (British politician)	1916
Ralph David Abernathy (civil rights leader)	1926

MARCH 12

Prince Henry the Navigator	1394
Gabriele d'Annunzio (poet)	1863
Hans Knappertsbusch (conductor)	1888
Jannis Spyropoulos (artist)	1912
Gordon MacRae (singer)	1921
Jack Kerouac (novelist)	1922
Walter Schirra (astronaut)	1923
Edward Albee (playwright)	1928
Vernon Law (baseball player)	1930
Valery Panov (ballet dancer)	1939
Liza Minnelli (singer)	1946
James Taylor (singer)	1948

MARCH 13

Percival Lowell (astronomer)	1855
Hugo Wolf (composer)	1860
Fritz Busch (conductor)	1890
Leona Powers (actress)	1896
L. Ron Hubbard	

(Scientologist)	1911
Igor Youskevitch (ballet dancer)	1912
Judith Evelyn (actress)	1913
Sammy Kaye (orchestra leader)	1913

MARCH 14

Georg Philipp Telemann (composer)	1681
Thomas Hart Benton (painter)	1782
James Bogardus (architect)	1800
Casey Jones (railroadsman)	1864
Olive Fremstad (opera singer)	1871
Albert Einstein (physicist)	1879
Osa Johnson (explorer)	1894
John Garfield (actor)	1913
Max Shulman (humorist)	1919
Hank Ketcham (cartoonist)	1920
Frank Borman (astronaut)	1928
Michael Caine (actor)	1933
Quincy Jones (jazz musician)	1933
Eugene Cernan (astronaut)	1934
Rita Tushingham (actress)	1942

MARCH 15

Michelangelo Buonarroti (artist)	1475
Andrew Jackson (politician)	1767
Lady Gregory (playwright)	1852
Mrs. Marjorie Merriweather Post (philanthropist)	1887
George Brent (actor)	1904
Margaret Webster (director)	1905
Lightnin Hopkins (blues singer)	1912
Macdonald Carey (actor)	1913

March 15 (*continued*)
Harry James (trumpeter) 1916
Sabu (actor) 1924
David Hayes (sculptor) 1931
Sly Stone (rock musician) 1944

Rudolf Nureyev (ballet dancer) 1938
Monique Van Vooren (actress) 1938
Paul Kantner (rock musician) 1942
Kurt Russell (actor) 1951

MARCH 16

Mme. de La Fayette (novelist) 1634
James Madison (politician) 1751
Georg Simon Ohm (physicist) 1787
Mike Mansfield (politician) 1903
Pat Nixon (first lady) 1912
Jean Rosenthal (lighting designer) 1912
Leo McKern (actor) 1920
Charles Ellsworth Goodell (politician) 1926
Jerry Lewis (comedian) 1926
Olga San Juan (actress) 1927
Christa Ludwig (opera singer) 1928
Mary Hinkson (dancer) 1930
Teresa Berganza (opera singer) 1935
Bernardo Bertolucci (film maker) 1940

MARCH 17

Edmund Kean (actor) 1787
Manuel Garcia II (singing teacher) 1805
Chaim Gross (artist) 1904
Bayard Rustin (civil rights leader) 1910
Mercedes McCambridge (actress) 1918
Nat King Cole (singer) 1919

MARCH 18

Ovid (poet) 43 B.C.
Amerigo Vespucci (explorer) 1454
John C. Calhoun (politician) 1782
Grover Cleveland (politician) 1837
Stephane Mallarme (poet) 1842
Nicolai Rimski-Korsakov (composer) 1844
Rudolf Diesel (engineer) 1858
Anna Held (actress) 1873
Edgar Cayce (psychic) 1877
Edward Everett Horton (actor) 1887
Wilfred Owen (poet) 1893
Manly Palmer Hall (occultist) 1901
Robert Donat (actor) 1905
Rene Clement (film maker) 1913
Peter Graves (actor) 1926
George Plimpton (playboy) 1927
John Updike (novelist) 1932
Wilson Pickett (singer) 1941

MARCH 19

King Henry II of England 1133
King Henry IV of England 1367
Georges de la Tour (painter) 1593
David Livingstone (explorer) 1813
Richard Burton (explorer) 1821
Albert Pinkham Ryder (painter) 1847

March 19 (*continued*)

Wyatt Earp (lawman)	1848
William Jennings Bryan (politician)	1860
Sergei Diaghilev (impresario)	1872
Max Reger (composer)	1873
Josef Albers (painter)	1888
Earl Warren (jurist)	1891
Moms Mabley (comedienne)	1894
Jo Mielziner (stage designer)	1901
John J. Sirica (jurist)	1904
Adolf Eichmann (Nazi official)	1906
Kent Smith (actor)	1907
Patricia Morison (actress)	1915
Irving Wallace (novelist)	1916
Dinu Lipatti (pianist)	1917
Ornette Coleman (jazz musician)	1930
Philip Roth (novelist)	1933
Phyllis Newman (actress)	1935
Ursula Andress (actress)	1936
Lynda Bird Johnson Robb (politician's daughter)	1944

MARCH 20

King Ferdinand of Castile	1452

Johann C. F. Hoelderlin (poet)	1770
Henrik Ibsen (playwright)	1828
Sepharial (astrologer)	1864
Beniamino Gigli (opera singer)	1890
Lauritz Melchior (opera singer)	1890
Serge Jaroff (choral conductor)	1896
B. F. Skinner (psychologist)	1904
Abraham Beame (politician)	1906
Ozzie Nelson (actor)	1907
Patrick McDermott (actor)	1908
Michael Redgrave (actor)	1908
Frank Stanton (broadcasting executive)	1908
Wendell Corey (actor)	1914
Sviatoslav Richter (pianist)	1915
Jack Barry (TV personality)	1918
Ray Goulding (comedian)	1922
Carl Reiner (comedian)	1922
John D. Ehrlichman (government official)	1925
Roland Peugeot (automobile executive)	1926
Fred Rogers (TV producer)	1928
Hal Linden (actor)	1931
Bobby Orr (hockey player)	1948
Carl Palmer (rock musician)	1950

THE MOON TABLES

The following tables of the moon's passage through the signs of the zodiac are an abbreviation of the information contained in any astrological ephemeris. The ephemeris gives precise calculations of daily planetary motions, in order that the exact position at any particular moment of the sun, moon, or planets may be ascertained, but for present purposes only the date is given on which the moon moves into a new sign, which occurs every two or three days. Thus, if the moon is shown to be entering Leo on the sixteenth of a given month, it will remain in Leo through the sixteenth and seventeenth and move into the next sign, Virgo, probably on the eighteenth. The change of sign can take place at any time of day, so in many cases it will not be certain which of two signs the moon occupied at the time a person was born; this can be determined conclusively, if the time of birth is known, only by consulting an ephemeris, but it is frequently possible to guess correctly which of the two signs is the right one, judging by the life and personality traits of the subject in question.

The energies symbolized by the moon are applied to the practical expression, as seen by others around a person, of the central drive that the sun represents. The manner in which these lunar energies are exercised depends on the sign in which the moon was positioned at a person's birth, in the same way that the sun's figurative ray is seen focused through the lens of the sign it occupied. The nature of the various signs has been described, and the way that the sun manifests itself through each of them; the moon's mode of operation in a sign is to be interpreted in the same way, according to the nature of that sign.

1890

JAN	FEB	MAR	APR	MAY	JUN	JUL	AUG	SEP	OCT	NOV	DEC
2 Gem	1 Can	2 Leo	1 Vir	1 Lib	2 Sag	1 Cap	2 Pis	2 Tau	2 Gem	1 Can	1 L…
4 Can	3 Leo	5 Vir	4 Lib	3 Sco	4 Cap	3 Aqu	4 Ari	5 Gem	4 Can	3 Leo	3 V…
7 Leo	6 Vir	7 Lib	6 Sco	5 Sag	6 Aqu	5 Pis	6 Tau	7 Can	7 Leo	6 Vir	5 L…
9 Vir	8 Lib	10 Sco	8 Sag	8 Cap	8 Pis	7 Ari	8 Gem	9 Leo	9 Vir	8 Lib	8 S…
12 Lib	10 Sco	12 Sag	10 Cap	10 Aqu	10 Ari	10 Tau	11 Can	12 Vir	12 Lib	10 Sco	10 S…
14 Sco	13 Sag	14 Cap	12 Aqu	12 Pis	12 Tau	12 Gem	13 Leo	14 Lib	14 Sco	13 Sag	12 C…
16 Sag	15 Cap	16 Aqu	15 Pis	14 Ari	15 Gem	14 Can	16 Vir	17 Sco	16 Sag	15 Cap	14 A…
18 Cap	17 Aqu	18 Pis	17 Ari	16 Tau	17 Can	17 Leo	18 Lib	19 Sag	17 Cap	17 Aqu	16 P…
20 Aqu	19 Pis	20 Ari	19 Tau	18 Gem	20 Leo	19 Vir	21 Sco	21 Cap	21 Aqu	19 Pis	18 A…
22 Pis	21 Ari	22 Tau	21 Gem	21 Can	22 Vir	22 Lib	23 Sag	23 Aqu	23 Pis	21 Ari	21 T…
24 Ari	23 Tau	25 Gem	24 Can	23 Leo	25 Lib	24 Sco	25 Cap	26 Pis	25 Ari	23 Tau	23 G…
27 Tau	25 Gem	27 Can	26 Leo	26 Vir	27 Sco	27 Sag	27 Aqu	28 Ari	27 Tau	26 Gem	25 C…
29 Gem	28 Can	30 Leo	29 Vir	28 Lib	29 Sag	29 Cap	29 Pis	30 Tau	29 Gem	28 Can	28 L…
				31 Sco		31 Aqu	31 Ari				30 V…

1891

JAN	FEB	MAR	APR	MAY	JUN	JUL	AUG	SEP	OCT	NOV	DEC
2 Lib	1 Sco	2 Sag	1 Cap	2 Pis	1 Ari	2 Gem	1 Can	2 Vir	2 Lib	1 Sco	3 C…
4 Sco	3 Sag	4 Cap	3 Aqu	4 Ari	3 Tau	4 Can	3 Leo	4 Lib	4 Sco	3 Sag	5 A…
7 Sag	5 Cap	7 Aqu	5 Pis	6 Tau	5 Gem	7 Leo	6 Vir	7 Sco	7 Sag	5 Cap	7 P…
9 Cap	7 Aqu	9 Pis	7 Ari	9 Gem	7 Can	9 Vir	8 Lib	9 Sag	9 Cap	8 Aqu	9 A…
11 Aqu	9 Pis	11 Ari	9 Tau	11 Can	10 Leo	12 Lib	11 Sco	12 Cap	11 Aqu	10 Pis	11 T…
13 Pis	11 Ari	13 Tau	11 Gem	13 Leo	12 Vir	14 Sco	13 Sag	14 Aqu	13 Pis	12 Ari	13 G…
15 Ari	13 Tau	15 Gem	13 Can	16 Vir	14 Lib	17 Sag	15 Cap	16 Pis	15 Ari	14 Tau	15 C…
17 Tau	15 Gem	17 Can	16 Leo	18 Lib	17 Sco	19 Cap	18 Aqu	18 Ari	17 Tau	16 Gem	18 L…
19 Gem	18 Can	20 Leo	18 Vir	21 Sco	19 Sag	21 Aqu	20 Pis	20 Tau	19 Gem	18 Can	20 V…
22 Can	20 Leo	22 Vir	21 Lib	23 Sag	22 Cap	23 Pis	22 Ari	22 Gem	22 Can	20 Leo	23 L…
24 Leo	23 Vir	25 Lib	23 Sco	25 Cap	24 Aqu	25 Ari	24 Tau	24 Can	24 Leo	23 Vir	25 S…
27 Vir	25 Lib	27 Sco	26 Sag	27 Aqu	26 Pis	27 Tau	26 Gem	27 Leo	26 Vir	25 Lib	28 Sa…
29 Lib	28 Sco	29 Sag	28 Cap	30 Pis	28 Ari	29 Gem	28 Can	29 Vir	29 Lib	28 Sco	30 Ca…
			30 Aqu		30 Tau		30 Leo			30 Sag	

1892

JAN	FEB	MAR	APR	MAY	JUN	JUL	AUG	SEP	OCT	NOV	DEC
1 Aqu	2 Ari	2 Tau	3 Can	2 Leo	1 Vir	1 Lib	2 Sag	1 Cap	1 Aqu	1 Ari	1 Ta…
3 Pis	4 Tau	4 Gem	5 Leo	5 Vir	3 Lib	3 Sco	4 Cap	3 Aqu	3 Pis	3 Tau	3 Ge…
5 Ari	6 Gem	6 Can	7 Vir	7 Lib	6 Sco	6 Sag	7 Aqu	5 Pis	5 Ari	5 Gem	5 Ca…
7 Tau	8 Can	9 Leo	10 Lib	10 Sco	8 Sag	8 Cap	9 Pis	7 Ari	7 Tau	7 Can	7 Le…
10 Gem	10 Leo	11 Vir	12 Sco	12 Sag	11 Cap	11 Aqu	11 Ari	9 Tau	9 Gem	9 Leo	9 V…
12 Can	13 Vir	13 Lib	15 Sag	14 Cap	13 Aqu	13 Pis	13 Tau	11 Gem	11 Can	12 Vir	11 L…
14 Leo	15 Lib	16 Sco	17 Cap	17 Aqu	15 Pis	15 Ari	15 Gem	14 Can	13 Leo	14 Lib	14 Sc…
16 Vir	18 Sco	19 Sag	20 Aqu	19 Pis	17 Ari	17 Tau	17 Can	16 Leo	15 Vir	17 Sco	16 Sa…
19 Lib	20 Sag	21 Cap	22 Pis	21 Ari	20 Tau	20 Gem	20 Leo	18 Vir	17 Lib	19 Sag	19 Ca…
21 Sco	23 Cap	23 Aqu	24 Ari	23 Tau	22 Gem	23 Leo	22 Vir	20 Lib	20 Sco	21 Cap	21 Ag…
24 Sag	25 Aqu	25 Pis	26 Tau	25 Gem	24 Can	26 Vir	24 Lib	23 Sco	23 Sag	24 Aqu	24 Pi…
26 Cap	27 Pis	27 Ari	28 Gem	27 Can	26 Leo	28 Lib	26 Sco	25 Sag	25 Cap	26 Pis	26 Ar…
28 Aqu	29 Ari	29 Tau	30 Can	29 Leo	28 Vir	30 Sco	29 Sag	28 Cap	28 Aqu	29 Ari	28 Ta…
31 Pis		31 Gem						30 Pis	30 Pis		30 Ge…

1893

JAN	FEB	MAR	APR	MAY	JUN	JUL	AUG	SEP	OCT	NOV	DEC
1 Can	2 Vir	1 Vir	2 Sco	2 Sag	1 Cap	1 Aqu	2 Ari	2 Gem	1 Can	2 Vir	1 Li…
3 Leo	4 Lib	3 Lib	5 Sag	5 Cap	3 Aqu	3 Pis	4 Tau	4 Can	4 Leo	4 Lib	4 Sc…
5 Vir	6 Sco	6 Sco	7 Cap	7 Aqu	6 Pis	5 Ari	6 Gem	6 Leo	6 Vir	7 Sco	6 Sa…
8 Lib	9 Sag	8 Sag	10 Aqu	9 Pis	8 Ari	7 Tau	8 Can	8 Vir	8 Lib	9 Sag	9 Ca…
10 Sco	11 Cap	11 Cap	12 Pis	12 Ari	10 Tau	10 Gem	10 Leo	10 Lib	10 Sco	12 Cap	11 Ag…
13 Sag	14 Aqu	13 Aqu	14 Ari	14 Tau	12 Gem	12 Can	12 Vir	13 Sco	12 Sag	14 Aqu	14 Pi…
15 Cap	16 Pis	16 Pis	16 Tau	16 Gem	14 Can	14 Leo	14 Lib	15 Sag	15 Cap	17 Pis	16 Ar…
18 Aqu	18 Ari	18 Ari	18 Gem	18 Can	16 Leo	16 Vir	17 Sco	18 Cap	17 Aqu	19 Ari	18 Ta…
20 Pis	20 Tau	20 Tau	20 Can	20 Leo	18 Vir	18 Lib	19 Sag	20 Aqu	20 Pis	21 Tau	21 Ge…
22 Ari	23 Gem	22 Gem	22 Leo	22 Vir	21 Lib	20 Sco	22 Cap	23 Pis	22 Ari	23 Gem	23 Ca…
24 Tau	25 Can	24 Can	25 Vir	24 Lib	23 Sco	23 Sag	24 Aqu	25 Ari	25 Tau	25 Can	25 Le…
26 Gem	27 Leo	26 Leo	27 Lib	27 Sco	25 Sag	25 Cap	26 Pis	27 Tau	27 Gem	27 Leo	27 Vi…
28 Can		28 Vir	29 Sco	29 Sag	28 Cap	28 Aqu	27 Tau	29 Gem	29 Can	29 Vir	29 Li…
31 Leo		31 Lib				30 Pis	31 Tau		31 Leo		31 Sc…

Table 1

JAN	FEB	MAR	APR	MAY	JUN	JUL	AUG	SEP	OCT	NOV	DEC
3 Sag	1 Cap	1 Cap	2 Pis	2 Ari	3 Gem	2 Can	2 Vir	1 Lib	3 Sag	2 Cap	1 Aqu
5 Cap	4 Aqu	3 Aqu	4 Ari	4 Tau	5 Can	4 Leo	4 Lib	3 Sco	5 Cap	4 Aqu	4 Pis
8 Aqu	6 Pis	6 Pis	7 Tau	6 Gem	7 Leo	6 Vir	7 Sco	5 Sag	8 Aqu	6 Pis	6 Ari
10 Pis	9 Ari	8 Ari	9 Gem	8 Can	9 Vir	8 Lib	9 Sag	8 Cap	10 Pis	9 Ari	9 Tau
13 Ari	11 Tau	10 Tau	11 Can	10 Leo	11 Lib	10 Sco	11 Cap	10 Aqu	13 Ari	11 Tau	11 Gem
15 Tau	13 Gem	12 Gem	13 Leo	12 Vir	13 Sco	13 Sag	14 Aqu	13 Pis	15 Tau	13 Gem	13 Can
17 Gem	15 Can	15 Can	15 Vir	14 Lib	15 Sag	15 Cap	16 Pis	15 Ari	17 Gem	15 Can	15 Leo
19 Can	17 Leo	17 Leo	17 Lib	17 Sco	18 Cap	18 Aqu	19 Ari	18 Tau	19 Can	18 Leo	17 Vir
21 Leo	19 Vir	19 Vir	19 Sco	19 Sag	20 Aqu	20 Pis	21 Tau	20 Gem	21 Leo	20 Vir	19 Lib
23 Vir	22 Lib	21 Lib	22 Sag	22 Cap	23 Pis	23 Ari	24 Gem	22 Can	23 Vir	22 Lib	21 Sco
25 Lib	24 Sco	23 Sco	24 Cap	24 Aqu	25 Ari	25 Tau	26 Can	24 Leo	26 Lib	24 Sco	24 Sag
27 Sco	26 Sag	26 Sag	27 Aqu	27 Pis	28 Tau	27 Gem	28 Leo	26 Vir	28 Sco	26 Sag	26 Cap
30 Sag		28 Cap	29 Pis	29 Ari	30 Gem	29 Can	30 Vir	28 Lib	30 Sag	29 Cap	29 Aqu
		31 Aqu		31 Tau		31 Leo		30 Sco			31 Pis

Table 2

JAN	FEB	MAR	APR	MAY	JUN	JUL	AUG	SEP	OCT	NOV	DEC
3 Ari	1 Tau	1 Tau	1 Can	1 Leo	1 Lib	1 Sco	2 Cap	3 Pis	2 Ari	1 Tau	1 Gem
5 Tau	4 Gem	3 Gem	4 Leo	3 Vir	3 Sco	3 Sag	4 Aqu	5 Ari	5 Tau	4 Gem	3 Can
7 Gem	6 Can	5 Can	6 Vir	5 Lib	6 Sag	5 Cap	6 Pis	8 Tau	7 Gem	6 Can	5 Leo
9 Can	8 Leo	7 Leo	8 Lib	7 Sco	8 Cap	8 Aqu	9 Ari	10 Gem	10 Can	8 Leo	8 Vir
11 Leo	10 Vir	9 Vir	10 Sco	9 Sag	10 Aqu	10 Pis	11 Tau	12 Can	12 Leo	10 Vir	10 Lib
13 Vir	12 Lib	11 Lib	12 Sag	12 Cap	13 Pis	13 Ari	14 Gem	15 Leo	14 Vir	12 Lib	12 Sco
15 Lib	14 Sco	13 Sco	14 Cap	14 Aqu	15 Ari	15 Tau	16 Can	17 Vir	16 Lib	14 Sco	14 Sag
18 Sco	16 Sag	16 Sag	17 Aqu	17 Pis	18 Tau	17 Gem	18 Leo	19 Lib	18 Sco	17 Sag	16 Cap
20 Sag	18 Cap	18 Cap	19 Pis	19 Ari	20 Gem	20 Can	20 Vir	21 Sco	20 Sag	19 Cap	18 Aqu
22 Cap	21 Aqu	20 Aqu	22 Ari	21 Tau	22 Can	22 Leo	22 Lib	23 Sag	22 Cap	21 Aqu	21 Pis
25 Aqu	24 Pis	23 Pis	24 Tau	24 Gem	24 Leo	24 Vir	24 Sco	25 Cap	24 Aqu	24 Pis	23 Ari
27 Pis	26 Ari	25 Ari	26 Gem	26 Can	26 Vir	26 Lib	26 Sag	27 Aqu	27 Pis	26 Ari	26 Tau
30 Ari		28 Tau	29 Can	28 Leo	28 Lib	28 Sco	29 Cap	30 Pis	30 Ari	29 Tau	28 Gem
		30 Gem		30 Vir		30 Sag	31 Aqu				31 Can

Table 3

JAN	FEB	MAR	APR	MAY	JUN	JUL	AUG	SEP	OCT	NOV	DEC
2 Leo	2 Lib	1 Lib	1 Sag	1 Cap	2 Pis	2 Ari	3 Gem	2 Can	1 Leo	2 Lib	1 Sco
4 Vir	4 Sco	3 Sco	3 Cap	3 Aqu	4 Ari	4 Tau	5 Can	4 Leo	3 Vir	4 Sco	3 Sag
6 Lib	6 Sag	5 Sag	6 Aqu	5 Pis	7 Tau	6 Gem	7 Leo	6 Vir	5 Lib	6 Sag	5 Cap
8 Sco	9 Cap	7 Cap	8 Pis	8 Ari	9 Gem	9 Can	10 Vir	8 Lib	7 Sco	8 Cap	7 Aqu
10 Sag	11 Aqu	9 Aqu	11 Ari	10 Tau	11 Can	11 Leo	12 Lib	10 Sco	9 Sag	10 Aqu	9 Pis
12 Cap	13 Pis	12 Pis	13 Tau	13 Gem	14 Leo	13 Vir	14 Sco	12 Sag	11 Cap	12 Pis	12 Ari
15 Aqu	16 Ari	14 Ari	16 Gem	15 Can	16 Vir	15 Lib	16 Sag	14 Cap	14 Aqu	15 Ari	14 Tau
17 Pis	19 Tau	17 Tau	18 Can	18 Leo	18 Lib	17 Sco	18 Cap	17 Aqu	16 Pis	17 Tau	17 Gem
20 Ari	21 Gem	19 Gem	20 Leo	20 Vir	20 Sco	20 Sag	20 Aqu	19 Pis	19 Ari	20 Gem	19 Can
22 Tau	23 Can	22 Can	22 Vir	22 Lib	22 Sag	22 Cap	23 Pis	22 Ari	21 Tau	22 Can	22 Leo
25 Gem	26 Leo	24 Leo	24 Lib	24 Sco	24 Cap	24 Aqu	25 Ari	24 Tau	24 Gem	25 Leo	24 Vir
27 Can	28 Vir	26 Vir	27 Sco	26 Sag	27 Aqu	26 Pis	28 Tau	26 Gem	26 Can	27 Vir	26 Lib
29 Leo		28 Lib	29 Sag	28 Cap	29 Pis	29 Ari	30 Gem	29 Can	29 Leo	29 Lib	29 Sco
31 Vir		30 Sco		30 Aqu		31 Tau			31 Vir		31 Sag

Table 4

JAN	FEB	MAR	APR	MAY	JUN	JUL	AUG	SEP	OCT	NOV	DEC
2 Cap	3 Pis	2 Pis	1 Ari	3 Gem	2 Can	1 Leo	2 Lib	1 Sco	2 Cap	3 Pis	2 Ari
4 Aqu	5 Ari	4 Ari	3 Tau	5 Can	4 Leo	4 Vir	4 Sco	3 Sag	4 Aqu	5 Ari	5 Tau
6 Pis	7 Tau	7 Tau	5 Gem	8 Leo	6 Vir	6 Lib	6 Sag	5 Cap	6 Pis	7 Tau	7 Gem
9 Ari	10 Gem	9 Gem	8 Can	10 Vir	9 Lib	8 Sco	8 Cap	7 Aqu	9 Ari	10 Gem	10 Can
11 Tau	12 Can	12 Can	10 Leo	12 Lib	11 Sco	10 Sag	11 Aqu	9 Pis	11 Tau	12 Can	12 Leo
14 Gem	15 Leo	14 Leo	13 Vir	15 Sco	13 Sag	13 Cap	13 Pis	11 Ari	13 Gem	15 Leo	15 Vir
16 Can	17 Vir	16 Vir	15 Lib	17 Sag	15 Cap	15 Aqu	15 Ari	14 Tau	16 Can	17 Vir	17 Lib
18 Leo	19 Lib	18 Lib	17 Sco	20 Cap	17 Aqu	17 Pis	17 Tau	16 Gem	19 Leo	20 Lib	19 Sco
21 Vir	21 Sco	20 Sco	19 Sag	22 Aqu	19 Pis	19 Ari	20 Gem	19 Can	21 Vir	22 Sco	21 Sag
23 Lib	23 Sag	22 Sag	21 Cap	24 Pis	21 Ari	21 Tau	22 Can	21 Leo	23 Lib	24 Sag	23 Cap
25 Sco	25 Cap	25 Cap	23 Aqu	26 Ari	24 Tau	24 Gem	25 Leo	24 Vir	25 Sco	26 Cap	25 Aqu
27 Sag	28 Aqu	27 Aqu	25 Pis	28 Tau	26 Gem	26 Can	27 Vir	26 Lib	27 Sag	28 Aqu	27 Pis
29 Cap		29 Pis	28 Ari	30 Gem	29 Can	29 Leo	29 Lib	28 Sco	29 Cap	30 Pis	30 Ari
31 Aqu			30 Tau			31 Vir		30 Sag	31 Aqu		

1898

JAN	FEB	MAR	APR	MAY	JUN	JUL	AUG	SEP	OCT	NOV	DEC
1 Tau	2 Can	2 Can	1 Leo	3 Lib	1 Sco	1 Sag	1 Aqu	1 Ari	1 Tau	2 Can	2 Can
3 Gem	5 Leo	4 Leo	3 Vir	5 Sco	3 Sag	3 Cap	3 Pis	4 Tau	3 Gem	5 Leo	5 Vir
6 Can	7 Vir	6 Vir	5 Lib	7 Sag	5 Cap	5 Aqu	5 Ari	6 Gem	6 Can	7 Vir	7 Lib
8 Leo	9 Lib	9 Lib	7 Sco	9 Cap	7 Aqu	7 Pis	7 Tau	9 Can	8 Leo	10 Lib	9 Sco
11 Vir	12 Sco	11 Sco	9 Sag	11 Aqu	9 Pis	9 Ari	10 Gem	11 Leo	11 Vir	12 Sco	11 Sag
13 Lib	14 Sag	13 Sag	11 Cap	13 Pis	11 Ari	11 Tau	12 Can	14 Vir	13 Lib	14 Sag	14 Cap
15 Sco	16 Cap	15 Cap	13 Aqu	15 Ari	14 Tau	13 Gem	14 Leo	16 Lib	16 Sco	16 Cap	16 Aqu
18 Sag	18 Aqu	17 Aqu	16 Pis	18 Tau	16 Gem	16 Can	17 Vir	18 Sco	18 Sag	18 Aqu	18 Pis
20 Cap	20 Pis	19 Pis	18 Ari	20 Gem	19 Can	19 Leo	20 Lib	20 Sag	20 Cap	20 Pis	20 Ari
22 Aqu	22 Ari	22 Ari	20 Tau	22 Can	21 Leo	21 Vir	22 Sco	23 Cap	22 Aqu	22 Ari	22 Tau
24 Pis	25 Tau	24 Tau	23 Gem	25 Leo	24 Vir	23 Lib	24 Sag	25 Aqu	24 Pis	25 Tau	24 Gem
26 Ari	27 Gem	26 Gem	25 Can	28 Vir	26 Lib	26 Sco	26 Cap	27 Pis	26 Ari	27 Gem	27 Can
28 Tau		29 Can	28 Leo	30 Lib	28 Sco	28 Sag	28 Aqu	29 Ari	28 Tau	30 Can	29 Leo
31 Gem			30 Vir			30 Cap	30 Pis		31 Gem		

1899

JAN	FEB	MAR	APR	MAY	JUN	JUL	AUG	SEP	OCT	NOV	DEC
1 Vir	2 Sco	1 Sco	2 Cap	1 Aqu	2 Ari	1 Tau	2 Can	1 Leo	1 Vir	2 Sco	2 Sag
3 Lib	4 Sag	4 Sag	4 Aqu	3 Pis	4 Tau	4 Gem	4 Leo	4 Vir	3 Lib	4 Sag	4 Cap
6 Sco	6 Cap	6 Cap	6 Pis	6 Ari	6 Gem	6 Can	7 Vir	6 Lib	6 Sco	7 Cap	6 Aqu
8 Sag	8 Aqu	8 Aqu	8 Ari	8 Tau	9 Can	8 Leo	10 Lib	8 Sco	8 Sag	9 Aqu	8 Pis
10 Cap	10 Pis	10 Pis	10 Tau	10 Gem	11 Leo	11 Vir	12 Sco	11 Sag	10 Cap	11 Pis	10 Ari
12 Aqu	12 Ari	12 Ari	13 Gem	12 Can	14 Vir	14 Lib	15 Sag	13 Cap	12 Aqu	13 Ari	12 Tau
14 Pis	15 Tau	14 Tau	15 Can	15 Leo	16 Lib	17 Sco	17 Cap	15 Aqu	15 Pis	15 Tau	14 Gem
16 Ari	17 Gem	16 Gem	17 Leo	17 Vir	19 Sco	18 Sag	19 Aqu	17 Pis	17 Ari	17 Gem	17 Can
18 Tau	19 Can	19 Can	20 Vir	20 Lib	21 Sag	20 Cap	21 Pis	19 Ari	19 Tau	20 Can	19 Leo
21 Gem	22 Leo	21 Leo	23 Lib	22 Sco	23 Cap	22 Aqu	23 Ari	21 Tau	21 Gem	22 Leo	22 Vir
23 Can	24 Vir	24 Vir	25 Sco	24 Sag	25 Aqu	24 Pis	25 Tau	23 Gem	23 Can	25 Vir	24 Lib
26 Leo	27 Lib	26 Lib	27 Sag	26 Cap	27 Pis	26 Ari	27 Gem	26 Can	26 Leo	27 Lib	27 Sco
28 Vir		29 Sco	29 Cap	29 Aqu	29 Ari	29 Tau	29 Can	28 Leo	29 Vir	29 Sco	29 Sag
31 Lib		31 Sag		31 Pis		31 Gem			31 Lib		31 Cap

1900

JAN	FEB	MAR	APR	MAY	JUN	JUL	AUG	SEP	OCT	NOV	DEC
2 Aqu	1 Pis	2 Ari	1 Tau	2 Can	1 Leo	1 Vir	2 Sco	1 Sag	1 Cap	1 Pis	1 Ari
4 Pis	3 Ari	4 Tau	3 Gem	5 Leo	4 Vir	3 Lib	5 Sag	3 Cap	3 Aqu	3 Ari	3 Tau
6 Ari	5 Tau	6 Gem	5 Can	7 Vir	6 Lib	6 Sco	7 Cap	5 Aqu	5 Pis	5 Tau	5 Gem
9 Tau	7 Gem	8 Can	7 Leo	10 Lib	9 Sco	8 Sag	9 Aqu	8 Pis	7 Ari	7 Gem	7 Can
11 Gem	9 Can	11 Leo	10 Vir	12 Sco	11 Sag	11 Cap	11 Pis	10 Ari	9 Tau	10 Can	9 Leo
13 Can	12 Leo	14 Vir	12 Lib	15 Sag	13 Cap	13 Aqu	13 Ari	12 Tau	11 Gem	12 Leo	12 Vir
16 Leo	14 Vir	16 Lib	15 Sco	17 Cap	15 Aqu	15 Pis	15 Tau	14 Gem	14 Can	14 Vir	14 Lib
18 Vir	17 Lib	19 Sco	17 Sag	19 Aqu	17 Pis	17 Ari	17 Gem	16 Can	16 Leo	17 Lib	17 Sco
21 Lib	19 Sco	21 Sag	20 Cap	21 Pis	20 Ari	19 Tau	20 Can	18 Leo	18 Vir	19 Sco	19 Sag
23 Sco	22 Sag	23 Cap	22 Aqu	23 Ari	22 Tau	21 Gem	22 Leo	21 Vir	21 Lib	22 Sag	21 Cap
26 Sag	24 Cap	26 Aqu	24 Pis	25 Tau	24 Gem	23 Can	24 Vir	23 Lib	23 Sco	24 Cap	24 Aqu
28 Cap	26 Aqu	28 Pis	26 Ari	28 Gem	26 Can	26 Leo	27 Lib	26 Sco	25 Sag	26 Aqu	26 Pis
30 Aqu	28 Pis	30 Ari	28 Tau	30 Can	28 Leo	28 Vir	29 Sco	28 Sag	28 Cap	29 Pis	28 Ari
			30 Gem			31 Lib			30 Aqu		30 Tau

1901

JAN	FEB	MAR	APR	MAY	JUN	JUL	AUG	SEP	OCT	NOV	DEC
1 Gem	2 Leo	1 Leo	2 Lib	2 Sco	1 Sag	1 Cap	2 Pis	2 Tau	1 Gem	2 Leo	2 Vir
3 Can	4 Vir	4 Vir	5 Sco	5 Sag	3 Cap	3 Aqu	4 Ari	4 Gem	3 Can	4 Vir	4 Lib
6 Leo	7 Lib	6 Lib	7 Sag	7 Cap	6 Aqu	5 Pis	6 Tau	6 Can	6 Leo	7 Lib	6 Sco
8 Vir	9 Sco	9 Sco	10 Cap	9 Aqu	8 Pis	7 Ari	8 Gem	8 Leo	9 Vir	9 Sco	9 Sag
10 Lib	12 Sag	11 Sag	12 Aqu	12 Pis	10 Ari	10 Tau	10 Can	11 Vir	10 Lib	12 Sag	11 Cap
13 Sco	14 Cap	14 Cap	14 Pis	14 Ari	12 Tau	12 Gem	12 Leo	13 Lib	13 Sco	14 Cap	14 Aqu
15 Sag	16 Aqu	16 Aqu	16 Ari	16 Tau	14 Gem	14 Can	15 Vir	16 Sco	15 Sag	17 Aqu	16 Pis
18 Cap	19 Pis	18 Pis	18 Tau	18 Gem	16 Can	16 Leo	17 Lib	18 Sag	18 Cap	19 Pis	19 Ari
20 Aqu	21 Ari	20 Ari	20 Gem	20 Can	18 Leo	18 Vir	19 Sco	20 Cap	20 Aqu	21 Ari	21 Tau
22 Pis	23 Tau	22 Tau	23 Can	22 Leo	21 Vir	20 Lib	22 Sag	23 Aqu	23 Pis	23 Tau	23 Gem
24 Ari	25 Gem	24 Gem	25 Leo	24 Vir	23 Lib	23 Sco	24 Cap	25 Pis	25 Ari	25 Gem	25 Can
26 Tau	27 Can	26 Can	27 Vir	27 Lib	26 Sco	26 Sag	27 Aqu	27 Ari	27 Tau	27 Can	27 Leo
29 Gem		28 Leo	30 Lib	29 Sco	28 Sag	28 Cap	29 Pis	29 Tau	29 Gem	29 Leo	29 Vir
31 Can		31 Vir				30 Aqu	31 Ari		31 Can		31 Lib

JAN	FEB	MAR	APR	MAY	JUN	JUL	AUG	SEP	OCT	NOV	DEC
3 Sco	2 Sag	1 Sag	2 Aqu	2 Pis	1 Ari	2 Gem	1 Can	1 Vir	1 Lib	2 Sag	1 Cap
5 Sag	4 Cap	3 Cap	5 Pis	4 Ari	3 Tau	4 Can	3 Leo	3 Lib	3 Sco	4 Cap	4 Aqu
8 Cap	7 Aqu	6 Aqu	7 Ari	6 Tau	5 Gem	6 Leo	5 Vir	6 Sco	5 Sag	7 Aqu	6 Pis
10 Aqu	9 Pis	8 Pis	9 Tau	8 Gem	7 Can	8 Vir	7 Lib	8 Sag	8 Cap	9 Pis	9 Ari
13 Pis	11 Ari	10 Ari	11 Gem	10 Can	9 Leo	10 Lib	9 Sco	10 Cap	10 Aqu	11 Ari	11 Tau
15 Ari	13 Tau	12 Tau	13 Can	12 Leo	11 Vir	13 Sco	12 Sag	13 Aqu	13 Pis	14 Tau	13 Gem
17 Tau	15 Gem	15 Gem	15 Leo	15 Vir	13 Lib	15 Sag	14 Cap	15 Pis	15 Ari	16 Gem	15 Can
19 Gem	17 Can	17 Can	17 Vir	17 Lib	16 Sco	18 Cap	17 Aqu	18 Ari	17 Tau	18 Can	17 Leo
21 Can	20 Leo	19 Leo	20 Lib	19 Sco	18 Sag	20 Aqu	19 Pis	20 Tau	19 Gem	20 Leo	19 Vir
23 Leo	22 Vir	21 Vir	22 Sco	22 Sag	20 Cap	23 Pis	21 Ari	22 Gem	21 Can	22 Vir	21 Lib
25 Vir	24 Lib	23 Lib	25 Sag	24 Cap	23 Aqu	25 Ari	24 Tau	24 Can	23 Leo	24 Lib	24 Sco
28 Lib	26 Sco	26 Sco	27 Cap	27 Aqu	26 Pis	27 Tau	26 Gem	26 Leo	26 Vir	27 Sco	26 Sag
30 Sco		28 Sag	30 Aqu	29 Pis	28 Ari	29 Gem	28 Can	28 Vir	28 Lib	29 Sag	29 Cap
		31 Cap			30 Tau		30 Leo		30 Sco		31 Aqu

JAN	FEB	MAR	APR	MAY	JUN	JUL	AUG	SEP	OCT	NOV	DEC
3 Pis	1 Ari	1 Ari	1 Gem	1 Can	1 Vir	1 Lib	2 Sag	3 Aqu	3 Pis	1 Ari	1 Tau
5 Ari	4 Tau	3 Tau	4 Can	3 Leo	3 Lib	3 Sco	4 Cap	5 Pis	5 Ari	4 Tau	3 Gem
7 Tau	6 Gem	5 Gem	6 Leo	5 Vir	6 Sco	5 Sag	7 Aqu	8 Ari	7 Tau	6 Gem	5 Can
10 Gem	8 Can	7 Can	8 Vir	7 Lib	8 Sag	8 Cap	9 Pis	10 Tau	10 Gem	8 Can	8 Leo
12 Can	10 Leo	9 Leo	10 Lib	9 Sco	11 Cap	11 Aqu	12 Ari	12 Gem	12 Can	10 Leo	10 Vir
14 Leo	12 Vir	11 Vir	12 Sco	12 Sag	13 Aqu	13 Pis	14 Tau	15 Can	14 Leo	12 Vir	12 Lib
16 Vir	14 Lib	14 Lib	15 Sag	14 Cap	16 Pis	15 Ari	16 Gem	17 Leo	16 Vir	15 Lib	14 Sco
18 Lib	16 Sco	16 Sco	17 Cap	17 Aqu	18 Ari	18 Tau	18 Can	19 Vir	18 Lib	17 Sco	16 Sag
20 Sco	19 Sag	18 Sag	19 Aqu	19 Pis	20 Tau	20 Gem	20 Leo	21 Lib	20 Sco	19 Sag	19 Cap
22 Sag	21 Cap	21 Cap	22 Pis	22 Ari	23 Gem	22 Can	22 Vir	23 Sco	23 Sag	21 Cap	21 Aqu
25 Cap	24 Aqu	23 Aqu	24 Ari	24 Tau	25 Can	24 Leo	24 Lib	25 Sag	25 Cap	24 Aqu	24 Pis
27 Aqu	26 Pis	26 Pis	27 Tau	26 Gem	27 Leo	26 Vir	27 Sco	28 Cap	27 Aqu	26 Pis	26 Ari
30 Pis		28 Ari	29 Gem	28 Can	29 Vir	28 Lib	29 Sag	30 Aqu	30 Pis	29 Ari	29 Tau
		30 Tau		30 Leo		30 Sco	31 Cap				31 Gem

JAN	FEB	MAR	APR	MAY	JUN	JUL	AUG	SEP	OCT	NOV	DEC
2 Can	2 Vir	1 Vir	1 Sco	1 Sag	2 Aqu	2 Pis	1 Ari	2 Gem	1 Can	2 Vir	1 Lib
4 Leo	4 Lib	3 Lib	3 Sag	3 Cap	5 Pis	4 Ari	3 Tau	4 Can	4 Leo	4 Lib	3 Sco
6 Vir	6 Sco	5 Sco	6 Cap	6 Aqu	7 Ari	7 Tau	5 Gem	6 Leo	6 Vir	6 Sco	6 Sag
8 Lib	9 Sag	7 Sag	8 Aqu	8 Pis	9 Tau	9 Gem	8 Can	8 Vir	8 Lib	8 Sag	8 Cap
10 Sco	11 Cap	9 Cap	11 Pis	11 Ari	12 Gem	11 Can	10 Leo	10 Lib	10 Sco	10 Cap	10 Aqu
13 Sag	14 Aqu	12 Aqu	13 Ari	13 Tau	14 Can	13 Leo	12 Vir	12 Sco	12 Sag	13 Aqu	12 Pis
15 Cap	16 Pis	15 Pis	16 Tau	15 Gem	16 Leo	15 Vir	14 Lib	14 Sag	14 Cap	15 Pis	15 Ari
17 Aqu	19 Ari	17 Ari	18 Gem	18 Can	18 Vir	17 Lib	16 Sco	17 Cap	16 Aqu	18 Ari	17 Tau
20 Pis	21 Tau	19 Tau	20 Can	20 Leo	20 Lib	20 Sco	18 Sag	19 Aqu	19 Pis	20 Tau	20 Gem
22 Ari	24 Gem	22 Gem	22 Leo	22 Vir	22 Sco	22 Sag	20 Cap	21 Pis	21 Ari	23 Gem	22 Can
25 Tau		24 Can	25 Vir	24 Lib	25 Sag	24 Cap	23 Aqu	24 Ari	24 Tau	25 Can	24 Leo
27 Gem	28 Leo	26 Leo	27 Lib	26 Sco	27 Cap	26 Aqu	25 Pis	26 Tau	26 Gem	27 Leo	26 Vir
29 Can		28 Vir	29 Sco	28 Sag	29 Aqu	29 Pis	28 Ari	29 Gem	29 Can	29 Vir	29 Lib
31 Leo		30 Lib		31 Cap			30 Tau		31 Leo		31 Sco

JAN	FEB	MAR	APR	MAY	JUN	JUL	AUG	SEP	OCT	NOV	DEC
2 Sag	3 Aqu	2 Aqu	1 Pis	3 Tau	2 Gem	1 Can	2 Vir	1 Lib	2 Sag	3 Aqu	2 Pis
4 Cap	5 Pis	4 Pis	3 Ari	5 Gem	4 Can	4 Leo	4 Lib	3 Sco	4 Cap	5 Pis	5 Ari
6 Aqu	8 Ari	7 Ari	6 Tau	8 Can	6 Leo	6 Vir	6 Sco	5 Sag	6 Aqu	7 Ari	7 Tau
9 Pis	10 Tau	9 Tau	8 Gem	10 Leo	9 Vir	8 Lib	8 Sag	7 Cap	9 Pis	10 Tau	10 Gem
11 Ari	13 Gem	12 Gem	11 Can	12 Vir	11 Lib	10 Sco	11 Cap	9 Aqu	11 Ari	13 Gem	12 Can
14 Tau	15 Can	14 Can	13 Leo	15 Lib	13 Sco	13 Sag	13 Aqu	12 Pis	14 Tau	15 Can	15 Leo
16 Gem	17 Leo	17 Leo	15 Vir	17 Sco	15 Sag	14 Cap	15 Pis	14 Ari	16 Gem	17 Leo	17 Vir
19 Can	19 Vir	19 Vir	17 Lib	19 Sag	17 Cap	17 Aqu	18 Ari	16 Tau	19 Can	20 Vir	19 Lib
21 Leo	21 Lib	21 Lib	19 Sco	21 Cap	19 Aqu	19 Pis	20 Tau	19 Gem	21 Leo	22 Lib	21 Sco
23 Vir	23 Sco	23 Sco	21 Sag	23 Aqu	22 Pis	21 Ari	23 Gem	21 Can	23 Vir	24 Sco	23 Sag
25 Lib	25 Sag	25 Sag	23 Cap	25 Pis	24 Ari	24 Tau	25 Can	24 Leo	25 Lib	26 Sag	25 Cap
27 Sco	28 Cap	27 Cap	25 Aqu	28 Ari	27 Tau	26 Gem	27 Leo	26 Vir	27 Sco	28 Cap	27 Aqu
29 Sag		29 Aqu	28 Pis	30 Tau	29 Gem	29 Can	30 Vir	28 Lib	29 Sag	30 Aqu	30 Pis
31 Cap			30 Ari			31 Leo		30 Sco	31 Cap		

1906

JAN	FEB	MAR	APR	MAY	JUN	JUL	AUG	SEP	OCT	NOV	DEC
1 Ari	2 Gem	2 Gem	1 Can	3 Vir	1 Lib	1 Sco	1 Cap	2 Pis	1 Ari	2 Gem	2 Ca
4 Tau	5 Can	4 Can	3 Leo	5 Lib	3 Sco	3 Sag	3 Aqu	4 Ari	4 Tau	5 Can	5 Le
6 Gem	7 Leo	7 Leo	5 Vir	7 Sco	5 Sag	5 Cap	5 Pis	6 Tau	6 Gem	7 Leo	7 Vi
9 Can	9 Vir	9 Vir	7 Lib	9 Sag	7 Cap	7 Aqu	8 Ari	9 Gem	9 Can	10 Vir	10 Li
11 Leo	12 Lib	11 Lib	19 Sco	11 Cap	9 Aqu	9 Pis	10 Tau	11 Can	11 Leo	12 Lib	12 Sc
13 Vir	14 Sco	13 Sco	11 Sag	13 Aqu	12 Pis	11 Ari	12 Gem	14 Leo	14 Vir	14 Sco	14 Sa
15 Lib	16 Sag	15 Sag	13 Cap	15 Pis	14 Ari	14 Tau	15 Can	16 Vir	16 Lib	16 Sag	16 Ca
18 Sco	18 Cap	17 Cap	16 Aqu	18 Ari	16 Tau	16 Gem	17 Leo	18 Lib	18 Sco	18 Cap	18 Aq
20 Sag	20 Aqu	19 Aqu	18 Pis	20 Tau	19 Gem	19 Can	20 Vir	20 Sco	20 Sag	20 Aqu	20 Pi
22 Cap	22 Pis	22 Pis	20 Ari	23 Gem	21 Can	21 Leo	22 Lib	22 Sag	22 Cap	22 Pis	22 Ar
24 Aqu	25 Ari	24 Ari	23 Tau	25 Can	24 Leo	24 Vir	24 Sco	25 Cap	24 Aqu	25 Ari	24 Ta
26 Pis	27 Tau	27 Tau	25 Gem	28 Leo	26 Vir	26 Lib	26 Sag	27 Aqu	26 Pis	27 Tau	27 Ge
28 Ari		29 Gem	28 Can	30 Vir	29 Lib	28 Sco	28 Cap	29 Pis	29 Ari	30 Gem	29 Ca
31 Tau			30 Leo			30 Sag	31 Aqu		31 Tau		

1907

JAN	FEB	MAR	APR	MAY	JUN	JUL	AUG	SEP	OCT	NOV	DEC
1 Leo	2 Lib	1 Lib	2 Sag	1 Cap	2 Pis	1 Ari	2 Gem	1 Can	1 Leo	2 Lib	2 Sc
3 Vir	4 Sco	4 Sco	4 Cap	3 Aqu	4 Ari	4 Tau	5 Can	4 Leo	3 Vir	4 Sco	4 Sa
6 Lib	6 Sag	6 Sag	6 Aqu	6 Pis	6 Tau	6 Gem	7 Leo	6 Vir	6 Lib	7 Sag	6 Ca
8 Sco	9 Cap	8 Cap	8 Pis	8 Ari	9 Gem	9 Can	10 Vir	9 Lib	8 Sco	9 Cap	8 Ag
10 Sag	11 Aqu	10 Aqu	11 Ari	10 Tau	11 Can	11 Leo	12 Lib	11 Sco	10 Sag	11 Aqu	10 Pi
12 Cap	13 Pis	12 Pis	13 Tau	13 Gem	14 Leo	14 Vir	15 Sco	13 Sag	12 Cap	13 Pis	12 Ar
14 Aqu	15 Ari	14 Ari	15 Gem	15 Can	16 Vir	16 Lib	17 Sag	15 Cap	15 Aqu	15 Ari	15 Ta
16 Pis	17 Tau	17 Tau	18 Can	18 Leo	19 Lib	18 Sco	19 Cap	17 Aqu	17 Pis	17 Tau	17 Ge
18 Ari	20 Gem	19 Gem	20 Leo	20 Vir	21 Sco	21 Sag	21 Aqu	19 Pis	19 Ari	19 Gem	19 Ca
21 Tau	22 Can	21 Can	23 Vir	22 Lib	23 Sag	23 Cap	23 Pis	21 Ari	21 Tau	22 Can	22 Le
23 Gem	25 Leo	24 Leo	25 Lib	25 Sco	25 Cap	25 Aqu	25 Ari	24 Tau	23 Gem	25 Leo	24 Vi
26 Can	27 Vir	26 Vir	27 Sco	27 Sag	27 Aqu	27 Pis	27 Tau	26 Gem	26 Can	27 Vir	27 Li
28 Leo		29 Lib	29 Sag	29 Cap	29 Pis	29 Ari	30 Gem	28 Can	28 Leo	30 Lib	29 Sc
31 Vir		31 Sco		31 Aqu		31 Tau			31 Vir		

1908

JAN	FEB	MAR	APR	MAY	JUN	JUL	AUG	SEP	OCT	NOV	DEC
1 Sag	1 Aqu	2 Pis	2 Tau	2 Gem	3 Leo	3 Vir	2 Lib	3 Sag	2 Cap	1 Aqu	2 Ar
3 Cap	3 Pis	4 Ari	4 Gem	4 Can	6 Vir	5 Lib	4 Sco	5 Cap	4 Aqu	3 Pis	4 Ta
5 Aqu	5 Ari	6 Tau	7 Can	7 Leo	8 Lib	8 Sco	6 Sag	7 Aqu	6 Pis	5 Ari	6 Ge
7 Pis	7 Tau	8 Gem	9 Leo	9 Vir	10 Sco	10 Sag	8 Cap	9 Pis	8 Ari	7 Tau	9 Ca
9 Ari	10 Gem	10 Can	12 Vir	12 Lib	12 Sag	12 Cap	10 Aqu	11 Ari	10 Tau	9 Gem	11 Le
11 Tau	12 Can	13 Leo	14 Lib	14 Sco	15 Cap	14 Aqu	12 Pis	13 Tau	13 Gem	11 Can	14 Vi
13 Gem	15 Leo	15 Vir	16 Sco	16 Sag	17 Aqu	16 Pis	14 Ari	15 Gem	15 Can	14 Leo	16 Li
16 Can	17 Vir	18 Lib	19 Sag	18 Cap	19 Pis	18 Ari	16 Tau	17 Can	17 Leo	16 Vir	19 Sc
18 Leo	20 Lib	20 Sco	21 Cap	20 Aqu	21 Ari	20 Tau	19 Gem	20 Leo	20 Vir	19 Lib	21 Sa
21 Vir	22 Sco	23 Sag	23 Aqu	22 Pis	23 Tau	22 Gem	21 Can	22 Vir	22 Lib	21 Sco	23 Ca
23 Lib	24 Sag	25 Cap	25 Pis	25 Ari	25 Gem	25 Can	24 Leo	25 Lib	25 Sco	23 Sag	25 Aq
26 Sco	26 Cap	27 Aqu	27 Ari	27 Tau	28 Can	28 Leo	26 Vir	28 Sco	27 Sag	26 Cap	27 Pi
28 Sag	29 Aqu	29 Pis	30 Tau	29 Gem	30 Leo	30 Vir	29 Lib	30 Sag	29 Cap	28 Aqu	29 Ar
30 Cap		31 Ari		31 Can			31 Sco			30 Pis	31 Ta

1909

JAN	FEB	MAR	APR	MAY	JUN	JUL	AUG	SEP	OCT	NOV	DEC
3 Gem	1 Can	1 Can	2 Vir	2 Lib	3 Sag	2 Cap	1 Aqu	1 Ari	1 Tau	1 Can	1 Le
5 Can	4 Leo	3 Leo	4 Lib	4 Sco	5 Cap	5 Aqu	3 Pis	3 Tau	3 Gem	3 Leo	3 Vi
7 Leo	6 Vir	6 Vir	7 Sco	6 Sag	7 Aqu	7 Pis	5 Ari	5 Gem	5 Can	6 Vir	6 Li
10 Vir	9 Lib	8 Lib	9 Sag	9 Cap	9 Pis	9 Ari	7 Tau	7 Can	7 Leo	8 Lib	8 Sc
12 Lib	11 Sco	11 Sco	12 Cap	11 Aqu	11 Ari	11 Tau	9 Gem	10 Leo	10 Vir	11 Sco	11 Sa
15 Sco	14 Sag	13 Sag	14 Aqu	13 Pis	14 Tau	13 Gem	11 Can	12 Vir	12 Lib	14 Sag	13 Ca
17 Sag	16 Cap	15 Cap	16 Pis	15 Ari	16 Gem	15 Can	14 Leo	15 Lib	15 Sco	16 Cap	15 Aq
19 Cap	18 Aqu	17 Aqu	18 Ari	17 Tau	18 Can	18 Leo	16 Vir	17 Sco	17 Sag	18 Aqu	18 Pi
22 Aqu	20 Pis	19 Pis	20 Tau	19 Gem	20 Leo	20 Vir	19 Lib	20 Sag	20 Cap	20 Pis	20 Ar
24 Pis	22 Ari	21 Ari	22 Gem	22 Can	23 Vir	23 Lib	21 Sco	22 Cap	22 Aqu	23 Ari	22 Ta
26 Ari	24 Tau	23 Tau	24 Can	24 Leo	25 Lib	25 Sco	24 Sag	25 Aqu	24 Pis	25 Tau	24 Ge
28 Tau	26 Gem	26 Gem	27 Leo	26 Vir	28 Sco	27 Sag	26 Cap	27 Pis	26 Ari	27 Gem	26 Ca
30 Gem		28 Can	29 Vir	29 Lib	30 Sag	30 Cap	28 Aqu	29 Ari	28 Tau	29 Can	28 Le
		30 Leo		31 Sco			30 Pis		30 Gem		31 Vi

JAN	FEB	MAR	APR	MAY	JUN	JUL	AUG	SEP	OCT	NOV	DEC
2 Lib	1 Sco	3 Sag	2 Cap	1 Aqu	2 Ari	1 Tau	2 Can	3 Vir	2 Lib	1 Sco	1 Sag
5 Sco	4 Sag	5 Cap	4 Aqu	4 Pis	4 Tau	3 Gem	4 Leo	5 Lib	5 Sco	4 Sag	3 Cap
7 Sag	6 Cap	8 Aqu	6 Pis	6 Ari	6 Gem	6 Can	6 Vir	8 Sco	7 Sag	6 Cap	6 Aqu
10 Cap	8 Aqu	10 Pis	8 Ari	8 Tau	8 Can	8 Leo	9 Lib	10 Sag	10 Cap	9 Aqu	8 Pis
12 Aqu	10 Pis	12 Ari	10 Tau	10 Gem	10 Leo	10 Vir	11 Sco	13 Cap	12 Aqu	11 Pis	10 Ari
14 Pis	12 Ari	14 Tau	12 Gem	12 Can	13 Vir	12 Lib	14 Sag	15 Aqu	14 Pis	13 Ari	12 Tau
16 Ari	14 Tau	16 Gem	14 Can	14 Leo	15 Lib	15 Sco	16 Cap	17 Pis	17 Ari	15 Tau	14 Gem
18 Tau	17 Gem	18 Can	17 Leo	16 Vir	18 Sco	17 Sag	18 Aqu	19 Ari	19 Tau	17 Gem	16 Can
20 Gem	19 Can	20 Leo	19 Vir	19 Lib	20 Sag	20 Cap	21 Pis	21 Tau	21 Gem	19 Can	19 Leo
23 Can	21 Leo	23 Vir	21 Lib	21 Sco	23 Cap	22 Aqu	23 Ari	23 Gem	23 Can	21 Leo	21 Vir
25 Leo	23 Vir	25 Lib	24 Sco	24 Sag	25 Aqu	24 Pis	25 Tau	25 Can	25 Leo	23 Vir	23 Lib
27 Vir	26 Lib	28 Sco	27 Sag	26 Cap	27 Pis	27 Ari	27 Gem	28 Leo	27 Vir	26 Lib	26 Sco
30 Lib	28 Sco	30 Sag	29 Cap	29 Aqu	29 Ari	29 Tau	29 Can	30 Vir	30 Lib	28 Sco	28 Sag
				31 Pis		31 Gem	31 Leo				31 Cap

JAN	FEB	MAR	APR	MAY	JUN	JUL	AUG	SEP	OCT	NOV	DEC
2 Aqu	1 Pis	2 Ari	1 Tau	2 Can	3 Vir	2 Lib	1 Sco	2 Cap	2 Aqu	1 Pis	1 Ari
4 Pis	3 Ari	4 Tau	3 Gem	4 Leo	5 Lib	5 Sco	3 Sag	5 Aqu	5 Pis	3 Ari	3 Tau
7 Ari	5 Tau	6 Gem	5 Can	6 Vir	7 Sco	7 Sag	6 Cap	7 Pis	7 Ari	5 Tau	5 Gem
9 Tau	7 Gem	9 Can	7 Leo	9 Lib	10 Sag	10 Cap	8 Aqu	9 Ari	9 Tau	7 Gem	7 Can
11 Gem	9 Can	11 Leo	9 Vir	11 Sco	12 Cap	12 Aqu	11 Pis	12 Tau	11 Gem	9 Can	9 Leo
13 Can	11 Leo	13 Vir	12 Lib	14 Sag	15 Aqu	15 Pis	13 Ari	14 Gem	13 Can	12 Leo	11 Vir
15 Leo	14 Vir	15 Lib	14 Sco	16 Cap	17 Pis	17 Ari	15 Tau	16 Can	15 Leo	14 Vir	13 Lib
17 Vir	16 Lib	18 Sco	16 Sag	19 Aqu	20 Ari	19 Tau	18 Gem	18 Leo	17 Vir	16 Lib	16 Sco
19 Lib	18 Sco	20 Sag	19 Cap	21 Pis	22 Tau	21 Gem	20 Can	20 Vir	20 Lib	18 Sco	18 Sag
22 Sco	21 Sag	23 Cap	21 Aqu	23 Ari	24 Gem	23 Can	22 Leo	22 Lib	22 Sco	21 Sag	20 Cap
24 Sag	23 Cap	25 Aqu	24 Pis	25 Tau	26 Can	25 Leo	24 Vir	25 Sco	25 Sag	23 Cap	23 Aqu
27 Cap	26 Aqu	27 Pis	26 Ari	26 Gem	28 Leo	27 Vir	26 Lib	27 Sag	27 Cap	26 Aqu	26 Pis
29 Aqu	28 Pis	30 Ari	28 Tau	29 Can	30 Vir	30 Lib	28 Sco	30 Cap	30 Aqu	28 Pis	28 Ari
			30 Gem	31 Leo			31 Sag				30 Tau

JAN	FEB	MAR	APR	MAY	JUN	JUL	AUG	SEP	OCT	NOV	DEC
1 Gem	2 Leo	2 Vir	1 Lib	3 Sag	1 Cap	1 Aqu	2 Ari	1 Tau	1 Gem	1 Leo	3 Lib
3 Can	4 Vir	4 Lib	3 Sco	5 Cap	4 Aqu	4 Pis	5 Tau	3 Gem	3 Can	3 Vir	5 Sco
5 Leo	6 Lib	7 Sco	5 Sag	8 Aqu	6 Pis	6 Ari	7 Gem	5 Can	5 Leo	5 Lib	7 Sag
7 Vir	8 Sco	9 Sag	8 Cap	10 Pis	9 Ari	9 Tau	9 Can	8 Leo	7 Vir	8 Sco	10 Cap
9 Lib	11 Sag	11 Cap	10 Aqu	12 Ari	11 Tau	11 Gem	11 Leo	10 Vir	9 Lib	10 Sag	12 Aqu
12 Sco	13 Cap	14 Aqu	13 Pis	15 Tau	13 Gem	13 Can	13 Vir	12 Lib	11 Sco	12 Cap	15 Pis
14 Sag	16 Aqu	16 Pis	15 Ari	17 Gem	15 Can	15 Leo	15 Lib	14 Sco	13 Sag	15 Aqu	17 Ari
17 Cap	18 Pis	19 Ari	17 Tau	19 Can	17 Leo	17 Vir	17 Sco	16 Sag	16 Cap	17 Pis	19 Tau
19 Aqu	20 Ari	21 Tau	20 Gem	21 Leo	19 Vir	19 Lib	20 Sag	18 Cap	18 Aqu	20 Ari	22 Gem
22 Pis	23 Tau	23 Gem	22 Can	23 Vir	22 Lib	21 Sco	22 Cap	21 Aqu	21 Pis	22 Tau	24 Can
24 Ari	25 Gem	25 Can	24 Leo	25 Lib	24 Sco	23 Sag	25 Aqu	23 Pis	24 Ari	24 Gem	26 Leo
27 Tau	26 Can	27 Leo	26 Vir	27 Sco	26 Sag	26 Cap	27 Pis	26 Ari	26 Tau	26 Can	28 Vir
29 Gem	29 Leo	30 Vir	28 Lib	30 Sag	29 Cap	28 Aqu	30 Ari	28 Tau	28 Gem	28 Leo	30 Lib
31 Can			30 Sco			31 Pis			30 Can	30 Vir	

JAN	FEB	MAR	APR	MAY	JUN	JUL	AUG	SEP	OCT	NOV	DEC
1 Sco	2 Cap	1 Cap	3 Pis	2 Ari	1 Tau	1 Gem	1 Leo	2 Lib	1 Sco	2 Cap	2 Aqu
3 Sag	5 Aqu	4 Aqu	5 Ari	5 Tau	3 Gem	3 Can	3 Vir	4 Sco	3 Sag	4 Aqu	4 Pis
6 Cap	7 Pis	6 Pis	8 Tau	7 Gem	6 Can	5 Leo	6 Lib	6 Sag	6 Cap	7 Pis	7 Ari
8 Aqu	10 Ari	9 Ari	10 Gem	9 Can	8 Leo	7 Vir	8 Sco	8 Cap	8 Aqu	9 Ari	9 Tau
11 Pis	12 Tau	11 Tau	12 Can	12 Leo	10 Vir	9 Lib	10 Sag	11 Aqu	11 Pis	12 Tau	12 Gem
13 Ari	14 Gem	14 Gem	14 Leo	14 Vir	12 Lib	11 Sco	12 Cap	13 Pis	13 Ari	14 Gem	14 Can
16 Tau	17 Can	16 Can	16 Vir	16 Lib	14 Sco	14 Sag	15 Aqu	16 Ari	16 Tau	17 Can	16 Leo
18 Gem	19 Leo	18 Leo	18 Lib	18 Sco	16 Sag	16 Cap	17 Pis	18 Tau	18 Gem	19 Leo	18 Vir
20 Can	21 Vir	20 Vir	20 Sco	20 Sag	19 Cap	18 Aqu	20 Ari	21 Gem	20 Can	21 Vir	20 Lib
22 Leo	23 Lib	22 Lib	23 Sag	22 Cap	21 Aqu	21 Pis	22 Tau	23 Can	23 Leo	23 Lib	23 Sco
24 Vir	25 Sco	24 Sco	25 Cap	25 Aqu	24 Pis	23 Ari	25 Gem	25 Leo	25 Vir	25 Sco	25 Sag
26 Lib	27 Sag	27 Sag	27 Aqu	27 Pis	26 Ari	26 Tau	27 Can	27 Vir	27 Lib	27 Sag	27 Cap
28 Sco		29 Cap	30 Pis	30 Ari	29 Tau	28 Gem	29 Leo	29 Lib	29 Sco	29 Cap	29 Aqu
31 Sag		31 Aqu				30 Can	31 Vir		31 Sag		

1914

JAN	FEB	MAR	APR	MAY	JUN	JUL	AUG	SEP	OCT	NOV	DEC
1 Pis	2 Tau	1 Tau	2 Can	2 Leo	3 Lib	2 Sco	2 Cap	1 Aqu	1 Pis	2 Tau	2 Gem
3 Ari	4 Gem	4 Gem	5 Leo	4 Vir	5 Sco	4 Sag	5 Aqu	3 Pis	3 Ari	4 Gem	4 Can
6 Tau	7 Can	6 Can	7 Vir	6 Lib	7 Sag	6 Cap	7 Pis	6 Ari	6 Tau	6 Can	7 Leo
8 Gem	9 Leo	8 Leo	9 Lib	8 Sco	9 Cap	8 Aqu	10 Ari	8 Tau	8 Gem	9 Leo	9 Vir
10 Can	11 Vir	10 Vir	11 Sco	10 Sag	11 Aqu	11 Pis	12 Tau	11 Gem	11 Can	12 Vir	11 Lib
12 Leo	13 Lib	12 Lib	13 Sag	12 Cap	13 Pis	13 Ari	15 Gem	13 Can	13 Leo	14 Lib	13 Sco
15 Vir	15 Sco	14 Sco	15 Cap	15 Aqu	16 Ari	16 Tau	17 Can	16 Leo	15 Vir	16 Sco	15 Sag
17 Lib	17 Sag	16 Sag	17 Aqu	17 Pis	18 Tau	18 Gem	19 Leo	18 Vir	17 Lib	18 Sag	17 Cap
19 Sco	19 Cap	19 Cap	20 Pis	20 Ari	21 Gem	21 Can	21 Vir	20 Lib	19 Sco	20 Cap	19 Aqu
21 Sag	22 Aqu	21 Aqu	22 Ari	22 Tau	23 Can	23 Leo	23 Lib	22 Sco	21 Sag	22 Aqu	21 Pis
23 Cap	24 Pis	24 Pis	25 Tau	25 Gem	26 Leo	25 Vir	25 Sco	24 Sag	23 Cap	24 Pis	24 Ari
26 Aqu	27 Ari	26 Ari	27 Gem	27 Can	28 Vir	27 Lib	28 Sag	26 Cap	25 Aqu	27 Ari	26 Tau
28 Pis		29 Tau	30 Can	29 Leo	30 Lib	29 Sco	30 Cap	28 Aqu	28 Pis	29 Tau	29 Gem
30 Ari		31 Gem		31 Vir		31 Sag			30 Ari		31 Can

1915

JAN	FEB	MAR	APR	MAY	JUN	JUL	AUG	SEP	OCT	NOV	DEC
3 Leo	1 Vir	1 Vir	1 Sco	1 Sag	1 Aqu	1 Pis	2 Tau	1 Gem	1 Can	2 Vir	1 Lib
5 Vir	3 Lib	3 Lib	3 Sag	3 Cap	3 Pis	3 Ari	4 Gem	3 Can	3 Leo	4 Lib	3 Sco
7 Lib	6 Sco	5 Sco	5 Cap	5 Aqu	6 Ari	6 Tau	7 Can	6 Leo	5 Vir	6 Sco	5 Sag
9 Sco	8 Sag	7 Sag	8 Aqu	7 Pis	8 Tau	8 Gem	9 Leo	8 Vir	8 Lib	8 Sag	7 Cap
11 Sag	10 Cap	9 Cap	10 Pis	10 Ari	11 Gem	11 Can	12 Vir	10 Lib	10 Sco	10 Cap	9 Aqu
14 Cap	12 Aqu	11 Aqu	12 Ari	12 Tau	13 Can	13 Leo	14 Lib	12 Sco	12 Sag	12 Aqu	12 Pis
16 Aqu	14 Pis	14 Pis	15 Tau	15 Gem	16 Leo	15 Vir	16 Sco	14 Sag	14 Cap	14 Pis	14 Ari
18 Pis	17 Ari	16 Ari	17 Gem	18 Can	18 Vir	18 Lib	18 Sag	16 Cap	16 Aqu	17 Ari	16 Tau
20 Ari	19 Tau	18 Tau	20 Can	20 Leo	20 Lib	20 Sco	20 Cap	19 Aqu	18 Pis	19 Tau	19 Gem
23 Tau	22 Gem	21 Gem	22 Leo	22 Vir	22 Sco	22 Sag	22 Aqu	21 Pis	20 Ari	22 Gem	21 Can
25 Gem	24 Can	23 Can	25 Vir	24 Lib	24 Sag	24 Cap	25 Pis	23 Ari	23 Tau	24 Can	24 Leo
28 Can	26 Leo	26 Leo	27 Lib	26 Sco	26 Cap	26 Aqu	27 Ari	26 Tau	25 Gem	27 Leo	26 Vir
30 Leo		28 Vir	29 Sco	28 Sag	29 Aqu	28 Pis	29 Tau	28 Gem	28 Can	29 Vir	29 Lib
		30 Lib		30 Cap		30 Ari			30 Leo		31 Sco

1916

JAN	FEB	MAR	APR	MAY	JUN	JUL	AUG	SEP	OCT	NOV	DEC
2 Sag	2 Aqu	1 Aqu	1 Ari	1 Tau	2 Can	2 Leo	1 Vir	2 Sco	1 Sag	2 Aqu	1 Pis
4 Cap	4 Pis	3 Pis	4 Tau	3 Gem	5 Leo	5 Vir	3 Lib	4 Sag	3 Cap	4 Pis	3 Ari
6 Aqu	7 Ari	5 Ari	6 Gem	6 Can	7 Vir	7 Lib	5 Sco	6 Cap	5 Aqu	6 Ari	5 Tau
8 Pis	9 Tau	7 Tau	9 Can	8 Leo	10 Lib	9 Sco	8 Sag	8 Aqu	8 Pis	8 Tau	8 Gem
10 Ari	11 Gem	10 Gem	11 Leo	11 Vir	12 Sco	11 Sag	10 Cap	10 Pis	10 Ari	11 Gem	10 Can
12 Tau	14 Can	12 Can	14 Vir	13 Lib	14 Sag	13 Cap	12 Aqu	12 Ari	12 Tau	13 Can	13 Leo
15 Gem	16 Leo	15 Leo	16 Lib	15 Sco	16 Cap	15 Aqu	14 Pis	14 Tau	14 Gem	16 Leo	15 Vir
18 Can	19 Vir	17 Vir	18 Sco	17 Sag	18 Aqu	17 Pis	16 Ari	17 Gem	16 Can	18 Vir	18 Lib
20 Leo	21 Lib	19 Lib	20 Sag	19 Cap	20 Pis	19 Ari	18 Tau	19 Can	19 Leo	20 Lib	20 Sco
23 Vir	23 Sco	22 Sco	22 Cap	22 Aqu	22 Ari	22 Tau	20 Gem	22 Leo	22 Vir	23 Sco	22 Sag
25 Lib	26 Sag	24 Sag	24 Aqu	24 Pis	25 Tau	24 Gem	23 Can	24 Vir	24 Lib	25 Sag	24 Cap
27 Sco	28 Cap	26 Cap	26 Pis	26 Ari	27 Gem	27 Can	26 Leo	27 Lib	26 Sco	27 Cap	26 Aqu
29 Sag		28 Aqu	29 Ari	28 Tau	29 Can	29 Leo	28 Vir	29 Sco	28 Sag	29 Aqu	28 Pis
31 Cap		30 Pis		31 Gem			30 Lib		31 Cap		30 Ari

1917

JAN	FEB	MAR	APR	MAY	JUN	JUL	AUG	SEP	OCT	NOV	DEC
2 Tau	3 Can	2 Can	1 Leo	1 Vir	2 Sco	2 Sag	2 Aqu	1 Pis	2 Tau	1 Gem	3 Leo
4 Gem	5 Leo	5 Leo	3 Vir	3 Lib	4 Sag	4 Cap	4 Pis	3 Ari	4 Gem	3 Can	5 Vir
7 Can	8 Vir	7 Vir	6 Lib	6 Sco	6 Cap	6 Aqu	6 Ari	5 Tau	7 Can	5 Leo	8 Lib
9 Leo	10 Lib	10 Lib	8 Sco	8 Sag	8 Aqu	8 Pis	8 Tau	7 Gem	9 Leo	8 Vir	10 Sco
12 Vir	13 Sco	12 Sco	11 Sag	10 Cap	10 Pis	10 Ari	11 Gem	9 Can	12 Vir	10 Lib	12 Sag
14 Lib	15 Sag	14 Sag	13 Cap	12 Aqu	13 Ari	12 Tau	13 Can	12 Leo	14 Lib	13 Sco	15 Cap
16 Sco	17 Cap	16 Cap	15 Aqu	14 Pis	15 Tau	14 Gem	15 Leo	14 Vir	16 Sco	15 Sag	17 Aqu
19 Sag	19 Aqu	19 Aqu	17 Pis	16 Ari	17 Gem	17 Can	18 Vir	17 Lib	19 Sag	17 Cap	19 Pis
21 Cap	21 Pis	21 Pis	19 Ari	19 Tau	19 Can	19 Leo	21 Lib	19 Sco	21 Cap	19 Aqu	21 Tau
23 Aqu	23 Ari	23 Ari	21 Tau	21 Gem	22 Leo	22 Vir	23 Sco	22 Sag	23 Aqu	22 Pis	23 Tau
25 Pis	25 Tau	25 Tau	23 Gem	23 Can	24 Vir	24 Lib	25 Sag	24 Cap	25 Pis	24 Ari	25 Gem
27 Ari	28 Gem	27 Gem	26 Can	26 Leo	27 Lib	27 Sco	28 Cap	26 Aqu	27 Ari	26 Tau	28 Can
29 Tau		29 Can	28 Leo	28 Vir	29 Sco	29 Sag	30 Aqu	28 Pis	29 Tau	28 Gem	30 Ari
31 Gem				31 Lib		31 Cap			30 Ari		30 Can

JAN	FEB	MAR	APR	MAY	JUN	JUL	AUG	SEP	OCT	NOV	DEC
2 Vir	3 Sco	2 Sco	1 Sag	3 Aqu	1 Pis	2 Tau	1 Gem	2 Leo	1 Vir	3 Sco	2 Sag
4 Lib	5 Sag	5 Sag	3 Cap	5 Pis	3 Ari	5 Gem	3 Can	4 Vir	4 Lib	5 Sag	5 Cap
7 Sco	7 Cap	7 Cap	5 Aqu	7 Ari	5 Tau	7 Can	5 Leo	7 Lib	6 Sco	8 Cap	7 Aqu
9 Sag	10 Aqu	9 Aqu	7 Pis	9 Tau	7 Gem	9 Leo	8 Vir	9 Sco	9 Sag	10 Aqu	9 Pis
11 Cap	12 Pis	11 Pis	9 Ari	11 Gem	9 Can	12 Vir	10 Lib	12 Sag	11 Cap	12 Pis	12 Ari
13 Aqu	14 Ari	13 Ari	11 Tau	13 Can	12 Leo	14 Lib	13 Sco	14 Cap	14 Aqu	14 Ari	14 Tau
15 Pis	16 Tau	15 Tau	13 Gem	15 Leo	14 Vir	17 Sco	15 Sag	16 Aqu	16 Pis	16 Tau	16 Gem
17 Ari	18 Gem	17 Gem	16 Can	18 Vir	17 Lib	19 Sag	18 Cap	18 Pis	18 Ari	18 Gem	18 Can
19 Tau	20 Can	19 Can	18 Leo	20 Lib	19 Sco	21 Cap	20 Aqu	20 Ari	20 Tau	20 Can	20 Leo
22 Gem	23 Leo	22 Leo	21 Vir	23 Sco	22 Sag	23 Aqu	22 Pis	22 Tau	22 Gem	23 Leo	22 Vir
24 Can	25 Vir	24 Vir	23 Lib	25 Sag	24 Cap	26 Pis	24 Ari	24 Gem	24 Can	25 Vir	25 Lib
26 Leo	28 Lib	27 Lib	26 Sco	28 Cap	26 Aqu	28 Ari	26 Tau	27 Can	26 Leo	27 Lib	27 Sco
29 Vir		29 Sco	28 Sag	30 Aqu	28 Pis	30 Tau	28 Gem	29 Leo	29 Vir	30 Sco	30 Sag
31 Lib			30 Cap		30 Ari		30 Can		31 Lib		

JAN	FEB	MAR	APR	MAY	JUN	JUL	AUG	SEP	OCT	NOV	DEC
1 Cap	2 Pis	1 Pis	2 Tau	1 Gem	2 Leo	1 Vir	3 Sco	1 Sag	1 Cap	2 Pis	2 Ari
3 Aqu	4 Ari	3 Ari	4 Gem	3 Can	4 Vir	3 Lib	5 Sag	4 Cap	4 Aqu	5 Ari	4 Tau
6 Pis	6 Tau	5 Tau	6 Can	5 Leo	7 Lib	6 Sco	8 Cap	6 Aqu	6 Pis	7 Tau	6 Gem
8 Ari	8 Gem	8 Gem	8 Leo	8 Vir	9 Sco	9 Sag	10 Aqu	9 Pis	8 Ari	9 Gem	8 Can
10 Tau	10 Can	10 Can	11 Vir	10 Lib	12 Sag	11 Cap	12 Pis	11 Ari	10 Tau	11 Can	10 Leo
12 Gem	12 Leo	12 Leo	13 Lib	13 Sco	14 Cap	14 Aqu	14 Ari	13 Tau	12 Gem	13 Leo	12 Cap
14 Can	15 Vir	14 Vir	16 Sco	15 Sag	16 Aqu	16 Pis	17 Tau	15 Gem	14 Can	15 Vir	15 Lib
16 Leo	17 Lib	17 Lib	18 Sag	18 Cap	19 Pis	18 Ari	19 Gem	17 Can	16 Leo	17 Lib	17 Sco
19 Vir	20 Sco	19 Sco	21 Cap	20 Aqu	21 Ari	20 Tau	21 Can	19 Leo	19 Vir	20 Sco	20 Aqu
21 Lib	23 Sag	22 Sag	23 Aqu	23 Pis	23 Tau	22 Gem	23 Leo	21 Vir	21 Lib	22 Sag	22 Aqu
24 Sco	25 Cap	24 Cap	25 Pis	25 Ari	25 Gem	25 Can	25 Vir	24 Lib	24 Sco	25 Cap	25 Aqu
26 Sag	27 Aqu	27 Aqu	27 Ari	27 Tau	27 Can	27 Leo	28 Lib	26 Sco	26 Sag	27 Aqu	27 Pis
29 Cap		29 Pis	29 Tau	29 Gem	29 Leo	29 Vir	30 Sco	29 Sag	29 Cap	30 Pis	29 Ari
31 Aqu		31 Ari		31 Can		31 Lib			31 Aqu		31 Tau

JAN	FEB	MAR	APR	MAY	JUN	JUL	AUG	SEP	OCT	NOV	DEC
3 Gem	1 Can	1 Leo	2 Lib	2 Sco	3 Cap	3 Aqu	2 Pis	2 Tau	2 Gem	2 Leo	2 Vir
5 Can	3 Leo	4 Vir	4 Sco	4 Sag	6 Aqu	5 Pis	4 Ari	5 Gem	4 Can	4 Vir	4 Lib
7 Leo	5 Vir	6 Lib	7 Sag	7 Cap	8 Pis	8 Ari	6 Tau	7 Can	6 Leo	7 Lib	6 Sco
9 Vir	7 Lib	8 Sco	9 Cap	9 Aqu	10 Ari	10 Tau	8 Gem	9 Leo	8 Vir	9 Sco	9 Sag
11 Lib	10 Sco	11 Sag	12 Aqu	12 Pis	12 Tau	12 Gem	10 Can	11 Vir	10 Lib	11 Sag	11 Cap
13 Sco	12 Sag	13 Cap	14 Pis	14 Ari	14 Gem	14 Can	12 Leo	13 Lib	13 Sco	14 Cap	14 Aqu
16 Sag	15 Cap	16 Aqu	16 Ari	16 Tau	16 Can	16 Leo	14 Vir	15 Sco	15 Sag	16 Aqu	16 Pis
19 Cap	17 Aqu	18 Pis	19 Tau	18 Gem	18 Leo	18 Vir	17 Lib	18 Sag	18 Cap	19 Pis	19 Ari
21 Aqu	20 Pis	20 Ari	21 Gem	20 Can	21 Vir	20 Lib	19 Sco	20 Cap	20 Aqu	21 Ari	21 Tau
23 Pis	22 Ari	22 Tau	23 Can	22 Leo	23 Lib	23 Sco	21 Sag	23 Aqu	22 Pis	23 Tau	23 Gem
26 Ari	24 Tau	24 Gem	25 Leo	24 Vir	25 Sco	25 Sag	24 Cap	25 Pis	25 Ari	25 Gem	25 Can
28 Tau	26 Gem	26 Can	27 Vir	27 Lib	28 Sag	28 Cap	26 Aqu	27 Ari	27 Tau	27 Can	27 Leo
30 Gem	28 Can	29 Leo	29 Lib	29 Sco	30 Cap	30 Aqu	29 Pis	30 Tau	29 Gem	29 Leo	29 Vir
		31 Vir		31 Sag			31 Ari		31 Can		31 Lib

JAN	FEB	MAR	APR	MAY	JUN	JUL	AUG	SEP	OCT	NOV	DEC
2 Sco	1 Sag	3 Cap	2 Aqu	2 Pis	3 Tau	2 Gem	1 Can	1 Vir	1 Lib	1 Sag	1 Cap
5 Sag	4 Cap	5 Aqu	4 Pis	4 Ari	5 Gem	4 Can	3 Leo	3 Lib	3 Sco	4 Cap	4 Aqu
7 Cap	6 Aqu	8 Pis	6 Ari	6 Tau	7 Can	6 Leo	5 Vir	5 Sco	5 Sag	6 Aqu	6 Pis
10 Aqu	9 Pis	10 Ari	9 Tau	8 Gem	9 Leo	8 Vir	7 Lib	8 Sag	7 Cap	9 Pis	9 Ari
12 Pis	11 Ari	13 Tau	11 Gem	11 Can	11 Vir	10 Lib	9 Sco	10 Cap	10 Aqu	11 Ari	11 Tau
15 Ari	13 Tau	15 Gem	13 Can	13 Leo	13 Lib	13 Sco	11 Sag	13 Aqu	12 Pis	14 Tau	13 Gem
17 Tau	16 Gem	17 Can	15 Leo	15 Vir	15 Sco	15 Sag	14 Cap	15 Pis	15 Ari	16 Gem	15 Can
19 Gem	18 Can	19 Leo	18 Vir	17 Lib	18 Sag	18 Cap	16 Aqu	18 Ari	17 Tau	18 Can	17 Leo
21 Can	20 Leo	21 Vir	20 Lib	19 Sco	20 Cap	20 Aqu	19 Pis	20 Tau	19 Gem	20 Leo	19 Vir
23 Leo	22 Vir	23 Lib	22 Sco	22 Sag	23 Aqu	23 Pis	21 Ari	22 Gem	22 Can	22 Vir	22 Lib
25 Vir	24 Lib	25 Sco	24 Sag	24 Cap	25 Pis	25 Ari	24 Tau	24 Can	24 Leo	24 Lib	24 Sco
27 Lib	26 Sco	28 Sag	27 Cap	26 Aqu	28 Ari	28 Tau	26 Gem	27 Leo	26 Vir	26 Sco	26 Sag
30 Sco	28 Sag	30 Cap	29 Aqu	28 Ari	30 Tau	30 Gem	28 Can	29 Vir	28 Lib	28 Sag	28 Cap
				31 Ari			30 Leo		30 Sco		31 Aqu

1922

JAN	FEB	MAR	APR	MAY	JUN	JUL	AUG	SEP	OCT	NOV	DEC
2 Pis	1 Ari	3 Tau	2 Gem	1 Can	2 Vir	1 Lib	2 Sag	2 Aqu	2 Pis	1 Ari	1 Tau
5 Ari	4 Tau	5 Gem	4 Can	3 Leo	4 Lib	3 Sco	4 Cap	5 Pis	5 Ari	4 Tau	3 Gem
7 Tau	6 Gem	8 Can	6 Leo	5 Vir	6 Sco	5 Sag	6 Aqu	8 Ari	7 Tau	6 Gem	6 Can
10 Can	8 Can	10 Leo	8 Vir	7 Lib	8 Sag	8 Cap	9 Pis	10 Tau	10 Gem	8 Can	8 Leo
12 Can	10 Leo	12 Vir	10 Lib	9 Sco	10 Cap	10 Aqu	11 Ari	12 Gem	12 Can	11 Leo	10 Vir
14 Leo	12 Vir	14 Lib	12 Sco	12 Sag	13 Aqu	12 Pis	14 Tau	15 Can	14 Leo	13 Vir	12 Lib
16 Vir	14 Lib	16 Sco	14 Sag	14 Cap	15 Pis	15 Ari	16 Gem	17 Leo	16 Vir	15 Lib	14 Sco
18 Lib	16 Sco	18 Sag	16 Cap	16 Aqu	18 Ari	17 Tau	18 Can	19 Vir	18 Lib	17 Sco	16 Sag
20 Sco	18 Sag	20 Cap	19 Aqu	19 Pis	20 Tau	20 Gem	21 Leo	21 Lib	20 Sco	19 Sag	18 Cap
22 Sag	21 Cap	23 Aqu	21 Pis	21 Ari	22 Gem	22 Can	23 Vir	23 Sco	22 Sag	21 Cap	21 Aqu
25 Cap	23 Aqu	25 Pis	24 Ari	24 Tau	25 Can	24 Leo	25 Lib	25 Sag	25 Cap	23 Aqu	23 Pis
27 Aqu	26 Pis	28 Ari	26 Tau	26 Gem	27 Leo	26 Vir	27 Sco	27 Cap	27 Aqu	26 Pis	26 Ari
30 Pis	28 Ari	30 Tau	29 Gem	28 Can	29 Vir	28 Lib	29 Sag	30 Aqu	29 Pis	28 Ari	28 Tau
				30 Leo		30 Sco	31 Cap				31 Gem

1923

JAN	FEB	MAR	APR	MAY	JUN	JUL	AUG	SEP	OCT	NOV	DEC
2 Can	3 Vir	2 Vir	2 Sco	2 Sag	3 Aqu	2 Pis	1 Ari	2 Gem	2 Can	1 Leo	3 Lib
4 Leo	5 Lib	4 Lib	4 Sag	4 Cap	5 Pis	5 Ari	4 Tau	5 Can	5 Leo	3 Vir	5 Sco
6 Vir	7 Sco	6 Sco	7 Cap	6 Aqu	7 Ari	7 Tau	6 Gem	7 Leo	7 Vir	5 Lib	7 Sag
8 Lib	9 Sag	8 Sag	9 Aqu	9 Pis	10 Tau	10 Gem	8 Can	9 Vir	9 Lib	7 Sco	9 Cap
10 Sco	11 Cap	10 Cap	11 Pis	11 Ari	12 Gem	12 Can	11 Leo	11 Lib	11 Sco	9 Sag	11 Aqu
13 Sag	13 Aqu	14 Ari	14 Ari	14 Tau	15 Can	14 Leo	13 Vir	13 Sco	13 Sag	11 Cap	13 Pis
15 Cap	16 Pis	15 Pis	16 Tau	16 Gem	17 Leo	17 Vir	15 Lib	15 Sag	15 Cap	13 Aqu	15 Ari
17 Aqu	18 Ari	18 Ari	19 Gem	19 Can	19 Vir	19 Lib	17 Sco	18 Cap	17 Aqu	16 Pis	18 Tau
20 Pis	20 Tau	20 Tau	21 Can	21 Leo	22 Lib	21 Sco	19 Sag	20 Aqu	19 Pis	18 Ari	21 Gem
22 Ari	23 Gem	23 Gem	24 Leo	23 Vir	24 Sco	23 Sag	21 Cap	22 Pis	22 Ari	21 Tau	23 Can
25 Tau	26 Can	25 Can	26 Vir	25 Lib	26 Sag	25 Cap	24 Aqu	25 Ari	24 Tau	23 Gem	25 Leo
27 Gem	28 Leo	27 Leo	28 Lib	27 Sco	28 Cap	27 Aqu	26 Pis	27 Tau	27 Gem	26 Can	28 Vir
29 Can		29 Vir	30 Sco	29 Sag	30 Aqu	30 Pis	28 Ari	30 Gem	30 Can	28 Leo	30 Lib
31 Leo		31 Lib		31 Cap			31 Tau			30 Vir	

1924

JAN	FEB	MAR	APR	MAY	JUN	JUL	AUG	SEP	OCT	NOV	DEC
1 Sco	1 Cap	2 Aqu	3 Ari	3 Tau	1 Gem	2 Can	2 Vir	1 Lib	2 Sag	1 Cap	2 Pis
3 Sag	4 Aqu	4 Pis	5 Tau	5 Gem	4 Can	4 Leo	5 Lib	3 Sco	4 Cap	3 Aqu	5 Ari
5 Cap	6 Pis	7 Ari	8 Gem	8 Can	6 Leo	6 Vir	7 Sco	5 Sag	7 Aqu	5 Pis	7 Tau
7 Aqu	8 Ari	9 Tau	10 Can	10 Leo	9 Vir	8 Lib	9 Sag	7 Cap	9 Pis	7 Ari	9 Gem
9 Pis	11 Tau	12 Gem	13 Leo	12 Vir	11 Lib	10 Sco	11 Cap	9 Aqu	11 Ari	10 Tau	12 Can
12 Ari	13 Gem	14 Can	15 Vir	15 Lib	13 Sco	12 Sag	13 Aqu	11 Pis	13 Tau	12 Gem	15 Leo
14 Tau	16 Can	16 Leo	17 Lib	17 Sco	15 Sag	14 Cap	15 Pis	14 Ari	16 Gem	15 Can	17 Vir
17 Gem	18 Leo	19 Vir	19 Sco	19 Sag	17 Cap	17 Aqu	17 Ari	16 Tau	18 Can	17 Leo	19 Lib
19 Can	20 Vir	21 Lib	21 Sag	21 Cap	19 Aqu	19 Pis	20 Tau	18 Gem	21 Leo	20 Vir	21 Sco
22 Leo	22 Lib	23 Sco	23 Cap	23 Aqu	21 Pis	21 Ari	22 Gem	21 Can	23 Vir	22 Lib	23 Sag
24 Vir	25 Sco	25 Sag	25 Aqu	25 Pis	24 Ari	23 Tau	24 Can	24 Leo	26 Lib	24 Sco	25 Cap
26 Lib	27 Sag	27 Cap	28 Pis	27 Ari	26 Tau	26 Gem	27 Leo	26 Vir	28 Sco	26 Sag	27 Aqu
28 Sco	29 Cap	29 Aqu	30 Ari	30 Tau	29 Gem	28 Can	30 Vir	28 Lib	30 Sag	28 Cap	30 Pis
30 Sag		31 Pis				31 Leo		30 Sco		30 Aqu	

1925

JAN	FEB	MAR	APR	MAY	JUN	JUL	AUG	SEP	OCT	NOV	DEC
1 Ari	2 Gem	1 Gem	3 Leo	2 Vir	1 Lib	1 Sco	1 Cap	2 Pis	1 Ari	2 Gem	2 Can
3 Tau	4 Can	4 Can	5 Vir	5 Lib	3 Sco	3 Sag	3 Aqu	4 Ari	3 Tau	5 Can	4 Leo
6 Gem	7 Leo	6 Leo	7 Lib	7 Sco	5 Sag	5 Cap	5 Pis	6 Tau	6 Gem	7 Leo	7 Vir
8 Can	9 Vir	9 Vir	10 Sco	9 Sag	7 Cap	7 Aqu	7 Ari	8 Gem	8 Can	10 Vir	9 Lib
11 Leo	12 Lib	11 Lib	12 Sag	11 Cap	9 Aqu	9 Pis	10 Tau	11 Can	11 Leo	12 Lib	12 Sco
13 Vir	14 Sco	13 Sco	14 Cap	13 Aqu	12 Pis	11 Ari	12 Gem	13 Leo	13 Vir	14 Sco	14 Sag
16 Lib	16 Sag	15 Sag	16 Aqu	15 Pis	14 Ari	13 Tau	15 Can	16 Vir	16 Lib	16 Sag	16 Cap
18 Sco	18 Cap	18 Cap	18 Pis	18 Ari	16 Tau	16 Gem	17 Leo	18 Lib	18 Sco	18 Cap	18 Aqu
20 Sag	20 Aqu	20 Aqu	20 Ari	20 Tau	19 Gem	18 Can	20 Vir	21 Sco	20 Sag	21 Aqu	20 Pis
22 Cap	22 Pis	22 Pis	23 Tau	22 Gem	21 Can	21 Leo	22 Lib	23 Sag	22 Cap	23 Pis	22 Ari
24 Aqu	25 Ari	24 Ari	25 Gem	25 Can	23 Leo	23 Vir	24 Sco	25 Cap	24 Aqu	24 Ari	24 Tau
26 Pis	27 Tau	26 Tau	27 Can	27 Leo	26 Vir	26 Lib	27 Sag	27 Aqu	26 Pis	27 Tau	27 Gem
28 Ari		29 Gem	30 Leo	30 Vir	29 Lib	28 Sco	29 Cap	29 Pis	29 Ari	29 Gem	29 Can
30 Tau		31 Can				30 Sag	31 Aqu		31 Tau		

Table 1

JAN	FEB	MAR	APR	MAY	JUN	JUL	AUG	SEP	OCT	NOV	DEC
1 Leo	2 Lib	1 Lib	2 Sag	2 Cap	2 Pis	1 Ari	2 Gem	1 Can	1 Leo	2 Lib	2 Sco
3 Vir	4 Sco	4 Sco	4 Cap	4 Aqu	4 Ari	4 Tau	5 Can	3 Leo	3 Vir	4 Sco	4 Sag
6 Lib	7 Sag	6 Sag	7 Aqu	6 Pis	6 Tau	6 Gem	7 Leo	6 Vir	6 Lib	7 Sag	6 Cap
8 Sco	9 Cap	8 Cap	9 Pis	8 Ari	9 Gem	8 Can	10 Vir	8 Lib	8 Sco	9 Cap	8 Aqu
10 Sag	11 Aqu	10 Aqu	11 Ari	10 Tau	11 Can	11 Leo	12 Lib	11 Sco	10 Sag	11 Aqu	11 Pis
12 Cap	13 Pis	12 Pis	13 Tau	12 Gem	13 Leo	13 Vir	15 Sco	13 Sag	13 Cap	13 Pis	13 Ari
14 Aqu	15 Ari	14 Ari	15 Gem	15 Can	16 Vir	16 Lib	17 Sag	15 Cap	15 Aqu	15 Ari	15 Tau
16 Pis	17 Tau	16 Tau	17 Can	17 Leo	18 Lib	18 Sco	19 Cap	17 Aqu	17 Pis	17 Tau	17 Gem
18 Ari	19 Gem	19 Gem	20 Leo	19 Vir	21 Sco	21 Sag	21 Aqu	20 Pis	19 Ari	20 Gem	19 Can
21 Tau	22 Can	21 Can	22 Vir	22 Lib	23 Sag	23 Cap	23 Pis	22 Ari	21 Tau	22 Can	22 Leo
23 Gem	24 Leo	23 Leo	25 Lib	25 Sco	25 Cap	25 Aqu	25 Ari	24 Tau	23 Gem	24 Leo	24 Vir
25 Can	27 Vir	26 Vir	27 Sco	27 Sag	27 Aqu	27 Pis	27 Tau	26 Gem	25 Can	27 Vir	26 Lib
28 Leo		28 Lib	29 Sag	29 Cap	29 Pis	29 Ari	29 Gem	28 Can	28 Leo	29 Lib	29 Sco
30 Vir		31 Sco		31 Aqu		31 Tau			30 Vir		31 Sag

Table 2

JAN	FRB	MAR	APR	MAY	JUN	JUL	AUG	SEP	OCT	NOV	DEC
3 Cap	1 Aqu	1 Aqu	1 Ari	2 Gem	1 Can	1 Leo	2 Lib	1 Sco	1 Sag	2 Aqu	1 Pis
5 Aqu	3 Pis	4 Pis	3 Tau	5 Can	3 Leo	3 Vir	4 Sco	3 Sag	3 Cap	4 Pis	3 Ari
7 Pis	5 Ari	5 Ari	5 Gem	7 Leo	6 Vir	6 Lib	7 Sag	6 Cap	5 Aqu	6 Ari	5 Tau
9 Ari	7 Tau	7 Tau	7 Can	9 Vir	8 Lib	8 Sco	9 Cap	8 Aqu	7 Pis	8 Tau	7 Gem
11 Tau	9 Gem	9 Gem	10 Leo	11 Lib	11 Sco	11 Sag	11 Aqu	10 Pis	9 Ari	10 Gem	9 Can
13 Gem	12 Can	11 Can	12 Vir	14 Sco	13 Sag	13 Cap	14 Pis	12 Ari	11 Tau	12 Can	12 Leo
16 Can	14 Leo	13 Leo	15 Lib	17 Sag	16 Cap	15 Aqu	16 Ari	14 Tau	13 Gem	14 Leo	14 Vir
18 Leo	17 Vir	16 Vir	17 Sco	19 Cap	18 Aqu	17 Pis	18 Tau	16 Gem	16 Can	17 Vir	16 Lib
20 Vir	19 Lib	18 Lib	20 Sag	22 Aqu	20 Pis	19 Ari	20 Gem	18 Can	18 Leo	19 Lib	19 Sco
23 Lib	22 Sco	21 Sco	22 Cap	24 Pis	22 Ari	21 Tau	22 Can	21 Leo	20 Vir	22 Sco	21 Sag
25 Sco	24 Sag	23 Sag	24 Aqu	26 Ari	24 Tau	24 Gem	24 Leo	23 Vir	23 Lib	24 Sag	24 Cap
28 Sag	26 Cap	26 Cap	26 Pis	28 Tau	26 Gem	26 Can	27 Vir	26 Lib	25 Sco	27 Cap	26 Aqu
30 Cap		28 Aqu	28 Ari	30 Gem	28 Can	28 Leo	29 Lib	28 Sco	28 Sag	29 Aqu	28 Pis
		30 Pis	30 Tau			30 Vir			30 Cap		30 Ari

Table 3

JAN	FEB	MAR	APR	MAY	JUN	JUL	AUG	SEP	OCT	NOV	DEC
2 Tau	2 Can	3 Leo	1 Vir	1 Lib	2 Sag	2 Cap	1 Aqu	1 Ari	1 Tau	1 Can	1 Leo
4 Gem	4 Leo	5 Vir	4 Lib	3 Sco	5 Cap	4 Aqu	3 Pis	3 Tau	3 Gem	3 Leo	3 Vir
6 Can	7 Vir	7 Lib	6 Sco	6 Sag	7 Aqu	7 Pis	5 Ari	6 Gem	5 Can	6 Vir	5 Lib
8 Leo	9 Lib	10 Sco	9 Sag	8 Cap	9 Pis	9 Ari	7 Tau	8 Can	7 Leo	8 Lib	8 Sco
10 Vir	12 Sco	12 Sag	11 Cap	11 Aqu	12 Ari	11 Tau	9 Gem	11 Leo	10 Vir	10 Sco	10 Sag
13 Lib	14 Sag	15 Cap	14 Aqu	14 Pis	14 Tau	13 Gem	11 Can	14 Vir	12 Lib	13 Sag	13 Cap
15 Sco	16 Cap	17 Aqu	16 Pis	15 Ari	16 Gem	15 Can	14 Leo	14 Lib	14 Sco	16 Cap	15 Aqu
18 Sag	19 Aqu	19 Pis	18 Ari	17 Tau	18 Can	17 Leo	16 Vir	17 Sco	17 Sag	18 Aqu	18 Pis
20 Cap	21 Pis	21 Ari	20 Tau	19 Gem	20 Leo	19 Vir	18 Lib	19 Sag	19 Cap	20 Pis	20 Ari
22 Aqu	23 Ari	23 Tau	22 Gem	21 Can	22 Vir	22 Lib	21 Sco	22 Cap	22 Aqu	23 Ari	22 Tau
25 Pis	25 Tau	25 Gem	24 Can	23 Leo	24 Lib	24 Sco	23 Sag	24 Aqu	24 Pis	25 Tau	24 Gem
27 Ari	27 Gem	28 Can	26 Leo	26 Vir	27 Sco	27 Sag	26 Cap	27 Pis	26 Ari	27 Gem	26 Can
29 Tau	29 Can	30 Leo	28 Vir	28 Lib	29 Sag	29 Cap	28 Aqu	29 Ari	28 Tau	29 Can	28 Leo
31 Gem				31 Sco			30 Pis		30 Gem		30 Vir

Table 4

JAN	FEB	MAR	APR	MAY	JUN	JUL	AUG	SEP	OCT	NOV	DEC
2 Lib	3 Sag	2 Sag	1 Cap	1 Aqu	2 Ari	1 Tau	2 Can	2 Vir	2 Lib	1 Sco	3 Cap
4 Sco	5 Cap	5 Cap	4 Aqu	3 Pis	4 Tau	3 Gem	4 Leo	5 Lib	4 Sco	3 Sag	5 Aqu
7 Sag	8 Aqu	7 Aqu	6 Pis	6 Ari	6 Gem	5 Can	6 Vir	7 Sco	7 Sag	5 Cap	8 Pis
9 Cap	10 Pis	9 Pis	8 Ari	8 Tau	8 Can	7 Leo	8 Lib	9 Sag	9 Cap	8 Aqu	10 Ari
12 Aqu	12 Ari	12 Ari	10 Tau	10 Gem	10 Leo	10 Vir	10 Sco	12 Cap	12 Aqu	10 Pis	12 Tau
14 Pis	15 Tau	14 Tau	12 Gem	12 Can	12 Vir	12 Lib	13 Sag	14 Aqu	14 Pis	13 Ari	14 Gem
16 Ari	17 Gem	16 Gem	14 Can	14 Leo	14 Lib	14 Sco	15 Cap	17 Pis	16 Ari	15 Tau	16 Can
18 Tau	19 Can	18 Can	17 Leo	16 Vir	17 Sco	17 Sag	18 Aqu	19 Ari	19 Tau	17 Gem	18 Leo
21 Gem	21 Leo	20 Leo	19 Vir	18 Lib	19 Sag	19 Cap	20 Pis	21 Tau	21 Gem	19 Can	21 Vir
23 Can	23 Vir	22 Vir	21 Lib	21 Sco	22 Cap	22 Aqu	23 Ari	23 Gem	23 Can	21 Leo	23 Lib
25 Leo	25 Lib	25 Lib	23 Sco	23 Sag	24 Aqu	24 Pis	25 Tau	25 Can	25 Leo	23 Vir	25 Sco
27 Vir	28 Sco	27 Sco	26 Sag	26 Cap	27 Pis	26 Ari	27 Gem	28 Leo	27 Vir	25 Lib	27 Sag
29 Lib		30 Sag	28 Cap	28 Aqu	29 Ari	29 Tau	29 Can	30 Vir	29 Lib	28 Sco	30 Cap
31 Sco				31 Pis		31 Gem	31 Leo			30 Sag	

1930

JAN	FEB	MAR	APR	MAY	JUN	JUL	AUG	SEP	OCT	NOV	DEC
2 Aqu	3 Ari	2 Ari	1 Tau	2 Can	1 Leo	2 Lib	1 Sco	2 Cap	1 Aqu	3 Ari	2 Tau
4 Pis	5 Tau	4 Tau	3 Gem	4 Leo	3 Vir	4 Sco	3 Sag	4 Aqu	4 Pis	5 Tau	5 Gem
6 Ari	7 Gem	7 Gem	5 Can	6 Vir	5 Lib	7 Sag	5 Cap	7 Pis	6 Ari	7 Gem	7 Can
9 Tau	9 Can	9 Can	7 Leo	9 Lib	7 Sco	9 Cap	8 Aqu	9 Ari	9 Tau	10 Can	9 Leo
11 Gem	11 Leo	11 Leo	9 Vir	11 Sco	9 Sag	12 Aqu	10 Pis	12 Tau	11 Gem	12 Leo	11 Vir
13 Can	13 Vir	13 Vir	11 Lib	13 Sag	12 Cap	14 Pis	13 Ari	14 Gem	13 Can	14 Vir	13 Lib
15 Leo	15 Lib	15 Lib	13 Sco	15 Cap	14 Aqu	17 Ari	15 Tau	16 Can	15 Leo	16 Lib	15 Sco
17 Vir	18 Sco	17 Sco	16 Sag	18 Aqu	17 Pis	19 Tau	18 Gem	18 Leo	18 Vir	18 Sco	18 Sag
19 Lib	20 Sag	19 Sag	18 Cap	21 Pis	19 Ari	21 Gem	20 Can	20 Vir	20 Lib	20 Sag	20 Cap
21 Sco	22 Cap	22 Cap	21 Aqu	23 Ari	22 Tau	23 Can	22 Leo	22 Lib	22 Sco	23 Cap	22 Aqu
24 Sag	25 Aqu	24 Aqu	23 Pis	25 Tau	24 Gem	25 Leo	24 Vir	24 Sco	24 Sag	25 Aqu	25 Pis
26 Cap	27 Pis	27 Pis	26 Ari	27 Gem	26 Can	27 Vir	26 Lib	26 Sag	26 Cap	28 Pis	27 Ari
29 Aqu		29 Ari	28 Tau	29 Can	28 Leo	29 Lib	28 Sco	29 Cap	29 Aqu	30 Ari	30 Tau
31 Pis			30 Gem		30 Vir		30 Sag		31 Pis		

1931

JAN	FEB	MAR	APR	MAY	JUN	JUL	AUG	SEP	OCT	NOV	DEC
1 Gem	2 Leo	1 Leo	2 Lib	1 Sco	2 Cap	1 Aqu	3 Ari	2 Tau	1 Gem	2 Leo	2 Vir
3 Can	4 Vir	3 Vir	4 Sco	3 Sag	4 Aqu	4 Pis	5 Tau	4 Gem	4 Can	4 Vir	4 Lib
5 Leo	6 Lib	5 Lib	6 Sag	5 Cap	7 Pis	6 Ari	8 Gem	6 Can	6 Leo	6 Lib	6 Sco
7 Vir	8 Sco	7 Sco	8 Cap	8 Aqu	9 Ari	9 Tau	10 Can	9 Leo	8 Vir	8 Sco	8 Sag
9 Lib	10 Sag	9 Sag	10 Aqu	10 Pis	11 Tau	11 Gem	12 Leo	11 Vir	10 Lib	10 Sag	10 Cap
12 Sco	12 Cap	12 Cap	13 Pis	13 Ari	14 Gem	14 Can	14 Vir	13 Lib	13 Sco	13 Cap	12 Aqu
14 Sag	15 Aqu	14 Aqu	16 Ari	15 Tau	16 Can	16 Leo	16 Lib	15 Sco	15 Sag	15 Aqu	15 Pis
16 Cap	17 Pis	17 Pis	18 Tau	18 Gem	18 Leo	18 Vir	18 Sco	17 Sag	17 Cap	17 Pis	17 Ari
19 Aqu	20 Ari	19 Ari	20 Gem	20 Can	20 Vir	20 Lib	20 Sag	19 Cap	19 Aqu	20 Ari	20 Tau
21 Pis	23 Tau	22 Tau	23 Can	23 Leo	23 Lib	22 Sco	22 Cap	21 Aqu	22 Pis	22 Tau	22 Gem
24 Ari	25 Gem	24 Gem	25 Leo	24 Vir	25 Sco	24 Sag	25 Aqu	24 Pis	24 Ari	25 Gem	25 Can
26 Tau	27 Can	26 Can	27 Vir	26 Lib	27 Sag	26 Cap	28 Pis	26 Ari	26 Tau	27 Can	27 Leo
29 Gem		29 Leo	29 Lib	28 Sco	29 Cap	29 Aqu	30 Ari	29 Tau	29 Gem	29 Leo	29 Vir
31 Can		31 Vir		31 Sag		31 Pis			31 Can		31 Lib

1932

JAN	FEB	MAR	APR	MAY	JUN	JUL	AUG	SEP	OCT	NOV	DEC
2 Sco	1 Sag	1 Cap	2 Pis	2 Ari	3 Gem	3 Can	1 Leo	2 Lib	1 Sco	2 Cap	1 Aqu
4 Sag	3 Cap	3 Aqu	4 Ari	4 Tau	5 Can	5 Leo	4 Vir	4 Sco	4 Sag	4 Aqu	4 Pis
6 Cap	5 Aqu	6 Pis	7 Tau	7 Gem	8 Leo	7 Vir	6 Lib	6 Sag	6 Cap	6 Pis	6 Ari
9 Aqu	7 Pis	8 Ari	10 Gem	9 Can	10 Vir	9 Lib	8 Sco	8 Cap	8 Aqu	9 Ari	9 Tau
11 Pis	10 Ari	11 Tau	12 Can	12 Leo	12 Lib	12 Sco	10 Sag	10 Aqu	10 Pis	11 Tau	11 Gem
14 Ari	12 Tau	13 Gem	14 Leo	14 Vir	14 Sco	14 Sag	12 Cap	13 Pis	13 Ari	14 Gem	14 Can
16 Tau	15 Gem	16 Can	16 Vir	16 Lib	16 Sag	16 Cap	14 Aqu	15 Ari	15 Tau	16 Can	16 Leo
19 Gem	17 Can	18 Leo	18 Lib	18 Sco	18 Cap	18 Aqu	17 Pis	18 Tau	18 Gem	19 Leo	18 Vir
21 Can	19 Leo	20 Vir	20 Sco	20 Sag	20 Aqu	20 Pis	19 Ari	20 Gem	20 Can	21 Vir	21 Lib
23 Leo	22 Vir	22 Lib	22 Sag	22 Cap	23 Pis	23 Ari	21 Tau	23 Can	23 Leo	23 Lib	23 Sco
25 Vir	24 Lib	24 Sco	25 Cap	24 Aqu	25 Ari	25 Tau	24 Gem	25 Leo	25 Vir	25 Sco	25 Sag
27 Lib	26 Sco	26 Sag	27 Aqu	26 Pis	28 Tau	28 Gem	26 Can	27 Vir	27 Lib	27 Sag	27 Cap
29 Sco	28 Sag	28 Cap	29 Pis	29 Ari	30 Gem	30 Can	29 Leo	29 Lib	29 Sco	29 Cap	29 Aqu
		31 Aqu		31 Tau					31 Sag		31 Pis

1933

JAN	FEB	MAR	APR	MAY	JUN	JUL	AUG	SEP	OCT	NOV	DEC
2 Ari	1 Tau	1 Tau	2 Can	2 Leo	3 Lib	2 Sco	2 Cap	1 Aqu	3 Ari	1 Tau	1 Gem
5 Tau	4 Gem	3 Gem	4 Leo	4 Vir	5 Sco	4 Sag	4 Aqu	3 Pis	5 Tau	4 Gem	4 Can
7 Gem	6 Can	6 Can	7 Vir	6 Lib	7 Sag	6 Cap	6 Pis	5 Ari	7 Gem	6 Can	6 Leo
10 Can	9 Leo	8 Leo	9 Lib	8 Sco	9 Cap	8 Aqu	9 Ari	7 Tau	10 Can	9 Leo	9 Vir
12 Leo	11 Vir	10 Vir	11 Sco	10 Sag	11 Aqu	10 Pis	11 Tau	10 Gem	12 Leo	11 Vir	11 Lib
15 Vir	13 Lib	12 Lib	13 Sag	12 Cap	13 Pis	12 Ari	13 Gem	13 Can	15 Vir	13 Lib	13 Sco
17 Lib	15 Sco	14 Sco	15 Cap	14 Aqu	15 Ari	15 Tau	16 Can	15 Leo	17 Lib	16 Sco	15 Sag
19 Sco	17 Sag	17 Sag	17 Aqu	17 Pis	18 Tau	17 Gem	18 Leo	17 Vir	19 Sco	18 Sag	17 Cap
21 Sag	19 Cap	19 Cap	19 Pis	19 Ari	20 Gem	20 Can	21 Vir	20 Lib	21 Sag	20 Cap	19 Aqu
23 Cap	22 Aqu	21 Aqu	22 Ari	21 Tau	23 Can	22 Leo	23 Lib	22 Sco	23 Cap	22 Aqu	21 Pis
25 Aqu	24 Pis	23 Pis	24 Tau	24 Gem	25 Leo	25 Vir	26 Sco	24 Sag	25 Aqu	24 Pis	23 Ari
27 Pis	26 Ari	25 Ari	27 Gem	26 Can	28 Vir	27 Lib	28 Sag	26 Cap	28 Pis	26 Ari	26 Tau
30 Ari		28 Tau	29 Can	29 Leo	30 Lib	29 Sco	30 Cap	28 Aqu	30 Ari	29 Tau	28 Gem
		30 Gem		31 Vir		31 Sag		30 Pis			31 Can

JAN	FEB	MAR	APR	MAY	JUN	JUL	AUG	SEP	OCT	NOV	DEC
2 Leo	1 Vir	3 Lib	1 Sco	1 Sag	1 Aqu	1 Pis	1 Tau	2 Can	2 Leo	1 Vir	1 Lib
5 Vir	3 Lib	5 Sco	3 Sag	3 Cap	3 Pis	3 Ari	4 Gem	5 Leo	5 Vir	4 Lib	3 Sco
7 Lib	6 Sco	7 Sag	5 Cap	5 Aqu	5 Ari	5 Tau	6 Can	7 Vir	7 Lib	6 Sco	5 Sag
9 Sco	8 Sag	9 Cap	8 Aqu	7 Pis	8 Tau	7 Gem	9 Leo	10 Lib	9 Sco	8 Sag	7 Cap
12 Cap	10 Cap	11 Aqu	10 Pis	9 Ari	10 Gem	10 Can	11 Vir	12 Sag	12 Sag	10 Cap	10 Aqu
14 Aqu	12 Aqu	13 Pis	12 Ari	11 Tau	13 Can	12 Leo	14 Lib	14 Sag	14 Cap	12 Aqu	12 Pis
16 Aqu	14 Pis	16 Ari	14 Tau	14 Gem	15 Leo	15 Vir	16 Sco	17 Cap	16 Aqu	14 Pis	14 Ari
18 Pis	16 Ari	18 Tau	17 Gem	16 Can	18 Vir	17 Lib	18 Sag	19 Aqu	18 Pis	17 Ari	16 Tau
20 Ari	18 Tau	20 Gem	19 Can	19 Leo	20 Lib	20 Sco	20 Cap	21 Pis	20 Ari	19 Tau	18 Gem
22 Tau	21 Gem	23 Can	22 Leo	21 Vir	22 Sco	22 Sag	22 Aqu	23 Ari	22 Tau	21 Gem	21 Can
25 Gem	23 Can	25 Leo	24 Vir	24 Lib	24 Sag	24 Cap	24 Pis	25 Tau	25 Gem	23 Can	23 Leo
27 Can	26 Leo	28 Vir	26 Lib	26 Sco	26 Cap	26 Aqu	26 Ari	27 Gem	27 Can	26 Leo	26 Vir
30 Leo	28 Vir	30 Lib	29 Sco	28 Sag	28 Aqu	28 Pis	29 Tau	30 Can	30 Leo	28 Vir	28 Lib
				30 Cap		30 Ari	31 Gem				31 Sco

JAN	FEB	MAR	APR	MAY	JUN	JUL	AUG	SEP	OCT	NOV	DEC
2 Sag	2 Aqu	2 Aqu	2 Ari	2 Tau	3 Can	2 Leo	1 Vir	2 Sco	2 Sag	1 Cap	2 Pis
4 Cap	4 Pis	4 Pis	4 Tau	4 Gem	5 Leo	5 Vir	4 Lib	5 Sag	4 Cap	3 Aqu	4 Ari
6 Aqu	6 Ari	6 Ari	6 Gem	6 Can	8 Vir	7 Lib	6 Sco	7 Cap	7 Aqu	5 Pis	6 Tau
8 Pis	8 Tau	8 Tau	9 Can	9 Leo	10 Lib	10 Sco	8 Sag	9 Aqu	9 Pis	7 Ari	9 Gem
10 Ari	10 Gem	11 Gem	11 Leo	11 Vir	12 Sco	12 Sag	11 Cap	11 Pis	11 Ari	9 Tau	11 Can
12 Tau	13 Can	13 Can	14 Vir	14 Lib	15 Sag	14 Cap	13 Aqu	13 Ari	13 Tau	11 Gem	13 Leo
15 Gem	16 Leo	15 Leo	16 Lib	16 Sco	17 Cap	16 Aqu	15 Pis	15 Tau	15 Gem	13 Can	16 Vir
17 Can	18 Vir	18 Vir	19 Sco	18 Sag	19 Aqu	18 Pis	17 Ari	17 Gem	17 Can	16 Leo	18 Lib
20 Leo	21 Lib	20 Lib	21 Sag	21 Cap	21 Pis	20 Ari	19 Tau	20 Can	19 Leo	18 Vir	21 Sco
22 Vir	23 Sco	22 Sco	23 Cap	23 Aqu	23 Ari	23 Tau	21 Gem	22 Leo	22 Vir	21 Lib	23 Sag
25 Lib	26 Sag	25 Sag	25 Aqu	25 Pis	25 Tau	25 Gem	23 Can	25 Vir	24 Lib	23 Sco	25 Cap
27 Sco	28 Cap	27 Cap	28 Pis	27 Ari	28 Gem	27 Can	26 Leo	27 Lib	27 Sco	26 Sag	27 Aqu
29 Sag		29 Aqu	31 Ari	29 Tau	30 Can	30 Leo	28 Vir	30 Sco	29 Sag	28 Cap	29 Pis
31 Cap		31 Pis		31 Gem			31 Lib			30 Aqu	

JAN	FEB	MAR	APR	MAY	JUN	JUL	AUG	SEP	OCT	NOV	DEC
1 Ari	1 Gem	2 Can	3 Vir	3 Lib	1 Sco	1 Sag	2 Aqu	1 Pis	2 Tau	2 Can	2 Leo
3 Tau	3 Can	4 Leo	5 Lib	5 Sco	4 Sag	3 Cap	4 Pis	3 Ari	4 Gem	5 Leo	4 Vir
5 Gem	6 Leo	6 Vir	8 Sco	8 Sag	6 Cap	6 Aqu	6 Ari	5 Tau	6 Can	7 Vir	7 Lib
7 Can	8 Vir	9 Lib	10 Sag	10 Cap	8 Aqu	8 Pis	8 Tau	7 Gem	8 Leo	10 Lib	9 Sco
9 Leo	11 Lib	12 Sco	13 Cap	12 Aqu	11 Pis	10 Ari	10 Gem	9 Can	11 Vir	12 Sco	12 Sag
12 Vir	13 Sco	14 Sag	15 Aqu	14 Pis	13 Ari	12 Tau	13 Can	11 Leo	13 Lib	15 Sag	14 Cap
14 Lib	16 Sag	16 Cap	17 Pis	16 Ari	15 Tau	14 Gem	15 Leo	14 Vir	16 Sco	17 Cap	17 Aqu
17 Sco	18 Cap	19 Aqu	19 Ari	18 Tau	17 Gem	16 Can	17 Vir	16 Lib	18 Sag	19 Aqu	19 Pis
19 Sag	20 Aqu	21 Pis	21 Tau	20 Gem	19 Can	19 Leo	20 Lib	19 Sco	21 Cap	22 Pis	21 Ari
22 Cap	22 Pis	23 Ari	23 Gem	23 Can	21 Leo	21 Vir	22 Sco	21 Sag	23 Aqu	24 Ari	23 Tau
24 Aqu	24 Ari	25 Tau	25 Can	25 Leo	24 Vir	23 Lib	25 Sag	24 Cap	25 Pis	26 Tau	25 Gem
26 Pis	26 Tau	27 Gem	28 Leo	27 Vir	26 Lib	26 Sco	27 Cap	26 Aqu	27 Ari	28 Gem	27 Can
28 Ari	28 Gem	29 Can	30 Vir	30 Lib	29 Sco	28 Sag	29 Aqu	28 Pis	29 Tau	30 Can	29 Leo
30 Tau		31 Leo				31 Cap		30 Ari	31 Gem		

JAN	FEB	MAR	APR	MAY	JUN	JUL	AUG	SEP	OCT	NOV	DEC
1 Vir	2 Sco	1 Sco	3 Cap	2 Aqu	1 Pis	1 Ari	1 Gem	2 Leo	1 Vir	2 Sco	2 Sag
3 Lib	4 Sag	3 Sag	5 Aqu	5 Pis	3 Ari	3 Tau	3 Can	4 Vir	3 Lib	5 Sag	4 Cap
5 Sco	7 Cap	6 Cap	7 Pis	7 Ari	5 Tau	5 Gem	5 Leo	6 Lib	6 Sco	7 Cap	7 Aqu
8 Sag	9 Aqu	9 Aqu	9 Ari	9 Tau	7 Gem	7 Can	7 Vir	8 Sco	8 Sag	10 Aqu	9 Pis
11 Cap	12 Pis	11 Pis	11 Tau	11 Gem	9 Can	9 Leo	10 Lib	11 Sag	11 Cap	12 Pis	12 Ari
13 Aqu	14 Ari	13 Ari	13 Gem	13 Can	11 Leo	11 Vir	12 Sco	13 Cap	13 Aqu	14 Ari	14 Tau
15 Pis	16 Tau	15 Tau	16 Can	15 Leo	14 Vir	13 Lib	15 Sag	16 Aqu	16 Pis	16 Tau	16 Gem
17 Ari	18 Gem	17 Gem	18 Leo	17 Vir	16 Lib	16 Sco	17 Cap	18 Pis	18 Ari	18 Gem	18 Can
20 Tau	20 Can	19 Can	20 Vir	20 Lib	18 Sco	18 Sag	20 Aqu	20 Ari	20 Tau	20 Can	20 Leo
22 Gem	22 Leo	21 Leo	22 Lib	22 Sco	21 Sag	21 Cap	22 Pis	22 Tau	22 Gem	22 Leo	22 Vir
24 Can	25 Vir	24 Vir	25 Sco	25 Sag	23 Cap	23 Aqu	24 Ari	24 Gem	24 Can	24 Vir	24 Lib
26 Leo	27 Lib	26 Lib	27 Sag	27 Cap	26 Aqu	26 Pis	26 Tau	27 Can	26 Leo	27 Lib	27 Sco
28 Vir		29 Sco	30 Cap	30 Aqu	28 Pis	28 Ari	28 Gem	29 Leo	28 Vir	29 Sco	29 Sag
31 Lib		31 Sag				30 Tau	30 Can		31 Lib		31 Cap

1938

JAN	FEB	MAR	APR	MAY	JUN	JUL	AUG	SEP	OCT	NOV	DEC
3 Aqu	2 Pis	1 Pis	2 Tau	1 Gem	1 Leo	1 Vir	2 Sco	3 Cap	3 Aqu	2 Pis	1 Ari
5 Pis	4 Ari	3 Ari	4 Gem	3 Can	4 Vir	3 Lib	4 Sag	5 Aqu	5 Pis	4 Ari	4 Tau
8 Ari	6 Tau	6 Tau	6 Can	5 Leo	6 Lib	5 Sco	7 Cap	8 Pis	8 Ari	6 Tau	6 Gem
10 Tau	8 Gem	8 Gem	8 Leo	7 Vir	8 Sco	8 Sag	9 Aqu	10 Ari	10 Tau	8 Gem	8 Can
12 Gem	11 Can	10 Can	10 Vir	10 Lib	11 Sag	10 Cap	12 Pis	13 Tau	12 Gem	10 Can	10 Leo
14 Can	13 Leo	12 Leo	12 Lib	12 Sco	13 Cap	13 Aqu	14 Ari	15 Gem	14 Can	13 Leo	12 Vir
16 Leo	15 Vir	14 Vir	15 Sco	14 Sag	16 Aqu	15 Pis	16 Tau	17 Can	16 Leo	15 Vir	14 Lib
18 Vir	17 Lib	16 Lib	17 Sag	17 Cap	18 Pis	18 Ari	19 Gem	19 Leo	18 Vir	17 Lib	16 Sco
20 Lib	19 Sco	18 Sco	20 Cap	19 Aqu	21 Ari	20 Tau	21 Can	21 Vir	21 Lib	19 Sco	19 Sag
23 Sco	22 Sag	21 Sag	22 Aqu	22 Pis	23 Tau	22 Gem	23 Leo	23 Lib	23 Sco	22 Sag	21 Cap
25 Sag	24 Cap	23 Cap	25 Pis	24 Ari	25 Gem	24 Can	25 Vir	25 Sco	25 Sag	24 Cap	24 Aqu
28 Cap	27 Aqu	26 Aqu	27 Ari	26 Tau	27 Can	26 Leo	27 Lib	28 Sag	28 Cap	26 Aqu	26 Pis
30 Aqu		28 Pis	29 Tau	28 Gem	29 Leo	28 Vir	29 Sco	30 Cap	30 Aqu	29 Pis	29 Ari
		31 Ari		30 Can		30 Lib	31 Sag				31 Tau

1939

JAN	FEB	MAR	APR	MAY	JUN	JUL	AUG	SEP	OCT	NOV	DEC
2 Gem	1 Can	2 Leo	1 Vir	2 Sco	1 Sag	3 Aqu	2 Pis	3 Tau	2 Gem	1 Can	3 Vir
4 Can	3 Leo	4 Vir	3 Lib	4 Sag	3 Cap	5 Pis	4 Ari	5 Gem	5 Can	3 Leo	5 Lib
6 Leo	5 Vir	6 Lib	5 Sco	7 Cap	6 Aqu	8 Ari	7 Tau	8 Can	7 Leo	5 Vir	7 Sco
8 Vir	7 Lib	8 Sco	7 Sag	9 Aqu	8 Pis	10 Tau	9 Gem	10 Leo	9 Vir	7 Lib	9 Sag
13 Sco	12 Sag	11 Sag	9 Cap	12 Pis	11 Ari	13 Gem	11 Can	12 Vir	11 Lib	9 Sco	11 Cap
15 Sag	14 Cap	13 Cap	12 Aqu	14 Ari	13 Tau	15 Can	13 Leo	14 Lib	13 Sco	12 Sag	14 Aqu
18 Cap	17 Aqu	16 Aqu	14 Pis	17 Tau	15 Gem	17 Leo	15 Vir	16 Sco	15 Sag	14 Cap	16 Pis
20 Aqu	19 Pis	18 Pis	17 Ari	19 Gem	17 Can	19 Vir	17 Lib	18 Sag	17 Cap	16 Aqu	19 Ari
23 Pis	22 Ari	21 Ari	19 Tau	21 Can	19 Leo	21 Lib	19 Sco	20 Cap	20 Aqu	19 Pis	21 Tau
25 Ari	24 Tau	23 Tau	22 Gem	23 Leo	21 Vir	23 Sco	21 Sag	22 Aqu	22 Pis	21 Ari	23 Gem
28 Tau	26 Gem	25 Gem	24 Can	25 Vir	23 Lib	25 Sag	24 Cap	25 Pis	25 Ari	23 Tau	26 Can
30 Gem	28 Can	27 Can	26 Leo	27 Lib	26 Sco	28 Cap	26 Aqu	28 Ari	27 Tau	26 Gem	28 Leo
		29 Leo	28 Vir	29 Sco	28 Sag	30 Aqu	29 Pis	30 Tau	30 Gem	28 Can	30 Vir
			30 Lib		30 Cap		31 Ari			30 Leo	

1940

JAN	FEB	MAR	APR	MAY	JUN	JUL	AUG	SEP	OCT	NOV	DEC
1 Lib	2 Sag	2 Cap	1 Aqu	3 Ari	2 Tau	2 Gem	2 Leo	1 Vir	2 Sco	1 Sag	3 Aqu
3 Sco	4 Cap	4 Aqu	3 Pis	6 Tau	4 Gem	4 Can	4 Vir	3 Lib	4 Sag	4 Cap	5 Pis
6 Sag	7 Aqu	7 Pis	6 Ari	8 Gem	7 Can	6 Leo	6 Lib	5 Sco	7 Cap	6 Aqu	7 Ari
8 Cap	9 Pis	9 Ari	8 Tau	10 Can	9 Leo	8 Vir	9 Sco	7 Sag	9 Aqu	8 Pis	10 Tau
10 Aqu	11 Ari	12 Tau	11 Gem	13 Leo	11 Vir	10 Lib	11 Sag	9 Cap	11 Pis	10 Ari	12 Gem
13 Pis	14 Tau	14 Gem	13 Can	15 Vir	13 Lib	12 Sco	13 Cap	11 Aqu	14 Ari	13 Tau	15 Can
15 Ari	16 Gem	17 Can	15 Leo	17 Lib	15 Sco	15 Sag	15 Aqu	14 Pis	16 Tau	15 Gem	17 Leo
18 Tau	19 Can	19 Leo	17 Vir	19 Sco	17 Sag	17 Cap	18 Pis	16 Ari	19 Gem	18 Can	19 Vir
20 Gem	21 Leo	21 Vir	19 Lib	21 Sag	19 Cap	19 Aqu	20 Ari	19 Tau	21 Can	20 Leo	21 Lib
22 Can	23 Vir	23 Lib	21 Sco	23 Cap	22 Aqu	21 Pis	23 Tau	21 Gem	24 Leo	22 Vir	24 Sco
24 Leo	25 Lib	25 Sco	23 Sag	25 Aqu	24 Pis	24 Ari	25 Gem	24 Can	26 Vir	24 Lib	26 Sag
26 Vir	27 Sco	27 Sag	26 Cap	28 Pis	27 Ari	27 Tau	28 Can	26 Leo	28 Lib	26 Sco	28 Cap
28 Lib	29 Sag	29 Cap	28 Aqu	30 Ari	29 Tau	29 Gem	30 Leo	28 Vir	30 Sco	28 Sag	30 Aqu
30 Sco			30 Pis			31 Can		30 Lib		30 Cap	

1941

JAN	FEB	MAR	APR	MAY	JUN	JUL	AUG	SEP	OCT	NOV	DEC
2 Pis	3 Tau	2 Tau	1 Gem	3 Leo	1 Vir	1 Lib	1 Sag	2 Aqu	1 Pis	3 Tau	2 Gem
4 Ari	5 Gem	4 Gem	3 Can	5 Vir	4 Lib	3 Sco	3 Cap	4 Pis	4 Ari	5 Gem	5 Can
7 Tau	8 Can	7 Can	6 Leo	7 Lib	6 Sco	5 Sag	6 Aqu	7 Ari	6 Tau	8 Can	7 Leo
9 Gem	10 Leo	9 Leo	8 Vir	9 Sco	8 Sag	7 Cap	8 Pis	9 Tau	9 Gem	10 Leo	10 Vir
11 Can	12 Vir	11 Vir	10 Lib	11 Sag	10 Cap	9 Aqu	10 Ari	11 Gem	11 Can	12 Vir	12 Lib
14 Leo	14 Lib	13 Lib	12 Sco	13 Cap	12 Aqu	11 Pis	13 Tau	14 Can	14 Leo	15 Lib	14 Sco
16 Vir	16 Sco	16 Sco	14 Sag	15 Aqu	14 Pis	14 Ari	15 Gem	16 Leo	16 Vir	17 Sco	16 Sag
18 Lib	18 Sag	18 Sag	16 Cap	18 Pis	16 Ari	16 Tau	18 Can	19 Vir	18 Lib	19 Sag	18 Cap
20 Sco	21 Cap	20 Cap	18 Aqu	20 Ari	19 Tau	19 Gem	20 Leo	21 Lib	20 Sco	21 Cap	20 Aqu
22 Sag	23 Aqu	22 Aqu	20 Pis	23 Tau	21 Gem	21 Can	22 Vir	23 Sco	22 Sag	23 Aqu	22 Pis
24 Cap	25 Pis	24 Pis	23 Ari	25 Gem	24 Can	24 Leo	24 Lib	25 Sag	24 Cap	25 Pis	25 Ari
27 Aqu	28 Ari	27 Ari	25 Tau	28 Can	26 Leo	26 Vir	27 Sco	27 Cap	26 Aqu	27 Ari	27 Tau
29 Pis		29 Tau	28 Gem	30 Leo	29 Vir	28 Lib	29 Sag	29 Aqu	29 Pis	30 Tau	30 Gem
31 Ari			30 Can			30 Sco	31 Cap		31 Ari		

1942

	JAN	FEB	MAR	APR	MAY	JUN	JUL	AUG	SEP	OCT	NOV	DEC
	1 Can	2 Vir	2 Vir	2 Sco	2 Sag	2 Aqu	2 Pis	3 Tau	1 Gem	1 Can	3 Vir	2 Lib
	4 Leo	4 Lib	4 Lib	4 Sag	4 Cap	4 Pis	4 Ari	5 Gem	4 Can	4 Leo	5 Lib	4 Sco
	6 Vir	7 Sco	6 Sco	6 Cap	6 Aqu	7 Ari	6 Tau	7 Can	6 Leo	6 Vir	7 Sco	7 Sag
	8 Lib	9 Sag	8 Sag	9 Aqu	8 Pis	9 Tau	9 Gem	10 Leo	9 Vir	8 Lib	9 Sag	9 Cap
	10 Sco	11 Cap	10 Cap	11 Pis	10 Ari	11 Gem	11 Can	12 Vir	11 Lib	11 Sco	11 Cap	11 Aqu
	13 Sag	13 Aqu	12 Aqu	13 Ari	13 Tau	14 Can	14 Leo	15 Lib	13 Sco	13 Sag	13 Aqu	13 Pis
	15 Cap	15 Pis	14 Pis	15 Tau	15 Gem	16 Leo	16 Vir	17 Sco	15 Sag	15 Cap	15 Pis	15 Ari
	17 Aqu	17 Ari	17 Ari	18 Gem	18 Can	19 Vir	19 Lib	19 Sag	18 Cap	17 Aqu	17 Ari	17 Tau
	19 Pis	20 Tau	19 Tau	20 Can	20 Leo	21 Lib	21 Sco	21 Cap	20 Aqu	19 Pis	20 Tau	19 Gem
	21 Ari	22 Gem	22 Gem	23 Leo	23 Vir	23 Sco	23 Sag	23 Aqu	22 Pis	21 Ari	22 Gem	22 Can
	23 Tau	25 Can	24 Can	25 Vir	25 Lib	26 Sag	25 Cap	25 Pis	24 Ari	24 Tau	25 Can	24 Leo
	26 Gem	27 Leo	27 Leo	28 Lib	27 Sco	28 Cap	27 Aqu	28 Ari	26 Tau	26 Gem	27 Leo	27 Vir
	28 Can		29 Vir	30 Sco	29 Sag	30 Aqu	29 Pis	30 Tau	29 Gem	28 Can	30 Vir	29 Lib
	31 Leo		31 Lib		31 Cap		31 Ari			31 Leo		

1943

	JAN	FEB	MAR	APR	MAY	JUN	JUL	AUG	SEP	OCT	NOV	DEC
	1 Sco	1 Cap	1 Cap	1 Pis	1 Ari	1 Gem	1 Can	2 Vir	1 Lib	1 Sco	2 Cap	1 Aqu
	3 Sag	3 Aqu	3 Aqu	3 Ari	3 Tau	4 Can	4 Leo	5 Lib	4 Sco	3 Sag	4 Aqu	3 Pis
	5 Cap	5 Pis	5 Pis	6 Tau	5 Gem	6 Leo	6 Vir	7 Sco	6 Sag	5 Cap	6 Pis	5 Ari
	7 Aqu	7 Ari	7 Ari	8 Gem	8 Can	9 Vir	9 Lib	10 Sag	8 Cap	7 Aqu	8 Ari	7 Tau
	9 Pis	10 Tau	9 Tau	10 Can	10 Leo	11 Lib	11 Sco	12 Cap	10 Aqu	10 Pis	10 Tau	10 Gem
	11 Ari	12 Gem	11 Gem	13 Leo	13 Vir	14 Sco	13 Sag	14 Aqu	12 Pis	12 Ari	12 Gem	12 Can
	13 Tau	15 Can	14 Can	15 Vir	15 Lib	16 Sag	15 Cap	16 Pis	14 Ari	14 Tau	15 Can	14 Leo
	16 Gem	17 Leo	16 Leo	17 Lib	17 Sco	18 Cap	17 Aqu	18 Ari	16 Tau	16 Gem	17 Leo	17 Vir
	18 Can	20 Vir	19 Vir	20 Sco	19 Sag	20 Aqu	19 Pis	20 Tau	19 Gem	18 Can	20 Vir	19 Lib
	21 Leo	22 Lib	21 Lib	22 Sag	22 Cap	22 Pis	21 Ari	22 Gem	21 Can	21 Leo	22 Lib	22 Sco
	23 Vir	24 Sco	24 Sco	24 Cap	24 Aqu	24 Ari	24 Tau	25 Can	23 Leo	23 Vir	24 Sco	24 Sag
	26 Lib	27 Sag	26 Sag	26 Aqu	26 Pis	26 Tau	26 Gem	27 Leo	26 Vir	26 Lib	27 Sag	26 Cap
	28 Sco		28 Cap	28 Pis	28 Ari	29 Gem	28 Can	30 Vir	28 Lib	28 Sco	29 Cap	28 Aqu
	30 Sag		30 Aqu		30 Tau		31 Leo			30 Sag		30 Pis

1944

	JAN	FEB	MAR	APR	MAY	JUN	JUL	AUG	SEP	OCT	NOV	DEC
	1 Ari	2 Gem	1 Gem	2 Leo	1 Vir	3 Sco	2 Sag	1 Cap	2 Pis	1 Ari	1 Gem	1 Can
	4 Tau	5 Can	3 Can	4 Vir	4 Lib	5 Sag	5 Cap	3 Aqu	4 Ari	3 Tau	4 Can	3 Leo
	6 Gem	7 Leo	5 Leo	7 Lib	6 Sco	7 Cap	7 Aqu	5 Pis	6 Tau	5 Gem	6 Leo	6 Vir
	8 Can	10 Vir	8 Vir	9 Sco	9 Sag	9 Aqu	9 Pis	7 Ari	8 Gem	7 Can	8 Vir	8 Lib
	11 Leo	12 Lib	10 Lib	11 Sag	11 Cap	11 Pis	11 Ari	9 Tau	10 Can	10 Leo	11 Lib	11 Sco
	13 Vir	15 Sco	13 Sco	14 Cap	13 Aqu	14 Ari	13 Tau	11 Gem	12 Leo	12 Vir	13 Sco	13 Sag
	16 Lib	17 Sag	15 Sag	16 Aqu	15 Pis	16 Tau	15 Gem	14 Can	15 Vir	15 Lib	16 Sag	15 Cap
	18 Sco	19 Cap	17 Cap	18 Pis	17 Ari	18 Gem	17 Can	16 Leo	17 Lib	17 Sco	18 Cap	18 Aqu
	21 Sag	21 Aqu	20 Aqu	20 Ari	19 Tau	20 Can	20 Leo	19 Vir	20 Sco	20 Sag	20 Aqu	20 Pis
	23 Cap	23 Pis	22 Pis	22 Tau	22 Gem	23 Leo	22 Vir	21 Lib	22 Sag	22 Cap	23 Pis	22 Ari
	25 Aqu	25 Ari	24 Ari	24 Gem	24 Can	25 Vir	25 Lib	24 Sco	25 Cap	24 Aqu	25 Ari	24 Tau
	27 Pis	27 Tau	26 Tau	26 Can	26 Leo	28 Lib	27 Sco	26 Sag	27 Aqu	26 Pis	27 Tau	26 Gem
	29 Ari		28 Gem	29 Leo	29 Vir	30 Sco	30 Sag	28 Cap	29 Pis	28 Ari	29 Gem	28 Can
	31 Tau		30 Can		31 Lib			31 Aqu		30 Tau		31 Leo

1945

	JAN	FEB	MAR	APR	MAY	JUN	JUL	AUG	SEP	OCT	NOV	DEC
	2 Vir	1 Lib	3 Sco	2 Sag	1 Cap	2 Pis	1 Ari	2 Gem	3 Leo	2 Vir	1 Lib	1 Sco
	5 Lib	3 Sco	5 Sag	4 Cap	4 Aqu	4 Ari	4 Tau	4 Can	5 Vir	5 Lib	3 Sco	3 Sag
	7 Sco	6 Sag	8 Cap	6 Aqu	6 Pis	6 Tau	6 Gem	6 Leo	7 Lib	7 Sco	6 Sag	6 Cap
	10 Sag	8 Cap	10 Aqu	8 Pis	8 Ari	8 Gem	8 Can	9 Vir	10 Sco	10 Sag	8 Cap	8 Aqu
	12 Cap	11 Aqu	12 Pis	10 Ari	10 Tau	10 Can	10 Leo	11 Lib	12 Sag	12 Cap	11 Aqu	10 Pis
	14 Aqu	13 Pis	14 Ari	12 Tau	12 Gem	13 Leo	12 Vir	13 Sco	15 Cap	14 Aqu	13 Pis	13 Ari
	16 Pis	15 Ari	16 Tau	14 Gem	14 Can	15 Vir	15 Lib	16 Sag	17 Aqu	17 Pis	15 Ari	15 Tau
	18 Ari	17 Tau	18 Gem	17 Can	16 Leo	17 Lib	17 Sco	18 Cap	19 Pis	19 Ari	17 Tau	17 Gem
	20 Tau	20 Gem	20 Can	19 Leo	19 Vir	20 Sco	20 Sag	21 Aqu	21 Ari	21 Tau	19 Gem	19 Can
	23 Gem	21 Can	23 Leo	21 Vir	21 Lib	22 Sag	22 Cap	23 Pis	23 Tau	23 Gem	21 Can	21 Leo
	25 Can	23 Leo	25 Vir	24 Lib	24 Sco	25 Cap	24 Aqu	25 Ari	25 Gem	25 Can	23 Leo	23 Vir
	27 Leo	26 Vir	27 Lib	26 Sco	26 Sag	27 Aqu	27 Pis	27 Tau	28 Can	27 Leo	26 Vir	25 Lib
	29 Vir	28 Lib	30 Sco	29 Sag	28 Cap	29 Pis	29 Ari	29 Gem	30 Leo	29 Vir	28 Lib	28 Sco
					31 Aqu		31 Tau	31 Can				30 Sag

1946

JAN	FEB	MAR	APR	MAY	JUN	JUL	AUG	SEP	OCT	NOV	DEC
2 Cap	1 Aqu	2 Pis	1 Ari	2 Gem	1 Can	2 Vir	1 Lib	2 Sag	2 Cap	1 Aqu	1 Pis
4 Aqu	3 Pis	4 Ari	3 Tau	4 Can	3 Leo	5 Lib	3 Sco	5 Cap	4 Aqu	3 Pis	3 Ari
7 Pis	5 Ari	6 Tau	5 Gem	6 Leo	5 Vir	7 Sco	6 Sag	7 Aqu	7 Pis	6 Ari	5 Tau
9 Ari	7 Tau	9 Gem	7 Can	9 Vir	7 Lib	9 Sag	8 Cap	10 Pis	9 Ari	8 Tau	7 Gem
11 Tau	9 Gem	11 Can	9 Leo	11 Lib	10 Sco	12 Cap	11 Aqu	12 Ari	11 Tau	10 Gem	9 Can
13 Gem	11 Can	13 Leo	11 Vir	13 Sco	12 Sag	15 Aqu	13 Pis	14 Tau	13 Gem	12 Can	11 Can
15 Can	14 Leo	15 Vir	14 Lib	16 Sag	15 Cap	17 Pis	15 Ari	16 Gem	15 Can	14 Leo	13 Vir
17 Leo	16 Vir	18 Lib	16 Sco	19 Cap	17 Aqu	19 Ari	18 Tau	18 Can	17 Leo	16 Vir	15 Lib
19 Vir	18 Lib	20 Sco	19 Sag	21 Aqu	20 Pis	21 Tau	20 Gem	20 Leo	20 Vir	18 Lib	18 Sco
22 Lib	21 Sco	22 Sag	21 Cap	23 Pis	22 Ari	23 Gem	22 Can	22 Vir	22 Lib	21 Sco	20 Sag
24 Sco	23 Sag	25 Cap	24 Aqu	26 Ari	24 Tau	26 Can	24 Leo	25 Lib	24 Sco	23 Sag	23 Cap
27 Sag	26 Cap	27 Aqu	26 Pis	28 Tau	26 Gem	28 Leo	26 Vir	27 Sco	27 Sag	26 Cap	25 Aqu
29 Cap	28 Aqu	30 Pis	28 Ari	30 Gem	28 Can	30 Vir	28 Lib	29 Sag	29 Cap	28 Aqu	28 Pis
			30 Tau		30 Leo		31 Sco				31 Ari

1947

JAN	FEB	MAR	APR	MAY	JUN	JUL	AUG	SEP	OCT	NOV	DEC
1 Tau	2 Can	1 Can	2 Vir	1 Lib	2 Sag	2 Cap	1 Aqu	2 Ari	1 Tau	2 Can	2 Leo
4 Gem	4 Leo	3 Leo	4 Lib	3 Sco	5 Cap	4 Aqu	3 Pis	4 Tau	4 Gem	4 Leo	4 Vir
6 Can	6 Vir	5 Vir	6 Sco	6 Sag	7 Aqu	7 Pis	6 Ari	7 Gem	6 Can	6 Vir	6 Lib
8 Leo	8 Lib	8 Lib	9 Sag	8 Cap	10 Pis	9 Ari	8 Tau	9 Can	8 Leo	9 Lib	8 Sco
10 Vir	10 Sco	10 Sco	11 Cap	11 Aqu	12 Ari	12 Tau	10 Gem	11 Leo	11 Vir	11 Sco	10 Sag
12 Lib	13 Sag	12 Sag	14 Aqu	13 Pis	14 Tau	14 Gem	12 Can	13 Vir	12 Lib	13 Sag	13 Cap
14 Sco	15 Cap	15 Cap	16 Pis	16 Ari	16 Gem	16 Can	14 Leo	15 Lib	14 Sco	15 Cap	15 Aqu
17 Sag	18 Aqu	17 Aqu	18 Ari	18 Tau	19 Can	18 Leo	16 Vir	17 Sco	17 Sag	18 Aqu	18 Pis
19 Cap	20 Pis	19 Pis	21 Tau	20 Gem	21 Leo	20 Vir	18 Lib	19 Sag	19 Cap	20 Pis	20 Ari
22 Aqu	23 Ari	22 Ari	23 Gem	22 Can	23 Vir	22 Lib	21 Sco	22 Cap	20 Aqu	23 Ari	23 Tau
24 Pis	25 Tau	24 Tau	25 Can	24 Leo	25 Lib	24 Sco	23 Sag	24 Aqu	24 Pis	25 Tau	25 Gem
26 Ari	27 Gem	26 Gem	27 Leo	26 Vir	27 Sco	27 Sag	25 Cap	27 Pis	27 Ari	27 Gem	27 Can
29 Tau		29 Can	29 Vir	28 Lib	30 Sag	29 Cap	28 Aqu	29 Ari	29 Tau	30 Can	29 Leo
31 Gem		31 Leo		31 Sco			30 Pis		31 Gem		31 Vir

1948

JAN	FEB	MAR	APR	MAY	JUN	JUL	AUG	SEP	OCT	NOV	DEC
2 Lib	1 Sco	1 Sag	2 Aqu	2 Pis	1 Ari	1 Tau	2 Can	2 Vir	2 Lib	2 Sag	2 Cap
4 Vir	3 Sag	4 Cap	5 Pis	5 Ari	4 Tau	3 Gem	4 Leo	4 Lib	4 Sco	4 Cap	4 Aqu
7 Sag	5 Cap	6 Aqu	7 Ari	7 Tau	6 Gem	5 Can	6 Vir	6 Sco	6 Sag	7 Aqu	7 Pis
9 Cap	8 Aqu	9 Pis	10 Tau	9 Gem	8 Can	7 Leo	8 Lib	8 Sag	8 Cap	9 Pis	9 Ari
12 Aqu	10 Pis	11 Ari	12 Gem	12 Can	10 Leo	9 Vir	10 Sco	11 Cap	10 Aqu	12 Ari	12 Tau
14 Pis	13 Ari	14 Tau	14 Can	14 Leo	12 Vir	11 Lib	12 Sag	13 Aqu	13 Pis	14 Tau	14 Gem
17 Ari	15 Tau	16 Gem	16 Leo	16 Vir	14 Lib	14 Sco	14 Cap	16 Pis	15 Ari	17 Gem	16 Can
19 Tau	18 Gem	18 Can	19 Vir	18 Lib	16 Sco	16 Sag	17 Aqu	18 Ari	18 Tau	19 Can	18 Leo
21 Gem	20 Can	20 Leo	21 Lib	20 Sco	19 Sag	18 Cap	19 Pis	21 Tau	20 Gem	21 Leo	20 Vir
23 Can	22 Leo	22 Vir	23 Sco	22 Sag	21 Cap	21 Aqu	22 Ari	23 Gem	23 Can	23 Vir	23 Lib
25 Leo	24 Vir	24 Lib	25 Sag	25 Cap	23 Aqu	23 Pis	24 Tau	25 Can	25 Leo	25 Lib	25 Sag
27 Vir	26 Lib	26 Sco	27 Cap	27 Aqu	26 Pis	26 Ari	27 Gem	28 Leo	27 Vir	27 Sco	27 Sag
29 Lib	28 Sco	29 Sag	30 Aqu	30 Pis	28 Ari	28 Tau	29 Can	30 Vir	29 Lib	30 Sag	29 Cap
		31 Cap				31 Gem	31 Leo		31 Sco		

1949

JAN	FEB	MAR	APR	MAY	JUN	JUL	AUG	SEP	OCT	NOV	DEC
1 Aqu	2 Ari	1 Ari	2 Gem	2 Can	3 Vir	2 Lib	2 Sag	1 Cap	1 Aqu	2 Ari	1 Tau
3 Pis	4 Tau	4 Tau	5 Can	4 Leo	5 Lib	4 Sco	5 Cap	3 Aqu	3 Pis	4 Tau	4 Gem
5 Ari	7 Gem	6 Gem	7 Leo	6 Vir	7 Sco	6 Sag	7 Aqu	6 Pis	5 Ari	7 Gem	6 Can
8 Tau	9 Can	8 Can	9 Vir	8 Lib	9 Sag	8 Cap	9 Pis	8 Ari	8 Tau	9 Can	9 Leo
10 Gem	11 Leo	11 Leo	11 Lib	11 Sco	11 Cap	11 Aqu	12 Ari	11 Tau	10 Gem	11 Leo	11 Vir
13 Can	13 Vir	13 Vir	13 Sco	13 Sag	13 Aqu	13 Pis	14 Tau	13 Gem	13 Can	14 Vir	13 Lib
15 Leo	15 Lib	15 Lib	15 Sag	15 Cap	16 Pis	16 Ari	17 Gem	16 Can	15 Leo	16 Lib	15 Sco
17 Vir	17 Sco	17 Sco	17 Cap	17 Aqu	18 Ari	18 Tau	19 Can	18 Leo	17 Vir	18 Sco	17 Sag
19 Lib	19 Sag	19 Sag	20 Aqu	19 Pis	21 Tau	21 Gem	21 Leo	20 Vir	19 Lib	20 Sag	19 Cap
21 Sco	22 Cap	22 Cap	22 Pis	22 Ari	23 Gem	23 Can	24 Vir	22 Lib	22 Sco	22 Cap	22 Aqu
23 Sag	24 Aqu	23 Aqu	25 Ari	24 Tau	25 Can	26 Leo	26 Lib	24 Sco	23 Sag	24 Aqu	24 Pis
25 Cap	27 Pis	26 Pis	27 Tau	27 Gem	28 Leo	27 Vir	28 Sco	26 Sag	26 Cap	26 Pis	26 Ari
28 Aqu		28 Ari	30 Gem	29 Can	30 Vir	29 Lib	30 Sag	28 Cap	28 Aqu	29 Ari	29 Tau
30 Pis		31 Tau		31 Leo		31 Sco			30 Pis		31 Gem

JAN	FEB	MAR	APR	MAY	JUN	JUL	AUG	SEP	OCT	NOV	DEC
3 Can	1 Leo	1 Leo	1 Lib	1 Sco	1 Cap	1 Aqu	2 Ari	1 Tau	3 Can	2 Leo	1 Vir
5 Leo	4 Vir	3 Vir	3 Sco	3 Sag	3 Aqu	3 Pis	4 Tau	3 Gem	5 Leo	4 Vir	4 Lib
7 Vir	6 Lib	5 Lib	5 Sag	5 Cap	6 Pis	5 Ari	7 Gem	6 Can	8 Vir	6 Lib	6 Sco
9 Lib	8 Sco	7 Sco	8 Cap	7 Aqu	8 Ari	8 Tau	9 Can	8 Leo	10 Lib	8 Sco	8 Sag
12 Sco	10 Sag	9 Sag	10 Aqu	9 Pis	11 Tau	10 Gem	12 Leo	10 Vir	12 Sco	10 Sag	10 Cap
14 Sag	12 Cap	11 Cap	12 Pis	12 Ari	13 Gem	13 Can	14 Vir	12 Lib	14 Sag	12 Cap	12 Aqu
16 Cap	14 Aqu	14 Aqu	15 Ari	14 Tau	16 Can	15 Leo	16 Lib	14 Sco	16 Cap	14 Aqu	14 Pis
18 Aqu	17 Pis	16 Pis	17 Tau	17 Gem	18 Leo	18 Vir	18 Sco	16 Sag	18 Aqu	17 Pis	16 Ari
20 Pis	19 Ari	18 Ari	20 Gem	19 Can	20 Vir	20 Lib	20 Sag	19 Cap	20 Pis	19 Ari	19 Tau
23 Ari	21 Tau	21 Tau	22 Can	22 Leo	23 Lib	22 Sco	22 Cap	21 Aqu	23 Ari	21 Tau	21 Gem
25 Tau	24 Gem	23 Gem	25 Leo	24 Vir	25 Sco	24 Sag	25 Aqu	23 Pis	25 Tau	24 Gem	24 Can
28 Gem	26 Can	26 Can	27 Vir	26 Lib	27 Sag	26 Cap	27 Pis	25 Ari	28 Gem	26 Can	26 Leo
30 Can		28 Leo	29 Lib	28 Sco	29 Cap	28 Aqu	29 Ari	28 Tau	30 Can	29 Leo	29 Vir
		30 Vir		30 Sag		30 Pis		30 Gem			31 Lib